CHAMPs

A Proactive and Positive Approach to Classroom Management

Randy Sprick, Ph.D.

Mickey Garrison, Ph.D.

Lisa M. Howard, M.S.

07 06 05 13 12 11 10

ISBN 1-57035-166-X

Edited by Lisa DeShantz-Cook

Text layout and design by Tracy Katzenberger

Cover Design by Katherine Getta

Printed in the United States of America
Published and Distributed by:

3880 West 11th Avenue • Eugene, OR 97402
(866) 542-1490 • (541) 345-1490
FAX: (541) 345-1507 • www.pacificnwpublish.com

65CHAMPS/BANTA/12-01/10M/241

ACKNOWLEDGMENTS

This book would not have been possible without the contributions of many individuals. We would like to thank all the students (children and adults) who have taught us to look first at our own behavior and to be intentional and proactive in our approach.

We would also like to acknowledge the skill and dedication of the Mt. Vernon staff, and to thank the *entire* staff for their patience and their willingness to try new ideas during the field tryout of this material. We especially appreciate the generous and skillful feedback (positive and corrective) provided by Debbie Egan, Pat Gagnon, Melva Schumacher, and Dianne Yonker.

To the school psychology graduate students making up the Schoolwide Support Team—Rachelle Berry, Jonathon Flojo, Christina Rameriz, Kindle Perkins, Kristen Peterson, and Robin Thurber—a special thanks for trying out the coaching/self-assessment tools and for providing feedback on the early drafts of the manuscript. We are additionally indebted to Kindle for her help with the final edits.

Many thanks to the entire Sopris staff. In particular, we wish to acknowledge the skill, dedication, and professionalism of Lynne Timmons in guiding the editorial and design process. In addition, we wish to acknowledge Tracy Katzenberger, designer, and Lisa DeShantz-Cook, editor.

Finally, thanks to the staff of Teaching Strategies, Judy Shinn, Dani Smith, and Marilyn Sprick, for all their help, support, patience, feedback, and humor.

ABOUT THE AUTHORS

Randall S. Sprick, Ph.D., is a nationally-known educational consultant and teacher trainer based in Eugene, Oregon. Much of his work involves helping teachers learn how to encourage student responsibility and motivation and how to effectively teach misbehaving students to behave more responsibly. Dr. Sprick is the author of numerous books and articles, as well as audio and videotape programs, dealing with discipline and classroom management. He is currently an adjunct faculty member of the University of Oregon and Seattle Pacific University.

Mickey Garrison, Ph.D., has worked in the field of education for over 20 years. She has been a teacher, an administrator, and a consultant for regular education programs and programs for students with emotional and/or behavioral disorders. She has had experience in public and private schools, at both the elementary and secondary levels. Dr. Garrison is co-author, with Dr. Randall Sprick, of *Interventions: Collaborative Planning for Students At-Risk* and *Foundations: Establishing Positive Discipline Policies.*

Lisa Howard, B.A., is a former special and general education teacher of students in grades K-12. She has worked on a number of school-based research projects in both reading and mathematics in Oregon, Washington, and California. With Dr. Randall Sprick, Ms. Howard is a co-author of *The Teacher's Encyclopedia of Behavior Management* and *The Administrator's Desk Reference of Behavior Management*. She is also a co-author, with Marilyn Sprick and Ann Fidanque, of the primary reading program *Read Well.*

OVERVIEW OF RANDY SPRICK'S SAFE AND CIVIL SCHOOLS SERIES

The Safe and Civil Schools *series* is a collection of practical materials designed to help school personnel ensure that all school settings are safe and civil. In so doing, they lay the foundation to enhance student engagement and learning. The goal of all the series' materials is to empower school personnel with techniques to help all students behave responsibly and respectfully. The materials are full of specific "how-to" information. Though each resource stands alone, all are integrated and share some basic processes and beliefs.

The processes include:

1. Self-reflection—if student behavior is irresponsible, school staff should reflect on what they can do to help the student.
2. Utilization of data—objective information about behavior is important in planning and making decisions about behavior.
3. Structuring for success—all school settings should be organized to promote successful behavior from students.
4. Collaboration—helping students behave responsibly is a shared responsibility of all school staff members.

The beliefs include:

1. All students must be treated with dignity and respect.
2. Students should be taught the skills and behaviors necessary for success.
3. Staff members should encourage motivation through positive interactions and building relationships with students.
4. Student misbehavior provides a teaching opportunity.

These processes and beliefs form a structure that supports procedures and techniques for keeping students from "falling through the cracks" into school failure. The procedures and techniques can be categorized as schoolwide (affecting all students in all settings), classroom (for teachers in their own classrooms), and those tailored to the needs of individual students. The figure at right represents these procedures as an inverted triangle, with schoolwide at the top.

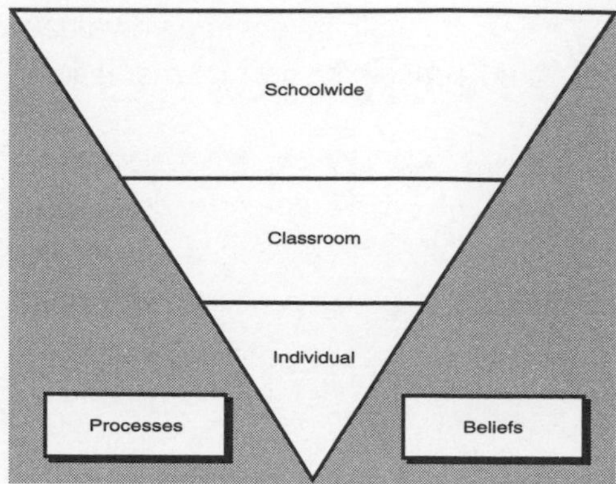

The idea is that if large numbers of students are misbehaving, modifying schoolwide procedures is the best intervention. If large numbers of students are having trouble in classrooms, classwide interventions are necessary. As needed, individualized interventions designed to help specific students who require more support are implemented. If too many students require individualized interventions, school staff should focus more time, effort, and energy on schoolwide and classwide interventions.

Schoolwide Resources in the Series

Foundations: Establishing Positive Discipline Policies assists a school staff in creating a calm, safe, and positive school environment, clarifying expectations, increasing positive interactions, improving student motivation, and reducing office referrals. Video and print materials provide step-by-step information on how to write, implement, and maintain a schoolwide policy that actually guides daily practice.

Bus Discipline is a four-tape video program designed to help bus drivers and classroom teachers improve student behavior on buses. The program also contains information for administrators on how to assess, revise, and implement transportation policies.

Cafeteria Discipline can help you turn your school's lunchroom into a calm, orderly place that staff and students will enjoy. This two-tape video program provides information on how to better prepare students to behave appropriately in the cafeteria, as well as specific strategies for lunchroom supervisors on how to manage behavior more effectively. The program also includes reproducible materials that can be used by staff.

Playground Discipline is an ideal inservice tool for teaching staff how to teach playground behavior, diagnose danger areas on the playground, establish clear procedures for crisis situations, interact positively with students during recess, etc. It consists of two video training sessions and accompanying print materials.

STP: Stop, Think, Plan shows educators how to teach and encourage students to calmly resolve their own conflicts. The program includes four videotapes, along with viewer outlines, a complete set of reproducible forms and lesson plans, and a comprehensive bibliography.

STP can help students gain valuable, life-long skills and free school staff and parents from time-consuming conflict mediation.

Administrator's Desk Reference of Behavior Management
Volume I of this three-volume set provides a building principal (and/or assistant principal) with information on guiding a school staff in the development and implementation of proactive schoolwide behavior management policies and procedures. Volume II presents suggestions for dealing with disciplinary referrals and for supporting teachers and students when chronic or severe misbehavior occurs. Volume III includes everything an administrator needs to implement a program of meaningful work for students. Meaningful Work is a proven program that can reduce behavior problems and increase student success.

ParaPro: Supporting the Instructional Process serves as a resource for ensuring that noncertified staff members are given the information and training they need to effectively manage student behavior in the settings they supervise. It addresses specific techniques for being part of the school team, managing small groups, helping in a classroom, supervising common areas, and working with an individual student.

Resources for the Classroom Teacher

CHAMPs: A Proactive and Positive Approach to Classroom Management is a systematic guide for classroom teachers who want to improve their current classroom management plans. The eight modules are structured to help teachers identify and maintain the effective parts of their current plans, while concurrently identifying and strengthening any weak parts of their management plans. This resource will help any teacher manage the behavior of students more positively and effectively.

CHAMPs Video Inservice Series
This series, with ten videotapes and print materials, provides everything necessary to lead a class or study group working through the *CHAMPs* book. The fast-paced videos provide a wealth of information to help bring the *CHAMPs* book to life and to guide groups of teachers in discussion and self-assessment activities that ensure effective implementation.

The Teacher's Encyclopedia of Behavior Management is a comprehensive reference for elementary and middle/junior high school teachers. It provides practical solutions to more than 100 common classroom problems. For each problem covered, there are three to five step-by-step intervention plans that teachers can choose from or modify to fit their particular situations. Arranged alphabetically, the book has an extensive index and cross-referencing among the problems, making it easy to use. The *Encyclopedia* is an indispensable tool for teachers wishing to help their students learn to be responsible for their own behavior.

Resources for Designing Plans for Individual Students

Interventions: Collaborative Planning for Students At Risk is both a resource and a process for education professionals. Through consultation and collaboration, staff members learn to share their expertise in developing practical intervention plans. Individual booklets describe how to set up, implement, and fade 16 specific interventions. The interventions presented include Managing Physically Dangerous Behavior, Managing Severely Disruptive Behavior, Self-Monitoring, Self-Control Training, Restructuring Self-Talk, and Academic Assistance. An optional 20-cassette audiotape album is available to accompany this resource.

The Teacher's Encyclopedia of Behavior Management also provides a wealth of information about setting up individualized behavior management plans.

CONTENTS

INTRODUCTION

CHAMPs is a modular series of materials designed to help you, as a classroom teacher, develop (or fine tune) an effective classroom management plan that is proactive and positive. In the last twenty years, a large and varied body of research literature has identified consistent and reliable findings concerning how effective teachers manage student behavior and enhance student motivation. The techniques included in this program have been derived from that literature and are based on the following principles or beliefs:

1. Classroom organization has a huge impact on student behavior; therefore, teachers should carefully structure their classrooms in ways that prompt responsible student behavior.
2. Teachers should overtly teach students how to behave responsibly (i.e., be successful) in every classroom situation.
3. Teachers should focus more time, attention, and energy on acknowledging responsible behavior than on responding to misbehavior.
4. Teachers should preplan their responses to misbehavior to ensure that they will respond in a brief, calm, and consistent manner.

We called this program *CHAMPs* for two reasons. First, we believe that by using effective management practices, teachers can help every student exhibit behavior that will make that student feel like a champion. Second, the acronym *CHAMPs* reflects the "categories" or "types" of expectations that you, as a teacher, need to clarify for students about every major activity and transition that occurs in your classroom. That is, for each classroom activity and transition, if you identify and then teach students *precisely* what your expectations are, you will significantly reduce the amount of misbehavior and increase the amount of learning that takes place in your classroom. Following are brief descriptions of the types of expectations that need to be clarified:

C	**Conversation**	(Can students talk to each other during this activity/transition?)
H	**Help**	(How can students get questions answered during this activity/transition? How do they get your attention?)
A	**Activity**	(What is the task/objective of this activity/transition? What is the expected end product?)
M	**Movement**	(Can students move about during this activity/transition? e.g., Are they allowed to get up to sharpen a pencil?)
P	**Participation**	(What does appropriate student behavior for this activity/transition look/sound like? How do students show that they are fully participating?)

NOTE

The specifics of how to clarify, and teach, your expectations are covered in detail in Module 3.)

CHAMPs is organized into eight modules, each of which focuses on one important aspect of effective classroom management. Within each module, we present specific tasks that will help you address that module's particular aspect, and offer detailed suggestions on how to accomplish the tasks themselves. Each module also includes a self-assessment tool that you can use to identify which of the tasks (or which parts of the tasks) you have completed and which you still need to address. Finally, every module ends with suggested discussion questions and activities that can be used by two or more teachers working together in a formal or informal study group. These questions and activities are designed to prompt group members to examine their beliefs and practices in a supportive environment and use each other as resources in their professional development efforts. Figure 1, on the following page, shows the basic organization of the material.

How to Use *CHAMPs*

This program can be used anytime during the year to evaluate and improve your classroom management and discipline plan. However, the most effective way to use this program is to work through all of the modules before the school year begins. Modules 1, 2, 3, and 4 will help you develop a detailed classroom management plan that focuses on directly teaching students how to behave responsibly from the very first day of school. Modules 5, 6, 7, and 8 can be skimmed before the school year begins, but are really designed to be implemented during the school year. These modules will help you develop and implement essential behavior management strategies for motivating students to behave responsibly throughout the year.

Figure 1: Organization of the CHAMPs Behavior Program

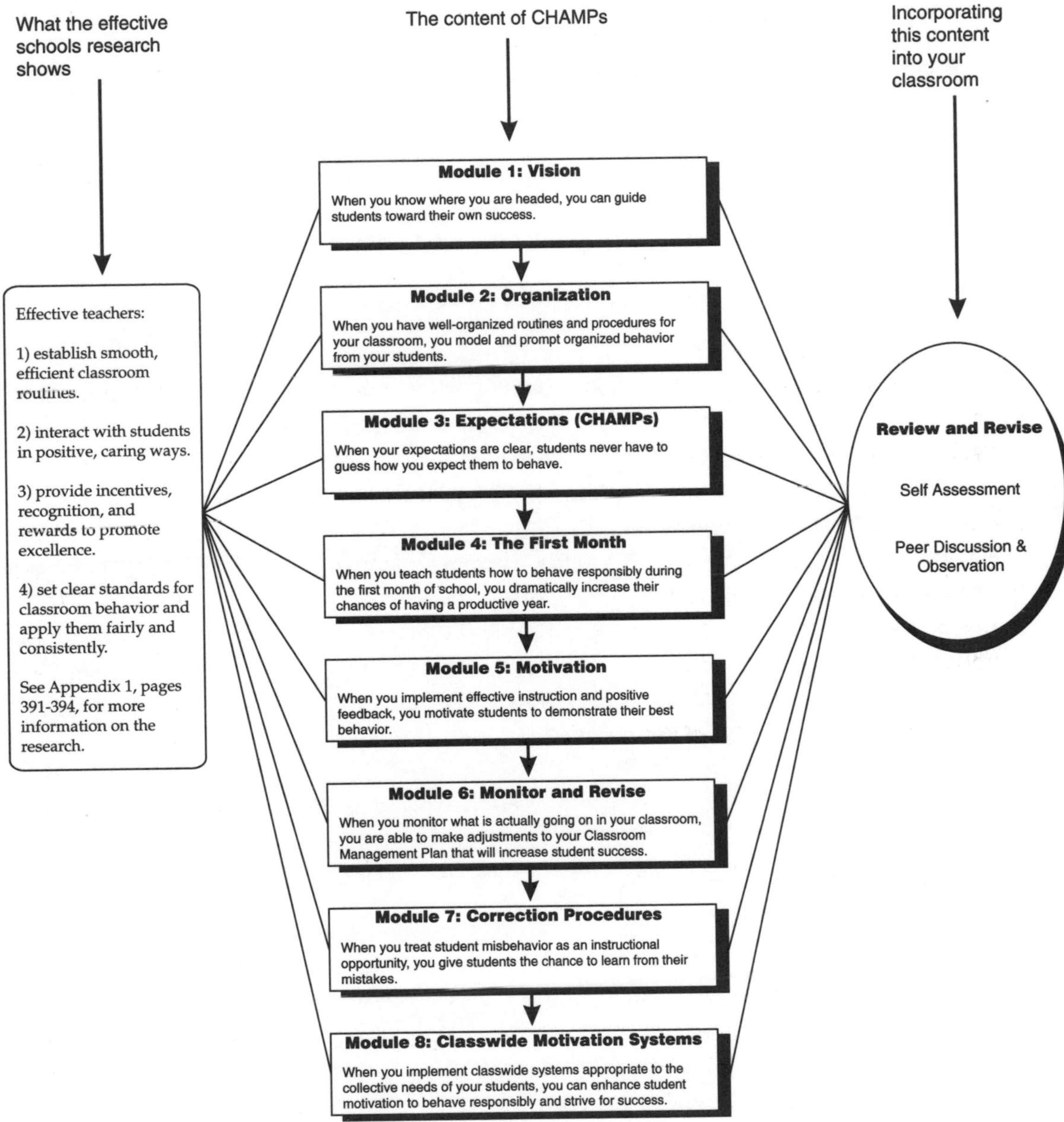

What the effective schools research shows
The content of CHAMPs
Incorporating this content into your classroom
Effective teachers:
1) establish smooth, efficient classroom routines.
2) interact with students in positive, caring ways.
3) provide incentives, recognition, and rewards to promote excellence.
4) set clear standards for classroom behavior and apply them fairly and consistently.
See Appendix 1, pages 391-394, for more information on the research.
Module 1: Vision
When you know where you are headed, you can guide students toward their own success.
Module 2: Organization
When you have well-organized routines and procedures for your classroom, you model and prompt organized behavior from your students.
Module 3: Expectations (CHAMPs)
When your expectations are clear, students never have to guess how you expect them to behave.
Module 4: The First Month
When you teach students how to behave responsibly during the first month of school, you dramatically increase their chances of having a productive year.
Module 5: Motivation
When you implement effective instruction and positive feedback, you motivate students to demonstrate their best behavior.
Module 6: Monitor and Revise
When you monitor what is actually going on in your classroom, you are able to make adjustments to your Classroom Management Plan that will increase student success.
Module 7: Correction Procedures
When you treat student misbehavior as an instructional opportunity, you give students the chance to learn from their mistakes.
Module 8: Classwide Motivation Systems
When you implement classwide systems appropriate to the collective needs of your students, you can enhance student motivation to behave responsibly and strive for success.
Review and Revise
Self Assessment
Peer Discussion & Observation

To get the most from this program, we also recommend that you use some of the activities throughout the year to help you identify which techniques and strategies will have the greatest positive impact on student behavior. Therefore, we suggest that *right now*, you write the prompts from Figure 2 on the appropriate week of your calendar/planbook. When you get to these prompts during the school year, go to the indicated module and task in the manual and follow the directions for collecting information about what is going on in your classroom. Note that because some schools are on semesters and some on trimesters, some times are indicated by the approximate week or month of the school year.

Figure 2: Calendar Planning of CHAMPs Activities

WEEK 3	Conduct Student Interviews or Quiz (Module 4, Task 3)
WEEK 4 OR 5	Use CHAMPs versus Daily Reality Rating Scale (Module 6, Tool 1)
2ND MONTH	Use Ratio of Interactions Monitoring Forms (Module 6, Tool 2)
3RD MONTH (EARLY)	Use Misbehavior(s) Recording Sheet (Module 6, Tool 3)
3RD MONTH (LATE)	Use Gradebook Analysis Worksheet (Module 6, Tool 4)
4TH MONTH	Use On-Task Behavior Observation Sheet (Module 6, Tool 5)
JANUARY (EARLY)	Use CHAMPs versus Daily Reality Rating Scale (Module 6, Tool 1)
JANUARY (LATE)	Use Misbehavior(s) Recording Sheet (Module 6, Tool 3)
FEBRUARY (EARLY)	Use Ratio of Interactions Monitoring Sheet (Module 6, Tool 2)
FEBRUARY (LATE)	Use On-Task Behavior Observation Sheet (Module 6, Tool 5)
MARCH (EARLY)	Use Gradebook Analysis Worksheet (Module 6, Tool 4)
APRIL (AFTER SPRING BREAK)	Use CHAMPs versus Daily Reality Rating Scale (Module 6, Tool 1)
LAST TWO WEEKS	Use Family/Student Satisfaction Survey (Module 6, Tool 6)

If you start using this program during the school year, plan to carefully read and implement the suggestions in Modules 3 and 4. These modules focus on ensuring that you have clarified your expectations and have directly taught those expectations to students. Then, as time permits, skim each of the modules and work through the self assessment suggestions. As you review each module, identify the tasks in which you feel you are sufficiently skilled and those in which you feel you need to improve. For tasks that may need improvement, review the materials on how to implement the task(s) in your classroom. Figure 3 is a "troubleshooting" guide that can help you identify which specific modules may help in solving particular problems.

Figure 3: Troubleshooting Guide to Using CHAMPs

Many different students misbehave in almost all types of activities.	Implement Module 3: Expectations and 4: The First Month to clarify expectations. Use Module 8: Classwide Motivational Systems to help you develop a class-wide motivation plan for a class needing high structure. Then work through Module 1: Vision and Module 2: Organization to analyze and improve your classroom management plan. Finally, work through Modules 5: Motivation Procedures, Module 6: Monitor and Revise, and Module 7: Correction Procedures to improve your behavior management practices.
The classroom climate needs to be more positive and/or you feel you are constantly nagging.	Implement Module 5: Motivation Procedures.
Students need to be more responsible about completing work.	Implement Module 2: Organization
Students need to behave more responsibly during independent work periods.	Implement Modules 2: Organization, Module 3: Expectations, and Module 4: The First Month to improve your plan for managing work times and for clarifying and teaching students how to work independently.
Many students exhibit a specific misbehavior (e.g., treating each other disrespectfully).	Implement Module 7: Correction Procedures to develop a plan for responding to the misbehavior and implement the strategies in Module 5: Motivation Procedures to increase student motivation to improve the behavior. Implement one or more procedures from Module 8: Classwide Motivational Systems
Students are apathetic.	Implement Modules 5: Motivation Procedures and Module 8: Classwide Motivational Systems to increase student enthusiasm and effort.

Whether you are using this program during the summer or during the year, and whether you are working through the material on your own or with colleagues, the information in *CHAMPs* is designed to help the experienced teacher fine tune current skills and the less experienced teacher develop a comprehensive plan for both classroom organization and for behavior management.

Remember, each module ends with discussion questions that you and your colleagues can use to further analyze your own procedures and as a structured means of sharing ideas with each other. If you are working with a colleague, spend one or two weeks working through a module on your own (i.e., reading and assessing your knowledge of the information). Then, get together for about an hour to review some or all of the suggested discussion topics. Repeat the process for each of the eight modules. In addition to discussion topics, there are optional non-evaluative activities that involve spending time in each others' classrooms. The self-assessment and peer activities in the modules will help you determine which tasks you already implement effectively and which may require more of your time and effort. NOTE: If your school or district has the *CHAMPs* Coaching Handbook (1999) and/or the *CHAMPs* Video Inservice Series, there may be district staff members who are available to lead discussion groups and/or observe and coach individual teachers on the various tasks presented in the program.

It is our sincere hope that the *CHAMPs* Behavior Program will help you expand and improve your skills in managing your classroom and motivating your students to achieve their fullest potential.

What the Research Says

The procedures within *CHAMPs* are well supported by a large body of educational research literature. If you are interested in reviewing a summary of the school effectiveness literature related to classroom and behavior management, see Appendix 1: What the Research Says at the end of this book.

MODULE 1: VISION

When you know where you are headed, you can guide students toward their own success.

Introduction

To effectively manage and motivate a class (or classes) of students, you need to have a clear vision of what you want your classroom to be like—what it should look like, what it should sound like, what it should feel like to a class member or a visitor, what you want your students to accomplish, etc. Once you have a clear idea of what you want your class to be like, you can design procedures that will ensure that you achieve those goals. In this module, we describe seven tasks that will help you clarify your vision of your classroom. The first two have to do with what you want your students to accomplish and what they will need to do to be successful. The next three tasks involve expectations that you have for your classroom. And the final two tasks describe knowledge that you will need in order to accomplish your vision. We believe that by attending to all seven of these tasks you can create a clear vision of what you want your class to be like and, therefore, the foundation upon which to build a management plan that will help achieve your vision.

The seven tasks presented and explained in this module are:

TASK 1: Long-Range Classroom Goals
Identify several major goals (instructional and behavioral) that you want to accomplish with all your students by the end of the year.

TASK 2: Guidelines for Success
Develop, and plan to actively share with your students, "guidelines" that describe basic attitudes, traits, and behaviors that will help students be successful in your classroom and throughout their lives.

TASK 3: Positive Expectations
Ensure that you have, and that you convey, high positive expectations for the success of all your students.

TASK 4: Family Contacts
Build positive relationships with your students' families (parents, guardian, grandparents) by making initial contact with them at the beginning of the year and maintaining regular contact throughout the year.

TASK 5: Professionalism
Demonstrate professionalism at all times.

TASK 6: Behavior Management Principles
Develop an understanding of fundamental behavior management principles so that you can make effective decisions and take appropriate actions to help your students learn to behave responsibly.

TASK 7: Level of Classroom Structure
Determine whether your students need you to implement a classroom management plan that involves high, medium, or low structure.

Immediately following the explanations of the tasks in this module is a Self-Assessment Checklist designed to help you determine which (or which parts) of the tasks you have done/are doing and which you still need to do. The module ends with a Peer Study Worksheet. This worksheet presents a series of discussion questions and activities that can be used by two or more teachers who want to share information and collegial support as they work to improve their classroom management practices.

Task 1: Long-Range Classroom Goals

Identify several major goals (instructional and behavioral) that you want to accomplish with all your students by the end of the year.

Without a destination in mind, you may arrive at a place you don't want to be.

This somewhat silly statement is one reason why it is so important to determine, before school begins, what you hope to accomplish with your students by the end of the school year. We recommend coming up with four to seven *major* goals that summarize why being in your classroom will be a worthwhile experience for your students. Specifically, you need to identify what it is you want your students to know or be able to do differently at the end of the year that they didn't know or were unable to do on the first day of school.

Long-range goals can be a mix of instructional/academic goals and/or behavioral/social goals. Instructional goals will focus on what students will be able to do differently relative to the academic content you will teach. Behavior goals focus on the attitudes or traits you hope to instill in your students. Whether your goals are predominantly behavioral or predominantly academic is entirely up to you.

Having long-range goals will help you plan and make decisions on a daily basis throughout the year. For example, if one of your goals is for students to plan long-range projects and bring them to completion, you should plan on devoting instructional time to several long-range projects over the course of the year. On the other hand, if this isn't a goal of yours, your plans may call for students to engage in more short daily activities and spend less time and energy on long-range projects.

Your goals should also help you make decisions regarding what you want to emphasize with students. If one of your goals is that students will "learn to study independently and stay on task," then you need to make an effort throughout the year to discuss, model, and provide feedback regarding students' on-task behavior. A teacher who does not have this goal may emphasize another behavior with his/her students.

Sharing your goals with your students and their families at the beginning of the year will let them know what you feel is important and where you hope to guide students. Detailed information about how to share goals with students and their families will be discussed in Module 4: The First Month.

Keeping your long-range goals in mind can be particularly important as you move further into the school year. We all know how easy it is for teachers to get so busy and so immersed in daily details that they lose sight of what they are trying to do and what they hope to accomplish. With long-range goals in mind, you can "keep your eyes on the prize" and periodically ask yourself if what you are doing on a daily basis is aiding (or hindering) your efforts to help students reach these goals.

Following are examples of long-range goals for different grade levels and subject areas.

NOTE

We have included these samples to prompt your thinking. In no way are we suggesting that they should be your long-range goals.

1st Grade: All students will:

- Develop basic decoding and comprehension skills and develop a love of good books.
- Develop basic math concepts, including mastering single digit addition and subtraction facts.
- Learn to work independently and finish assigned tasks.
- Learn to work cooperatively in groups.
- Learn to listen and follow directions.
- Treat everyone with courtesy and respect.

4th Grade: All students will:

- Develop written expression skills that allow them to communicate in both narrative and expository styles.
- Master all basic addition, subtraction, multiplication, and division facts, and be able to use those facts accurately when doing computation and problem solving.
- Learn to work cooperatively in groups and to sometimes take the leadership role.
- Learn to plan long-range projects and bring them to completion (including two major reports and two major projects).
- Learn to speak in front of their peers with confidence and style.
- Learn to stay focused on and bring written tasks to completion.

8th Grade U.S. History: All students will:

- Memorize 10 key events in U.S. history (including the year the Constitution was ratified, the beginning and ending years of the Civil War, and the year the U.S. entered World War II) and be able to place those events on a timeline.
- Be able to describe and apply five essential concepts of the U.S Constitution (including the three branches of government and the First Amendment right of free speech).
- Be able to learn something new about U.S. history and analyze that event using the timeline events and constitutional concepts noted above.
- Learn to take notes from lectures, films, and readings and use those notes to analyze and synthesize information on tests and projects.

- Learn to study independently and stay on task during class and when working on homework.

To develop your long-range goals, you might start by considering the following suggestions to help you write goals for your class:

- Ask yourself what you want students to be able to know and do at the end of the year that they may not be able to do now. What knowledge, processes, attitudes, behaviors, or traits do you hope to instill in your students? What do you want students to remember about their year with you?
- Find out the building, district, and/or state level goals for your students in the grade level or subject you teach. Your goals should probably reflect some of these.
- Talk to other teachers at your grade level about the goals they have for their students. Ask your colleagues at the next grade level what they feel students coming to them will need to be successful.

NOTE

If you are starting CHAMPs during the school year, implementing this task may be a relatively low priority. However, before the next school year begins, you should give careful thought to what your long-range goals for that year will be.

Task 2: Guidelines for Success

Develop, and plan to actively share with your students, "guidelines" that describe basic attitudes, traits, and behaviors that will help students be successful in your classroom and throughout their lives.

In addition to academics, we believe that teachers need to provide their students with specific information about attitudes, traits, and behaviors that will help them succeed in school and throughout their lives. Sadly, there are some students and families who believe that school success is not possible if one doesn't come from an educated or a rich family. There are others who believe that school success depends on the color of one's skin or one's ethnicity. We would argue that part of your responsibility as a teacher is to let your students know that they *can* succeed in school and to give them "guidelines" regarding what will help them do so.

Your Guidelines for Success should reflect broad and, for want of a better word, noble ideals. They should represent what you really hope students will learn from you—not the content, but the attitudes or actions that will help students succeed in your class, in the classes they will have in the future, in their hobbies, and in life in general. Try to imagine your students as young adults, looking back on their elementary or middle school years and thinking, "I remember that my ___ grade teacher really taught me the importance of _____________."

Having Guidelines for Success is important regardless of the types of students you teach. However, it can be especially critical if your school or class has a large number of high-needs students. Unfortunately, high-needs students often lack the knowledge of and/or motivation to exhibit traits that educators want, need, and expect them to have (e.g., staying focused on a task, choosing a hard task over a more entertaining one because of the long-term benefits, etc.).

Some of your guidelines may overlap with or be taken directly from your long-range goals, but in general, they should be traits students can exhibit that will help them achieve the long-range goals. For example, if you have a goal about students becoming more proficient writers, you want to ask yourself what attitudes or traits will help your students become proficient writers. Figure 1.1 shows a sample of one school's Guidelines for Success.

Figure 1.1: Sample Guidelines for Success

- **Be responsible.**
- **Always try.**
- **Do your best.**
- **Cooperate with others.**
- **Treat everyone with respect (including yourself).**

NOTE

Optimally, Guidelines for Success are developed and used on a schoolwide basis. That is, an entire staff creates and agrees to use the same guidelines. Sprick, Howard, Wise, Marcum & Haykin (1998) provide suggestions for how to involve staff, students, and parents in developing schoolwide Guidelines for Success. If your school does not have schoolwide guidelines, you should plan on developing them for your own class.

When developing your own Guidelines for Success (or "Goals to Strive Toward," or whatever you choose to call them), frame them as brief phrases that describe the attitudes, traits, and characteristics you hope to instill in your students. Note that Guidelines for Success are different than classroom rules. Rules pertain to specific and observable behaviors, and they generally have consequences associated with failing to follow them. (Information on developing classroom rules is presented in Module 2.)

Developing your guidelines is just the first step. If students are truly going to learn to exhibit these attitudes, traits, and behaviors, you will need to make them a vibrant part of your classroom. There are several ways you can do this, including (but not limited to) the following.

Post your guidelines in a prominent place in your classroom where everyone can see them. Teach them to students at the beginning of the year. As with your long-range goals, let students' families know what your Guidelines for Success are. Keep them alive by using them frequently in the classroom. For example, you can use them to prompt motivation; that is, to "pump up" your students to strive for excellence. You should also use the guidelines as a basis for providing both positive and corrective feedback to students regarding their behavior. "Shelly, when you pick up litter in the class without needing to be asked, it is a great example of being responsible." "Fionna, you need to work quietly. Part of the guideline about treating everyone with respect means you do not disturb others when they are trying to get their work finished."

Guidelines for Success can be used as the basis for celebrations of progress (e.g., class awards at the end of the week), in the context of your classroom's monthly themes (October is Be Responsible Month), as part of writing assignments, class discussions, and so on. (More specific information on how to use the guidelines to elicit motivation will be provided in Modules 4 and 5.)

Remember, when students do not receive information about or modeling of these kinds of attitudes, traits, and behaviors at home, the emphasis that school personnel place on their guidelines may provide critical lifelong lessons. If you find that some of your students have less of a context for understanding and operating from your guidelines, plan to provide more instruction on how students can implement them and be prepared to give students more encouragement and "pep talks" about their benefits.

NOTE

Whether you are starting CHAMPs at the beginning of or during the school year, we suggest that you take the time to implement this task. Guidelines for Success give your students critical information about how they can accomplish what it is that you expect from them—and this is valuable at any point in the year.

Task 3: Positive Expectations

Ensure that you have, and that you convey, high positive expectations for the success of all your students.

Research has repeatedly demonstrated what common sense tells us: when a teacher has low expectations for an individual student or a group of students, the student or students achieve less than if the teacher has high expectations. In other words, your "vision" of student achievement and performance has a significant impact on the reality of your students' achievement and performance. Therefore, it is crucial for you to have and convey high expectations for *all* your students in terms of their academic achievement and their ability to behave responsibly.

Please note that we are not suggesting that you wear rose-colored glasses or that you ignore the problems and difficulties your students may have. What we are saying is that you must foster high, yet realistic, expectations for your students if they are going to accomplish what you want them to accomplish. To understand the difference, consider the following examples. Imagine that you have a student in your class who is permanently confined to a wheelchair due to a birth defect. While it would be unrealistic to ignore the student's disability and pretend that she is no different than the other students, it is both realistic and important for you to expect her to thrive and be successful in your classroom. Similarly, although it would be unrealistic to expect this student to get out of her chair and run with other students in physical education class, you can and should expect that if you get information on how to adapt the physical education class, she will be able to participate actively and successfully.

A more subtle example would involve having a student with a reputation for chronic and long-standing behavior problems placed in your class at the beginning of a new school year. It may be unrealistic to think that this student will never misbehave, however, it is important for you to *expect* that he will be able to learn to behave independently and responsibly in your classroom. This task is all about having a belief in the potential success of every student.

The first step in ensuring that you have positive expectations for all students is to honestly and objectively consider the kinds of things you think to yourself and/or say to others *about* students. Whether or not you make disparaging remarks directly to students, if you let yourself think or talk about students in unproductive ways, you will be communicating low expectations.

Statements that indicate you have low expectations for your students include:

- "This student can really press my buttons."
- "That kid is ADHD so he can't do it."
- "What can you expect from a student like this?"
- "I just wish this student would move to a different school."
- "I guess that kind of thing is expected with a student from that kind of a home."

If you find that you have such thoughts or are making such statements to others, you need to put a stop to them. Try to identify specific alternate phrases that you can use. When you begin to think or speak negatively, force yourself to substitute a more positive way of thinking or speaking.

Even when you start the year with positive feelings about and expectations for your students, it can be difficult to sustain them. It's easy to get so busy that you don't notice the negative thoughts/statements creeping in. Or, it may be that a particularly trying student or class wears you out and, without realizing it, your expectations are lowered. To buttress against this, you need to periodically check-in with yourself. On the Self Assessment Checklist at the end of this module, we suggest marking your calendar now for times during the year when you will take the time to thoroughly examine your thoughts and statements about students.

In addition, we recommend that once school is in session, you make a point of monitoring the kinds of statements you actually make *to* students themselves. At various times throughout the year, be honestly self-critical about whether you have been using statements such as the following:

- To a small group—"You students have to work with me because you can't work by yourself."
- "Are you that stupid that you can't figure it out?"
- "I am not even going to bother to answer that question."
- "Stop asking such stupid questions."
- "Why don't you just grow up?"
- "You can't do that. It is too difficult for you. You had better do this instead."
- "Why would you do something like that? Use your head."

NOTE

Remarks like these are not only damaging to students, they are unprofessional and unacceptable. All teachers need to make a commitment to never use this kind of language with students.

A college professor was once asked, "But, what do you do about the kid you just don't like?" He wisely and calmly responded, "You can't dislike kids on company time." The point is that although you do not have to personally like every student (you can even dislike some on your own time), during the hours you are being paid, you must maintain a high expectation for every student's success. The way you treat your students at school should have as little to do with "liking" or "disliking" them, as the quality of care your physician provides you depends on how much she likes or dislikes you. When you are feeling frustrated with a student or students, think before you speak. It is fine to address a misbehavior or problem, for example, "Jill, you must quit making noise when people around you are trying to work." However, calling the student names or otherwise passing judgment about the student will in no way help make the situation better and will probably damage any trust the student has in you.

Implementing one or more of the following suggestions can help you to keep positive attitudes and expectations toward your students:

- **Take care of yourself.** You are more likely to maintain positive expectations and attitudes if you are in good health. Design a "wellness" program for yourself to ensure you are getting adequate rest and exercise and that you have activities and interests outside of your career.
- **Maintain a positive, but realistic vision of students behaving successfully.** When problems occur, keep reminding yourself of the vision of students behaving successfully. This is especially important if you are dealing with students who repeatedly behave poorly. Set aside a minute or two each day to visualize the student being successful.
- **Be reflective about your behavior management plan.** Periodically ask yourself what is going well and what needs improvement in your behavior management plan. If you identify something that needs improvement, take steps to do something differently. Remember that even though you may not be able to directly control student behavior, you can modify various aspects of your classroom (e.g., seating arrangements, schedules, the way you interact with a student, and so on), which in turn may have a positive effect on student behavior.
- **Don't take it personally.** If a student misbehaves, try to remain objective. You are not the cause of the problem, but you do offer the best hope of positively reaching the student. Remind yourself that you are a professional and you can, eventually, solve any problem. It may also help to remember that you are probably not the only one—the student probably treats most adults the same way.
- **Make an overt effort to interact positively with each student.** All students should feel that you notice and have positive regard for them. Say "hello" to them, show an interest in their interests, and so on. When you make an effort to make contact with every student as an individual, they know that you value them and that reduces the likelihood that they will misbehave.
- **Consult with colleagues.** If an individual student or group becomes particularly challenging, discuss your concerns with fellow staff members. Be careful not to communicate low expectations, but describe the kinds of problems a student is having. Collegial problem solving is a powerful mechanism for getting ideas on how you might proceed to help the student.
- **Implement the tasks described in this program.** All of the tasks presented in the eight modules are designed to help you develop an effective and comprehensive approach to managing student behavior. Keep trying things until you find something that works for you.

It isn't enough to simply avoid having and/or communicating negative expectations about students. You also need to make a conscious effort to actively communicate high positive expectations to your students. Throughout this program we make a number of suggestions about how you can do that. They include things like sharing your Guidelines for Success and telling students that you know that they can achieve those guidelines; frequently reminding students that they are capable of achieving any goal they set their minds to; remembering to treat all students with dignity and respect; interacting with students in a friendly manner; etc.

NOTE

Whether you are starting CHAMPs at the beginning of or during the school year, we strongly recommend that you take the time to carefully consider this task. If you have low expectations for your students' behavior, they will live up to (or, perhaps more accurately, down to) those expectations. To successfully implement CHAMPs, you must have and communicate high expectations for every student's success.

Task 4: Family Contacts

Build positive relationships with your students' families by making initial contact with them at the beginning of the year and maintaining regular contact throughout the year.

NOTE

Given that more students than ever live in one-parent households, in foster care, with grandparents, and so on, we felt that it would often be inaccurate to refer to "the student's parents." Yet, we found it cumbersome to continually refer to "the student's parent(s), grandparent(s), or guardian(s)." Therefore, for accuracy and efficiency purposes, throughout this program we use the term "student's family" when talking about a student's primary caregivers.

There is no question that when school personnel and families work together to help meet the educational needs of students, the probability of effectively educating those students increases tremendously. That is why we believe that part of your classroom vision should be to have your class be a place where you, your students, and your students' families work collaboratively to ensure student success. Building the positive relationships necessary to work collaboratively with families, however, is not always easy. First of all, it requires communication, which takes time; and time can be a problem for both teachers and families.

Making the effort to communicate with your students' families, however, sends a powerful message that you want to include them in what happens at school. In addition, such efforts increase the probability that an individual student's family will be receptive should you need to inform them about and enlist their assistance in solving a behavioral or academic problem the student is having. (Note: Specific information on how to work with families when behavior problems occur is included in Module 7: Correction Procedures.) You can increase the likelihood of communicating efficiently and effectively with your students' families, if you develop a specific plan for how you will make initial contact with them at the beginning of the school year and how you will maintain ongoing contact with them throughout the year.

Family contacts are especially important when you have a large number of high-needs students. Unfortunately, the families of high-needs students may be more likely to feel alienated from the school, and more of those students may come from troubled homes. Because it's also possible that contacts will be more difficult to achieve with families of high-needs students, we urge you to remember that the greater the needs of your students, the greater the need for you to establish and maintain contact with their families.

The more personal you can make both initial and ongoing contacts, the more effective they will be in helping you build friendly and productive relationships with your students' families.

Face to face contacts are more personal than phone calls, which are more personal than notes, which are more personal than form letters. At the same time, however, more personal contacts generally require more time than less personal contacts. Thus, although we believe it is critical for teachers to establish and maintain contact with their students' families, we realize that each teacher will have to determine the nature and amount of contact that is realistically possible for him or her. Obviously, a middle school teacher who sees 150 students every day will not be able to have as many, or as personal, contacts with families of his/her students as a special education teacher who has 12 students.

NOTE

If the families of some (or many) of your students are non- and/or limited-English speaking, you will face an additional challenge. We recommend that you check with building and/or district personnel for information about getting some kind of assistance in communicating with the families' in their native languages. For example, maybe someone can translate written communications or an interpreter can be present for at-school events like conferences or Open House or possibly even during phone contacts. If your school is so diverse that there are many different primary languages, it may not be feasible to make adaptation arrangements for all the languages. However, if half your students come from Spanish-speaking homes, for example, arranging for important information to be translated into Spanish demonstrates to families the value you place on communicating with them.

Initial Contact

Because your initial contact with a student's family results in that family's "first impression" of you, it's important to make the contact friendly and inviting, yet also highly professional. When possible, try to establish initial contact with your students' families before the first day of school. If that is not possible, we recommend making initial contact within the first two weeks of school.

The purpose of an initial contact is twofold: to begin to establish a productive relationship with the students' families; and to give the student and their families important information about yourself and your vision of the upcoming school year. The type of information that we suggest you provide during an initial contact with students' families includes the following:

- A welcome indicating that you are looking forward to an exciting year.
- Some information about your background (e.g., I have taught for fifteen years, the last three years at the middle school level).
- A statement that you are looking forward to working with the student and getting to know the family.

- A statement stressing that you anticipate a very good year.
- Your major goals (academic and behavioral) for the year.
- Information about when and how the family can get in touch with you if they have questions and/or want to share information about the student that may be helpful for you to know.
- Information about when and how you will maintain ongoing communication with them (e.g., "I will be sending home a classroom newsletter every other week, and the first will be going home next Friday.").
- (Optional) A copy of your classroom rules, with a slip that can be signed by the student and a family member to indicate that they have discussed the rules.
- (Optional for middle school teachers) A syllabus that orients students to some of the detailed expectations of the class, such as homework schedules, routines, and so on.
- Invite comments or questions and give families a chance to let you know how you can reach them.

What follows are descriptions of four possible strategies for making initial contact with students' families, along with brief discussions of their relative pros and cons. As you read through them, consider whether one (or some combination) of the strategies might work for you. It's also possible that you already have or will need to develop a strategy that better meets your needs. However you decide to make initial contact with students' families, the important thing is that you take steps to do it.

Face to Face Contact Prior to the First Day of School

Some schools hold an "Open House" a day or so before school starts in order for students and families to meet their teachers and see their classrooms. If there is any possibility of implementing this wonderful idea at your school, you may wish to encourage it. Because it is so important for the families of students who are most likely to have trouble (e.g., those with a past history of behavioral or academic problems) to attend, we suggest that you also consider phoning those families to specifically invite them to the event. In addition, you should prepare a letter that contains the important initial contact information (see Figure 1.2), and give it to those students and families that attend the Open House. *NOTE: You will have to make sure the letter also gets to those students/families that did not attend.*

If you like the idea of face to face family contact before school starts but your school doesn't hold an Open House, consider possible alternatives. For example, you might contact only the families of students who have had problems in the past (e.g., a student who is painfully shy or who has a history of acting out) and invite those students/families to come to school before the first day to meet you and get oriented to the classroom.

Your building principal or counselor can probably point out which students and families from your class would most benefit from a welcoming contact (if you are not sure).

Phone Contact Prior to the First Day of School

If you know who will be in your class, another option is to phone each student's family. Most families will appreciate this effort to contact them directly. If you prepare an outline of the information you want the students and their families to have, it may be possible to keep each call to only a few minutes. (Just make sure that you aren't sounding like a recording by the last calls.) Unfortunately, if, as frequently happens, families want to tell you a great deal about their student, this kind of contact can end up taking ten minutes or so per student. As with face-to-face contact, if contacting all families is not feasible, you might consider contacting only the families of those students who have experienced either academic or behavioral difficulty in the past.

Letter Sent Home (on the first day of school)

This may be the most common and least time consuming strategy. It also tends to be the least personal. Another drawback is that if a family is illiterate, a letter alone will be an ineffective method of communicating and may even make the family defensive. Finally, when you send a letter home on the first day of school, it may get lost in a blizzard of other papers (e.g., bus schedules, immunization information and lunch menus). Figure 1.2 shows a letter to families used by a 4th grade teacher.

Figure 1.2: Letter to Families

Dear Families,

Hi! My name is Ms. Veric and I am your child's teacher this year. I am looking forward to a very exciting and productive year. I have been a teacher for six years, but this will be my first year of teaching fourth grade. As the year goes on, I am looking forward to meeting you and getting to know you and your student.

I want you and your student to know that my major goals for this year are that all students in my class:

- Develop skills in written expression so they can communicate in both narrative and expository styles.
- master all basic addition, subtraction, multiplication and division facts and correctly apply those facts when doing computation and problem solving.
- learn to work cooperatively in groups and to sometimes take the leadership role.
- learn to plan long-range projects and bring them to completion including two major reports and two major projects.
- speak in front of groups with confidence and style.
- stay focused on written tasks and bring those tasks to completion.

I will be sending home a classroom newsletter every other week, and the first will be going home next Friday. In that letter, I will tell you about my "Guidelines for Success" and my classroom rules.

If you want to speak with me for any reason, don't hesitate to give me a call The best time to call is between 3:00 and 4:00 on Monday, Tuesday, Thursday or Friday at 555-1234. Or call any time between 8:00 and 4:00 and leave a message and I will get back to you.

Please feel free to let me know any information that may help me to be successful with your child, and let me know the best way (and time) to reach you.

Good-bye for now and let your child know that we will all have a great year in Room 17.

Sincerely,

Ms. Veric
4th Grade Teacher

Videotape Sent Home (during the first two weeks of school)

Most families today, even many low-income families, have a videocassette recorder (VCR). Another way to make initial contact with your students' families is to make a videotape introducing you and your classroom and send it home with students during the first week or two of school. A video may give students' families a better sense of who you are and create a greater sense of comfort and trust with you than a letter would. (A disadvantage is that it may put a student whose family does not have a VCR in an uncomfortable or embarrassing position.)

Teachers can pair up and help each other make their videotapes. As one teacher operates the camera, the other can greet his/her students' families, talk about his/her major goals for the year, and even give a brief tour of the classroom ("And over here is the science learning center. When students are done with their work, this is one of five centers they can choose to spend time in. Of course, they will have to clean up the center after they work here, but we will be working on how to use and take care of the centers during the first two weeks of school.") Once the first person has finished making his/her tape, the teachers can change roles. If you prepare an outline in advance, filming a video like this should take no longer than writing a letter.

To make sure that each student has the opportunity to take a tape home during the first two weeks of school, you will probably need seven to ten copies of the tape. The time and expense required to make multiple copies of the tape may be a major disadvantage to this strategy. Check with your district's media department to see if they can help you. NOTE: If there are many non-English speaking families in your class, you should also look into having a couple of tapes with a voice-over translation.

If you use a videotape, you may still want to have a letter that goes over your classroom rules and your major goals for the class that the family can sign and return. The letter also provides a back-up form of communication for any students who do not have a VCR at home.

Ongoing Contact

In addition to making initial contact with your students' families at the beginning of the year, you also need to maintain ongoing contact with them during the year. Remember, the more families feel you are making an effort to keep them informed, the greater the probability that they will work with you should their student have a behavioral or academic problem. The key here is to come up with a way of maintaining communication without burning yourself out.

Some contact opportunities will arise from regularly scheduled school events, such as parent-teacher conferences, Open House, or Back to School Night. Other ways of keeping families informed of major class priorities, activities, and/or issues, which may require more time and energy, include having a weekly, bi-weekly, or monthly class newsletter or newspaper, or sending families a letter from you on a regular basis.

We suggest that you record your ongoing contacts with families, using a class list and some form of coding. For example, you might write "9/22, Ph" and "10/4, Conf" next to a student's name to indicate that you made a phone contact on September 22nd and had a face-to-face conference at school on October 4th. A method like this will let you monitor how often and in what ways you have contacted each student's family. It also allows you to see at a glance whether there are any families with whom you have not had contact.

NOTE

When family contact is necessary because of some problem a student is having, it's important to pre-think what you want to say and how you are going to say it. This will reduce the chances that you will be misunderstood or inadvertently say something insensitive. Suggestions for handling this type of situation, and reproducible templates for making notes prior to contacting a family, are provided in Module 7: Correction Procedures.

NOTE

If you are starting CHAMPs during the school year, making initial contact with families will probably be a relatively low priority. However, you should put time and energy into maintaining as much positive contact as you can to build relationships with your students' families. Before the beginning of the next school year, make sure that you have a specific plan for both establishing and maintaining contact with families.

Task 5: Professionalism

Demonstrate professionalism at all times.

As a teacher, you are a professional. Effective teachers understand that it is important for them to behave in a manner that communicates their professionalism. Imagine how you would feel if you went to a professional (e.g., a physician, architect, attorney) who dressed like a slob, acted hesitant and unsure or arrogant and condescending, and/or talked about your personal issues with members of your community. It is doubtful that you would have much confidence in such a person, and consequently he or she probably wouldn't be very effective in helping you. We have chosen to include the issue of professionalism in this program on classroom management because teachers who fail to demonstrate professionalism tend to have more difficulty managing the behavior of their students.

We do not mean to imply that professionalism alone will ensure that your students won't have behavior problems—it's not that simple. However, a lack of professionalism can cause behavioral situations to be worse. Therefore, we urge you to maintain a vision of yourself as a professional and to demonstrate professionalism at all times. The following information provides a structure for considering whether there are attitudes or behaviors that you might modify to reflect more professionalism.

Be an active problem solver.

When faced with a problem (e.g., a student is not behaving responsibly and/or is not making adequate academic progress), the teacher demonstrating professionalism will analyze the problem and take responsibility for seeking and implementing a solution. On the other hand, a teacher not acting professionally will tend to blame the problem on someone else and/or feel that someone else should solve the problem. The teacher demonstrating professionalism will also continue to try various strategies until a solution is found—that is, he or she never gives up. As Eleanor Roosevelt once said, "We have never failed unless we have ceased to try."

Work cooperatively with colleagues.

Working cooperatively means both responding supportively when another teacher or a paraprofessional asks your advice about a particular student or situation, *and* being willing to ask your colleagues for help with a student or situation that is troubling you. If someone comes to you for help, give that person your full attention and work with him/her to identify possible strategies for addressing the situation in question. At the same time, if you have a student who consistently misbehaves and your attempts to help the student improve her behavior have been ineffective, you should not hesitate to ask a fellow teacher for additional ideas. Seeking collegial assistance is a sign of professional strength—not weakness. This may be most clearly demonstrated by professionals in the field of medicine. When faced with a puzzling situation, most physicians will discuss the case with other physicians. It is our belief that teachers can and should exhibit this same level of collegial problem-solving.

Another aspect of working with colleagues is being willing to provide emotional support to others. When someone has a problem or is going through a difficult time in his/her personal life, the support of colleagues can be invaluable. Finally, we urge you to remember that it is never appropriate to put a colleague down or talk about a colleague behind his or her back. In fact, you should even be very careful about how and when you use any form of sarcasm.

Respect the confidentiality of both students and colleagues.

You should not discuss your students' problems outside of school, especially if you live in the community in which you teach. In addition, unless you are participating in a school-sponsored problem-solving procedure, we suggest that you avoid talking about school business or the concerns of your co-workers. Consider, for example, a situation in which you feel that another teacher is not giving you the help and support you need regarding a problem student that both of you teach. The most professional response is to go directly to this person, discuss your concerns, and ask for more assistance. It would be highly unprofessional to discuss the problem with other teachers and/or bring the problem up during a parent-teacher conference. Again, look at the medical profession. A physician can and should discuss cases with colleagues at work, however it is inappropriate and unprofessional for her to talk about a patient with the guests at a dinner party. As a teaching professional, you owe your students and fellow staff members the same level of professionalism that they expect and deserve from their doctors. Be aware that in some schools, discussions in the faculty room may border on being unprofessional (e.g., discussing students in a hostile or sarcastic manner). If this is the case, just be sure that you are not a contributor. Regardless of the behavior of others, maintain your high level of professional behavior.

Engage in ongoing professional development, which includes reflecting on your own teaching practices.

Professionals are expected to continually learn and grow in their chosen fields. For example, most physicians who have been practicing medicine for over ten years are doing some things differently today than they did when they first started out as doctors. Professional development requires both keeping up-to-date on new information in your field and being willing to look at your own behavior with a critical eye. "What am I doing that is working effectively? What is not working effectively?" After identifying things that are not working effectively, the true professional is always on the lookout for a better way to do them—from peers, from professional books, and from the research literature.

It is our hope that the information in this program, along with the Self-Assessment Checklists and Peer Study Worksheets, will help you examine and, as necessary, modify your behavior management practices. In addition, we urge you to do your own review of the research on effective teaching. A great source for identifying strategies that have a solid research base is Effective Schooling Practices: A Research Synthesis, 1995 Update. This excellent summary of school and teacher effectiveness literature was compiled by Kathleen Cotton, and is updated every five years or so. To order a copy, you can call 503-275-9519. Excerpts from the manual can be found in Appendix 1: What the Research Says.

Act in a professional manner.

The concept of acting in a professional manner is somewhat hard to pin down. One way to approach it is to think about the kind of demeanor you want/expect when you go to someone for professional services (e.g., a physician, an attorney, or an architect). Most of us probably prefer someone who seems knowledgeable, confident, and comfortable—but not haughty and arrogant. We are generally uncomfortable with someone who seems extremely unsure of themselves, doesn't seem to like his/her job, complains about his/her working conditions, and/or someone who mumbles when he/she talks to us or doesn't make eye contact with us.

A teacher should try to always act in a relaxed and confident manner. Notice that we did not say you need to *be* relaxed and confident, just that you should act relaxed and confident. In fact, there may be times when you are unsure of yourself or unsure of how to handle a situation. While it's not necessary to give the impression that you know what to do when you don't, you do want to keep reminding yourself that you are a professional, that you provide a valuable service to your students and the community, and that you can solve any problem—eventually. Ask yourself whether you would rather go to physician who bluffs and blusters when he is unsure or one who confidently says, "I am unsure what is the best course of action, but I will find out."

Professionalism also includes dependability. As a professional, you need to arrive at work on time; fulfill your various duties (e.g., supervising a bus-waiting area for two weeks) without needing reminders; attend staff meetings and give your full attention to the business being conducted; stay on top of attendance and grade reports; and so on.

Present a professional appearance.

We may not always recognize how much our appearance affects the impression others have of us, but it does. In addition to making sure that you dress neatly and cleanly, we believe that you need to consider the degree of casualness/formality that is most appropriate for your work attire. While wearing high-powered business suits is not necessary for most teachers, a teacher who is dressed in baggy sweat pants and a sweater with holes and coffee stains definitely gives the wrong impression—to students, students' families, other teachers, and administrators.

We are not trying to give fashion advice here; nor are we saying that you need to be "fashionable." What we are suggesting is that you should carefully select an appropriate level of casualness/formality for your school attire. For a P.E. teacher who frequently provides demonstrations to students, wearing nice workout clothing is probably perfectly reasonable. However, we question whether sweats are appropriate for classroom teachers. Specific questions, like "Should men always wear a tie?" "Are casual pants acceptable?" etc., should be answered within the context of your particular school and its community's standards. As a general rule, we recommend that you dress with a level of formality that is typical of the most professional staff in your district. If you are unsure about what attire is considered appropriate, ask your administrator.

NOTE

If you are starting CHAMPs during the school year, addressing this task may be a relatively low priority. However, before the next school year begins, you should review the information presented here and examine your own attitudes and behaviors in terms of professionalism.

Task 6: Behavior Management Principles

Develop an understanding of fundamental behavior management principles so that you can make effective decisions and take appropriate actions to help your students learn to behave responsibly.

The focus of Module 1 is on creating a vision of what you want your classroom to be like. Because there will undoubtedly be times when your students will not behave as responsibly as you would like, your classroom vision should include something about how you will help them learn to behave more responsibly. We believe you can do this by developing an understanding of and skill in using fundamental behavior management principles. Specifically, as a teacher, you need to know why and how to: (1) structure your class to promote responsible student behavior; (2) effectively acknowledge responsible student behavior; and (3) effectively respond to irresponsible student behavior. The following pages present information that overviews the principles we believe to be most important. Modules 3-8 include more detailed information about the principles and specific actions that you can take.

The principles of behavior management are grounded in the assumption that people are constantly engaged in learning and that every experience adds to a person's knowledge base and influences (both consciously and unconsciously) his/her subsequent actions. For example, someone who has submitted scores of resumes, but hasn't gotten any job interviews might decide to write a new resume. If, after sending out the new resume, the person gets multiple interviews, he or she is more likely to use the new resume instead of the old one in the future. Similarly, someone who goes to a movie based on a friend's recommendation, but finds it to be a poor movie and a waste of money, isn't likely to take that friend's movie recommendations as seriously in the future.

Figure 1.3: Variables that Affect Behavior

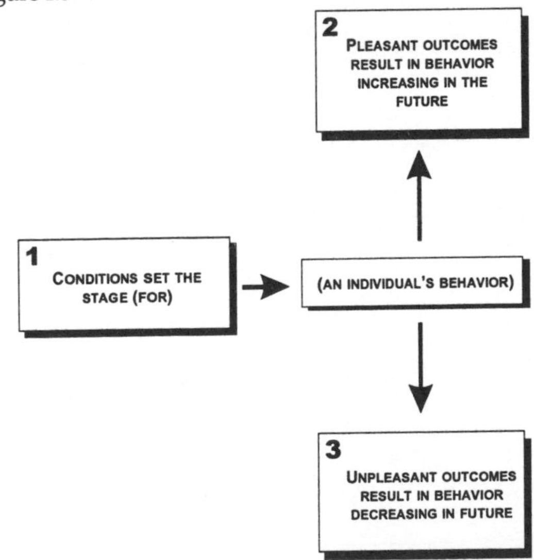

Scenarios such as these are repeated in each person's life many times per day, in uncountable and interwoven combinations, to create a rich fabric of experiences and learning. Simply put, a person's behavior is influenced by events and conditions he or she experiences, some of which will encourage that person to engage in certain behaviors and others of which will discourage that person from engaging in certain behaviors. Figure 1.3 shows a graphic representation (model) of the three main variables that affect behavior.

Those with behavioral training will recognize this to be a model of behavioral theory—expressed in common sense and pragmatic terms. We believe that this model provides a useful structure for helping teachers understand behavior management principles.

NOTE

Because the vocabulary typically associated with behavioral theory is so often misunderstood and/or misused, we have deliberately chosen to use less technical vocabulary and more common sense examples. In addition, although the fundamentals of school-based behavior management are based on a large and comprehensive body of research findings, we have chosen to include only that information that we believe will be most useful to teachers. As a result, what is presented here reflects a simple understanding of very complex principles.

To effectively apply the fundamental principles of behavior management to your classroom, there are two essential underlying concepts that you should keep in mind. We believe that these concepts have such important implications about where teachers should put their time and energy in terms of managing student behavior that we have used them to organize the remainder of the information.

1. Effective teachers spend more time promoting responsible behavior than responding to irresponsible behavior.

2. Effective teachers recognize that misbehavior (especially any chronic misbehavior) occurs for a reason, and take the reason into account when determining how to respond to the misbehavior.

Promoting Responsible Behavior

When you focus a majority of your time and energy on promoting responsible behavior by using effective instruction, providing appropriate positive feedback, and ensuring that there are no negative results for students when they behave responsibly, you will prevent most misbehavior from ever occurring. There are three main categories of teacher-based actions for promoting responsible behavior that you need to address:

1. Set up conditions that prompt responsible behavior and discourage irresponsible behavior. Specific actions can include:
   - Making sure students understand what the behavioral expectations are;
   - Making sure students know how to meet the behavioral expectations;

- Arranging the physical space so that it is more conducive to responsible behavior than irresponsible behavior;
- Designing a fast-paced schedule and providing interesting lessons;
- Running efficient transitions between activities;
- Interacting respectfully and positively with all students; and
- Showing an interest in student work.

2 Ensure that students experience positive results when they engage in responsible behavior. Specific actions can include:

- Giving verbal praise;
- Writing positive notes;
- Encouraging students to praise themselves;
- Contacting parents regarding responsible behavior; and
- Occasionally rewarding individuals or the whole class with a special activity.

3 Ensure that students *do not* experience negative results from exhibiting responsible behavior. Specific actions can include:

- Avoiding embarrassing students with praise;
- Ensuring that no student is laughed at for making a mistake during class participation;
- Ensuring that no student ever feels "like a geek" for behaving responsibly; and
- Ensuring that no one is ridiculed as a "teacher's pet" for behaving responsibly.

Misbehavior Occurs for a Reason

It is often difficult to understand why a student behaves irresponsibly, especially when the consequences of that behavior seem highly unpleasant. However, whenever a student or group of students exhibits irresponsible behavior on an *ongoing basis*, the behavior is occurring for a reason—it is not completely random. Therefore, the first thing you need to do is determine the reason for the misbehavior. Among the likely possibilities:

- The student doesn't know exactly what you expect.
- The student doesn't know how to exhibit the responsible behavior.
- The student is unaware that he or she is engaged in the misbehavior.
- The student is experiencing some pleasant outcome from exhibiting the misbehavior (e.g., she likes the attention she gets from adults or peers).
- The student is successfully avoiding some unpleasant outcome by exhibiting the misbehavior (e.g., she is getting out of assigned work).

Once you have a reasonable idea about why a chronic misbehavior is occurring, you can take actions to reduce and eventually eliminate it. Again, there are three major categories of teacher-based actions for you to consider:

1. Modify any conditions that may be perpetuating the misbehavior. Specific actions can include:
   - Providing lessons to teach the student how to behave responsibly;
   - Assigning different seats to two students who talk when they sit together;
   - Modifying work that is too difficult for the student not completing assignment;
   - Pacing lessons more quickly so students are less likely to get off task; and
   - Providing something for students to do when they have completed classwork.

2. Remove any pleasant outcomes that might be resulting from the misbehavior. Specific actions can include:
   - Ignoring misbehavior that is designed to get attention;
   - Responding calmly to a student who likes to make adults angry; and
   - Ensuring that a student is not getting out of doing assigned work as a result of the misbehavior.

3. Implement corrective consequences that will make exhibiting the misbehavior more unpleasant for the student. Examples include:
   - Using a system of demerits (e.g. three demerits results in an after school detention);
   - Taking away one minute of recess for each infraction;
   - Using a classroom point system and instituting point fines for particular infractions, and
   - Contacting the student's parents regarding problem behavior.

A Case Study—Taking Action to Improve Irresponsible Behavior

Our case study involves a seventh grade student who is chronically argumentative with staff (and has been since he entered the middle school). This student has been continually sent out of class and regularly assigned to detention. His parents must be called frequently, and he often faces school staff who are angry and frustrated with him.

The first thing to do is identify what positive function this student's behavior is serving for him. There are several possibilities to consider. For example, it may be that getting lots of attention from adults (i.e., direct and angry engagement) gives this student a sense of power. Or, he may be getting lots of attention from his peers (for appearing strong and powerful enough to fight with teachers). The following represent the main types of action that school personnel might take to influence this student's behavior. (The specific procedures included for each category might be used as a menu. Not all of the procedures would be implemented. Staff would select one or two from each category to implement with the argumentative student depending on the exact nature of the situation.)

1. Modify conditions (organization, schedule, physical structure, and so on) to encourage more responsible behavior and discourage the irresponsible behavior.
   - Give the student a high status job (to be performed daily) that will increase his sense of power and purpose in the school.
   - Because the student seems to behave better during teacher-directed instruction, consider arranging for a greater percentage of his daily schedule to be teacher-directed instruction.
   - To mitigate the possibility that the student is misbehaving because he is frustrated over academic difficulties, arrange for him to privately receive tutorial assistance in his most difficult subjects.
   - Assign the student a different place to sit in the room.
   - Tell all staff to make an effort to give the student very clear directions.
   - Remind staff to avoid power struggles with the student.

2. Implement procedures designed to encourage responsible behavior.
   - Tell all staff that whenever the student exhibits responsible behavior, they should give him specific praise.
   - Ask all staff members to make an effort to give the student frequent, unconditional, positive adult attention.
   - Remind all staff to *privately* praise the student when he follows directions without arguing.

3. Remove any aversive aspects of exhibiting responsible behavior.
   - Modify the student's academic assignments so that he can succeed.
   - Correct the student before he makes an error (e.g., privately say to the student, "This is the type of work period where you need to really try to stay calm and work with me without arguing. Let's have a good day today.")
   - Teach particularly difficult assignments to the student prior to presenting the assigment to the class.
   - Prearrange times during the day when the student can privately ask teachers questions and/or get assistance so he does not have to do so in front of his peers.
   - Remind staff to avoid publicly praising the student for following directions.

4. Remove any positive aspects of exhibiting irresponsible behavior.

- Remind staff *not* to engage in arguing with the student. Provide training as necessary.
- Train other students to ignore situations in which the student begins to argue.
- Train staff to maintain instructional momentum so the student doesn't get attention from peers when he attempts to argue.

5 Implement effective corrective consequences designed to reduce irresponsible behavior. Have all staff respond to the student's arguing with the following procedures:

- Give the student a warning when he begins to argue. (e.g., "This is an example of arguing.")
- Calmly implement a corrective consequence if the student continues to argue after the warning.
- Ignore any further attempts by the student to engage in arguing.
- Redirect the student into the activity he should be engaged in.
- Keep accurate records of the number of times and the duration of each arguing incident.

Implementing an intervention plan that includes procedures from some or all of these categories will increase the probability that staff efforts to help this student learn to behave more responsibly will be successful. The sample plan described above, for example, might not be effective if staff did nothing to remove positive aspects of exhibiting the irresponsible behavior. That is, the student's behavior would not improve if getting peer and teacher attention outweighed all the other steps taken.

NOTE

Whether you are starting CHAMPs at the beginning of or during the school year, this is an important task. Most of the suggestions in the rest of the program assume that you understand the basics of behavior management that have been presented here.

Task 7: Level of Classroom Structure

Determine whether your students need you to implement a classroom management plan that involves high, medium, or low structure.

A classroom management plan's level of structure refers to the degree of teacher orchestration for various classroom activities that is necessary to ensure that students will be successful. Whether your management plan needs low, medium, or high structure depends primarily on the risk factors for the students in your classroom. If you have significant numbers of immature or emotionally needy children, the risk factors are probably high and you will need a more tightly structured plan. If your class is composed of predominantly mature and independent students, the risk factors are likely to be low and a more loosely structured plan should be perfectly adequate.

When your class has high "risk factors" and you do not orchestrate things tightly enough, student behavior tends to be problematic. For example, although beginning instruction quickly is a good idea regardless of a class' risk factors, in a class with high risk factors, student behavior may be especially problematic if you do not orchestrate the beginning of class well. That is, if students in this class have nothing to do for the first five minutes of class because you are taking attendance and doing "housekeeping" activities, they are likely to be talking, out of their seats, and exhibiting other behaviors that may make it difficult to begin teaching once you have finished with the attendance and housekeeping procedures. On the other hand, if you begin instruction immediately after the bell rings, and then take attendance after students have begun working on a task, you will have established instructional momentum and increased the probability that students will behave appropriately.

As you read through the subsequent modules in this program, you will notice references to how various tasks might be implemented differently depending on whether your class has high risk factors or low risk factors. If you have high risk factors, you should plan to implement all of the tasks in all eight modules of the program. If you have low risk factors, you can implement only those tasks you think might facilitate student engagement with academic tasks, and avoid any procedures that might cut into instructional time. If you have medium risk factors, we recommend that you plan to implement most of the tasks in this program (except those that seem unnecessary because students will be engaged and motivated without them), but that you not worry about implementing them in a highly structured fashion. To summarize, the greater the number of risk factors, the greater the pressure on you, the teacher, to orchestrate carefully and to implement *all* of the tasks.

We recommend that you make a preliminary determination about the necessary level of structure before you begin designing your classroom management plan. You should also plan to re-evaluate the level of structure your class needs at various times throughout the year. For example, we suggest that sometime during the fourth or fifth week of school, and again after winter and spring break, you evaluate how well students are meeting your expectations.

If a significant number of students are not meeting expectations, you may need to move to a more highly structured management plan. Directions for collecting and analyzing the evaluation information will be provided in Module 6: Monitor and Revise.

What level of structure do you need?

The reproducible Management & Discipline Planning Questionnaire (Figure 1.4) is designed to help you determine the "risk factors" for your class and the level of structure that is most appropriate for your classroom management plan. It can also be used throughout the year to increase your awareness of those aspects of your classroom management plan that should be reviewed and revised to increase or decrease the level of structure in your classroom.

Figure 1.4: Reproducible

Management & Discipline Planning Questionnaire

For each question circle the number under the statement that best answers the question. If you are unsure about or do not know the answer to a question, circle the middle choice. When you are done, add all the numbers circled and enter the total on the line provided (you should have a number between 0 and 120).

Questions 1- 6 relate to the population of the entire school			
1 How would you describe overall behavior of students in your school?	Generally quite irresponsible. I frequently have to nag and/or assign consequences. 10	Most students behave responsibly, but about 10% put me in the position where I have to nag and/or assign consequences. 5	Generally responsible. I rarely find it necessary to nag and/or assign consequences. 0
2 What percentage of students in your school qualify for free or reduced lunch?	60% or more 10	10% to 60% 5	Less than 10% 0
3 What percentage of students in your school typically move in and/or out of the school during the course of the school year?	50% or more 10	10% to 50% 5	Less than 10% 0
4 How would you describe the overall attitude of students toward school?	A large percentage hate school and ridicule the students who are motivated. 10	It's a mix, but most students feel okay about school. 5	The vast majority of students like school and are highly motivated. 0
5 How would you describe the overall nature of the interactions between students and adults in your school?	There are frequent confrontations, which include sarcasm and/or disrespect. 10	There is a mix, but most interactions are respectful and positive. 5	The vast majority of interactions are respectful and positive. 0
6 How would you describe the level of interest and support provided by the parents of students in your school?	Many parents are openly antagonistic and many show no interest in school. 10	Most parents are at least somewhat supportive of school. 5	The majority are interested, involved, and supportive of what goes on in the school. 0
Questions 7- 11 relate to students in your class this year. Middle school teachers should use their most difficult class.			
7 What grade level do you teach?	K or 1 20	6, 7, or 8 10	Other 0
8 How many students do you have in your class?	30 or more 10	23 to 30 5	22 or less 0
9 What is the reputation of this group of students from previous years? For example, if you teach fifth grade, what was the reputation of these students as fourth graders?	This is the class from hell. 10	It's a mix, but most students work hard and cooperate. 5	This group is very hard working and cooperative. 0
10 How many students in your class have been identified as Severely Emotionally Disturbed (SED)? Note: This label varies from state to state (e.g., ED, EBD, BD, and so on.)	Two or more 10	One 5	Zero 0
11 Not including students identified as SED, how many students have a reputation for chronic discipline problems?	Three or more 10	One or two 5	Zero 0

Total ________

Use the following scale to interpret your risk factors and determine the most appropriate level of structure for your classroom management plan.

IF YOUR TOTAL IS:	YOUR RISK FACTORS ARE:
0 to 30	**Low,** which means your students can probably be successful with a classroom management plan that involves **Low, Medium or High Structure.**
31 to 60	**Medium,** which means that for your students to be successful, your classroom management plan should involve **Medium or High Structure.**
61 to 120	**High,** which means that for your students to be successful, your classroom management plan should involve **High Structure.**

Module 1: Vision

Self-Assessment Checklist

Use the worksheet on the following pages to identify which (or which parts) of the tasks described in this module you have completed. For any item that has not been completed, note what needs to be done to complete it. Then translate your notes onto your planning calendar in the form of specific actions that you can take (e.g., August 17, finish Guidelines for Success, write orientation letter for parents.)

COMPLETED	TASK	NOTES & IMPLEMENTATION IDEAS
	LONG-RANGE CLASSROOM GOALS I have developed and written down four to seven major goals (instructional and/or behavioral) that I want to accomplish with all my students by the end of the school year. I have identified specific ways in which I will use these goals to guide lesson planning and decision making throughout the year. I have a specific plan for letting my students and their families know what the long-range classroom goals are.	
	GUIDELINES FOR SUCCESS I have identified three to six basic attitudes, traits, and/or behaviors that are important for my students to succeed in my classroom and in their lives. From them I have created a set of "Guidelines for Success" (or "Guiding Principles," "Goals" etc.). I have posted the "Guidelines for Success" in my classroom.	

COMPLETED	TASK	NOTES & IMPLEMENTATION IDEAS
	I have identified specific ways in which I can and will make frequent use of the "Guidelines for Success," including: • as topics for class discussions about behavior or goals; • referring to them when providing positive or corrective feedback to students; • as monthly class themes, as part of class assignments, during classwide celebrations of progress, etc.	
	POSITIVE EXPECTATIONS I understand the importance of having high expectations for all my students. I will make a conscious effort not to say anything (to students, their families, or others) that would suggest that I have low expectations for any student. I have identified specific ways I can and will convey my high expectations to students, their families, and others. I have noted in my planning calendar times during the year when I will objectively examine my expectations for, language about, and behavior toward my students.	

COMPLETED	TASK	NOTES & IMPLEMENTATION IDEAS
	FAMILY CONTACTS I am committed to establishing positive relationships with my students' families as part of my classroom vision.	
	I have a specific plan for how I will make initial contact with my students' families at the beginning of the year.	
	I have a specific plan for how I will maintain ongoing contact with my student's families throughout the year.	
	PROFESSIONALISM I understand the importance of demonstrating professionalism at all times. Specifically, I will make an effort to: • be an active problem solver; • work cooperatively with my colleagues; • respect the confidentiality of all students and colleagues; • engage in professional development activities; and • dress and act in a professional manner.	

COMPLETED	TASK	NOTES & IMPLEMENTATION IDEAS
	BEHAVIOR MANAGEMENT PRINCIPLES I have sufficient knowledge of fundamental behavior management principles that I can effectively help my students learn to behave more responsibly. Specifically: 1. I know why and how to promote responsible behavior by: • setting up conditions that prompt responsible behavior; • ensuring that students experience positive results for engaging in responsible behavior; and • ensuring that students do not experience negative results from exhibiting responsible behavior; and 2. I know why and how to deal with misbehavior by: • recognizing that all misbehavior occurs for a reason, and taking that reason into account when designing an intervention; • identifying, and then modifying any conditions that may be perpetuating the misbehavior; • identifying, and then eliminating any positive outcomes that may be resulting from the misbehavior; and • implementing appropriate corrective consequences calmly and consistently when necessary.	

COMPLETED	TASK	NOTES & IMPLEMENTATION IDEAS
	LEVEL OF CLASSROOM STRUCTURE I have carefully considered all factors, especially the needs of my students, to determine whether my classroom management plan needs to involve high, medium, or low structure. I have noted in my planning calendar times throughout the year to re-evaluate the level of structure my classroom needs. Specifically: • during the fourth or fifth week of school I will conduct *CHAMPs* Assessments (Module 6). • shortly after winter and spring vacations I will conduct the *CHAMPs* Assessments (Module 6).	

Module 1: Vision

Peer Study Worksheet

Schedule one to two hours with one to five colleagues. Each participant should have read Module 1 and worked through the Self-Assessment activities in advance of this discussion time. By discussing each participant's policies, procedures and questions regarding the tasks in Module 1, each participant will gain a deeper understanding of Module 1 and will learn tips and techniques from colleagues. Begin the discussion by prioritizing the seven tasks—which task interests participants most (i.e., for which task do you most want to hear the procedures and policies of colleagues.)? Which task is the next highest priority? In this way, if there is not adequate time to discuss all seven tasks within the hour, discussion will focus on the tasks of greatest interest to you and the other participants. Work through the prioritized tasks by discussing the questions or topics within that task. Then go on to the next highest priority. Continue this process and complete as many of the tasks as possible within the scheduled time.

Task 1: Long-Range Classroom Goals

A. Have each group member share his/her goals and explain why he/she chose those goals.

B. As a group, examine each member's goals individually, giving positive and constructive feedback on their content and language.

C. Have each group member share how he/she plans to communicate his/her long-range goals to students and students' families.

Task 2: Guidelines for Success

A. If your school does not have schoolwide "Guidelines for Success," have each group member share his/her "guidelines" with the other group members.

B. Brainstorm at least six different strategies, other than those identified in the text, for using "Guidelines for Success" in the classroom to help students understand and internalize them.

C. If your school does not have schoolwide "Guidelines for Success," discuss: 1) whether it would be worth trying to develop schoolwide agreement so that all staff emphasize the same set of attitudes, characteristics, or traits; and 2) what actions would be necessary to get a schoolwide development process started.

Task 3: Positive Expectations

A. Have group members share what they do to avoid developing low expectations for a student who is chronically behaviorally challenging.

B. Objectively consider whether the atmosphere at your school is one of positive expectations for students (e.g., evaluate the kinds of comments about students that are made in the faculty room). If it is not, identify things those of you who are in the group might do to help your whole staff develop more positive expectations.

Task 4: Family Contacts

A. Have each group member share his/her strategies for making initial contact with families.
   - Discuss the utility and feasibility of contacting all students' families before the school year begins.
   - Discuss the utility and feasibility of contacting only the families of some of the more troubled students.
   - Have group members share any orientation letters they have used.
   - Discuss the utility and feasibility of making a "Welcome to My Classroom" videotape.

B. Have each group member share his/her strategies for maintaining ongoing contact with families.
   - Group members who use newsletters should bring samples.
   - Discuss how a "Contact Log" might be used to keep records of family contacts.

C. If relevant, discuss strategies for improving communication with families that are limited- and/or non-English speaking.

Task 5: Professionalism

A. Discuss each of the aspects of being professional that were discussed in the text. In particular, are there any items (summarized below) with which you disagree?
   - being an active problem solver
   - respecting the confidentiality of students and colleagues
   - acting in a professional manner
   - working cooperatively with colleagues
   - engaging in professional development activities
   - presenting a professional appearance

B. Identify and discuss other aspects of being a professional that were not presented in the text.

Task 6: Behavior Management Principles

A. Identify the three categories of procedures for promoting responsible behavior.

B. Identify the three categories of procedures to take into account once you have identified the reason a chronic misbehavior may be occurring (e.g., the student loves getting attention from other students by making rude comments in class).

C. Have group members discuss whether this organization for categorizing behavior management strategies is useful. Ask them to share specific examples.

Task 7: Level of Classroom Structure

A. Have each group member share his/her completed "Management & Discipline Planning Questionnaire."

B. Have group members discuss how the level of structure they have identified will affect their classroom management plan.

C. Briefly discuss why you should periodically re-evaluate the level of structure required for your class, and have each group member identify when he/she will re-evaluate the level of structure necessary for his/her class.

MODULE 2: ORGANIZATION

When you have well-organized routines and procedures for your classroom, you model and prompt organized behavior from your students.

Introduction

Think about two different college classes. In one class, the professor always begins class right on time, uses class time to focus on essential class concepts, and has clear assignments with definite due dates. Now, contrast that with a different class in which the professor never begins class on time because he is always sorting through his notes or organizing his transparencies. This professor often uses class time to just chat about whatever is on his mind. His assignments are unclear and you are never sure when they are due. Which of these classes are you likely to appreciate the most and in which class are you most likely to strive toward excellence? The organization (that is, the procedures and routines) within a classroom influences the behavior and motivation of students.

The seven tasks presented in this module are designed to help you organize your classroom in a manner that is both efficient and likely to prompt responsible behavior from your students. When possible, we recommend that you complete the tasks before the school year begins so that you have solid organizational structures in place from the first day of school. In addition, once you have finished the tasks, the essential information should be included on your Classroom Management Plan (see Task 7).

NOTE

If you are starting this module during the school year, it may be wise to address the tasks one at a time and implement them gradually so that you do not make too many changes to your classroom routine too quickly.

The seven tasks presented and explained in this module are:

TASK 1: Daily Schedule
Arrange (or modify) your daily schedule so that it maximizes instructional time and responsible behavior and minimizes wasted time and irresponsible behavior.

TASK 2: Physical Space
Arrange the physical space in your classroom so that it promotes positive student/teacher interactions and reduces the possibility of disruptions.

TASK 3: Attention Signal
Decide upon a signal you can use to get students' attention. Teach them to respond to the signal by focusing on you and maintaining complete silence.

TASK 4: Beginning and Ending Routines
Design efficient and effective procedures for beginning and ending the school day (or class period).

TASK 5: Classroom Rules
Identify and post three to six Classroom Rules that will be used as a basis for providing positive and corrective feedback.

TASK 6: Student Work
Design efficient and effective procedures for assigning, monitoring, and collecting student work.

TASK 7: Classroom Management Plan
Prepare a "Classroom Management Plan" with which you can summarize the important information, policies, and procedures that you will use to motivate students and address student misbehavior.

Immediately following the explanations of the tasks in this module is a Self-Assessment Checklist, designed to help you determine which (or which parts) of the tasks you have done/are doing and which you still need to do. The module ends with a Peer Study Worksheet. This worksheet presents a series of discussion questions and activities that can be used by two or more teachers who want to share information and collegial support as they work to improve their classroom management practices.

Task 1: Daily Schedule

Arrange (or modify) your daily schedule so that it maximizes instructional time and responsible behavior and minimizes wasted time and irresponsible behavior.

How you schedule subjects across a day and how you schedule tasks within an activity can have a tremendous influence on student behavior. For example, the middle school teacher who schedules independent work for the last half of the last period of the day will probably find that students engage in more off-task behavior. An effective schedule provides enough variety that, at any given time, students won't have a hard time keeping their attention focused on the task at hand. An effective schedule also takes into consideration the degree of skill that you (the teacher) have in presenting various tasks and activities, and the maturity level of your students.

The information in this task is designed to help you evaluate (and modify, if necessary) your schedule to ensure that it is more likely to prompt responsible student behavior than irresponsible behavior. Along with specific scheduling suggestions, we identify times of day during which students are most prone to irresponsible behavior and what you can do to help students handle those times in a more responsible manner.

We realize that most teachers cannot control all aspects of their daily schedule. For instance, if the teachers at your grade level share students for reading instruction, then you have to schedule reading for the same time as the other teachers. Or, you may have no choice about when your students will go to music and/or physical education. In this case, you will have to accept these time slots. The scheduling issues and decisions we suggest below will help you arrange those times that have not been predetermined by the school-wide schedule.

NOTE: LEVEL OF STRUCTURE AND SCHEDULE

The level of structure that you have determined to be most appropriate for your classroom management plan has a direct impact on how you approach this task. If you have determined that your students are likely to be successful with a low structure management plan, you may not need to attend as closely to daily schedule issues. Your students are probably able to stay focused on any type of activity for long periods and they may be able to settle down immediately after high-excitement times without teacher prompting. However, if your class requires a medium or high structure plan, we strongly suggest that you carefully consider the following information and use it to arrange (or modify) your daily schedule to facilitate instruction and responsible student behavior.

To work through the information in this task, first write down your schedule of daily subjects. Most middle school teachers will have the subject schedule pre-established, but elementary teachers need to make decisions about when and how long each subject will be taught. Once the schedule of subjects is established, list the activities that typically occur within each subject, the amount of time spent on each activity, and whether the activity is teacher directed (lecture, discussion, question/answer), independent work (seatwork, lab activities), or a cooperative group task. In other words, look at what a lesson plan might look like within that subject. For example, if you teach math from 9:30 to 10:30, it may look something like this:

5 minutes	Teacher-directed review of previous concepts
10 minutes	Teacher-directed introduction of new concepts
10 minutes	Teacher-directed guided practice, working on assignments
25 minutes	Independent work/cooperative tasks (depending on task)
10 minutes	Teacher-directed corrections/guided practice to help students identify errors or misunderstandings

Once you have your schedule of subjects written down and a sample schedule of activities within each subject, evaluate the variety and times for each activity using the following guidelines:

Make sure that you have a reasonable *balance* among the types of activities (i.e., teacher-directed instruction, independent seatwork, and cooperative/peer group) you use within and across subjects during the day.

The goal is to balance the kinds of tasks students do in a day. You especially want to watch for a tendency to schedule too much of a good thing. For example, if you like having students work in cooperative groups and feel strongly that students learn a lot by working cooperatively, you may have inadvertently scheduled a disproportionate amount of your daily schedule (or class period) for cooperative group tasks. Similarly, if you prefer teacher-directed activities (e.g., lectures, discussions, demonstrations), you may have a tendency to schedule an insufficient amount of independent work and cooperative group tasks.

Look at your daily schedule and estimate the approximate percentage of classtime (not counting lunch, passing periods, recesses) students spend in the various types of tasks. Middle school teachers should think about one particular class over the course of a week. For example, you may find your activities look something like the following:

- 40% teacher-directed
- 35% independent work periods (and, as appropriate, lab activities or learning centers)
- 25% cooperative groups

There are no absolute rules on what constitutes balance among major instructional tasks. A technology class, for example, will have far more independent work and less teacher-directed instruction than a history class. What you can do is look closely at what type of task takes up the highest percentage of your class time, and honestly ask yourself if this might represent "too much of a good thing."

Within each activity, avoid having any one type of task run overly long.

Whenever students engage in one particular type of task for too long, behavior problems can result. When teacher-directed instruction goes on too long, students will tend to become inattentive. When students have to sit and do independent work for an overly long time, they may get bored and stop working.

There are no absolute rules about how long is too long or how much is too much (although any activity can be problematic if it runs longer than thirty minutes). In part, it can depend on your skills and talents as a teacher. A teacher who designs clear, interesting, and fun independent assignments can successfully engage students in longer periods of independent work than a teacher who is not as talented in this regard. A teacher whose presentation style is dynamic, organized, and humorous can sustain student attention for longer periods of teacher-directed instruction than the teacher who is less skilled in presenting to the whole class. If you have found in the past that student behavior deteriorates as a task progresses (e.g., they do well at the start of independent work, but get increasingly off task after about fifteen minutes), schedule shorter time periods for that particular type of task.

Schedule independent work and cooperative/peer group tasks so that they immediately follow teacher-directed tasks.

Teacher-directed instruction is an excellent way to generate positive energy and momentum and get everyone thinking about the same topic. On the other hand, beginning a class period by having students working on independent projects can result in lower rates of on-task behavior. Starting the period by reviewing previous concepts, introducing some new concepts or skills, and then moving students into independent work or cooperative tasks allows you to clarify what students should be working on, creates a cohesive and clear expectation for on-task behavior, and has the power of instructional momentum.

There are exceptions to this suggestion. For example, many teachers have students work on review exercises (independently or cooperatively) or a challenge problem as soon as they enter the room, while the teacher takes attendance and/or deals with other housekeeping tasks. This strategy usually involves brief (two to five minutes) independent or cooperative activities, and is a structured part of the daily routine—and it can be a very effective practice. Another exception may involve a class in which students work mainly on extremely clear and highly motivating independent tasks; a computer lab class, for example. As you develop your daily schedule, remember that, in general, teacher-directed instruction is usually the best way to begin class and you want to avoid starting class with long periods of independent work time.

Implementing the preceding suggestions as you schedule daily subjects is one way to reduce the likelihood of irresponsible student behavior. Another way is to identify and proactively address those times of day and specific activities/tasks during which students typically exhibit the most misbehavior. We recommend that for problematic times/activities, you make a point of diligently teaching students *what* your expectations are and *how* to meet those expectations. What follows are descriptions of times that we have found to be particularly troublesome for many teachers, along with some suggestions on how to mitigate the problems.

- **Immediately following recesses or entry into class from hall**
  Misbehavior tends to be common right after recess. You can decrease misbehavior by directly teaching students how you want them to enter the classroom and settle down. The key here is to provide this instruction before they go out to recess every time during the first couple of days of school. (You should also plan for periodic re-teaching—especially after any long breaks, such as winter or spring break.) In addition, you should have a task or activity scheduled immediately after recess that helps students calm down and get mentally ready to pay attention to their work scheduled immediately after recess. For example, a primary teacher might have "Sharing" immediately after recess (rather than first thing in the morning) because it is largely teacher-directed but not overly intense. Or, an intermediate teacher might schedule a five to ten minute discussion period for "Current Events" or "What's New in My Life" (a type of sharing in which students are encouraged to discuss what they are doing and interested in).

- **The last hour of the day**
  Students (and teachers!) tend to be tired by the end of the day. Students may be more easily distracted and irritable than they were early in the day. That is why we suggest that you avoid scheduling too much independent work for the last hour. If you are a middle school teacher who has multiple sections of the same class, this may not seem feasible, but with a little creativity you can make easy modifications. Say you teach two classes of eighth grade English—one first period and one seventh period. Allowing the first period class to spend thirty minutes working on a long-range assignment may be reasonable. If you allow the same thirty minutes in the seventh period class, you will probably have high rates of off-task behavior. You would be better off to begin class with teacher-directed instruction, then give 15 minutes to work on their projects, then have more teacher-directed instruction and guided practice during the last 20 minutes of class.

- **The last five minutes of a class period**
  This suggestion applies primarily to middle school teachers. We recommend that you try to end each class period with a few minutes of teacher-directed instruction. If you schedule independent work time during the last part of the class, students can begin to think that when you stop direct teaching that the remainder of the class period is free time in which they can choose to do their work—or not. By scheduling the last activity as a teacher-directed task, you set a precedent that class time to work on assignments is for the purpose of working on assignments. "Class, you have fifteen minutes to work on your assignment, and then I am going to end the class by bringing us all back together to find out if any parts of the assignment need clarification."

  Arranging your schedule to end a subject with teacher-directed activities is not that hard to do. Say, for example, that you have students working—individually or in groups—on assignments during the second half of the class period. While they are working, you can monitor individual and group progress, noting common errors, misconceptions, and/or poor work habits. Then, as the period draws to a close, you can get everyone's attention and discuss the common errors and work habits. "Class, a few things you should keep in mind as you are working on a task such as this is . . ."

  In addition to giving students feedback or information about the current task, you can use the time to review homework expectations or to remind them about long-range projects or housekeeping details. "Class, do not forget that you should be done with your outline for the projects by Wednesday, and tomorrow is the last day to get your permission slips in for the field trip." If you do not end the class with teacher-directed instruction, students may begin to act as if independent work time is "free choice" time.

A well-designed schedule ensures that students experience a varied, but balanced, range of activities within subjects. If students are kept engaged with activities that are scheduled for reasonable lengths of time, responsible behavior will result. If students are required to engage in the same type of activity too much, or overly long, they may become bored, distracted and even disruptive.

Task 2: Physical Space

Arrange the physical space in your classroom so that it promotes positive student/teacher interactions and reduces the possibility of disruptions.

Just as the daily schedule of activities can influence student behavior, so too can the physical organization of the classroom. For example, if student desks are arranged in a manner that makes it difficult for the teacher to circulate throughout the room, student behavior is likely to be less responsible than if the teacher arranges the room so that he or she can easily be out among the students. In this task, we discuss five specific aspects of a classroom's physical arrangement that you can address to increase the probability of responsible student behavior and reduce the probability of irresponsible student behavior. If you have determined that you need a high structure classroom management plan, carefully consider how you can implement all five aspects of physical space presented in this task. Well designed physical space prevents a wide array of potential behavioral problems.

NOTE

We realize that teachers do not always have control over the physical arrangement of the space in which they teach. In some cases this is because you do not teach in your own classroom—e.g., you are a middle school teacher who teaches in a different classroom each period or an elementary music specialist who teaches students in their grade level classroom. In other cases, it may be because tables or workstations in your room are permanently attached to the floor (e.g., you are a middle school English teacher whose students must work at lab stations because the science lab was the only classroom available during first period). It is also possible that you have less flexibility in arranging your physical environment because your classroom is small and you have large numbers of students.

If any of these scenarios apply to your situation, the suggestions that follow may be difficult to implement. Thus, the basic rule regarding physical arrangements is, change what you can and make the best out of what you cannot change. For example, if you are forced to teach English in a science lab, you will probably have to put more energy into teaching your students to stay on task than you would if they could work at individual desks. You may also have to take the time to teach students not to play with the sinks and gas jets. In other words, manipulate those aspects of the physical space over which you have some control, and try to address issues that may arise from the less than desirable aspects of the physical setting over which you have no control.

To whatever extent you can control the physical space in which you teach, we urge you to consider the following suggestions:

Arrange student desks to optimize the most common types of instructional tasks that you will have students engaged in.

What follows are descriptions of four common arrangements for individual student desks (i.e., desks clustered in fours; desks in rows—front to back; desks in rows side to side; desks in a U shape around the perimeter of the classroom) and information about their relative pros and cons. Remember, as you consider what arrangement you want for your classroom (one of these or any other), you need to think about the instructional tasks students will be participating in and the level of classroom structure your students require.

Figure 2.1: Desks in Rows, Front to Back

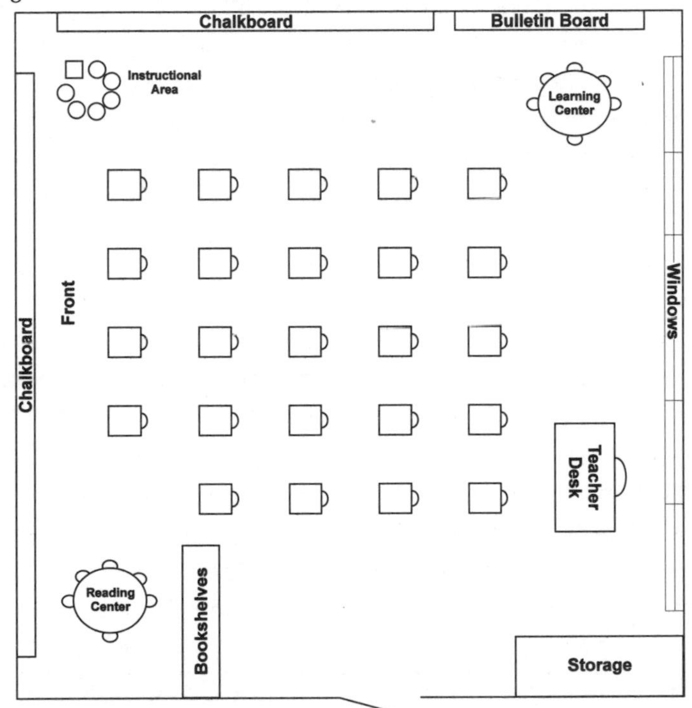

- Excellent if you schedule frequent whole class instruction or have students do tasks for which they must see the board.
- For occasional cooperative learning activities, students can be trained to move quickly from the rows into groups of four, and back to the rows when the cooperative activity is completed.
- Allows students to interact, but the space between desks helps to keep off-task conversation down.
- Implies student attention should be directed to the front of the room.
- Allows easy circulation among students.
- Useful for classes that need medium to high structure.

Figure 2.2: Desks in Rows, Side to Side

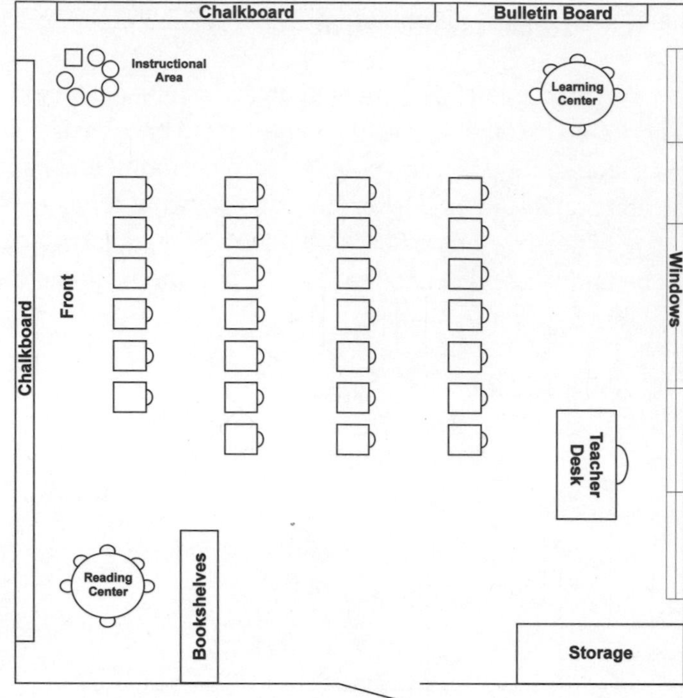

- Excellent if you use frequent whole class instruction where you have students do tasks for which they must see the board.
- For occasional cooperative learning activities, students can be trained to move quickly from the rows into groups of four, and back to the rows when the cooperative activity is completed.
- Allows for students to interact more easily than Desks in Rows, Front to Back, which may result in more off-task conversation than desired.
- Implies student attention should be directed to the front of the room.
- Maximizes available space in the room to allow for centers, work areas, and small group instruction around the perimeter of the room.
- May hinder easy circulation among students — unless you arrange for one or two aisles running perpendicular to the rows so you do not have to go all the way to either side of the room to get from one row to another.
- Best for classes that would benefit from low to medium classroom structure.

Figure 2.3: Desks in Clusters

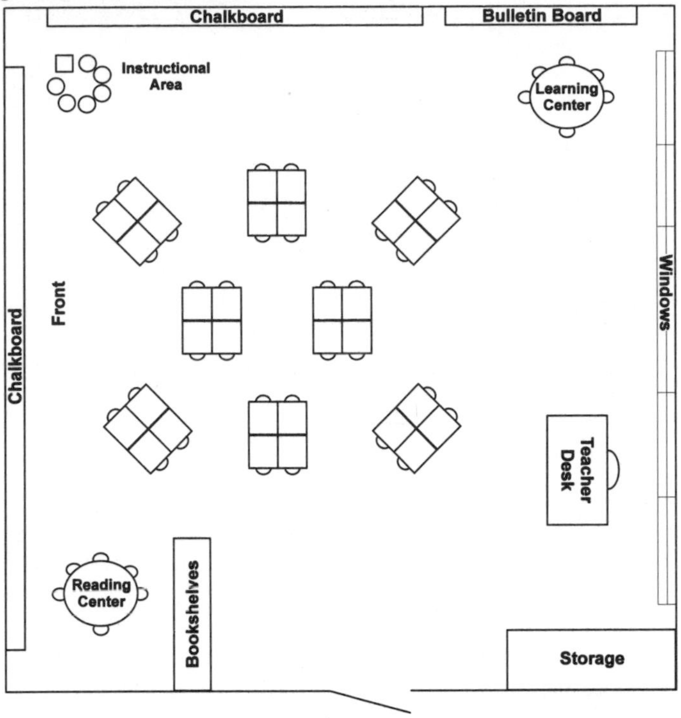

- Allows easy access from any one part of the room to any other part of the room, making it easy to circulate among students.
- Excellent if you schedule frequent cooperative learning tasks.
- Can be problematic if you have students who need less stimulation and distraction. Being part of a cluster may make it more difficult for them to behave responsibly, but separating them may make them feel excluded.
- Requires students to turn sideways or completely around to see the board or teacher-directed instruction.
- May result in frequent off-task conversation during independent work periods and during teacher-directed instruction.
- Usually best for classes of low to medium structure; clusters may prompt too much inappropriate student-to-student interaction for a class needing high structure.

Figure 2.4: Desks in U-Shape

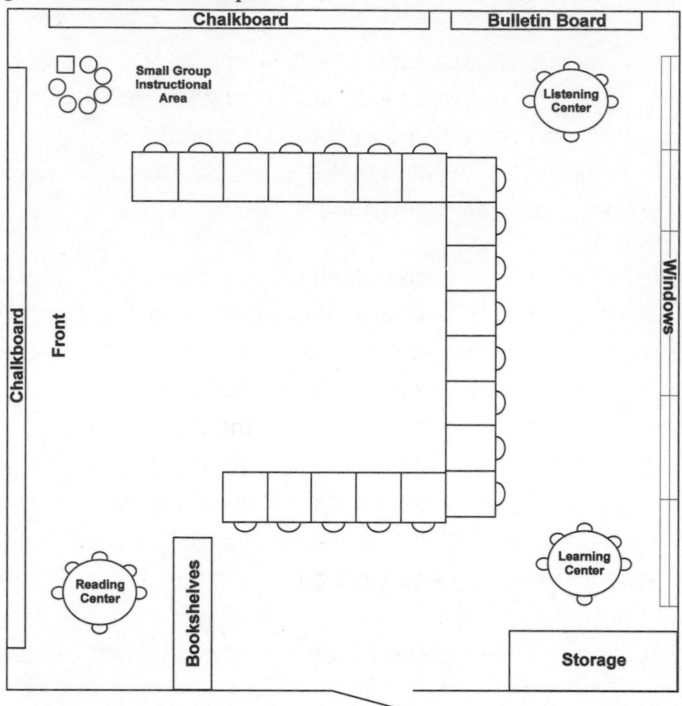

- Excellent for whole-class discussions and teacher-directed instruction in which you want students to participate with verbal responses.
- Excellent for teacher proximity and circulation—you can get quickly to any student.
- Does not lend itself to cooperative group activities.
- Does not make good use of space (the area in the center of the U is largely unused). May not allow room for learning centers, small group instruction, and so on.
- Probably not feasible if you have a large number of students.
- If used with a large class, you may need to have two rows. You need to make sure the inside U has space so you can easily interact with the students in the outside U.
- You need to arrange for access from the inside of the U to the outside, so you/students are able to cross the room to turn something in, etc.
- Best for classes that need low to medium classroom structure. (Can work for classes needing high structure if you monitor students closely, use proximity management effectively, and provide high rates of positive feedback.)

Make sure you have easy access to all parts of the room.

One of the most effective behavior management strategies a teacher can implement is to circulate throughout the room as much and as unpredictably as possible. You are more likely to circulate when you can move about the room easily. Thus, regardless of how you arrange student desks, you want to make sure that you can move easily from any one part of your room to any other part of the room.

When students are working independently or in groups, your proximity will have a moderating effect on their behavior. As you circulate, you will not only be able to provide corrective feedback to students who are off task, but also be able to give positive feedback to students using the work time well and answer the questions of students who need assistance. As you are helping one student, if you notice another student who is off task, you want to be able to go to the off-task student in a fairly direct route. When you have to go all the way to the outside edges of the classroom before going to the off-task student, you are more likely to find yourself frustrated and angry because you have to go "out of your way" to keep students engaged.

Minimize the disruptions caused by high traffic areas in the class.

There are a number of "legitimate" reasons why students need to move about the classroom during the day. Yet, any time students are out of their seats, there is a greater potential for misbehavior. What you want to do is think about what students might need to do away from their desks and then arrange the room so that students who are moving about will be less likely to distract students who are working at their seats. For example, we recommend that as much as possible, you keep student desks away from the areas where students will do the following:

- Get supplies;
- Sharpen their pencils;
- Turn in their work;
- Have small group instruction; or
- Use learning centers.

If you must have student desks near one or more of these high traffic areas, you will need to directly teach students how to be in the area(s) without distracting other students doing their work.

Arrange to devote some of your bulletin board/display space to student work.

We suggest that you save the most prominent display space in your classroom for student work. When their work is prominently displayed, it demonstrates to students that you are proud of what they have done and that you want to show others what they have accomplished. Artistic teachers sometimes feel that they must have every bit of wall space elaborately decorated. However, when all the decoration has been done by the teacher, students may get the sense that they are just visitors in "your" room.

If needed, arrange for a "Time Out" space in your classroom that is as unobtrusive as possible.

Time out procedures are probably most effective in grades K-3. If you are likely to be sending a misbehaving student to a quiet space, you will need to decide ahead of time where this area will be. When possible, we recommend that you avoid having it in a spot where the misbehaving student is on display to students who are working at their desks. You might also want to consider the possibility of having the area screened off for privacy. For more information on using a Time Out or Problem Solving Area, see Module 7: Correction Procedures.

The physical space in your classroom should be arranged to prompt responsible behavior from students. One way to accomplish this is to make sure that there is easy access from any one part of the room to any other part of the room, so that you can circulate unpredictably among students and so that students can move about without disturbing others. In addition, desks and traffic patterns should be arranged in a manner that takes into account the major types of instructional activities you use and the level of structure needed in your classroom management plan. Finally, thinking ahead of time about where to display student work and whether or not you need an in-class time out space will help you ensure that the physical space of your classroom is functional for both you and your students.

Task 3: Attention Signal

Decide upon a signal you can use to get students' attention. Teach them to respond to the signal by focusing on you and maintaining complete silence.

Getting and holding students' undivided attention is an important management responsibility for all teachers. An orchestra conductor uses a signal (e.g. tapping a baton while standing at the podium) to get the musicians to cease their individual warm up activities and pay attention so that everyone can start on the same beat. You need a signal to bring students from their individual efforts to having everyone focus on you so that you can give directions or provide instruction.

There are many situations in which an attention signal is useful. For example, imagine a class for 28 students working in cooperative groups. As she monitors the groups, the teacher realizes that the students do not fully understand what they are supposed to be doing. Using a well practiced signal, it can take the teacher no more than five seconds to get students to cease the group conversations and pay attention to her. After briefly clarifying the directions and answering any questions, she can then instruct them to resume their small group work. Without a well practiced signal, this teacher is likely to spend several minutes repeatedly asking students to stop working and/or yelling over the noise of the groups. It is entirely possible that she won't ever get all the students to stop talking so that she can clarify the task.

NOTE: LEVEL OF STRUCTURE AND ATTENTION SIGNAL

Whether your class requires a low, medium, or high structure classroom management plan, an attention signal is an important behavior management strategy for you to implement. That is, whatever level of structure your class needs, you still need a way to get students to transition from potentially active and noisy activities into activities that demand that everyone's attention be focused on the same thing.

To implement this task, the first thing you need to do is identify what you will use as a signal. We recommend something like saying in a firm (but not shouting) voice, "Class, your attention please," while at the same time swinging your right arm in a circular motion (from 9:00 to 12:00 on a clock face). Then, hold your hand in the 12:00 position, which prompts each student to stop talking, look at you, and raise his/her own hand—until all students are quiet and looking at you with their hands raised. (See Figure 2.5)

Figure 2.5: Attention Signal

"Class, your attention please."

This signal has several advantages. First of all, it can be given from any location in the room. Second, it can be used outside the classroom—for example, in the hall or even on a field trip. Third, it has both a visual (the sweeping motion and raised hand) and an auditory (the verbal statement) component—so students who don't hear the signal may see the sweeping arm motion and raised hand, and vice versa. Another advantage of this signal (or something similar) is its "ripple effect." Even a student who does not hear or see the teacher will find it hard to miss the raised hands of the other students.

Other commonly used signals may not have all the preceding advantages. For example, some teachers flick off the lights as a signal for attention. However, this signal requires the teacher to go to the light switch, and it cannot be used at all in the hall or on a field trip. Or a signal may be ineffective because it has to be repeated frequently before students pay attention (e.g., you use a clapping rhythm, that students echo back, but you find you have to use it three or four times in succession before you have all students' cease what they are doing). If you have a signal that is different from the one we recommend, but that works well for you, do not bother to change it. However, if you have used a different signal and it has not worked well, then you might want to consider using the signal described above.

Regardless of the signal you decide to use, you *must* teach students what the signal is and how to respond to it from the first day of school. Information on when and how to teach your attention signal will be provided in Module 4: The First Month. For now, just be sure that you know what you will use as a signal to gain students' attention.

Task 4: Beginning and Ending Routines

Design efficient and effective procedures for beginning and ending the school day (or class period).

How you start and end each school day (or class period) will have a significant influence on the climate of your classroom. Effective and efficient beginning and ending procedures create an invitational and supportive atmosphere, and communicate that time will not be wasted. These things, in turn, will make a difference in student behavior. Consider the following two middle school scenarios.

Teacher A begins the day by warmly greeting students as they enter the classroom. She has previously taught students that when they enter the room they are to immediately take their seats, get out any required materials (listed on the board), and begin working on the challenge problem that is on the overhead projector. Students who do not have their materials do not interrupt the teacher while she is greeting students because, starting on the second day of school, she taught them specific procedures for dealing with this situation. When the bell rings, the students continue to work on the challenge problem while the teacher uses her seating chart to take attendance. Within one minute after the bell rings, Teacher A has taken attendance, secured the attention of the class, and started teaching. Six minutes later and again four minutes after that a student enters late, but Teacher A does not stop teaching. She has previously taught students her procedures for tardiness (both excused and unexcused), which are designed to ensure accurate record keeping, but no disruption of class.

The situation is different in Teacher B's class. As students enter the class, Teacher B is seated at her desk trying to finish up last minute preparations for the lesson. Some of the students take their seats, others socialize in groups of two to five students. When the bell rings, Teacher B looks up from her work and acknowledges that students are there by saying, "Quit talking and go sit down. It is time to begin class." After two minutes of nagging and cajoling, the students are finally in their seats and reasonably quiet. The teacher instructs students to get out their materials, then spends several minutes helping a couple of students who are not prepared get what they need (letting them borrow books and pencils), all the while nagging them about "being responsible." Five minutes after the bell rings, the teacher finally begins teaching. One minute later and again four minutes after that a student enters late. Both times the teacher stops teaching to determine if the tardiness is excused or unexcused, and to fill out the necessary paper work.

Note that Teacher A spends only one minute on attendance, materials, and tardiness procedures, and even during that minute students are engaged in an instructional task. Teacher B spends seven minutes on attendance, materials, and tardiness. Students who arrived on time with all of their materials have been forced to sit and do nothing while the teacher deals with these procedures. In both scenarios, a couple of students did not have their materials and a couple of students arrived late—things that occasionally happen with even the most effective teacher. The difference is that Teacher A has anticipated these common problems and has taught her students procedures for handling them in ways that do not usurp teacher time and attention and do not waste the time of the students who are punctual and prepared.

In this task, we address how to begin and end your school day/class period with a positive tone, and how to maintain maximum time for instructional activities. We have identified eight critical times or issues related to beginning and ending the day/class period, developed a goal statement for each that describes optimal outcomes related to that time/issue, and then provided suggested routines and procedures for achieving the goal. While elementary teachers will find useful suggestions for beginning and ending their school day and for beginning and ending each subject period (e.g., beginning and ending science class), this task may be even more critical for middle school teachers who typically have five to seven different classes each day.

Keep in mind that our suggestions represent just one way of dealing with beginning and ending your day/class. If you already have efficient and effective beginning/ending routines (i.e., procedures that adequately address the goal statements), there is no reason to change what you do. If you do not, we recommend that you read our suggestions and/or talk to colleagues, then design beginning/ending procedures for your class that are time efficient and set a positive tone.

NOTE: LEVEL OF STRUCTURE AND BEGINNING AND ENDING ROUTINES

If you need a medium or high structure classroom management plan, we recommend that you address all of the issues covered in this task. In particular, it will be important for you to be in your classroom (or in the hall near your door) when students enter. You should also plan to keep students occupied with a task from the moment they enter the room. On the other hand, for a class that requires only a low structure management plan, it is probably reasonable to assume that students will take care of themselves even if you arrive a minute or two after they do and there is no assigned task to keep them occupied.

Entering Class

GOAL: Students will feel welcome and will immediately go to their seats and start on a productive task.

Greeting students as they enter your classroom helps them to feel welcome and reduces classroom behavior problems. A brief greeting communicates to students that you are aware of and interested in them, not just as students, but as individuals.

"Charlene, how did things go at the choir concert last night?" In addition, greeting students as they enter provides a subtle but powerful message that you are aware of students and what they are doing from the minute they enter class, not just when the bell rings.

In general, you want to greet students at the door. If you are supervising the hall outside your room, you can greet them before they even enter your door. Although you can greet students from a position within the classroom (e.g., while seated at your desk), the effect is not quite as powerful as being at or near the door and greeting them immediately as they enter.

In addition to greeting students as they enter your classroom, you also want to have a task prepared that students can work on as they sit down. The purpose is to give students something to do while they wait for the bell to ring, and while you take care of any attendance/housekeeping tasks in the first minute or two of class. Having students work on a daily task like this communicates to them that you value instructional time and plan to use every minute as efficiently as possible.

Keep the task relatively short, one that will require three to five minutes of work from students. It should be a review task that students can perform independently, but also something that is instructionally relevant—not just busy work. For example, math teachers might give a short daily quiz on the previous night's homework assignment or language arts teachers might have students work in their journals or do a power writing exercise. A primary teacher may have students work on a handwriting exercise or a practice page of math facts.

When you have finished taking attendance, give the students feedback on the correct responses for the task and have students grade their own papers or trade with a neighbor for corrections. Then collect the papers so that later in the day or that evening, you can enter the score or a check mark in your grade book to indicate students' completion of the task. If students know that this initial task does not "count" in any way, they will soon cease to work on the task.

Opening Activities (Middle School)

If you are a middle school teacher, you want to make sure that your procedures for opening activities accomplish the following three goals.

GOAL 1: Students will be instructionally engaged while you take attendance.

When the bell rings, and as students continue to work on the assigned task, use a seating chart—rather than calling out names and having students reply—to determine who is present and who is not. This allows you to take attendance and students to continue focusing on the work they are doing. Sitting and doing nothing except for the split second he or she responds to roll call is a very boring way for a student to begin class.

GOAL 2: Your procedures for dealing with tardiness will:

- Ensure that students who are tardy do not disrupt class or take your attention away from teaching;
- Allow you to keep accurate records of excused and unexcused tardies; and
- Let you assign consistent corrective consequences for unexcused tardiness.

One effective procedure for dealing with tardy students involves having a three ring binder with forms similar to the reproducible "Record of Tardies" (shown in Figure 2.6) on a table or shelf near the door to the classroom. Each day before students arrive, make sure that a new page is showing with the correct day and date filled in at the top. Attach a couple of paper clips to the page so that students with excused tardies can attach either the excuse slip from the attendance office or a note from the teacher who is excusing the tardy for them.

During the first week of school, train your students that when they are tardy, whether it is excused or unexcused, they are to quietly enter the classroom without interrupting you or any students in the class. They are to quietly go to the "tardy notebook," put their name in the box for the appropriate period, indicate "Excused" or "Unexcused," attach the excuse if they have one, and then quietly take their seat.

Figure 2.6: Reproducible

Record of Tardies

Teacher ______________________ Day ____________ Date ____________

Names	Excused or Unexcused? If your tardy is excused, attach the excuse slip from the attendance office or a note from the excusing teacher.
1st Period	
2nd Period	
3rd Period	
4th Period	
5th Period	
6th Period	
7th Period	

When a student enters late, do not stop what you are doing. Visually monitor to make sure that the tardy student goes to the notebook and writes something (you can check later to see that the student did write his/her name). If the student does not go to the notebook, provide a verbal reminder. "Paul, before you sit down, put your name in the notebook by the door and indicate if you have an excused or unexcused tardy. Now class, what I was saying was . . . "

Later in the period, when the class is engaged in independent work or cooperative groups, check the information on the tardy student(s) in the notebook. Record the information in your grade book, and follow any school-wide procedures for reporting unexcused tardies to the attendance office. With excused tardies, look at the note or slip to verify accuracy. If you need to talk to a student about being tardy, do it then, while the rest of the class is instructionally engaged. Note that following these procedures prevents the tardy student(s) from getting attention and/or interrupting your lesson.

There should be corrective consequences for unexcused tardies. Most middle schools have a schoolwide tardiness policy that is managed and implemented by the administration. For example, a school may have a policy such as:

2 unexcused tardies in a semester:	Family notification (notification occurs for each subsequent incident).
4 unexcused tardies:	After school detention.
6 unexcused tardies:	½ day in-school suspension.

If your school does not have such a policy, develop your own and inform students of it on the first day of school. A policy similar to the preceding schoolwide example above can work for you as an individual teacher, although you probably cannot assign an in-school suspension without administrative approval.

GOAL 3: Announcements and other housekeeping tasks will not take up too much time.

You want to begin instructional activities as soon after the beginning of the period as possible. Therefore, try to spend no more than a minute or two on announcements and housekeeping. Activities that are not directly related to the subject of the class (e.g., general social skills training or school spirit discussions) should be reserved for advisory or homeroom periods.

Opening Activities (Elementary Level)

If you are an elementary school teacher, you want to make sure that your procedures for opening activities accomplish the following two goals.

GOAL 1: Opening activities will be efficient and orderly, and will ease students into the school day.

Effective elementary teachers vary widely in the way they deal with the beginning of the school day. This variation reflects, among other things, grade level and personal style. For example, some teachers include "sharing" as an opening activity, others do not. Some teachers like to emphasize having students do class jobs, and take time each morning to assign these jobs. Some teachers do calendar and weather activities, others do not. Because there is not one single correct way to start the day, what follows are a couple of considerations for you to keep in mind:

- Opening activities should include accurate recording of attendance, lunch count, and so on.

- Opening activities that take more than a few minutes should have an educational objective. That is, if you take five minutes each day to discuss weather, it should be because one of your science objectives is that students master some basic concepts regarding weather—otherwise don't bother with this five minute activity. If you do a "sharing" activity, you should have some compelling reasons why you take class time for this activity each day.

- Opening activities should keep students actively engaged. If students are expected to sit and do nothing, you will have behavior problems. Therefore, as you think about your opening, if students have nothing to be engaged with, modify opening exercises. For example, if you have sharing, you need to structure the activity so it does not take overly long. With only one student talking at a time, the activity is largely passive and students (particularly primary level) will get restless if this goes on for more than five minutes or so.

If your procedures for opening activities address the preceding considerations, there is no reason to change. If they don't, we suggest you talk to other teachers about what they do first thing in the morning and how long it usually requires.

GOAL 2: Students will understand that school attendance and punctuality are important.

Periodically (every two weeks or so) have a brief discussion with your class about the importance of consistent attendance and punctuality. When punctuality and regular attendance are not high priorities for students' families, having teachers regularly emphasize that coming to school and getting there on time are important will help the students develop these values.

If either absenteeism or tardiness becomes a significant problem, one effective technique is to calculate, and publicly chart, the percentage of students who come to school and/or who arrive on time each day. This gives you an opportunity to talk to your class about the importance of attendance and/or punctuality. It can also put gentle pressure on students to put pressure on their parents to get them to school on time. If necessary and appropriate, you might also set up a small reward system (e.g., when everyone is on time, the class gets a point. When the class collects ten points the class gets to go to recess five minutes early.)

If the chronic tardiness involves only one or two students, do not use either of the preceding procedures. It is probably more effective in this case to ask your administrator for help in putting pressure on the family to get the student to school on time. You might also want to set up an individual contract and some form of reinforcement system with the student (see *The Teacher's Encyclopedia of Behavior Management: 100 Problems/500 Plans* for ideas on setting up such a system).

Being Prepared With Materials

GOAL: Your procedures for dealing with students who do not have materials and/or who are not prepared should:

- Ensure that a student who does not have the necessary materials to participate in class can get them in a way that does not disrupt or slow down instruction;
- Establish reasonable penalties that will reduce the likelihood the student will forget materials in the future; and
- Reduce the amount of time and energy that you (the teacher) spend dealing with this problem.

First of all, you have to make sure that you clearly communicate to students exactly what materials you expect them to have each day in your class, (e.g., two sharpened pencils, a binder with a divider for science class, lined notebook paper, and the science textbook). This information should be communicated verbally to students and in writing to students' families (as part of a syllabus or notice that goes home on the first day of school). At the end of each class period during the first week of school, remind students what materials they should have when they return to class the next day.

Next, develop procedures that allow a student who lacks any of the necessary materials to: get what he or she needs (to participate in the lesson); and receive a mild consequence designed to reduce the probability that the student will forget materials again. For example, you might inform students that, when possible, they should try to borrow the missing material from another student (e.g., a pencil or some paper) without involving you or interrupting instruction. Explain further that, if they need to borrow materials from you, it wastes time that you should be using to teach and so they will owe you a short amount of time after class (e.g., thirty seconds after class for middle school or a minute off of recess for elementary).

If it seems likely that there will be times when students will need to go to their lockers to get materials, you'll want to include procedures that minimize the teaching time you will lose to fill out hall passes. For example, you could inform students that if they have to go back to their locker for materials after class has begun, it will count as a tardy. Tell them that you will give them a hall pass that they must fill out for you to sign. That way, while the student is filling out the pass, you can continue with your other teaching responsibilities. Having the student fill out the pass reduces your involvement with this student from two or three minutes to only thirty seconds or so. (NOTE: Never let more than one student at a time leave class to go back to the lockers.)

If you ask other teachers in your building how they deal with students who do not have materials, you will probably hear a wide variety of procedures. Some teachers just give away pencils and loan books without any penalty. ("I don't make an issue of it, if they need a pencil, I give them one.") Other teachers impose penalties ("I think students must learn to be responsible. If they don't have a pencil and I have to give them one, the student owes me a quarter or an after-school detention.") There is no one right answer—the important thing is for you to decide in advance on how you will deal with this very common occurrence. If you aren't sure whether your planned procedure is fair and/or appropriate, ask your building administrator for feedback. Some administrators, for example, may not want teachers to impose a choice type penalty such as "a quarter or a detention, your choice."

It's important that you inform students, during the first couple of days of school, how you will respond if they do not have their materials. Then, a couple of days into the first week of school, you should start conducting periodic spot checks. "As you are working on the challenge problem on the overhead, I want to check that you came to class with the materials you need in this class each day. Put your extra pencil, not the one you are writing with, your notebook and your science book on your desk. While you are working I'll come around." If any students are missing one or more of the required materials, provide a gentle but firm reminder about the importance of being responsible for bringing their materials every day.

After the first couple of weeks, conduct unpredictable intermittent spot checks of materials. Any students who do not have what they need should receive a minor corrective consequence (e.g. they lose a point from their participation grade), while students who have all materials might receive a bonus point. If you plan to do this, be sure to inform students during the first week of school that you may conduct spot checks once or twice a week for the first few weeks of school.

When a student does come unprepared to class, try not to get upset or frustrated; simply follow through consistently with the procedures you told students would be implemented. Remember you want procedures that do not usurp too much of your time. If you start feeling frustrated because you are spending too much time dealing with students who have forgotten materials, ask colleagues for ideas on how to streamline procedures so that you can keep your focus on instruction.

Dealing With Students Returning After an Absence

GOAL: Students who have been absent can find out what assignments they have missed and get any handouts and/or returned papers in a way that does not involve a large amount of your time and energy.

We recommend setting up two baskets—one for "Absent, What You Missed" and one for "Absent, Assignments In"—that you keep in a consistent location on a counter or shelf or your desk. Anytime you give students an assignment, a handout (worksheets, reading materials, bulletins, or notices), and/or graded papers, put that same material in a folder for an absent student. The folder should have the date, the class period, and the student's name on it. Some teachers pair students in a buddy system. When one of the students is absent, it is the responsibility of his/her partner to copy any assignments and collect any handouts and graded papers, and to put that material in a file folder with the student's name and the date. The folders are placed in the basket marked "Absent, What You Missed."

Teach students that when they return after an absence, they should collect a folder with their name on it for each day they missed. This way, they can find out all the tasks they must do and have any handouts they might need without needing to interrupt you.

The basket marked "Absent, Assignments In" can be used in two ways. When a student returns on Tuesday from an absence on Monday, he can turn in any assignment that had been due on Monday to the "Absent, Assignments In" basket at the same time as he is picking up the folder from the "Absent, What You Missed" basket. In addition, when the student completes the work assigned on Monday (the day he was absent), he should also turn that work into the "Absent, Assignments In" basket.

A system like this can save you lots of time and interruptions, but it will only work if you keep the baskets up-to-date by checking them daily and reminding students who return from being absent to collect what they missed and hand in anything that was due.

As a general rule, we recommend letting students have the same number of days to complete missed assignments as the number of days they were absent. Thus, the student who returns Tuesday from being absent on Monday, has until Wednesday to turn in the work that was assigned on Monday and due Tuesday. If the student did not return until Thursday, he would have until the following Tuesday, or three school days following the day he returned, to turn in the missed assignments.

Wrap up/Clean up at the End of Day or Class Period

GOAL: Your procedures for wrapping up the day/class period/activity will:

- Ensure that students will not leave the classroom before they have organized their own materials and completed any necessary clean-up tasks;
- Ensure that you have enough time to give students both positive and corrective feedback, and to set a positive tone for ending the class.

You want to leave enough time at the conclusion of an activity/period/day to ensure that things end on a relaxed note. How much time this will entail will vary. For example, in a middle school math class, one minute will probably be sufficient; whereas in a middle school art class, it may take up to ten minutes to get all the supplies put away and the room ready for the next class. Elementary teachers may need five to ten minutes at the end of the day to help students get organized, make sure the room is clean, and provide last minute announcements. (NOTE: At the beginning of the year, plan to leave more time than you think is necessary. Remember that during the first week of school, you may have to take time to help students figure out which bus to take, where their family is going to pick them up, and so on. If the wrap-up/clean-up takes less time than you scheduled, you can always use the extra couple of minutes for a discussion, a song, or a word game.)

When students have finished organizing and cleaning up, give the class as a whole feedback on things they are doing well and things that may require more effort on their part. This is especially important during the first six weeks of school, but is also useful intermittently throughout the school year. "Class, I want to let you know that the way you have been using class time demonstrates a high level of responsibility. We should be very proud of how well we are all functioning as a group. One thing that a few people need to manage more effectively is remembering homework. Tomorrow, you have a math assignment and your science assignment due. Make a decision right now, when you are going to work on those assignments—this afternoon or this evening? I expect to see two completed homework assignments from each of you. (bell rings.) Thanks for a good day today. Have a nice evening. You are all excused to go."

Dismissal

GOAL: Students will not leave the classroom until they are dismissed by you (not by the bell ringing).

On the first day of school, and periodically thereafter, remind your students that they are not to leave their seats when the bell rings. Explain that the bell is the signal to you, and that you will excuse the class when things are reasonably quiet and when all wrap-up tasks have been completed. If you let students "bolt" for the door when the bell rings, it sets a precedent that your instructional control ends when the bell rings. By reserving the right to excuse the class, you can make judgments about whether you should excuse the whole class at once, or by rows (or table clusters). As a general rule, primary students should be excused by rows, and older students can be excused as a class. However, let the older students know that if there is rushing out of the room or crowding at the door, you will start excusing them by rows.

The beginning and ending of the day (class period) plays a major role in setting the climate of the classroom. Opening and dismissal routines that are welcoming, calm, efficient, and purposeful demonstrate to students that you are pleased to see them and that you care so much about class time that not a minute will be wasted.

Task 5: Classroom Rules

Identify and post three to six Classroom Rules that will be used as a basis for providing positive and corrective feedback.

Posted classroom rules communicate to students that you have specific expectations. Therefore, your rules should provide objective descriptions of the specific behaviors you expect from students and pre-inform them that certain behaviors are not acceptable and will result in corrective consequences. Because the rules should serve as the basis for implementing consequences for the most frequent misbehaviors, you want to develop them in such a way that if students follow the rules, the most likely misbehaviors will not occur. This means that before you develop your classroom rules, you should identify the misbehaviors that you think are most likely to occur. To do this, think about your grade level and the typical developmental level of students at that grade level. Also consider your schedule, your opening and dismissal routines, your procedures for managing work, and so on. The other important aspect to classroom rules is that once you have them, you need to teach students what the rules are and specifically how they can demonstrate that they are following the rules.

Decide who will have input into the rules.

The first thing you need to decide is whether you are going to develop the rules yourself or if you will work them out with the students. This decision is really a matter of style and expediency; both teacher-designed and student-designed rules have been highly correlated with teacher effectiveness. An advantage of student-developed rules is that the process itself may give students a greater sense of ownership in the classroom. The disadvantages to student-developed rules, though, include: (1) you will have no rules in place for the first day of school; (2) if you teach more than one class, it may be difficult to keep track of multiple sets of rules; and (3) the students may not come up with the rules you feel you need to have an orderly classroom. If you don't know whether to use teacher-designed or student-designed rules, and you have never involved students in rule development before, it might be best to design the rules yourself. However, if you like the idea of involving students in rule development and have been successful with the practice in the past, you certainly should feel free to continue doing so.

Make sure your rules will be "effective."

Regardless of whether you involve students or you draft the rules yourself, keep the following suggestions about effective rules in mind:

- You should have no more than six rules (three to five is probably best).

- The rules should be stated positively. (Using one or two negatively stated rules, for clarity reasons, is fine—e.g., "No food or drink in the computer room.")
- For the most part, the rules should be specific and refer to observable behaviors. "Arrive on time with all of your materials," is specific and observable. "Do your best," is not.
- The rules should be posted in a prominent place that is visible from all parts of the classroom.

Figure 2.7 shows a sample set of classroom rules.

Figure 2.7: Sample Classroom Rules

- **Arrive on time with all your materials.**
- **Keep hands, feet, and objects to yourself.**
- **Work during all work times.**
- **Follow directions immediately.**

NOTE

Your Classroom Rules should be different than your "Guidelines for Success." "Guidelines for Success" are more global and more like goals. For example, a statement such as "Do your Best" is something you want students to strive toward. It is too broad, subjective, and open to interpretation to be a rule that has consequences tied to it. That is, while you very well may want to have a discussion with a student about your perception that she is not doing her best, you are not going to impose penalties or fines for her not doing so. Rules should be specific, because infractions of those rules will have consequences.

Develop consequences for rule infractions.

If you developed your classroom rules with the students, this step should involve student input as well. If you developed your rules by yourself, you can decide whether or not to involve students in determining consequences. Either way, pre-think what the consequence for violating each of your rules should be. That is, identify what should happen if a student does not "arrive on time with all materials." Identify what an appropriate consequence would be for tardiness. Using corrective consequences when responding to misbehavior will be covered in much more detail in Module 7: Correction Procedures, but following are a few quick tips on developing consequences for rule infractions:

- For each rule, identify one or more consequence that will be implemented when a student breaks that rule. An example of a rule without a consequence is having a speed limit without ever getting a ticket.

- Make all consequences mild enough that you will follow through with assigning them consistently.

- Think about how you will record rule infractions so that you can ensure that consequences assigned are actually implemented. Telling a student he has lost time off recess and then letting him get the full recess time because you forgot, sends the message that the teacher does not follow through.

- Always assign the consequence for a rule infraction unemotionally; and address the behavior, not the person. The following statement is an example of how a consequence might be assigned in a middle school classroom. "Charlene, you need to get back to work. The consequence for not 'working during all work times' is one demerit. If you get three demerits, I'll contact your family and you will have a lunch time detention."

Teach students what the rules are and how they can demonstrate compliance.

How to teach your rules at the beginning of the year is covered in Module 4: The First Month. If you have a rule that is not specific, but that you feel is important in communicating your expectations, you will have to teach that rule in even more detail. For example, if you have a rule such as, "Work during all work periods," you will need to model for students exactly what you mean by work behavior in each different type of work activity. Demonstrate what work behavior looks like during teacher-directed instruction, independent seat work, cooperative groups, and so on. If you do not directly teach your definition of "work" behavior, the rule is too general. You should plan on repeatedly teaching the details of any somewhat subjective rules for at least the first two to three weeks of school. Finally, you should plan how you will provide positive feedback on rule-following behavior. This is covered in detail in Module 5: Motivation.

Classroom rules should be designed to correct (in advance) the most common misbehaviors that are likely to occur. Your three to six rules should be specific, observable, and for the most part stated positively. Design the consequences that you will assign and implement for rule violations. Clear rules and consistent corrective consequences will help reduce, and eventually eliminate, the majority of classroom misbehavior.

Task 6: Student Work

Design efficient and effective procedures for assigning, monitoring, and collecting student work.

An all-too-common frustration for most teachers is dealing with students who do not complete assigned classwork/homework. The problem is that students who do not complete assignments often do not get the practice necessary to achieve mastery of essential instructional objectives. In addition, without seeing students' completed assignments, you may not have sufficient information about whether they have mastered the skills or need more practice. Anything that you can do to increase the likelihood that students will complete assignments is worthwhile because you will significantly increase the rates of student learning and significantly decrease your level of frustration. In this task, we specifically address procedures and routines for managing student work. We believe that implementing well-designed and organized strategies for assigning, monitoring, and collecting student work can alleviate a lot of your potential frustration because they: (1) let students know that you put a high value on their completing work; (2) prompt more responsible student behavior regarding assigned tasks; and (3) help you effectively manage student work without taking unreasonable amounts of time.

We have identified five major areas related to managing student work for you to consider (see Figure 2.8). For each area, we describe the kinds of decisions you should think about and suggest some strategies that you might implement.

Figure 2.8: Five Major Areas to Consider for Managing Student Work

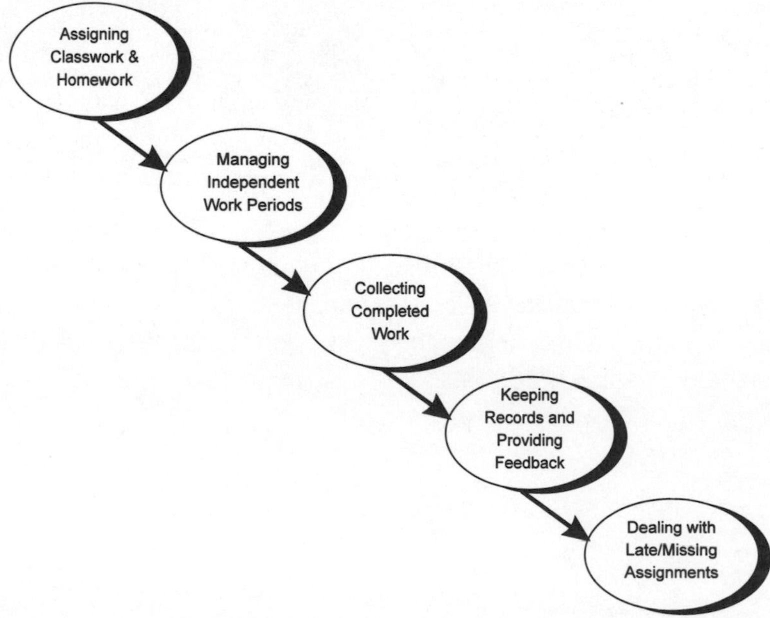

Assigning Classwork and Homework

One of the first things you need to consider is implementing a system which allows students to easily find out information about the tasks they have been assigned to complete. Students should have a consistent place to look (e.g., on the board or an assignment sheet) to find out what their assignments are. It is not enough to simply tell students what their assignments are or to write them on an overhead projector during the lessons. These methods do not create a *permanent place* for students to check to find out what they need to do. And, if there is no set place where students can check on what their assignments are, a student who forgets what the day's homework is will have no choice but to ask you or another student for the information. On the other hand, when assignments are written (and left) on the board or recorded on an assignment sheet, the student can simply look at the board or assignment sheet to determine what he needs to do.

You should also teach students to keep their own records of assigned homework so that when they get home they will know what they need to do. If your procedure is to write assignments on the board, then you'll want to teach students to copy the homework assignments onto notebook paper which they put in a consistent place in their notebook. If you give out a weekly assignment sheet, students should be taught to keep the assignment sheet in a consistent place in their notebooks. Be specific—tell students exactly how and where they should record the information. Show them a model and, especially at the beginning of the year, monitor whether they are following through. "Class, we have a couple of minutes before the bell. Open your notebooks to the page immediately after the divider for this class. I want to see that you have the Weekly Assignment Sheet in the correct place."

If you give both short-term daily assignments and long-term assignments (e.g., a term paper), you'll want to be sure to note both types of assignments on the board space or assignment sheet. Including daily reminders about a long-term task will help students remember that they should be working on the task on an ongoing basis, not putting it off to the last minute. It can also serve as a prompt to you to let students know what parts of an assignment they should have done by certain points in time. "Remember that your projects are due in one week, so by Monday you should have your outline and your first draft completed."

Figure 2.9 shows how you might use board space for recording assignments.

Figure 2.9: Sample of Assignments on Board

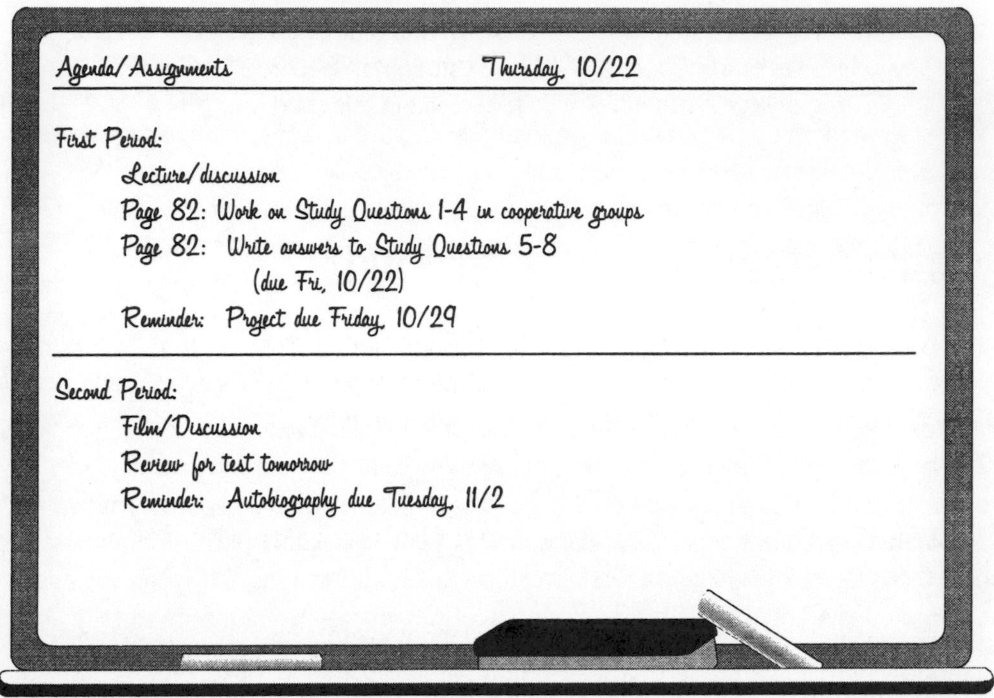

An alternative to using board space or assignment sheets, is to use a flip chart (or to designate a portion of the bulletin board to put up a large sheet of paper) and write each day's assignment(s) on one page (middle school teachers might use one page for each class period for a full week). Each day, you can flip over (or add) a new page for that day's assignments. This system has the additional advantage of facilitating easy access to information on previous assignments. When a student has been absent, she/he can simply go to the flip chart or bulletin board, find the page(s) for the day(s) she/he was absent, and copy down what needs to be done.

Because a class with high risk factors may be more likely to have frequent absences, having a permanent record of daily assignments is especially useful if you have determined that your students need a high structure classroom management plan.

As part of your plan to assign work, you should determine how students will be expected to organize materials and monitor assignments. That is, when you give an assignment, where will students keep a record of what they are expected to do? One effective strategy that is used in many schools involves having students keep a three ring binder with dividers for various subjects. (Specific information on how students can use a binder for assignments will be described later.) If your school has adopted a particular schoolwide study skills curriculum, you should follow the organizational strategies suggested in that curriculum.

If your school does not have a study skills curriculum, you might want to suggest that your staff consider a schoolwide adoption of *Skills for School Success*, by Anita Archer and Mary Gleason, published by Curriculum Associates. This excellent curriculum teaches strategies for organization and studying that will enhance the academic achievement of all students. Effective use of a three ring binder is heavily emphasized within this curriculum.

Managing Independent Work Periods

The following suggestions focus on how to effectively set up independent work periods. In Module 3: Expectations, we provide additional information on how to clarify and directly teach your behavioral expectations regarding independent work periods to students.

Be sure that any independent work you assign can be done independently by students.

If you assign students tasks that they cannot complete, you set them up to fail. When students have to do work that is beyond their ability, they are likely to: (1) do the work, but fail because of excessive errors; (2) not do the work and fail because they didn't complete the assignment; or (3) do the work, but deal with feeling and looking helpless because they ask for help day after day (from you or peers). Over time, a lot of students tend to slip into the second option because when they do nothing they look tough or bored, rather than stupid or helpless. Following are suggestions on how you can ensure that the independent work you assign can be done by all students:

- Modify assignments for the lower performing students in the class.

For more information on modifying instruction for meeting the needs of the lower performing students, see *Interventions: Collaborative Planning for High Risk Students* by Randall Sprick, Marilyn Sprick and Mickey Garrison, published by Sopris West.

- Provide alternative assignments for some of the students.
- Work with a few students in a small group and do the assignment together, while the rest of the class works independently.
- Have students work in pairs or cooperative groups to help each other. (Do not overuse this strategy or your higher performing students may get tired of always having to help someone else do his work.)

Schedule independent work times in a way that maximizes on-task behavior.

The following information summarizes the suggestions about how to improve student engagement during independent work periods that were presented in Task 1 of this module:

- Do not schedule overly long periods in which students are expected to stay on task while working independently. (There is no magic rule about how long students can stay focused, but in general, having students work on the same task for more than thirty minutes without some change in routine will result in high rates of off-task behavior. Even thirty minutes can be too long for primary grade students—unless you have built up to that amount. See Module 4: The First Month for ideas on how to teach primary age students to stay on task during independent work periods.)
- Do not schedule independent work periods to immediately follow high excitement times such as recess, assemblies, and so on.
- Do schedule independent work periods to follow some form of teacher-directed instruction.
- Do arrange for the independent work periods that occur at the end of the day to be shorter than the independent work periods that occur at the beginning of the day.

Develop a clear vision of what you want student behavior during work times to look and sound like.

This suggestion is covered in detail in Module 3: Expectations. For now remember that if you do not clarify and teach exactly what you want from students, some students are likely to assume that behaviors such as chatting in groups, moving about the room, or playing with toys are okay during independent work times. Once you have a vision of the behaviors you want students to exhibit (and correspondingly, the behaviors you do not want them to exhibit), teach students to meet those expectations.

Provide guided practice on tasks and assignments (i.e., work with students in a teacher-directed activity for the first 10 to 50% of an assignment).

When teaching a math lesson, for example, you might start by reviewing previously taught concepts, then introduce the day's new concept, then work through the first several exercises of the math assignment, and finally turn students loose to work on the remainder of the assignment independently or in groups. If there were 30 problems in the assignment, you might model and lead students through the first six. "Watch me do the first two problems on the overhead; and copy what I do." (You demonstrate and explain.) "OK, on the next two problems, I'll do the first part and you do the second half of the problem." (You demonstrate the first part and let students do the second part; correct the problems, and answer questions from students or reteach based on student mistakes.) "Now do the next two problems on your own. Stop when you finish problem 6, so we can correct." (Let all students do two problems while you monitor student performance. Then model or have individual students demonstrate the correct answer, answer any questions, and provide any additional instructions.) If students are doing well, you could then assign the remainder of problems as independent work. If many students are having problems, you should continue to work through the problems together until you are sure students understand the concepts and processes.

Guided practice is important because it increases the chance that students will really know what they need in order to successfully complete the task. It has the further advantage of creating "behavioral momentum." That is, if you have guided students through the first part of a task, a portion of the task is already completed by the time you say, "Now do the rest of the assignment on your own (or in groups)." Without guided practice, when you say "Get to work on your assignment," students are faced with a blank piece of paper. For many individuals, the hardest part of doing assigned tasks is getting started. Guided practice increases work completion because it ensures that tasks are begun before the independent part of the class period starts.

Develop a specific system for how students can get questions answered during independent work periods.

When students have a question about how to do something, they may feel that they cannot continue with their work until the question is answered. If you have not structured a way for students to get questions answered/help when necessary, you will have higher rates of off-task behavior. For those independent work periods in which you (or another adult—a co-teacher or paraprofessional) are available to answer questions, develop and teach your students to use some kind of a visual signal that they need assistance. We recommend having students put an upright book (other than the book they need for the assignment) or some kind of flag on the corner of their desk. Figure 2.10 shows how a flag taped to each student's desk can be used as a help signal. This idea was originally suggested by Paine, et. al. (1983).

Figure 2.10: Flag as a Help Signal

Another way students can indicate they need assistance is to write their name on the board, along with the question or problem number on which they need help. In this way, if several students have a question with the same item, you can gather those students together and provide assistance one time instead of helping each person individually. "Sandra, Mark, and Dani, please come to my desk so we can figure out problem number 5."

Note that none of these suggestions involve having students raise their hands when they want help. This is deliberate. The problems with the traditional "hand raising procedure" are that: (1) it is physically difficult to keep a hand in the air for the three to five minutes it may take you to respond; (2) the student is necessarily off task while he or she is waiting for your help; and (3) hand raising tends to draw more attention to a student, which may discourage some students from asking for help. With the open book or flag signal (or some variation), students can be trained to unobtrusively put up their signal, mark the question or problem that has them confused, and continue working on other problems.

For those independent work times that you are not available (e.g., you are working with a small reading group while other students are working on independent assignments), you will have to devise and teach students to use strategies for asking and helping each other. Be sure that students understand that this permitted talking is appropriate only to get needed help, not to talk about anything they want anytime they want.

NOTE TO ELEMENTARY LEVEL TEACHERS

If you feel that students need to have access to you even when you are teaching a small group, you might want to consider using a "Question Box." Place a masking tape box (approximately 18" square) on the floor near where you do small group teaching, and teach students that if they cannot get their question answered by asking another student, one student at a time can stand in the Question Box. When you get to a logical stopping place with your small group, the student in the Question Box can ask his/her question. When you have answered the question, the student can return to his/her seat and you can resume working with the small group. It will be important to teach the class that there can be only one student at a time in the Question Box and that no one else can be out of his/her seat.

Collecting Completed Work

Another issue for you to consider is how completed work, both in-class work and homework, will be turned in to you. Whenever possible, we recommend collecting the work personally from each student. "Class, put your homework on the upper right hand corner of your desk. While you are working on the challenge problem on the overhead, I will come around and collect it." The biggest advantage of this procedure is that you know immediately if students have not completed the work (and students know you know). If a student does not have his or her homework, you can take that moment to re-emphasize that work completion is an important aspect of responsible behavior in your class. Do not listen to excuses, but let the student know that she/he will need to speak to you later. When using this procedure, students should be doing something worthwhile while you are collecting their work. If they are doing nothing, it is too big a waste of students' time.

Because this procedure allows you to give students immediate feedback about their work (i.e., intermittent positive feedback to students being responsible for their work, and consistent corrective feedback as modeled above to students who have not done their work), we strongly recommend it if you have determined that your students need a high structure classroom management plan. On the other hand, the procedure has the disadvantage of being time and labor intensive for the teacher. If you require only a low or medium structure classroom management plan, you might prefer another procedure.

Having students hand in their work by rows or tables, or having a student helper collect assigned work, or having students put their work in a designated basket are all less time intensive procedures for collecting work. However, they lack the interpersonal contact and immediate feedback advantages that collecting work directly from each student has. That is, with these procedures, students don't actually see you handling their homework and class assignments, and you don't know until you grade the papers who has completed the assignment and who has not. Thus any feedback (positive or corrective) is delayed until the next day, or even longer. If you have used one of these methods in the past, and have been unhappy with the percentage of work completion by your students, you might try experimenting with collecting work directly from students and see if the rates of work completion improve.

Consider having students "check off" completed tasks.

If you give students a daily or weekly assignment sheet or have them use an assignment notebook, consider adding a place for students to check that they have completed a task. Another option is to display a wall chart (similar to the reproducible form shown in Figure 2.11) on which students can check off completed tasks. If you use some kind of wall chart in an elementary classroom, you would need to include all the major daily tasks on it, and should plan on putting up a fresh copy (with student names already on it) each day. In middle school, you would probably put up one sheet per class for the whole week. Note that an assignment check off sheet like this is not an official record and does not take the place of, or supersede, your grade records. It is simply an opportunity for students to put closure on the task.

Figure 2.11: Reproducible

Completed Assignments Checklist

Week of ________________________

Directions: When you turn in an assignment, put your initials in the space next to your name under that assignment.

Name							

Once you have taught students how to use a "check off" procedure, you might also teach them to self-reinforce in an age-appropriate manner. For example, with middle school students you might say, "When you check off that you have completed your math assignment, tell yourself, 'I am choosing to be successful in this class, because I am responsible for completing my work.'" You might even consider posting the statement above the chart so students can read the statement as they check off each completed task. It is no accident that the major time management systems used by adults include a place next to the list of daily tasks where the user is encouraged to "check off" each task as it is completed. Self-reinforcement and closure on tasks can be achieved using this simple, but powerful, idea of a "checking off" procedure.

Keeping Records and Providing Feedback

An important, yet often overlooked, aspect to managing student work involves providing regular feedback to students on their work completion and current grade status. Experienced teachers know that an accurate and complete gradebook is an essential part of a well run classroom. Gradebook information is critical for monitoring and evaluating student performance. Many teachers with complete and comprehensive gradebooks, though, do not have procedures for keeping students informed of their current grade status. A student who isn't aware of her current grade status in the middle of a term may not realize that she needs to improve.

If a student is falling behind by the second week of school, the student and the student's family should immediately be informed that adequate progress is not being made. In addition, we recommend having a standard policy to send notes and/or make phone calls regarding any students who have more than a certain number of missing assignments (e.g., five). Regular and gentle nagging will increase rates of work completion, and students need to learn that they are still accountable for completing assignments even though something was not completed on the due date.

Although regularly informing students of their grade status may not be useful or appropriate in primary classrooms, intermediate and middle school teachers should definitely have a system for keeping students up-to-date on a weekly basis about their current grade status. Descriptions of two such systems follow. Consider implementing the one that best fits your personal style.

Use a computer grade book, and print out a weekly report for each student on each subject.

If you are not currently keeping your grade records using one of the many fine computer programs for grading, consider doing so. In addition to saving time when you have to figure grades at the end of the term, most of the programs allow you to print out a grade record for every student each week. The print-out will show any missing assignments or tests, the score possible and the score earned on each assignment, the total points accumulated, and the current grade.

Have students keep a Student Grade Record

If you do not have access to a computer grading program, have each student keep his/her own records. You can design a form that includes the range of assignments and tests you anticipate are likely to occur during each grading period. (See Figure 2.12)

Figure 2.12: Sample of Student Grade Record Sheet

Sample Student Grade Record

Class Period ____________________

Student ____________________

TESTS

1 Score _____ /100 points
2 Score _____ /100 points
3 Score _____ /100 points
4 Score _____ /100 points
5 Score _____ /100 points
6 Score _____ /100 points
7 Score _____ /100 points
Total _____ /700 points

QUIZZES

1 Score _____ /20 points
2 Score _____ /20 points
3 Score _____ /20 points
4 Score _____ /20 points
5 Score _____ /20 points
6 Score _____ /20 points
7 Score _____ /20 points
Total _____ /100 points

TERM PAPER

Score _____ /200 points
Total _____ /200 points

HOMEWORK

1 Score _____ /10 points
2 Score _____ /10 points
3 Score _____ /10 points
4 Score _____ /10 points
5 Score _____ /10 points
6 Score _____ /10 points
7 Score _____ /10 points
8 Score _____ /10 points
9 Score _____ /10 points
10 Score _____ /10 points
Total _____ /100 points

WEEKLY PARTICIPATION

Week 1 _____ /20 points
Week 2 _____ /20 points
Week 3 _____ /20 points
Week 4 _____ /20 points
Week 5 _____ /20 points
Week 6 _____ /20 points
Week 7 _____ /20 points
Week 8 _____ /20 points
Week 9 _____ /20 points
Total _____ /180 points

Final Score ____ /1280 Points

If you choose to use some kind of Student Grade Record, remember that each time you hand something back to students, you should have them get their recording sheet out and enter the score they received in the appropriate space (e.g., a 92% on Test #2) . Approximately once a week, have students total the points they have earned (as recorded on the Student Grade Record). As students are adding up their points, you can put a breakdown of the point range for each letter grade on the board or an overhead (see the following example).

IF YOU HAVE BETWEEN:	YOUR CURRENT GRADE IS:
360-400 points	A
320-359	B
280-319	C
240-279	D
< 240	F

The major disadvantages of using a Student Grade Record rather than a computer generated print-out is that you have to depend on students to keep track of their forms and enter the scores they have earned each time you hand something back. This organizational dependence on the students can work, but it requires that you be very direct about your expectations and that you take class time, every time you hand back graded work, to have students record their scores.

An Extra Procedure for Classes Needing High Structure

In addition to ensuring that all students receive regular and ongoing feedback about their current grade status, you may be able to increase rates of work completion by providing feedback to the class as a whole on the classwide percentage of work being handed in. For example, if you want to increase rates of homework completion, you might use a large wall chart (or an overhead transparency if wall space is not available) on which you record the daily percentage of homework handed in. Simply take the number of completed homework assignments and divide it by the number of students present that day and you could have a chart like the one shown in Figure 2.13.

Figure 2.13: Sample of Homework Completion Chart

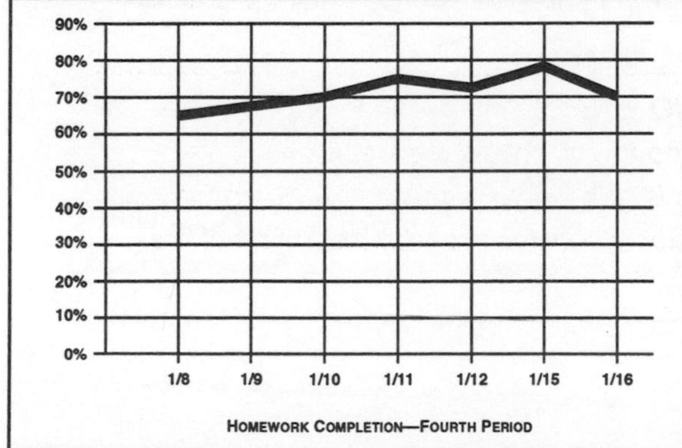

An advantage to using a charting procedure is that it gives you the opportunity, on a daily basis, to discuss the importance of being responsible for completing homework. In addition, it may create a bit of peer pressure for competing work as each student's completion, or lack thereof, affects the percentage of the class. If you wish to, you can tie small-scale rewards to achieving certain goals (e.g., "When the class percentage is 92 % or higher, the class earns the last five minutes of class as 'choice time.')

Dealing with Late/Missing Assignments

The last major consideration regarding managing student work is how you will deal with late and missing assignments. Some teachers choose to have no penalty for late work (i.e., students can hand in anything, anytime, and there is no cost), while others do not allow students to turn in any assignment late (i.e., a late assignment equals zero points). We suggest adopting some form of middle ground between these two extremes. When there is no penalty, some students will turn in everything late, possibly even handing in all assignments on the last day of the term. If students are allowed to do this, it is unfair to you (you should not have to stay up all night at the end of every grading period) and it is unfair to the students (they can learn that they do not really have to pay attention to due dates). On the other hand, an extreme "If it's late, it's a zero" policy does not take into account that an occasional late assignment is likely for even the most responsible student. Figure 2.14 shows a sample policy that might be implemented by a middle school science teacher.

Figure 2.14: Sample Late Assignments Policy

- Any assignment that is turned in late will receive an immediate 10% penalty (i.e., a 100-point lab will have 10 points deducted from whatever score you earn).
- No assignment will be accepted beyond one week late.
- Students who have more than ___ late or missing assignments will have their families informed.
- No more than four late assignments will be accepted during the quarter.

NOTE

The details of and/or criteria used in a policy will reflect the decisions of the individual teacher. The important thing is to develop a policy that works for you and inform students and their families about the policy at the beginning of the term/year.

In most classrooms, a large percentage of students' time will be spent working on written tasks. The way you manage assignments, work periods, and so on, will have a big impact on how responsible students will be for managing and completing their written tasks. If you effectively manage student work, students are more likely to complete that work, thus giving them the practice they need on essential instructional objectives. In addition, when students complete their work, you know whether they are achieving mastery of those objectives and can make judgments about when additional instruction is necessary.

Task 7: Classroom Management Plan

Prepare a "Classroom Management Plan" with which you can summarize the important information, policies, and procedures that you will use to motivate students and address student misbehavior.

Summarizing your organizational and discipline policies and strategies on a brief form (e.g., two pages) will help you determine whether your overall plan is clear and simple enough. If you have trouble highlighting the important features of your expectations and procedures on two pages, there is a good chance that your plan is overly complicated and/or poorly defined.

The major categories of information that we recommend be covered on a Classroom Management Plan (CMP) form are identified and briefly explained below. For each category, we have identified the module and task from this program that address that particular category. For example, the "M-1,#T2" notation next to Guidelines for Success means that you can find specific details about Guidelines for Success in Module 1, Task 2.

Level of Classroom Structure (M-1,#T7)—Based on the "risk factors" of your students, will you require a classroom management plan with low, medium, or high structure in order for students to be successful?

Guidelines for Success (M-1, #T2)—What attitudes, traits, and/or behaviors will help your students achieve success in your class and in life?

Rules (M-2, #T5)—What specific observable behaviors will define the expected behavior of students in your classroom?

Teaching Expectations (M-3, all tasks; M-4, #T2 & #T3)—What, how, and when will you teach students about behaving responsibly in your classroom?

Monitoring (M-6, #T1 & #T3)—How will you monitor what is occurring in your classroom so that you can be assured that both you and your students are meeting your expectations?

Encouragement Procedures (M-5, #T4, #T5, & #T6)—How will you encourage your students to demonstrate motivated and responsible behavior, and how will you let them know when they are doing well?

Correction Procedures (M-7, all tasks)—How will you respond to students' irresponsible behavior in order to increase the probability that they will not behave that way in the future?

Managing Student Work (M-2, #T-6)—What procedures and systems will you use to manage student work in an efficient and effective manner?

Figure 2.15 is a two-page reproducible template of a Classroom Management Plan (CMP) form that you can use to summarize your own management plan. Following the blank template is a completed sample CMP (Figure 2.16). Please note that the completed sample has been provided to give you an idea of what a CMP might look like. We do not mean to suggest that your CMP will/should be exactly like the sample.

If you are working through *CHAMPs* during the summer, you should start to fill out your CMP right now. Begin by working on those sections of the form that address information covered in Modules 1 and 2 (i.e., Level of Structure, Guidelines for Success, Classroom Rules, and Managing Student Work). To complete the form you will need to work through subsequent modules of the program. Specifically, you will find that Teaching Expectations are covered in Modules 3 and 4, Encouragement Procedures are covered in Module 5, Monitoring Procedures are covered in Module 6, and Correction Procedures are covered in Module 7.

If you are starting *CHAMPs* during the school year, examine the completed sample CMP that follows the blank template. Use the information in Modules 1 and 2, your review of the completed sample, and what you know from experience works well in your classroom, to complete your own CMP. Then, as you work through the Modules 3-8, modify aspects of that CMP so that it reflects an up-to-date description of your current policies and procedures.

NOTE

Once you have completed a written summary of your policies and procedures (i.e., your CMP), we recommend that you give a copy to your administrator so that she/he knows the basics of your classroom management plan. Ask your administrator to provide feedback or suggestions on how you might make your plan consistent with any building or district behavior management directives/policies. In addition, put a copy of the CMP in your "substitute folder" so that a substitute teacher can quickly review the basic elements of your plan.

Figure 2.15: Reproducible

Classroom Management Plan

Classroom Management Plan for ______________________________

Level of Structure: ☐ **H** ☐ **M** ☐ **L**

Guidelines for Success:

1. ______________________
2. ______________________
3. ______________________
4. ______________________
5. ______________________

Rules:

____

____

____

____

____

Teaching Expectations:

Monitoring Procedures

Encouragement Procedures

Class

Individual

Possible Corrective Consequences

Figure 2.15: Reproducible

Classroom Management Plan

Procedures for Managing Student Work

1. **Procedures for Assigning Classwork and Homework**

2. **Procedures for Managing Independent Work Periods**

3. **Procedures for Collecting Completed Work**

4. **Procedures for Keeping Records and Providing Feedback to Students**

5. **Procedures and Policies for Dealing with Late/Missing Assignments**

Figure 2.16: Completed Sample

Classroom Management Plan

Classroom Management Plan for Mr. Kuske

Level of Structure: ☐ H ☐ M ☐ L

Guidelines for Success:

1. Be responsible.
2. Always try.
3. Do your best.
4. Cooperate.
5. Treat everyone with dignity and respect.

Rules:

- Arrive on time with all materials.
- Keep hands, feet and objects to yourself.
- Follow directions.
- Stay on-task during work times.

TEACHING EXPECTATIONS:

- Teach students how to handle transitions between activities and lessons.
- Teach students how rules relate to different types of classroom activity.
- Conduct lessons on study strategies.
- Teach and review grading procedures with a course syllabus.

MONITORING PROCEDURES

1. Frequent scanning and use of proximity management to keep "in touch" with what the students are doing.
2. Weekly printout to each student on current grades and missing assignments--conference with students as necessary.
3. Use of the Weekly Record form to keep track of misbehavior.

ENCOURAGEMENT PROCEDURES

Class

Verbal feedback
Group activities--e.g., Game time or time outside
Cooperative groupings--train to encourage each other

Individual

Verbal feedback
Frequent non-contingent acknowledgment
Written feedback--notes on papers, certificates, thank you notes
Lottery tickets toward drawing (only some weeks--to maintain variety)
Parental contacts
Free "Homework" pass
Call the "Top Guns" at home--highest male and female on each test
Individualized contracts as necessary

POSSIBLE CORRECTIVE CONSEQUENCES

Verbal reprimand
Proximity management
Keep a record of the behavior
Time owed after class
In-class time out
Parental contacts
Restitution
Principal Notification Form
Disciplinary Referral

Figure 2.16: Completed Sample

Classroom Management Plan **Page 2 of 2**

Procedures for Managing Student Work

1. Procedures for Assigning Classwork and Homework

All assignments will be written on the board each day. In addition, assignments will be written on an 8.5x11 paper and placed in the "Absent: What You Missed" basket. When a student returns after the absence, this basket will have each day's assignments and any handouts or papers the student can pick up. In addition, all long-term assignments will be written on the daily assignment list on the board (e.g., "Science Projects due in two days.")

2. Procedures for Managing Independent Work Periods

A. Anytime a student is developing a pattern of not completing work, I will meet with the student privately to determine if the work is beyond the student's ability. If so, I will modify assignments or adapt instruction to help the student be successful.

B. I will not schedule seatwork periods that last longer than 30 minutes without creating some change in activity that allows students to move about somewhat.

C. During the first two weeks of school, I will directly teach students how to behave during independent work periods.

D. I will provide guided practice (doing 10 to 25 percent of the assignment together as a class-wide teacher-directed activity) before expecting students to complete any new type of task independently.

E. When students have questions, they can flip up a "????" flag that I will have on each desk.

3. Procedures for Collecting Completed Work

During the first month of school, I will collect all homework and classwork by having students put the completed assignment on their desk, and I will go around and take it from each student. After the first month, I will have students hand class-work into a basket and "check off" on a wall chart that they have handed it in. I will continue to physically collect homework from students at least until after winter break.

4. Procedures for Keeping Records and Providing Feedback to Students

I will enter all grades into my computer grade program. I will send a weekly print out of current grades, missing assignments and record of absenteeism/tardiness home with students. Parent (guardian) will be asked to sign and return.

I will also keep a class chart of Percentage of Homework Handed in On Time as a way to provide feedback and to motivate students to get their homework in on time.

5. Procedures and Policies for Dealing with Late/Missing Assignments

Any assignment that is turned in late will receive an immediate 10 percent penalty (a 100 point lab will have 10 deducted from the score you earn).

No assignment will be accepted beyond one week late.

Parents will be informed each week (on my Weekly Grade Report) of any missing assignments.

Module 2: Organization

Self-Assessment Checklist

Use the worksheet on the following pages to identify which (or which parts) of the tasks described in this module you have completed. For any item that has not been completed, note what needs to be done to complete it. Then translate your notes onto your planning calendar in the form of specific actions that you can take (e.g., August 17, finish developing procedures for Assigning Work.)

COMPLETED	TASK	NOTES & IMPLEMENTATION IDEAS
	DAILY SCHEDULE I have arranged my daily schedule to include a reasonable balance of teacher-directed, independent work, and cooperative group activities—both within a given subject and/or across subjects during the day. I have arranged my daily schedule so that no one type of activity (i.e., teacher-directed, independent work, or cooperative group) goes for too long a period of time. I have scheduled independent work and cooperative group activities to immediately follow teacher-directed tasks. I have identified and taken steps to pro-actively address those times of the class/day when students are more likely to misbehave.	
	PHYSICAL SPACE I have arranged the desks in my classroom to optimize the most common types of instructional activities students will engage in and to reflect the level of structure my students require. My classroom is arranged so that I have easy access to all parts of the room.	

COMPLETED	TASK	NOTES & IMPLEMENTATION IDEAS
	PHYSICAL SPACE (CONTINUED) My classroom is arranged in such a way that disruptions caused by activity in high traffic areas will be kept to a minimum. I have devoted some of my bulletin board/display space for student work. I have scheduled independent work and cooperative group activities to immediately follow teacher-directed tasks.	
	ATTENTION SIGNAL I have identified an attention signal that has both auditory and visual components to teach students. I have a specific plan for how I will provide both positive and corrective feedback to students regarding how they respond to the signal.	
	BEGINNING/ENDING ROUTINES I have identified how I will begin class/the school day in a way that makes students feel welcome and has them going immediately to their seats to work on a productive task. As a **middle school teacher,** I have determined how I will conduct opening activities to meet the following goals: • Students will be instructionally engaged while I take attendance. • My procedures for dealing with tardiness will insure that tardy students will not disrupt class or take my attention. • Announcements and housekeeping tasks will not take up too much time.	

COMPLETED	TASK	NOTES & IMPLEMENTATION IDEAS
	BEGINNING/ENDING ROUTINES (CONTINUED) As an **elementary school teacher,** I have determined how I will conduct opening activities to meet the following goals: • Opening activities will be efficient and orderly, and will ease students into the day. • Students will learn that school attendance and punctuality are important. I have identified procedures for dealing with students who do not have necessary materials and/or are unprepared that: • Ensure the student(s) can get needed materials in a way that does not disrupt instructions. • Establish reasonable penalties to reduce the likelihood the student(s) will forget materials in the future. • Reduce the amount of time and energy I have to spend dealing with this issue. I have identified how I will deal with students who return after an absence so that they can find out what assignments they have missed and get any handouts/returned papers in a way that does not involve a large amount of time and energy. I have developed procedures for wrapping up at the end of the school day and/or class period that: • Ensure that students will not leave the classroom before they have organized their own materials and completed any necessary clean-up tasks. • Ensure that I have enough time to give students both positive and corrective feedback, and set a positive tone for the class.	
	I have developed dismissal procedures that ensure that students will not leave the classroom until they have been dismissed by me (not by the bell ringing).	

COMPLETED	TASK	NOTES & IMPLEMENTATION IDEAS
	CLASSROOM RULES I have identified three to six positively stated rules that describe specific observable behaviors I expect students to exhibit, and specific observable behaviors I expect them not to exhibit. I have posted the Classroom Rules in a spot in the classroom that is easily visible from all parts of the room. I have identified possible corrective consequences that can be assigned for infractions of the Classroom Rules.	
	STUDENT WORK I have designed procedures for assigning classwork and homework that ensure that students can easily find out information about the tasks they have been assigned to complete. As I set up my independent work periods I will make sure that: • I only assign independent work that I know students can do independently. • The independent work times will be scheduled in a way that maximizes on-task behavior (see Task 1-Daily Schedule). • I have a clear vision of what I want student behavior to look and sound like during independent work times. • I will arrange to provide guided practice on tasks and assignments that I expect students to do independently. • I will develop a specific system for how students can get questions answered during independent work periods.	

COMPLETED	TASK	NOTES & IMPLEMENTATION IDEAS
	I have designed efficient and effective procedures for how I will collect student work. I have designed efficient and effective procedures for keeping records of students' work and giving them feedback about their progress. I have designed efficient and effective procedures for dealing with late and/or missing assignments.	
	CLASSROOM MANAGEMENT PLAN I have developed and/or completed a Classroom Management Plan form that summarizes the procedures and policies I plan to implement to keep students motivated and to address any misbehavior. I have given a copy of my Classroom Management Plan form to my administrator. I have placed a copy of my Classroom Management Plan form in my "substitute folder."	

Module 2: Organization

Peer Study Worksheet

With one or more of your colleagues, work through the following discussion topics and activities related to the tasks in Module 2. If necessary, refer back to the text to get additional ideas or for clarification. (See Module 1 Peer Study Worksheet for suggestions on structuring effective discussion sessions.)

Task 1: Daily Schedule

A. Have each group member share his/her daily schedule and explain the balance he or she has established among teacher-directed instruction, independent student work, and cooperative group activities.

B. As a group, identify those times/events during the day/class period that are likely to produce more irresponsible student behavior and discuss how you each might proactively address those times/events to reduce misbehavior.

Task 2: Physical Space

A. Arrange for the group to visit each group member's room, one at a time. When the group is in a particular room, have group members give feedback on the arrangement of desks, the use of bulletin board space, and the general effectiveness of (or potential problems with) the way the room is arranged.

Task 3: Attention Signal

A. Have each group member share what he or she has decided to use for an attention signal and get feedback from the other group members.

B. As a group, discuss how you will provide positive and corrective feedback to students regarding how they respond (or don't respond) to the signal.

Task 4: Beginning/Ending Routines

A. For each of the following designated areas, have each group member explain his or her procedures. Give each other feedback and help each other problem-solve any areas that have proven difficult to address:

- Before/immediately after the bell rings
- Taking attendance
- Dealing with tardy students
- Dealing with students who come to class without necessary materials
- Dealing with students upon their return from an absence
- Wrapping up the end of the day/class period
- Dismissal

Task 5: Classroom Rules

A. Have each group member share the Classroom Rules he or she has developed. As a group, give feedback to each individual.

B. As a group, discuss the possible corrective consequences that would be reasonable to assign for various infractions of Classroom Rules.

Task 6: Student Work (NOTE: Covering all aspects of this task may take an entire session itself.)

A. Have individual group members explain the procedures they use for managing the following aspects of student work. Give each other feedback.

- assigning classwork and homework
- collecting completed work
- keeping records and giving students feedback about their performance and progress
- setting up independent work periods
- dealing with late/missing work

Task 7: Classroom Management Plan

A. Have each group member share his/her completed “Classroom Management Plan” form. As a group, give feedback and problem-solve any areas that any one person is having difficulty with.

MODULE 3: EXPECTATIONS (*CHAMPS*)

When your expectations are clear, students never have to guess how you expect them to behave.

Introduction

The school and teacher effectiveness literature has consistently shown that successful teachers are very clear with students about exactly how they expect students to behave during the school day. If a teacher doesn't know and/or doesn't communicate his/her behavioral expectations to students, then the students have to guess at what constitutes responsible behavior. The problem with this is obvious when you consider the most common misbehaviors that occur in the typical classroom:

- Students talking too much or too loudly or about the wrong things;
- Students demanding attention by following the teacher around or by calling out to the teacher;
- Students doing math when they should be working on science;
- Students socializing when they should be cleaning up;
- Students wandering around the room or sharpening pencils when they are supposed to be listening to the teacher;
- Some students monopolizing classroom discussions and others not participating at all; and
- Some students disrupting lessons and others sitting and doing nothing during work periods.

We believe that you can avoid most (if not all) of these problems by clearly defining for yourself and then communicating to your students how you expect them to behave during each classroom activity and transition that occurs during the school day. If you do not, your students won't know whether or not it is all right to sharpen their pencils during cooperative group times; ask other students for help during a work period; ask you questions while you are taking attendance; etc.

Keep in mind that the answers to these kinds of questions can and will be different for different teachers. The important thing is that you know what your answers are. That is why the first two tasks in this module are designed to help you specifically define your behavioral expectations for students during major classroom activities (e.g. teacher-directed instruction, independent seat work, class discussions, cooperative group work, etc.) and common transition times (switching from one subject to another, getting textbooks open to a particular page, correcting papers, etc.). The foundation for completing the tasks is the *CHAMPs* acronym, which itself reflects the major issues that affect student behavior problems. The issues incorporated in *CHAMPs*, and the basic questions to be addressed for each issue, are:

C	**Conversation**	(Can students talk to each other?)
H	**Help**	(How do students get their questions answered? How do they get your attention?)
A	**Activity**	(What is the task/objective? What is the end product?)
M	**Movement**	(Can students move about?)
P	**Participation**	(What does the expected student behavior look/sound like? How do students show they are fully participating?)

Specifically defining your expectations is critical if you hope to have a positive and productive classroom. However, it is not—in and of itself—sufficient to achieve that goal. You also have to effectively communicate your expectations to your students. Thus, the third task in this module has to do with designing lessons to teach students the expectations you have defined. Teaching expectations is the first step in a three-step process for effectively communicating expectations to students (i.e., teaching expectations, monitoring student behavior during activities/transitions; and giving students feedback about their implementation of the expectations). This three-step process is summarized in Figure 3.1.

Figure 3.1: Three-step process for communicating expectations

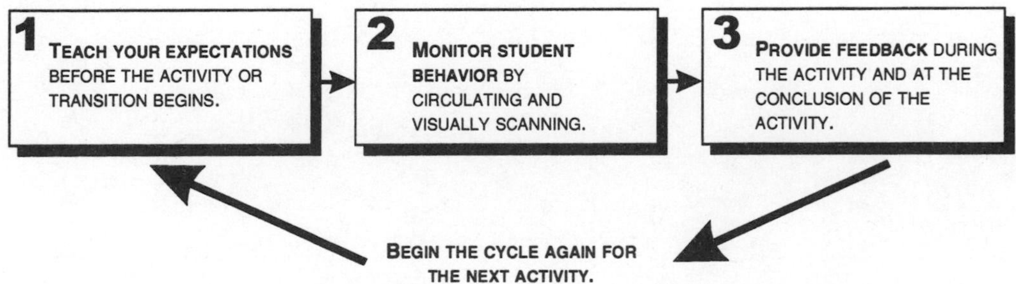

Detailed information about how to apply this three step communication process is presented in Module 4: The First Month. The three tasks described in this module are designed to ensure that you will be ready for the first day of school with clear expectations and lessons for teaching those expectations to students.

NOTE

Even if you are starting this program part way into the school year, it is critical that you to attend to the tasks in this module. Clarifying and teaching expectations is especially useful for any activities and/or transitions during which student behavior has been consistently problematic.

The three tasks presented and explained in this module are:

TASK 1: *CHAMPs* Expectations for Classroom Activities
Define clear and consistent behavioral expectations for all regularly scheduled classroom activities (e.g., small group instruction, independent work periods, etc.).

TASK 2: *CHAMPs* Expectations for Transitions
Define clear and consistent behavioral expectations for the common transitions (within and between activities) that occur during a typical school day.

TASK 3: Prepare Lessons on Expectations
Develop a preliminary plan and prepare lessons for teaching your *CHAMPs* expectations to students.

Immediately following the explanations of the tasks in this module is a Self-Assessment Checklist, designed to help you determine which (or which parts) of the tasks you have done/are doing and which you still need to do. The module ends with a Peer Study Worksheet. This worksheet presents a series of discussion questions and activities that can be used by two or more teachers who want to share information and collegial support as they work to improve their classroom management practices.

SPECIAL CONSIDERATIONS

The focus of this module is on student behavior in individual classrooms. However, there are two other related areas that need to be addressed, preferably on a schoolwide basis—a) student behavior in the school's common areas, and b) the schoolwide teaching of prosocial skills. While these two important areas are not specifically covered in this program, what follows is some basic information and suggested programs for addressing them.

Common Areas

Students need to know the behavioral expectations for common area settings (e.g., hallways, cafeteria, playground, bus waiting areas, buses, assemblies, substitutes, and so on). If your school has not clarified schoolwide expectations for them, ask your principal what you should teach your students about responsible behavior in these settings. For more information on defining and teaching behavioral expectations for common area settings, you may want to preview one or more of the following programs:

- Sprick, R.S. (1990). *Playground Discipline: Positive Techniques for Playground Supervision* (Video Program). Eugene, OR: Teaching Strategies.
- Sprick, R.S. (1995). *Cafeteria Discipline : Positive Techniques for Lunchroom Supervision* (Video Program). Eugene, OR: Teaching Strategies.
- Sprick, R.S. & Colvin, G. (1992). *Bus Discipline: A Positive Approach* (Video Program). Eugene, OR: Teaching Strategies.
- Sprick, R.S., & Howard, L. (1996). *Substitutes: Planning for Productivity and Consistency* (Video Program). Longmont, CO: Sopris West.
- Sprick, R.S., Sprick, M.S., & Garrison, M. (1993). *Foundations: Establishing Positive Discipline Policies, Vol. I: The Process*, *Vol. II: Sample Policies*, and *Vol. III: The Workbook* (Video Program). Longmont, CO: Sopris West.

Teaching of Social Skills

Sometimes when a teacher thinks a student has a behavior problem, it is in fact a skill problem. If many of the students in your school exhibit poor social skills, we urge you to encourage your whole staff to review one or more of the following programs for possible schoolwide implementation.

- Fister, S.L. & Kemp, K.A. (1995). *The One-Minute Skill Builder: Improving Student Social Skills*. Longmont, CO: Sopris West.
- Hartwig, L. & Meredith, G. (1994). *Got It!: Seven Steps for Teaching Students to Get On Top of Their Problems*. Longmont, CO: Sopris West.
- Huggins, P. (1990). *The ASSIST Program: Affective/Social Skills: Instructional Strategies and Techniques*. Longmont, CO: Sopris West.
- Sheridan, S.M. (1995). *The Tough Kid Social Skills Book*. Longmont, CO: Sopris West.
- Sprick, R.S. (1995). *STP: Stop, Think, Plan: A School-Wide Strategy for Teaching Conflict Resolution Skills* (Video Program). Eugene, OR: Teaching Strategies.
- Walker, H.M., Colvin, G., & Ramsey, E. (1995). *Antisocial Behavior In School: Strategies and Best Practices*. Pacific Grove, CA: Brooks/Cole.

- Walker, H.M., McConnell, S., Holmes, D., Todis, B., Walker, J., & Golden, N. (1983). *The Walker Social Skills Curriculum: The ACCEPTS Program.* Austin, TX: Pro-Ed.
- Walker, H.M., Todis, B., Holmes, D., & Horton, D. (1998). *The Walker Social Skills Curriculum: The ACCESS Program.* Austin, TX: Pro-Ed.

Task 1: *CHAMPs* Expectations for Classroom Activities

Define clear and consistent behavioral expectations for all regularly scheduled classroom activities (e.g., small group instruction, independent work periods, etc.).

The first step in defining your behavioral expectations for classroom activities is to make a list of the major types of activities that your students will engage in on a daily (or regular) basis. Your list might include things like:

- Opening/attendance routines.
- Teacher-directed instruction.
- Small group instruction.
- Independent work.
- Sustained silent reading.
- Cushion activities (what students do when they have finished assigned work and time still remains in the work period).
- Class meetings.
- Taking tests/quizzes.
- Centers/Lab stations.
- Peer tutoring sessions.
- Cooperative groups.

The idea is to identify specific activities and/or categories of activities for which you will have *different* behavioral expectations. For example, you may have a single item for teacher-directed instruction, because your expectations for student behavior during teacher-directed instruction are the same regardless of subject matter. Or, you may have one item for teacher-directed instruction in math and reading (because the behavioral expectations for them are the same), and another for teacher-directed instruction in science (because your expectations for teacher-directed instruction in science class are different than they are in math and reading). Middle school teachers will likely have the same basic classroom activities for each particular subject area they teach (e.g., the same activities for all foreign language sections), but different expectations for any other classes they teach, such as a science class.

Figure 3.2 is a reproducible "Classroom Activities List" form. Stop now, and use it to list your major classroom activities.

Figure 3.2: Reproducible

Teacher: ______________________________ **School Year:** ____________________

Classroom Activities List

List each major classroom activity and/or category of activity that will occur during a typical day in your classroom. Create a separate item for every activity (or category) during which you will have different behavioral expectations. For example, you may list "teacher-directed instruction (for math, reading, and language arts)" as one item or you may have three separate items, "teacher-directed instruction for math," "teacher-directed instruction for reading," and "teacher-directed instruction for language arts, depending upon whether your behavioral expectations for teacher-directed instruction will be the same regardless of content or different for the different content areas.

Once you have identified your major classroom activities, use the *CHAMPs* acronym as your guide to the important issues. For each activity, define *detailed* behavioral expectations for students in terms of the following:

C	**Conversation**	(Under what circumstances, if at all, can students talk to each other during the activity?)
H	**Help**	(How do students get their questions answered during the activity? How do they get your attention?)
A	**Activity**	(What is the activity? What is its intended objective/end product?)
M	**Movement**	(Under what circumstance, if at all, can students move about during the activity? e.g., Can they sharpen a pencil?)
P	**Participation**	(What does appropriate student work behavior during the activity look/sound like? How do students demonstrate their full participation?)

Remember, details are important. The more specific you can be in your own mind about exactly what you expect from students, the more clearly you will be able to communicate your expectations to your students. In addition, the more specific your expectations are, the more consistent you are likely to be in enforcing them.

Level of Structure and *CHAMPs* Expectations for Classroom Activities

Pay close attention to the "level of structure" your students need when defining your behavioral expectations. The greater the level of structure your students require, the more tightly you will need to design your expectations—to reduce the probability that students will make irresponsible behavioral choices. For example, with a class needing high structure, you should have narrowly-defined guidelines about when and how it is acceptable for students to sharpen their pencils (e.g., OK during independent work, but not OK during teacher-directed instruction). However, for a class needing only low structure, it is probably perfectly reasonable to have a broad guideline that permits pencil sharpening at anytime.

The other thing to keep in mind is that it's always easier to lessen highly structured procedures (gradually!) than to try to implement more structure because students are making bad choices. So, if students need high structure, it is probably advisable not to allow student-to-student talking during work periods at the beginning of the year. However, two weeks or three weeks into the year, after you've had a chance to see how the students behave, you might revise your expectations. "Class, starting today, if you have a question and I am not available, you can whisper to the person next to you, get the question answered and then get right back to quiet, independent work."

Figure 3.3 is a reproducible template of a *CHAMPs* Classroom Activity Worksheet. Make multiple copies of this form. Then document your behavioral expectations by filling out one worksheet for each major type of activity you identified. The completed worksheets will provide the content for your lessons to teach your students about your behavioral expectations. (Specific information on teaching your expectations is covered in Task 3 of this module and in Module 4: The First Month.)

NOTE

Immediately following the CHAMPs Classroom Activity Worksheet template are completed sample worksheets showing CHAMPs expectations for a variety of classroom activities (see Figures 3.4A - 3.4H). These completed samples have been provided as models only. We do not mean to imply that you should use the expectations included on them.

Figure 3.3: Reproducible

CHAMPs Classroom Activity Worksheet

Activity: ______________________________

C ONVERSATION

Can students engage in conversations with each other during this activity?

If yes, about what?

With whom?

How many students can be involved in a single conversation?

How long can the conversation last?

H ELP

How do students get questions answered? How do students get your attention?

If students have to wait for help, what should they do while they wait?

A CTIVITY

What is the expected end product of this activity? (Note: This may vary from day to day.)

M OVEMENT

Can students get out of their seats during the activity?

If yes, acceptable reasons include:

Pencil	Restroom
Drink	Hand in/pick up materials
Other:	

Do they need permission from you?

P ARTICIPATION

What behaviors show that students are participating fully and responsibly?

What behaviors show that a student is not participating?

Figure 3.4A: Completed Sample

CHAMPs Classroom Activity Worksheet

Activity: Independent seatwork while teacher is with small group

C ONVERSATION

Can students engage in conversations with each other during this activity? Yes

If yes, about what? If a student has a question about work assignment.

With whom? Other students at their table.

How many students can be involved in a single conversation? Two to four students.

How long can the conversation last? About a minute, then back to silent work.

H ELP

How do students get questions answered? How do students get your attention?
They should try to get answer without teacher help, but if no one at table can help, then come and stand in "Question Box."

If students have to wait for help, what should they do while they wait?
Stand quietly in the square.

A CTIVITY

What is the expected end product of this activity? (Note: This may vary from day to day.)
Students will complete seatwork packet; when done can go to book or science learning center.

M OVEMENT

Can students get out of their seats during the activity?

If yes, acceptable reasons include:

Pencil yes Restroom yes

Drink yes Hand in/pick up materials yes

Other: If they have a question, can come to the "Question Box."

Do they need permission from you? No

P ARTICIPATION

What behaviors show that students are participating fully and responsibly?
Looking at paper; writing or coloring. Talking with tablemate while looking at paper.

What behaviors show that a student is not participating?
Talking without looking at paper. Staring out window. Wandering around room.

Figure 3.4B: Completed Sample

CHAMPs Classroom Activity Worksheet

Activity: Small group reading instruction

CONVERSATION

Can students engage in conversations with each other during this activity? No

If yes, about what?

With whom?

How many students can be involved in a single conversation?

How long can the conversation last?

HELP

How do students get questions answered? How do students get your attention?
Raise their hands.

If students have to wait for help, what should they do while they wait?
Keep hand raised, wait quietly.

ACTIVITY

What is the expected end product of this activity? (Note: This may vary from day to day.)
Working on tasks and activities presented by the teacher. Verbal and written responses to teacher-presented tasks.

MOVEMENT

Can students get out of their seats during the activity?

If yes, acceptable reasons include:

Pencil no Restroom yes

Drink no Hand in/pick up materials no

Other:

Do they need permission from you? Yes, to leave group to use the restroom.

PARTICIPATION

What behaviors show that students are participating fully and responsibly?
Looking at teacher. Raising hand with something to say. Answering questions. Looking at reader or presentation book. Writing on individual chalkboard.

What behaviors show that a student is not participating?
Not answering questions. Talking to another student. Staring out window. Leaving circle without permission. Not following directions.

Figure 3.4C: Completed Sample

CHAMPs Classroom Activity Worksheet

Activity: Teacher directed instruction

C ONVERSATION

Can students engage in conversations with each other during this activity? No

If yes, about what?

With whom?

How many students can be involved in a single conversation?

How long can the conversation last?

H ELP

How do students get questions answered? How do students get your attention?
Raise their hand.

If students have to wait for help, what should they do while they wait?
Keep hand raised, wait quietly.

A CTIVITY

What is the expected end product of this activity? (Note: This may vary from day to day.)
Working on tasks and activities presented by the teacher. Verbal and written responses to teacher-presented tasks.

M OVEMENT

Can students get out of their seats during the activity?

If yes, acceptable reasons include:

Pencil no Restroom yes

Drink no Hand in/pick up materials Only if directed by teacher.

Other:

Do they need permission from you? Any leaving of seat must have permission.

P ARTICIPATION

What behaviors show that students are participating fully and responsibly?
Looking at teacher. Raising hand with something to say. Answering questions when called on or signaled to. Looking where teacher directs. Writing as directed by teacher.

What behaviors show that a student is not participating? Talking to another student. Getting out of seat without permission. Looking somewhere other than where directed. Not following teacher directions. Not raising hand. Not answering when signaled.

Figure 3.4D: Completed Sample

CHAMPs Classroom Activity Worksheet

Activity: Group activity

C ONVERSATION

Can students engage in conversations with each other during this activity? Yes, up to level 3. (so just those involved can hear you).

If yes, about what? The assignment they are working on.

With whom? Only students they are working with.

How many students can be involved in a single conversation? Those assigned to activity with you.

How long can the conversation last? Throughout activity, until signal is given.

H ELP

How do students get questions answered? How do students get your attention?
Put out sign that says "I need help, but I'm still working."

If students have to wait for help, what should they do while they wait?
Students will continue working on the rest of the assignment.

A CTIVITY

What is the expected end product of this activity? (Note: This may vary from day to day.)
Students will complete as much of assignment as possible during time given. If finished before time is up, read quietly or finish prior assignments at your desk.

M OVEMENT

Can students get out of their seats during the activity?

If yes, acceptable reasons include:

Pencil yes — Restroom no

Drink no — Hand in/pick up materials Yes, only relating to this assignment.

Do they need permission from you? Any movement must be assignment related.

P ARTICIPATION

What behaviors show that students are participating fully and responsibly?
Looking at paper or others in group. Writing or doing what task requires. Talking only with those in group. Staying with group until finished.

What behaviors show that a student is not participating?
Not working with group. Not writing or doing what task requires. Talking with others outside of group. Leaving group when not finished.

Figure 3.4E: Completed Sample

CHAMPs Classroom Activity Worksheet

Activity: Oral written tests (such as spelling)

C ONVERSATION

Can students engage in conversations with each other during this activity? No.

If yes, about what?

With whom?

How many students can be involved in a single conversation?

How long can the conversation last?

H ELP

How do students get questions answered? How do students get your attention?
Raise their hand.

If students have to wait for help, what should they do while they wait?
Keep hand raised, wait quietly.

A CTIVITY

What is the expected end product of this activity? (Note: This may vary from day to day.)
Listening and writing answers to oral test. When finished with test, sit quietly.

M OVEMENT

Can students get out of their seats during the activity?

If yes, acceptable reasons include:

Pencil no Restroom no

Drink no Hand in/pick up materials no

Other:

Do they need permission from you?

P ARTICIPATION

What behaviors show that students are participating fully and responsibly?
Looking at paper. Writing or doing what task requires. Not talking. Not leaving seat for any reason.

What behaviors show that a student is not participating?
Talking to another student. Getting out of seat. Not looking at paper. Not working on task.

Figure 3.4F: Completed Sample

CHAMPs Classroom Activity Worksheet

Activity: *Individual written tests*

C ONVERSATION

Can students engage in conversations with each other during this activity? *No.*

If yes, about what?

With whom?

How many students can be involved in a single conversation?

How long can the conversation last?

H ELP

How do students get questions answered? How do students get your attention?
Put out sign that says "I need help, but I'm still working." if it's an individual test..

If students have to wait for help, what should they do while they wait?
Student will continue working on the rest of the test.

A CTIVITY

What is the expected end product of this activity? (Note: This may vary from day to day.)
Working on written test. When finished with test, sit quietly and read.

M OVEMENT

Can students get out of their seats during the activity?

If yes, acceptable reasons include:

Pencil *no* Restroom *no*

Drink *no* Hand in/pick up materials *no*

Other:

Do they need permission from you?

P ARTICIPATION

What behaviors show that students are participating fully and responsibly?
Looking at paper. Writing or doing what task requires. Not talking. Not leaving seat for any reason.

What behaviors show that a student is not participating?
Talking to another student. Getting out of seat. Not looking at paper. Not working on task.

Figure 3.4G: Completed Sample

CHAMPs Classroom Activity Worksheet

Activity: Peer tutoring

C ONVERSATION

Can students engage in conversations with each other during this activity? Yes, level 2 only.

If yes, about what? The assignment they are working on.

With whom? Only student they are working with.

How many students can be involved in a single conversation? Only two students.

How long can the conversation last? Only about five minutes, then back to silent work.

H ELP

How do students get questions answered? How do students get your attention?
Put out sign that says "I need help, but I'm still working," and mark question for when the teacher gets to you.

If students have to wait for help, what should they do while they wait?
Students will continue working on the rest of the assignment.

A CTIVITY

What is the expected end product of this activity? (Note: This may vary from day to day.)
Helping another student to do an assignment.

M OVEMENT

Can students get out of their seats during the activity?

If yes, acceptable reasons include:

Pencil no Restroom no

Drink no Hand in/pick up materials no

Other:

Do they need permission from you?

P ARTICIPATION

What behaviors show that students are participating fully and responsibly?
Looking at paper. Writing or doing what task requires. Talking only with peer. Not leaving seat until finished. Giving help so the other student understands how to do it themselves.

What behaviors show that a student is not participating?
Giving answers instead of help. Getting out of seat. Not looking at paper. Not working on task. Talking to others not involved.

Figure 3.4H: Completed Sample

CHAMPs Classroom Activity Worksheet

Activity: *Individual seatwork*

C ONVERSATION

Can students engage in conversations with each other during this activity? *Yes, level 2 only.*

If yes, about what? *If a student has a question about work assigned.*

With whom? *Only students they sit next to.*

How many students can be involved in a single conversation? *Only two students.*

How long can the conversation last? *Only about a minute, then back to silent work.*

H ELP

How do students get questions answered? How do students get your attention?
Put out sign that says "I need help, but I'm still working," and mark question for when the teacher gets to you.

If students have to wait for help, what should they do while they wait?
Student will continue working on the rest of the assignment.

A CTIVITY

What is the expected end product of this activity? (Note: This may vary from day to day.)
Helping another student to do an assignment.

M OVEMENT

Can students get out of their seats during the activity?

If yes, acceptable reasons include:

Pencil *Yes*

Drink *Yes, as long as it doesn't create a line.*

Restroom *Yes, after signing out.*

Hand in/pick up materials *Yes*

Other:

Do they need permission from you? *Only for the restroom.*

P ARTICIPATION

What behaviors show that students are participating fully and responsibly?
Looking at paper. Writing or doing what task requires. Talking only under above circumstance.

What behaviors show that a student is not participating?
Talking outside above circumstance. Talking during movement. Wandering around the room. Looking somewhere other than at work. Not doing task.

Task 2: *CHAMPs* Expectations for Transitions

Define clear and consistent behavioral expectations for the common transitions (within and between activities) that occur during a typical school day.

In addition to the classroom "activities" that take place during the school day, there are also "transitions," or times when students transition from one task to another during an activity (e.g., in a math lesson, you present teacher-directed instruction and then have students get out their math books to work independently) or transition from one activity to another (e.g., reading time is ending and students will be going out to recess). Transitions are often problematic in terms of student behavior, and poorly managed transitions are troublesome—both because of their potential for student misbehavior and because they end up consuming valuable instructional time. When you clearly define and communicate your expectations for transitions, you will have well-managed and efficient transitions.

As with classroom activities, the first step in defining behavioral expectations for transitions involves listing the major transitions that typically occur during your school day or class period (use the reproducible Transitions List form, Figure 3.5). Be sure to identify all the specific transitions and/or categories of transitions for which you will have *different* behavioral expectations. A list of transitions might include the following:

- Before the bell rings.
- After the bell rings.
- Getting out paper, pencil, and heading paper.
- Getting a book out and opening to a particular page.
- Moving to and from a small group location.
- Students leaving and entering the classroom (e.g., grade level teachers homogeneously group across classes for math instruction).
- Putting things away (clearing their desks).
- Handing in work (e.g., after an in-class assignment or a quiz).
- Trading papers for corrections.
- Cleaning up after project activities.
- Leaving the classroom at end of day (or a class period).
- Moving as a class to a different and specific location (e.g., library, playground, and so on).
- Handing things out (e.g., an assignment sheet or art supplies).
- Handing things back (e.g. graded papers).
- Opening and dismissal routines (expectations for these transitions were discussed in Module 2, Task 4).

NOTE

An elementary teacher who has the same group of students all day will probably have more variety in types of transitions throughout the day than a middle school teacher.

Figure 3.5: Reproducible

Teacher: ______________________ School Year: ______________

Transitions List

List each common transition and/or category of transitions that will occur during a typical day in your classroom. Create a separate item for every transition (or category) during which you will have different behavioral expectations. For example, you may list "getting out the textbook and turning to a specific page (during math, reading, and language arts)" as one item or you may have three separate items, "getting out a book during math," "getting out a book during reading," and "getting out a book during language arts" -- depending upon whether your behavioral expectations for getting out a textbook during a lesson will be the same regardless of lesson content or different for the different content areas.

Once you have your list of transitions, use the *CHAMPs* acronym as a guide for defining your behavioral expectations for the important issues. Make copies of the reproducible *CHAMPs* Transition Worksheet template (Figure 3.6) for all of the transitions on your list. Then, complete one worksheet for each type of transition. Be thorough—remember, the more detailed you are, the more clearly you will be able to communicate your expectations to students and the more consistent you are likely to be in implementing your expectations. (Information on teaching expectations to students is covered in Task 3 of this module and in Module 4: The First Month.) You will notice that some of the specific questions included with the *CHAMPs* acronym for transitions are slightly different from those included for classroom activities. This is due to the unique nature of transitions.

C	**Conversation**	(Can students talk to each other during the transition activity?)
H	**Help**	(How can students get your attention during the transition?)
A	**Activity**	(What is the objective of the transition, or what will be different after the transition—e.g., location change, different materials to work with, and so on? How long should the transition take?)
M	**Movement**	(Can students move about during the transition? If so, for what purposes?)
P	**Participation**	(What does desired student behavior during the transition look/sound like?)

NOTE

Following the CHAMPs Transition Worksheet template are samples of completed worksheets showing CHAMPs expectations for a variety of transitions (see Figures 3.7A - 3.7I. These completed samples are included as models only, and are not meant to imply that the expectations on them should be your expectations.

Level of Structure and *CHAMPs* Expectations for Transitions

The more structure your class requires, the more specific and tightly orchestrated you need to make your expectations for transitions. For a low structure class, you probably don't need to specify the routes students are to take to the small-group instruction area. On the other hand, for students needing high structure, you should include the expectation that students need to take the most direct route and that they need to keep their hands, feet, and objects to themselves so they do not disturb students who are working at their seats.

Figure 3.6: Completed Sample

CHAMPs Transition Worksheet

Transition: ____

____

CONVERSATION

Can students engage in conversations with each other during this transition?

If yes, clarify how (so that they are keeping their attention on completing the transition).

HELP

How do students get questions answered? How do students get your attention?

ACTIVITY

Explain transition. What will be different afterwards? (e.g., change in location, use of different materials, etc.). Include time criteria (i.e., how long it should take).

MOVEMENT

If the transition itself DOES NOT involve getting out of seats, can students get out of their seat for any reason during the transition?
If "yes," what are acceptable reasons?

If the transition itself involves out-of-seat movement, can a student go elsewhere, for example, to sharpen a pencil?

PARTICIPATION

What behaviors show that students are participating in the transition fully and responsibly?

What behaviors show that a student is not participating appropriately in the transition?

Figure 3.7A: Completed Sample

CHAMPs Transition Worksheet

Transition: Getting a book out and opening to a particular page—e.g., for guided practice on problems during a math lesson

C ONVERSATION

Can students engage in conversations with each other during this transition?

Only if a student needs to ask to look on with a neighbor's book because he/she does not have his/her book in the desk.

If yes, clarify how (so that they are keeping their attention on completing the transition).

If a student needs to look on with a neighbor, he/she can quietly whisper the request to the neighbor, and can quietly move his/her chair so they can both see.

H ELP

How do students get questions answered? How do students get your attention?

Raise hand.

A CTIVITY

Explain transition. What will be different afterwards? (e.g., change in location, use of different materials, etc.) Include time criteria (i.e., how long it should take). Teacher will tell (and write on the board) the book and the page number. Within ten seconds, all students will have the book open to the correct page and should be waiting quietly. If a student does not have the book, they can ask to look on with a neighbor.

M OVEMENT

If the transition itself DOES NOT involve getting out of seats, can students get out of their seat for any reason during the transition? No

If "yes," what are acceptable reasons?

If the transition itself involves out-of-seat movement, can a student go elsewhere, for example, to sharpen a pencil?

P ARTICIPATION

What behaviors show that students are participating in the transition fully and responsibly?

As soon as the instruction is given, students will open the book quickly and quietly and will wait for further instruction to be given.

What behaviors show that a student is not participating appropriately in the transition?

Asking "What page?"

Talking (other than asking quietly to share book)

Wasting time (e.g., looking for book in messy desk or playing)

Figure 3.7B: Completed Sample

CHAMPs Transition Worksheet

Transition: Moving to and from small reading groups.

C ONVERSATION

Can students engage in conversations with each other during this transition?
No

If yes, clarify how (so that they are keeping their attention on completing the transition).

H ELP

How do students get questions answered? How do students get your attention?
Raise hand from their desk or from where they are seated for the small group.

A CTIVITY

Explain transition. What will be different afterwards? (e.g., change in location, use of different materials, etc.) Include time criteria (i.e., how long it should take). Teacher will announce which group should come to the reading area. Students in that group should gather their reading materials, push in their chairs, and come quickly and quietly to the reading area. All students should be in the reading area within 30 seconds of the announcement.

M OVEMENT

If the transition itself DOES NOT involve getting out of seats, can students get out of their seat for any reason during the transition? Yes

If "yes," what are acceptable reasons?
To come to or leave the reading area.

If the transition itself involves out-of-seat movement, can a student go elsewhere, for example, to sharpen a pencil? No

P ARTICIPATION

What behaviors show that students are participating in the transition fully and responsibly?
As soon as the direction is given, students will go directly to the correct location (to reading area or back to seats) quickly and quietly.

What behaviors show that a student is not participating appropriately in the transition?
Not moving immediately (e.g., continuing to work at desk).
Talking or poking someone or knocking things off desks as they pass by.
Running or making noise on the way.

Figure 3.7C: Completed Sample

CHAMPs Transition Worksheet

Transition: Getting out supplies (paper/pencil, etc.)

C ONVERSATION

Can students engage in conversations with each other during this transition?
No

If yes, clarify how (so that they are keeping their attention on completing the transition).

H ELP

How do students get questions answered? How do students get your attention?
Raise their hand.

A CTIVITY

Explain transition. What will be different afterwards? (e.g., change in location, use of different materials, etc.) Include time criteria (i.e., how long it should take). Teacher will tell (and write on the board) what supplies are needed. Within 10 seconds, all students will have the supplies out and should be waiting quietly.

M OVEMENT

Can students get out of their seat for any reason? If so, for what reasons? No
If "yes," what are acceptable reasons?

If the transition itself involves out-of-seat movement, can a student go elsewhere, for example, to sharpen a pencil?

P ARTICIPATION

What behaviors show that students are participating in the transition fully and responsibly?
As soon as the instruction is given, students will get out supplies quickly and quietly and will wait for further instruction to be given. They will be prepared for this by making sure they have supplies in the morning.

What behaviors show that a student is not participating appropriately in the transition?
Asking, "What do we need?"
Talking
Wasting time (looking for supplies in messy desk or playing)

Figure 3.7D: Completed Sample

CHAMPs Transition Worksheet

Transition: *Movement of small group*

C ONVERSATION

Can students engage in conversations with each other during this transition?
Yes, level 2 only.

If yes, clarify how (so that they are keeping their attention on completing the transition).
Conversation is only for the purpose of saying "excuse me," "thank you," and "please."

H ELP

How do students get questions answered? How do students get your attention?
Raise their hand.

A CTIVITY

Explain transition. What will be different afterwards? (e.g., change in location, use of different materials, etc.) Include time criteria (i.e., how long it should take). *Teacher will announce that it's group time (spelling, reading, etc.) Those leaving will get their supplies out, push in their chair, and go quickly and quietly to the small group area they are assigned to. All students should be in their area within 30 seconds of the announcement.*

M OVEMENT

Can students get out of their seat for any reason? If so, for what reasons? *Yes, when told to go to groups.*
If "yes," what are acceptable reasons?

If the transition itself involves out-of-seat movement, can a student go elsewhere, for example, to sharpen a pencil? *No, only to go to group.*

P ARTICIPATION

What behaviors show that students are participating in the transition fully and responsibly?
As soon as the instruction is given, students will go quickly and quietly and will wait for further instruction to be given. They will walk in single file. Talking only for above reasons.

What behaviors show that a student is not participating appropriately in the transition?
Talking without reasons given above. Not going when told to. Not going straight to group by most direct route or route given. Being next to someone instead of in front or behind when going.

Figure 3.7E: Completed Sample

CHAMPs Transition Worksheet

Transition: Handing out papers/supplies

C ONVERSATION

Can students engage in conversations with each other during this transition?
Yes, level 2 only.

If yes, clarify how (so that they are keeping their attention on completing the transition).
Conversation is only for the purpose of saying "excuse me," "thank you," and "please."

H ELP

How do students get questions answered? How do students get your attention?
Raise their hand.

A CTIVITY

Explain transition. What will be different afterwards? (e.g., change in location, use of different materials, etc.) Include time criteria (i.e., how long it should take). Teacher will hand papers to the person at the end of the row, and they will pass them to the next person, and so on. Passing out papers should take no longer than 30 seconds.

M OVEMENT

Can students get out of their seat for any reason? If so, for what reasons? No

If "yes," what are acceptable reasons?

If the transition itself involves out-of-seat movement, can a student go elsewhere, for example, to sharpen a pencil?

P ARTICIPATION

What behaviors show that students are participating in the transition fully and responsibly?
As soon as the papers are given, students will pass papers to the person next to them, making sure the papers don't fall on the floor. Talking only as above. Paying attention so everyone gets the papers quickly.

What behaviors show that a student is not participating appropriately in the transition?
Talking without reasons given above. Throwing papers to the next person. Getting up and passing papers to each person in your row. Not paying attention, so others don't get the papers.

Figure 3.7F: Completed Sample

CHAMPs Transition Worksheet

Transition: Handing in papers (tests, etc.)

C ONVERSATION

Can students engage in conversations with each other during this transition?
Yes, level 2 only.

If yes, clarify how (so that they are keeping their attention on completing the transition).
Conversation is only for the purpose of saying "excuse me," "thank you," and "please."

H ELP

How do students get questions answered? How do students get your attention?
Raise their hand.

A CTIVITY

Explain transition. What will be different afterwards? (e.g., change in location, use of different materials, etc.) Include time criteria (i.e., how long it should take). Students will pass their paper to the next person and so on in the direction the teacher indicates. Last person at the back row will come forward collecting papers from the other rows and giving papers to teacher. Collecting papers should take no longer than 30 seconds.

M OVEMENT

Can students get out of their seat for any reason? If so, for what reasons? Yes, only the last person in the back row to bring papers forward.

If "yes," what are acceptable reasons?

If the transition itself involves out-of-seat movement, can a student go elsewhere, for example, to sharpen a pencil? No

P ARTICIPATION

What behaviors show that students are participating in the transition fully and responsibly?
Students will collect papers from the person next to them, making sure the papers don't fall on the floor. Talking only as above. Paying attention so everyone gets the papers in quickly.

What behaviors show that a student is not participating appropriately in the transition?
Talking without reasons given above. Throwing papers to the next person. Getting up and collecting papers from each person in your row. Not paying attention, so others don't get their papers in.

Figure 3.7G: Completed Sample

CHAMPs Transition Worksheet

Transition: Before Bell

C ONVERSATION

Can students engage in conversations with each other during this transition?
No

If yes, clarify how (so that they are keeping their attention on completing the transition).
Conversation is only for the purpose of saying "excuse me," "thank you," and "please."

H ELP

How do students get questions answered? How do students get your attention?
Put out sign that says, "I need help, but I'm still working." I'll only be able to help when I'm finished greeting your classmates. I will eventually assign a few helpers for this time.

A CTIVITY

Explain transition. What will be different afterwards? (e.g., change in location, use of different materials, etc.) Include time criteria (i.e., how long it should take). Students come into the classroom quickly and quietly. They will take care of housekeeping details and will get the morning handout or check the overhead for the assignment and get to work in their seats by the time the bell rings.

M OVEMENT

Can students get out of their seat for any reason? If so, for what reasons? Yes, to sharpen pencils, to get silent reading book, and to get paper. Morning handout should be taken as they come in the door. To turn in assignments, check job chart, and put away backpack/coat.

If "yes," what are acceptable reasons?

If the transition itself involves out-of-seat movement, can a student go elsewhere, for example, to sharpen a pencil? Only with permission.

P ARTICIPATION

What behaviors show that students are participating in the transition fully and responsibly?
Students come into the classroom quietly then empty and put away backpack. Make sure they have two sharpened pencils for the day, silent reading book, and paper. Turn in any homework due (see chart next to baskets). On Mondays, check the job chart to see what their assigned job is. Put chairs down for their area. Get the morning handout or check the overhead for the assignment and get to work quickly and quietly.

What behaviors show that a student is not participating appropriately in the transition?
Come in noisily. Leave supplies and homework in backpack. Not get ready for day. Not check job chart. Not do morning work.

Figure 3.7H: Completed Sample

CHAMPs Transition Worksheet

Transition: Class travel

C ONVERSATION

Can students engage in conversations with each other during this transition?
Yes, level 2 only.

If yes, clarify how (so that they are keeping their attention on completing the transition).
Conversation is only for the purpose of saying "excuse me," "thank you," and "please."

H ELP

How do students get questions answered? How do students get your attention?
Raise their hand.

A CTIVITY

Explain transition. What will be different afterwards? (e.g., change in location, use of different materials, etc.) Include time criteria (i.e., how long it should take). Teacher will announce where class is going and then have line leader and door holder go to the door. Rows will quietly line up as called on. Students will push in their chair as they line up to go. All students will be lined up within 30 seconds.

M OVEMENT

Can students get out of their seat for any reason? If so, for what reasons? Yes, when called on to line up.

If "yes," what are acceptable reasons?

If the transition itself involves out-of-seat movement, can a student go elsewhere, for example, to sharpen a pencil? No, only to line up.

P ARTICIPATION

What behaviors show that students are participating in the transition fully and responsibly?
As soon as the instruction is given, students will line up quickly and quietly and will wait for further instruction to be given. They will be facing the back of the student in front of them. They will be in single file. Talking only for above reasons.

What behaviors show that a student is not participating appropriately in the transition?
Talking without reasons given above. Not lining up when told to. Not going straight to line by most direct route or route given. Being next to someone instead of in front or behind.

Figure 3.7I: Completed Sample

CHAMPs Transition Worksheet

Transition: *Clean up at end of day*

C ONVERSATION

Can students engage in conversations with each other during this transition?
Yes, level 2 only.

If yes, clarify how (so that they are keeping their attention on completing the transition).
Conversation is only for the purpose of saying "excuse me," "thank you," and "please."

H ELP

How do students get questions answered? How do students get your attention?
Raise their hand.

A CTIVITY

Explain transition. What will be different afterwards? (e.g., change in location, use of different materials, etc.) Include time criteria (i.e., how long it should take). *Students will get out their homework folder and see what they need to take home. They will make sure they have everything they need to accomplish homework on their desk, ready to put in their backpack. When called on by the teacher, students will go as rows first to the coatrack and then to their mailbox to collect their things. They will put everything going home into their backpack. They will stack up their chairs in front of the desk not used yesterday. They will stand quietly at their desks until told by row to line up. Complete within 10 minutes, then teacher will make any announcements.*

M OVEMENT

Can students get out of their seat for any reason? If so, for what reasons? *Yes, when directed by the teacher to do so.*

If "yes," what are acceptable reasons?

If the transition itself involves out-of-seat movement, can a student go elsewhere, for example, to sharpen a pencil? *Yes*

P ARTICIPATION

What behaviors show that students are participating in the transition fully and responsibly?
Students will get what they need from their desks, follow teacher directions, put items to go home in their backpack, stack chairs in a quiet and orderly manner, and wait quietly for instruction to line up.

What behaviors show that a student is not participating appropriately in the transition?
Talking without reasons given above. Putting papers from mailbox into desk. Not getting homework ready. Talking above level 2. Not being careful when stacking chairs.

Task 3: Prepare Lessons on Expectations

Develop a preliminary plan and prepare lessons for teaching your CHAMPs expectations to students.

As important as it is for you to define for yourself exactly how you expect students to behave during various classroom activities and transitions, identifying expectations alone is not enough. If students are going to be able to meet your expectations, you also need to communicate those expectations to students clearly and thoroughly. We believe that effectively communicating expectations can be accomplished through the three-step process introduced earlier in this module (and shown in Figure 3.8).

Figure 3.8: Three-step process for communicating expectations

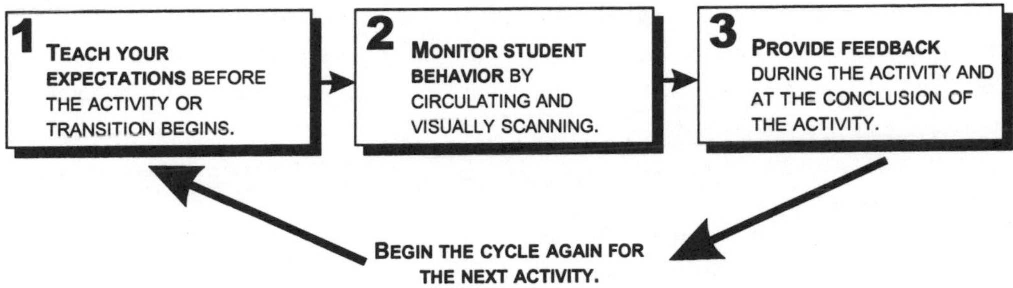

As you can see, the first step in the communication process is teaching your expectations to students. To do this effectively, you need to develop a preliminary plan for how you will teach students and then prepare lessons that you will use. The remainder of this module addresses those two issues.

NOTE

Detailed information on the second and third steps in the communication process—monitoring student behavior and giving students feedback on their implementation of the expectations—is presented in Tasks 2 and 3 of Module 4: The First Month.

Develop a preliminary plan for how you will teach your *CHAMPs* expectations.

Your plan for how you will teach your *CHAMPs* expectations should reflect answers to these three basic questions. How detailed do your lessons need to be? How long do you anticipate having to actively teach the lessons? What is the best way to organize the "content"? When answering these questions, you need to consider the complexity of the expectations you have defined, your own teaching style, and the age and sophistication of your students. For example, in settings with mature and responsible students (a class needing only a low-structure behavior plan), it may be sufficient to simply verbally describe your expectations on the first day of school, provide short verbal reviews on the second and third days, and thereafter use only occasional reminders. On the other hand, with students with more behavior problems (a class that needs a highly structured management plan) you should probably plan to teach your expectations—using visual displays, demonstrations, and perhaps even actual practice—every day for at least the first ten days of school.

If a verbal presentation alone will work with your students, you may not even need to prepare any lessons—you can just have your *CHAMPs* worksheets handy. However, when you anticipate that repeated teaching will be necessary, you will want to vary the instructional approach you use to keep things interesting. Therefore, if you believe that your class will need high structure, you should plan on preparing lessons that have maximal variety. Include student involvement so that you reduce the probability that students will get bored and ensure that they will fully understand the expectations.

Another consideration when developing your teaching plan is how you will organize the content. You may or may not want to actually use the *CHAMPs* acronym when teaching your expectations. With very young students (Pre-K to first grade), the acronym may not be very meaningful as most of the students may not even know the alphabet. At the other end of the spectrum, mature middle-school students may find the acronym "corny" or babyish. For second through sixth grade students though, the acronym can be a useful way to communicate that there is consistency regarding what students have to know to behave responsibly. Although the specific expected behaviors might be different between cooperative groups and teacher-directed instruction, for example, students will learn that the issues (i.e., conversation, help, movement, and participation) are the same from one activity/transition to another. It can also help students realize that for each classroom activity and transition, you have definite thoughts about each of those categories. Without the acronym as an anchor, students may feel that there are just thousands of unconnected expectations. Another advantage in using the *CHAMPs* acronym is that the content is already neatly organized for you—all you have to do is use your *CHAMPs* worksheets.

NOTE

Remember, whether or not you use the CHAMPs acronym with your students, you should use it when defining your expectations—to ensure that you cover all important aspects of student behavior.)

There are other options for organizing the content of your expectations. One possibility is to simply list the three or four main expectations you have for each activity or transition. This option might be appropriate if you have students who need only a low structure management plan. Another possibility is to organize your expectations into "T-Charts" of "looks like/sounds like" descriptors. Figure 3.9 shows a sample T-Chart for teacher-directed instruction/class discussions that might be used by a middle school teacher who conducts interactive lessons involving frequent discussion opportunities. T-Charts are appropriate for classes needing medium to high structure because of the amount and nature of detail they provide.

Figure 3.9: T-Chart Sample

Expectations for Teacher Directed Instruction & Discussions

LOOKS LIKE:	SOUNDS LIKE:
Eyes on speaker, overhead, or your own notes.	Only one voice at a time can be heard.
Everyone looks as if they are listening to the speaker.	Presentation voice is used when you are the speaker.
Hands raised before speaking.	Questions and comments from the speaker relate the lesson.
Notes being taken on essential points.	No noise other than writing or turning a page of your notes if you are not the current speaker.
Everyone in seat, except speaker.	All verbal participation sounds respectful–even when you are disagreeing.
If someone disagrees, s/he raises hand to become the speaker. There are no non-verbal expressions of disagreement.	

One last note. When developing your plan for teaching expectations (i.e., deciding how detailed your lessons will be, anticipating how many days you will actively teach the expectations, and choosing how you will organize the content), it is better to overplan than underplan. We recommend that you err on the side of more lessons and more detail than you might need because it is always easier to condense (or eliminate) some of what you have than to scramble to create new lessons once school has started.

Prepare lessons for teaching your *CHAMPs* expectations.

As you begin to prepare your lessons, keep in mind that you will teach the lesson for a particular activity/transition immediately before that activity/transition is scheduled to occur. Also keep in mind that the two main activities that must be included in all lessons on expectations are presenting (explaining) the expectations to students and verifying that students understand what the expectations are. Depending upon what you determined when you developed your teaching plan, you may or may not also need/want to include the following as part of your presentation: (1) some kind of textual and/or graphic visual display (e.g., overhead transparency, flip chart, flip notebook, bulletin board); (2) actual demonstrations of the expected behaviors (by you, by students); and/or (3) opportunities for students to practice and rehearse the expected behaviors. Given the amount of detail involved with most classroom expectations (which you may have noticed when you completed your *CHAMPs* worksheets), it's important that you structure your lessons so that they inform but do not overwhelm or intimidate students. Following are brief discussions of the various means of "embellishing" the way you present (explain) your expectations.

Visual Displays

Using a visual display as part of your presentation of expectations has several advantages. Visual displays can be used to summarize key expectations and to make the lessons more graphic for students. A visual display represents a permanent record of the expectations, to which students can refer during an activity or transition if they have any questions. It also provides a concrete object to which you can draw students' attention, both when you are explaining the expectations and as a prompt during an activity where students may not be following the expectations. If you decide to use a visual display of your expectations, you will have to make further decisions about the displays you will use. As you consider the following information, remember that you can create visual displays that best meet the needs of your students by using these ideas singly or in combination.

There are many forms for presenting visual displays of your expectations. Among the most useful that we have found are: (1) overhead transparencies; (2) flip charts; (3) notebook flip charts; and (4) bulletin boards.

Overhead Transparencies

One way to visually display your expectations is to put them on overhead transparencies. Immediately prior to any given activity or transition, you could put the transparency for that particular activity or transition on the overhead and use it as the focus for a short lesson on how students are expected to behave. If you do not otherwise need the overhead projector, you can even leave the transparency showing during the activity or transition. You can use overhead transparencies regardless of how you have decided to organize your lesson content. That is, you could create transparencies on which you list your expectations, or on which you have placed a T-Chart of "Looks Like/Sounds Like." A particularly simple way of using overhead transparencies is to just make transparencies of the various *CHAMPs* worksheets that you completed as part of Task 1.

Flip Charts

Another mode of visual display is flip charts. On each page of the flip chart you would put the expectations for one activity or transition. (Again, you could "organize" the content in any way that is comfortable for you — with the *CHAMPs* acronym, as a T-Chart, or simply as a list of major expectations.) You would keep the flip chart in a location that can be seen by all students. Then, as you are about to begin a particular activity or transition, you flip to the page for that activity/transition and have students follow along as you describe the activity or transition and what your expectations for student behavior are. When you get to the point that you no longer have to review your expectations with students, you can simply flip the chart to the correct page and point to the expectations and have a list of your major expectations for that activity/transition. (NOTE: You can use either a full size flip chart, such as you see in many elementary classrooms, or a notebook flip chart, which is just a large three-ring binder that can be set up on the teacher's desk or a file cabinet.) Figure 3.10 shows a sample of a notebook flip chart which has been turned to a page with a simple list of expectations on it.

Figure 3.10: Notebook as a Flip Chart

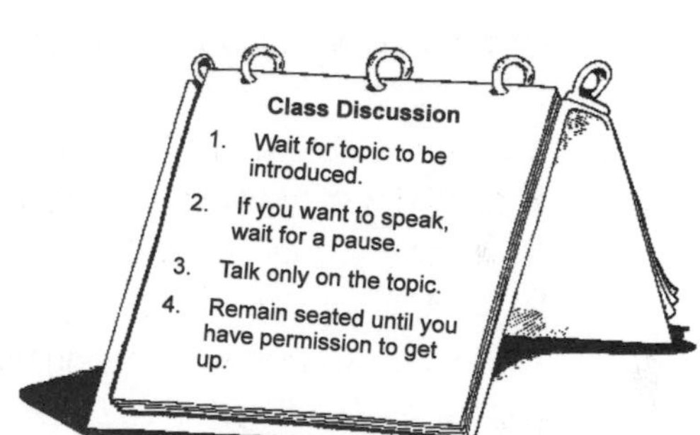

Visual displays, whether they are on overhead transparencies, flip charts, notebook flip charts, or bulletin boards can include text only, graphic icons only, or some combination of text and graphics. Again, the decision will depend on the complexity of your expectations, the age and sophistication of your students, and to a lesser extent, how you have chosen to organize the content of your expectations. Text-only displays are probably best for middle school students.

For primary students, visual displays that involve graphic icons rather than text will be more effective. The most obvious example involves students in grades K-2 who are probably not proficient enough readers for visual displays involving a lot of text to be meaningful. However, there may also be students in grades 3 and above who simply find graphic icons more appealing. In Appendix 2 of this program, you will find reproducible copies of icons that depict the major *CHAMPs* categories (e.g., conversation, help, movement, participation) and some common classroom activities and transitions (including seatwork, board work, discussion, circle times, music, library, P.E., hallway, free play, clean up, small group, and lining up). Feel free to use the icons to create your visual displays.

An example of how one teacher uses the icons with the *CHAMPs* acronym is shown in Figure 3.11. As you can see, the teacher has made a large chart with the *CHAMPs* acronym on it and pockets adjacent to each letter. Just before she begins a new activity or transition, she places the appropriate icons in the appropriate pockets of the chart. At the beginning of the year (and periodically thereafter), she explains what each icon means as she places it in the pocket. In Figure 3.11, the icons indicate that the activity is independent work, that there should be no talking, that a student who has a question should put up the "? Flag," and that it is okay to get out of seats to sharpen pencil, turn in work, or get a drink. The authors wish to thank Clerese Sprague from Hood River, Oregon for sharing this wonderful idea with us. Some teachers may prefer to use a bulletin board and use push pins to display the relevant icons.

Figure 3.11: CHAMPs Chart with Icons

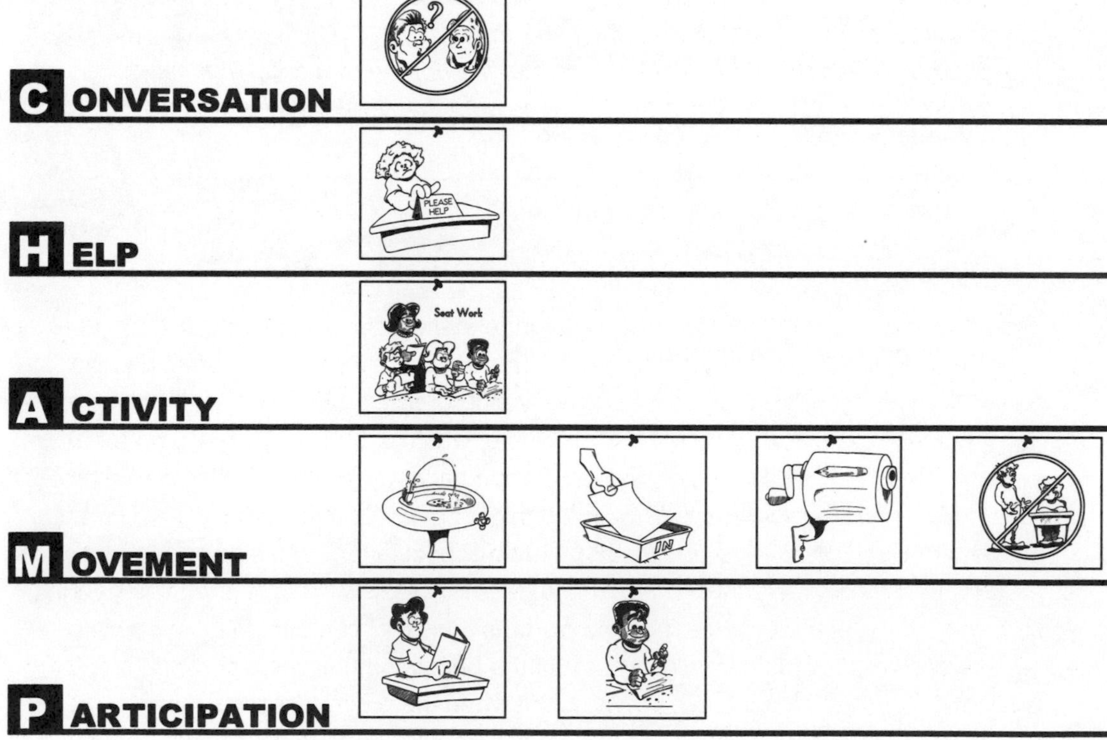

Demonstrations

Some aspects of behavioral expectations may be more clear to students if they are demonstrated. One way to do this is for you to model (i.e., act out) both positive and negative examples of what you expect. For example, when teaching students what participation (the P from the *CHAMPs* acronym) should look and sound like during independent work periods, you might want to model the right way and the wrong way for students to demonstrate participation. You can even "ham it up" a bit to make it more interesting for students. If you use modeling, it's a good idea to do so in the following manner. First provide a couple of positive models (the right ways to demonstrate participation). Then give the negative models (showing the most likely wrong ways students might misbehave). Finally, end by briefly redemonstrating the positive models. By beginning and ending with positive models, you reduce the chance that students will mistakenly view the negative models as the way to do things.

NOTE

You may also wish to involve students when modeling expectations. Students at both the elementary and middle school levels enjoy participating in role-play situations, in which student volunteers demonstrate (model) one or more aspects of the expectations. The advantage of involving students in role-play situations is that it gets them more actively involved in the lesson. Ask for a couple of volunteers, and have them demonstrate a positive model of one or more aspects of your expectations. Then, unless you think they will get overly silly or act irresponsibly, have the students demonstrate one or more negative examples. Just as when you model the expectations, be sure the students' final role plays demonstrate positive examples.

Practice and Rehearsal Opportunities

In some situations, students will not really understand what is expected of them until they have experienced the activity or transition. This is especially true for transitions that are complex or potentially problematic. One way of addressing this "problem" is to have the class practice the actual behavior. For example, washing hands and lining up for lunch tends to be a complex set of expectations for primary age students. Therefore, sometime before lunch on the first day of school, you might have students actually practice the behavior. At the intermediate grade and middle school levels, you could have students practice getting out materials and getting a paper headed within a reasonable period of time (e.g., 30 seconds). Other activities or transitions that can benefit from practice include entering the room from recess or at the beginning of class, appropriate noise level within cooperative groups, getting quiet when the attention signal is given, moving to and from small groups or lab stations, moving desks into and out of cooperative group activities, and so on.

Verification

Regardless of exactly how you teach your expectations for a given activity or transition, you should probably ask students a few questions about the expectations before you actually start the activity or transition. The answers students give (or fail to give) will help you determine whether or not you have adequately explained the essential information. If students can answer your questions, you are probably ready to start the activity or transition. On the other hand, if students seem unsure of their answers or if they are unable to answer the questions at all, you should go over the information again more thoroughly. That is, you need to plan on "reteaching" the expectations until students know what you expect.

Do not ask for volunteers to answer the questions. Students who do not know the answer are unlikely to volunteer; so you will not get accurate information about whether all students understand the expectations. A more effective approach is to ask the question first, give everyone time to think, and then assign one individual student to answer. "Everyone, get ready to answer a few questions. During the time we will be working in cooperative groups, can you get out of your seat for any reason? If so, what are the reasons? (Pause to provide think time.) Jared, please answer."

Level of Structure and Lessons to Teach Expectations

The greater the level of structure needed in your classroom, the more detailed you are going to have to be when teaching your expectations, and the more time you should plan to spend explaining and reviewing your expectations. If your expectations are relatively simple and your students are relatively sophisticated, it might be enough to just tell them the expectations before any particular activity begins. However, if your expectations are complex and/or students are less mature, your lessons should be more involved—perhaps using the *CHAMPs* acronym, visual displays, modeling, practice, and verifying student understanding. The goal is to ensure that your lessons communicate to students exactly what behaviors you expect from them.

Module 3: Expectations

Self-Assessment Checklist

Use the worksheet on the following pages to identify which (or which parts) of the tasks described in this module you have completed. For any item that has not been completed, note what needs to be done to complete it. As appropriate, translate your notes onto your planning calendar in the form of specific actions that you can take (e.g., August 17, finish developing *CHAMPs* expectations for math class.)

COMPLETED	TASK	NOTES & IMPLEMENTATION IDEAS
	CHAMPs EXPECTATIONS FOR CLASSROOM ACTIVITIES I have made a list of the major classroom activities and/or categories of activities that will take place during a typical day. For each activity (or category) that I have listed, I have defined, specifically and in detail, my behavioral expectations for students. For each activity (or category), I have considered the level of classroom structure my students need as I addressed the following issues/questions: • Conversation – How much and what type of conversation among students is allowed? • Help – How are students to request help and what should they do while they are waiting for help? • Activity – What is the activity, task, or assignment students will be engaged in? What is its purpose? What is the expected end product?	

COMPLETED	TASK	NOTES & IMPLEMENTATION IDEAS
	• Movement – How much and under what circumstances can students move about? • Participation – What student behaviors will show active and responsible participation in the activity and what student behaviors will show lack of appropriate participation in the activity?	
	***CHAMPs* EXPECTATIONS FOR TRANSITIONS** I have made a list of the common transitions and/or categories of transitions (within and between activities) that will take place during a typical day. For each transition (or category) that I have listed, I have defined, specifically and in detail, my behavioral expectations for students. For each transition (or category), I have considered the level of classroom structure my students need as I addressed the following issues/questions: • Conversation – How much and what type of conversation among students is allowed? • Help – How are students to request help and what should they do while they are waiting for help? • Activity – What is the transition? What is its purpose? What will be different after the transition is complete? What is the time criteria for how long the transition should take?	

COMPLETED	TASK	NOTES & IMPLEMENTATION IDEAS
	***CHAMPS* EXPECTATIONS FOR TRANSITIONS (CONT'D)** • Movement – If the transition itself does not involve movement, how much and under what circumstances can students move about? If the transition does involve movement, are there any restrictions to student movement? • Participation – What student behaviors will show active and responsible participation in the transition and what student behaviors will show lack of appropriate participation in the transition?	
	LESSONS TO COMMUNICATE EXPECTATIONS Based on the needs of my students, I have developed a plan to teach my CHAMPs expectations for activities and transitions. In developing my plan, I considered whether and how to use the following: • The *CHAMPs* acronym • Visual displays • Modeling and/or role-play demonstrations • Practice by the class • Verification of students' understanding of expectations Based on my plan, I have prepared *CHAMPs* lessons that I will use at the beginning of the school year to communicate behavioral expectations to students.	

Module 3: Expectations

Peer Study Worksheet

With one or more of your colleagues, work through the following discussion topics and activities related to the tasks in Module 3. If necessary, refer back to the text to get additional ideas or for clarification. (See the Module 1 Peer Study Worksheet for suggestions on structuring effective discussion sessions.)

Task 1: *CHAMPs* Expectations for Classroom Activities

A. Have each group member share his/her list of major classroom activities or categories of classroom activities. As a group, help each person identify whether he or she has omitted any important activities from the list.

B. Have group members share their *CHAMPs* Expectations Worksheets for Classroom Activities. As a group, give individuals feedback on the clarity and thoroughness of their expectations. (Remember, group members do not have to agree with each other's expectations—their feedback should focus on whether the expectations are specific and detailed enough that lessons for students could be taught from them.)

Task 2: *CHAMPs* Expectations for Transitions

A. Have each group member share his/her list of common transitions or categories of transitions. As a group, help each person identify whether he or she omitted any important transitions from the list.

B. Have group members share their *CHAMPs* Expectations Worksheets for Transitions. As a group give individuals feedback on the clarity and thoroughness of their expectations. (Remember, group members do not have to agree with each other's expectations—their feedback should focus on whether the expectations are specific and detailed enough that lessons for students could be taught from them.)

Task 3: Prepare Lessons to Communicate Expectations

A. Have each group member share his/her ideas for lessons on communicating expectations. In particular, discuss the decisions you have made regarding the answers to the following questions about your lessons:

- Do you plan to use the *CHAMPs* acronym with your students?

- Will you use visual displays within your lessons on expectations?
- Will you use modeling and role-playing within your lessons?
- Will you have students actually practice some of the expectations?
- Will you verify students' understanding of expectations prior to beginning activities?
- Share any samples of visual displays, ideas for modeling/role-playing, and so on.

B. Discuss how many days of repetition of these lessons you anticipate at the beginning of the school year. Identify strategies that will reduce the probability that students will get bored with whatever repetition is likely to be required.

MODULE 4: THE FIRST MONTH

When you teach students how to behave responsibly during the first month of school, you dramatically increase their chances of having a productive year.

Introduction

Through your efforts to develop your classroom vision and organization, and to define your *CHAMPs* expectations for student behavior during the school day, you have created the potential for a wonderful classroom. In this module we offer suggestions on how you can implement all the creative work you have done — and make the first month of school a highly productive one that sets the stage for the rest of the year. The first month of school is an incredibly important time. If you do not get students "on board" and behaving responsibly from the start, it can be very difficult (not impossible, but very difficult) to change any negative behavior patterns later. The information and strategies in this module are designed to ensure that during the first month of school you build positive relationships with students and communicate your expectations so clearly that you and your students are working productively as a team by the end of the first four weeks of school.

The four tasks in this module are presented chronologically. That is, they address final preparations you should make before school starts; what to do on the first day of school; procedures and considerations to deal with during the remainder of the first month; and preparations for special circumstances that may come up later.

Task 1 begins with the suggestion that you review your implementation of the most essential concepts from Modules 1 - 3 to ensure you are ready for the first day. In addition, we describe a few final ideas that may help the first day of school go more smoothly. These ideas include making it easy for students to find your classroom, planning for how you will get students into the room and settled down, and preparing to make effective use of the first ten minutes of class.

In Task 2, we provide specific "how to" information for "the first day of school." Most students are somewhat apprehensive about that first day. They have questions such as—"Where will I go? Will there be any of my friends in the class? What will my teacher be like? Will the teacher be mean? Will I feel stupid? Will other students think my new clothes look awful?" The more things you can do to help students feel safe and comfortable, the greater the probability that students will feel a sense of appreciation and loyalty to you. It's also important to give careful thought to the first impression students will form about you and your classroom. You want students to leave at the end of their first day (or class period) with an idea of what you and the class will be like, what you view as the major goals for the year, and what will be expected of them.

We also discuss, in detail, how to use the three-step process for communicating expectations on the first day of school. The information includes ideas on teaching the lessons you have developed about your expectations (Step 1), comprehensive suggestions on monitoring student behavior using circulating and visual scanning (Step 2), and specific strategies for providing feedback to students about their performance in meeting expectations during and after each activity/transition (Step 3).

The third task in this module focuses on the process of communicating your behavioral expectations throughout the first month of school. You need to ensure that students have a thorough understanding of how to behave during each type of classroom activity and transition by the end of the first week. In addition, if you are an elementary teacher, you should have coordinated with specialists (e.g., media, music, physical education) so that your students know the behavioral expectations for when they are with each specialist. During weeks two and three, you continue to teach, monitor, and give feedback on your expectations, and eventually to objectively verify student understanding of the expectations (using a brief quiz and/or interviews with students). If you find that students do not fully understand what is expected of them, you will need to reteach your *CHAMPs* expectations.

The module ends with a task that addresses two issues related to communicating expectations: how to teach your *CHAMPs* expectations to any new students (i.e., students who did not participate in your *CHAMPs* lessons during the first couple of weeks of school); and how to design *CHAMPs* lessons on any special or unique activities (e.g., guest speakers or field trips).

The four tasks presented and explained in this module are:

TASK 1: Final Preparations
Review and complete the essential tasks from Modules 1 - 3, and make final preparations for the first day of school.

TASK 2: Day One
Be prepared to implement strategies on the first day of school that will allow you to make a great impression on your students.

TASK 3: Days 2 Through 20 (The First Four Weeks)
During the first month of school, continue to implement the three-step process for communicating expectations, and take the time to verify that students understand what is expected of them.

TASK 4: Special Circumstances
Be prepared to teach your *CHAMPs* expectations to any new students who enter your class, and be prepared to develop and teach all students your expectations for any unique events that may occur.

Immediately following the explanations of the tasks in this module is a Self-Assessment Checklist, designed to help you determine which (or which parts) of the tasks you have done/are doing and which you still need to do. The module ends with a Peer Study Worksheet. This worksheet presents a series of discussion questions and activities that can be used by two or more teachers who want to share information and collegial support as they work to improve their classroom management practices.

Task 1: Final Preparations

Review and complete the essential tasks from Modules 1 - 3, and make final preparations for the first day of school.

Being fully prepared for the first day of school will allow you to be relaxed and ready to handle whatever takes place. To help you, we have identified the most essential preparation tasks from Modules 1, 2, and 3, and suggest that you first double-check that you have completed them. In addition, we recommend that you develop a first-day schedule, create a classroom sign so that students will be able to easily find your classroom, and plan the procedures you will use to ensure that when the bell rings on the first day students will be in their seats and ready to begin a positive and productive school year.

- Review (and complete) the following essential tasks from Modules 1 - 3.

  The first step in finalizing your preparations for the beginning of school should be to complete the important tasks from the preceding modules. The following list represents the essential minimums we believe are necessary to ensure a productive year. If time permits, we recommend that you also address the tasks from Modules 1 and 2 that are not included on this list.

- Develop and post Guidelines for Success (Module 1, #T-2)
- Maintain positive expectations for all students (Module 1, #T-3)
- Understand the basic principles of behavior management (Module 1, #T-6)
- Identify your level of classroom structure (Module 1, #T-7)
- Develop your daily schedule (Module 2, #T-1)
- Arrange your physical space (Module 2, #T-2)
- Develop your attention signal (Module 2, #T-3)
- Prepare beginning and ending routines (Module 2, #T-4)
- Identify and post classroom rules (Module 2, #T-5)
- Develop procedures for managing student work (Module 2, #T-6)
- Create a Classroom Management Plan (CMP) (Module 2, #T-7)
- Define/prepare lessons on behavioral expectations (Module 3, #T-1, #T 2, & #T3)

Develop a modified daily (class) schedule for the first day of school.

In Module 2 (Task 1), we recommended that you develop a well thought-out daily (class) schedule. That schedule needs to be modified for the first day of school—to ensure the inclusion of the unique tasks and activities that must occur on the first day. Your goal is to have the day be as representative of a typical day as possible, yet to include activities that will accomplish such important first day functions as helping students feel comfortable and settled; communicating your classroom goals, rules, guidelines, and expectations; communicating any schoolwide rules and expectations; and dealing with logistics such as distributing textbooks.

Elementary teachers will probably want to plan "get acquainted" activities for the first day—to help the class begin to function as a group. We caution you not to fill the entire first day with games, however. Students should leave at the end of the day feeling that the class provides a welcome and enjoyable environment, and fully aware that they will be expected to work and study to the best of their abilities.

At the middle school level, "get acquainted" activities can be included in advisory or homeroom periods, but should not be part of every class period. Imagine how you would feel if you had to play the "Get to Know the Names" game in six different class periods on the first day of school!

Before you create your first day schedule, find out from your building administrator whether there will be any schoolwide activities (e.g., assemblies, testing, and so on) that you need to take into account. Be sure to schedule the first few minutes of the day for going over your goals, classroom rules, Guidelines for Success, and other essential information. Other activities that you need to think about including are how and when to pass out books, assign storage space, and otherwise get students settled. Plan on allowing more time for each activity on the first day—in order to acquaint students with how you do things. For example, something as simple as having second grade students line up at the door for recess, which should eventually take no more than thirty seconds, may take anywhere between two and five minutes on the first day of school.

NOTE

Module 3, Task 3 presents detailed information on how to introduce and communicate your expectations to students.

Figure 4.1 shows two sample first day schedules (as they might be posted)—one for an elementary classroom and one for a middle school classroom.

Figure 4.1: Sample First-Day Schedules

Elementary Example		Middle School Example 7th Grade Science (Per. 1,3, & 6)	
8:30	Welcome, goals, & rules	10 min.	Welcome, goals, & rules
8:45	Getting organized	10 min.	Grading & homework
9:00	Reading	15 min.	Activity to identify what you know about science (This is not graded, so relax!)
9:45	Getting ready for recess		
10:00	Recess	10 min.	Tips on being successful in this class
10:15	Math	3 min.	Wrap up and dismissal
11:00	Getting to know each other		
11:30	Getting ready for lunch		
11:45	Lunch		
12:30	Spelling/writing		
1:15	Science (Weather & Climate)		
2:00	Afternoon break		
2:10	Getting to know each other		
2:30	Wrap up and get ready to go		
2:45	The end of a great school day!		

Make a sign for your room.

Create an easy-to-read sign that you can place in the hall, on or near the door, to help your students find your room. Include your name, your grade level or subject, and the room number. Be sure to print large enough that students will be able to see the information from fairly far away. Remember, your students are likely to be self-conscious about looking as if they do not know what they are doing—a nice clear sign will keep them from having to go from door to door looking at small room numbers or teacher names.

Prepare an initial activity for students to work on when they enter the room.

Having an initial activity will serve several important functions. First, it will give students something to do while they wait for the bell to ring and for things to begin. This can reduce the self-consciousness that some students may feel about not having someone to talk to. In addition, having an activity to work on will keep students who do know each other from congregating and conversing in groups. Without an activity, groups of students may become so engrossed in conversations that when the bell rings, you are put in the position of having to interrupt them and/or of trying to get them into their seats so that class can begin. If students have a task to work on when they enter the room, you can keep most of your attention on greeting all students as they arrive. Finally, having an initial task will communicate the expectation that when students are in your class, they will be actively engaged, not just sitting around.

Choose any task that students can do independently—i.e., a task that will not require assistance from you. Ideally it should be reasonably short and somewhat open-ended. Don't forget that students who enter the room first will have longer to work on the task than students who don't enter until just before the final bell rings. Following are some suggestions for this initial first-day task.

At the kindergarten and first grade levels:

- give students a coloring sheet and a couple of crayons.

At the second grade level and beyond:

- have students fill out a general information form (e.g., with name, phone number, address, etc.).
- have students write answers to one or two open-ended questions that will help you get to know them better. For example, you might ask students in grades 2- 5 to identify the two school activities or subjects they like most, and why; and the two school activities they like the least, and why. Middle school students could be asked to identify two things for which they like to receive public praise and two things for which they prefer to get feedback in a more private manner.

Prepare a plan for dealing with families who want to take your time on the first day.

This is an especially important consideration for teachers of primary students (kindergartners in particular). Families of young students often want to spend time helping their student adjust or telling you about the unique needs or interests of their child. Spending five minutes with the families of just three students, however, would cost you the first 15 minutes of school. One solution is to have a prepared "Note to Families" that you can distribute to families who drop into the classroom on the first day.

NOTE

If you know that the families of several of your students speak a language other than English, see if you can arrange to have the note written on one side in English and on the other side in the language the students' families are more likely to be able to read. A sample "Note to Families" is shown in Figure 4.2.

Figure 4.2: Sample Note to Families Regarding When to Contact Teacher

Dear Families:

Welcome! My name is Mrs. Morales and I will be your child's teacher this year. I want to get to know you and your child as quickly as possible, but on this first day, I need to give all of my attention to helping the children adjust and feel comfortable in my classroom. It will probably be easier for your child to adjust if you are not here. If there are things I should know about your child right away (for example, he or she has allergies that are not on the school records), please go to the office and let the office staff know. They will inform me. If there is other information I should know, or if you just want to talk to me, please feel free to call me at 555-1111. The best time to reach me is between 3:00 and 3:45 p.m. on any day other than Tuesday.

I look forward to a great year with your child and you.

Mrs. Morales

Mrs. Morales

If you are a kindergarten teacher, you may also want to ask the school counselor (or someone else who has time flexibility on the first day of school) to assist you in getting families to leave their students behind. You can interact with the student while the counselor gently escorts the student's family into the hall. "Hi, Mrs. Thompson, I am Mr. Verner, the school counselor. While Mrs. Morales takes Joanie and helps her find her desk, why don't you and I go out in the hall. I can give you some information about Mrs. Morales' program and how you can get in touch with her."

The procedures suggested in this task have been designed to ensure that the first day of school will go smoothly; that students will feel comfortable and know what you want them to do from the moment they arrive at your classroom. Implementing them will help you head into the first day feeling confident, organized, and prepared to guide your students toward responsible, motivated behavior.

Task 2: Day One

Be prepared to implement strategies on the first day of school that will allow you to make a great impression on your students.

The first day of school is an important one for both you and the students. When managed well, students will leave at the end of the first day thinking, "This teacher is organized, friendly, and expects a lot from us. Being in this class will be quite a bit of work, but should be exciting and fun. This teacher really wants to help me be successful!" Your goal is to conduct the first day of school in a manner that will make students feel welcome and will help them learn to behave responsibly from the beginning. We believe the following strategies can help you do just that.

Write your "Day One Schedule" on the board, an overhead transparency, or a flip chart.

When students enter the room, they will want to know what the day (class period) will be like. Seeing a schedule or an agenda can give students a sense of "what they are in for." In addition, it provides a subtle message that you are prepared, organized, and very clear about exactly what you want the day (period) to be like. Middle school teachers who have different classes may want to put the first day schedule information for each class on a separate page of a flip chart. Before class starts, flip to the appropriate page so students will only see the schedule for their class period. (NOTE: Obviously for kindergarten and first grade students, most of whom probably cannot read, it would be silly and even intimidating to have a written schedule.)

Greet the students individually as they enter your room.

The logistics of how you greet your students will depend on how long a time span will occur between when the first students enter and when the opening bell rings. If the time is less than ten minutes, arrange to be near the door so you can greet each student as he or she enters. Ask the students their names and introduce yourself. Then instruct (or help) them to take their seats and start on the task you have prepared (e.g., coloring, filling out the information form, answering the questions). Then go back to greeting other entering students. By the time the bell rings, all students should be in their seats and quietly working on the task.

In schools where the building is opened early, you may have some students enter the classroom up to 30 minutes before the opening bell rings. In this case, still greet individual students as they enter the room, but realize that you probably cannot be at the door the entire time. Get the early-arriving students seated and started on the initial task. Let the students know that if they complete the task, they can raise their hand and wait for you to call on them and give them something else to do. Decide in advance whether you will give these students other tasks to do quietly at their seats, if you will chat with them in small groups or if you will have them assist you with some last minute classroom tasks. You may want to ask other teachers what they do to keep students occupied when there will be a lengthy waiting period for the official beginning of the school day.

Get students' attention as soon as the bell rings.

Use your attention signal (e.g., Raise your hand and say, "Class, your attention please"—see Module 2, Task 3) to get students to focus on you. Even though students will not yet know your signal, it is likely to be effective because students will be working quietly at their seats. If students look at you, thank them for their attention and explain that whether or not they have completed the task, they should put their pencils down and pay attention to you. If students fail to give you their attention, repeat the signal and wait with your hand up until everyone is quiet and looking at you. Even if this takes several minutes (it probably won't), simply maintain the visual aspect of the signal and wait quietly. Resist the urge to shout at the students to get their attention. The fact is, if you start shouting for students' attention at the beginning of the year, you are likely to be shouting at them from then on.

Communicate the essential classroom information in the first ten minutes.

Once you have the full attention of all students, introduce yourself and tell the students one or two personal or interesting things about yourself. Do not go into great detail. Then describe your long-range goals for the year, both academically and behaviorally. "Thank you for giving me your attention. Please put your pencils down for now; you will be able to complete the questions later in the period. My name is Mr. Younce [write it on the board] and I will be your teacher this year. Over the year we will get to know each other better, but for now I just want to tell you a couple of things about myself. I have two children of my own. They are both older than you; my daughter is 13 and my son is 17. My hobby is bicycling and I sometimes bike as much as 100 miles in a day. We will have a chance to learn more about each other as the year goes on." Next explain to students what your Guidelines for Success and *classroom rules* are. As you share these pieces of information, involve the students in age-appropriate ways. "Raise your hand if you have an idea about why I might have a rule that says 'Keep hands and feet and objects to yourself.'"

At the conclusion of this first ten minutes, students should have a preliminary sense of who you are, what will be expected of them, and what they will learn. Do not spend more than ten minutes on this orientation. If you talk too much or provide too many details students may get overwhelmed or may tune you out.

Teach your attention signal.

Demonstrate the signal you will be using to get students' attention and tell them why the signal will be important. "I appreciate how well all of you are keeping your attention on me while I am speaking. During class when you are working at your seats, or in groups, or at one of the centers, there will be times when I need you to stop what you are doing and look at and listen to me. At those times, I will say, 'Class, your attention please,' while I am making this big circular motion with my arm. Then I will hold my hand in the air. When you hear me say those words and/or see me make that motion, stop whatever you are doing, stop talking or walking, look at me, and raise your own hand. When you raise your hand, it will help get the attention of other students who may not have seen or heard my signal.

"Stopping immediately when I give that signal is very important. There will be many times when we will all need to start an activity together. This way, even if each person is doing something different—working at their seats, in the learning centers, or on the way to the pencil sharpener—I can give the signal and everyone will be quiet and paying attention within five seconds. Then we can all be together for the next activity. I'm going to show you my signal one more time, and show you how long five seconds is. This is how quickly I expect the whole class to be quiet and looking at me." Demonstrate the signal and count the five seconds.

Orient students to the posted First Day Schedule and begin using the three-step process for communicating your expectations.

Start by giving students a clear idea of what the day (class period) is going to be like. For students in second grade and higher, point out the schedule you have posted for the day (class period). Then, for each activity throughout the day (class period), use the three-step process for communicating expectations. This cycle, which was introduced in Module 3, is summarized in Figure 4.3, and then explained.

Figure 4.3: Three-step process for communicating expectations

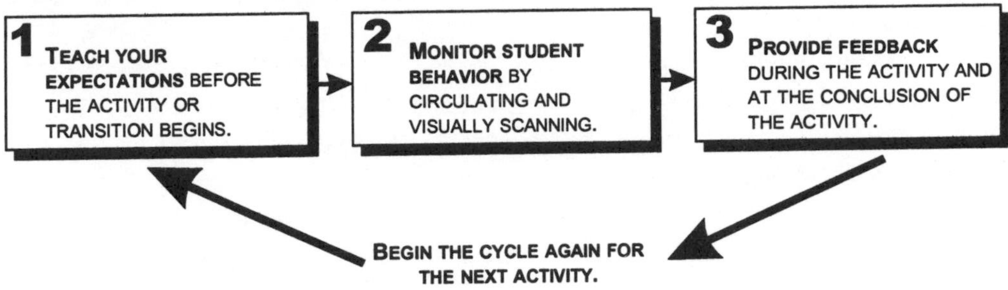

Teach your expectations (Step 1).

The first step in this process is teaching students what your expectations are. That is, just before students engage in any activity or transition, you will use the lessons you have developed (see Module 3, Task 3) to prepare students for what you expect during that activity/transition. It's important to note that you will teach your lesson for each particular activity/transition immediately before that activity/transition occurs. You *do not* want to teach the expectations for all (or even several) activities or transitions at one time.

Be prepared to spend as much time as necessary at the beginning of an activity or transition to ensure that students understand what is expected of them. If the lesson you have prepared (see Module 3) involves modeling or practicing of a behavior, you will need to allow for more time than if you are simply going to describe your expectations to students. For example, say you have scheduled a 15-minute teacher-directed instructional period. It is possible that, on the first day, five to seven of those 15 minutes will be spent explaining and modeling your expectations for student behavior during that activity. In other words, you should be prepared to spend anywhere from 20% to 50% of the time scheduled for a given activity on teaching your expectations for that activity during the first day(s) of school. Some of you may feel that you do not have time to do that because there is so much content to cover. We believe that taking the time to thoroughly teach your expectations will make such a positive difference in student behavior that you will actually save time in the long run (fewer disruptions, better on-task behavior for the rest of the year).

Monitor student behavior (Step 2).

The only way to know how well students are meeting your behavioral expectations for classroom activities and transitions is for you to monitor their behavior in some way, which is the second step in the three-step process for effectively communicating expectations. Two of the most useful and efficient ways to monitor student behavior during an activity or transition are to circulate among students and to visually scan all parts of the classroom. These two basic (but absolutely essential) strategies will allow you to know exactly what is going on at all times. Then you can use the information you gain from circulating and scanning to help you make sound decisions about the type and frequency of feedback you should provide students concerning their behavior. Circulating has an additional benefit because your physical presence tends to reduce student misbehavior. It's human nature. Just as most drivers are more likely to adhere to the speed limit when a police officer is present, so too are students more likely to follow classroom rules and procedures when you are physically close to them. What follows are further explanations of and suggestions about the strategies of circulating and scanning.

Circulating:

Whenever possible, circulate throughout the classroom in unpredictable patterns. That is, do not spend the majority of your time in any one part of the room and do not move in predictable ways that would permit students to know that you would not be near them for a significant amount of time. This is especially important during independent work periods and cooperative group activities. Your nearness will communicate your concern for and interest in the students. It will also make it clear that if someone chooses to engage in something other than the expected behaviors, you will be likely to notice it.

Obviously there are times (e.g., when you are teaching a small group or presenting to the class using an overhead) when circulating is difficult to do. However, whenever you can, try to move about the room. For example, in the middle of teaching a 30-minute small reading group, you might consider giving the students in the group a short task to perform independently while you quickly circulate among the other students. Then you can come back and resume instruction in the small group. Or, while teaching a math lesson to the whole class with an overhead projector, you might give students a couple of problems to work, and then circulate through the room. After looking at students' work, you can come back to the overhead and continue with the teacher-directed portion of the lesson.

Remember, as you circulate, give positive feedback to students meeting your expectations, answer any questions students may have, and provide gentle reprimands or consequences to students who are not meeting expectations. And, always try to avoid staying too long in any one place.

Visual Scanning:

Regardless of what you and the students are doing, you should frequently visually scan all settings in the classroom. For example, when you are circulating, don't just look at the students nearest to you—visually sweep any place students are—even a learning center across the room. When you are conducting a whole-class activity, visually scan the back rows and the front corners. When you are helping an individual student with her work, plan to occasionally stand up and look around the room. When you are teaching a small group, look up from the group periodically and find out what is going on with students who are working at their seats.

As you scan, look for any misbehaviors that require correction. If a student is engaged in a misbehavior, go to the student and issue a gentle reprimand or assign an appropriate consequence. Also look for opportunities to acknowledge and encourage responsible behavior. For example, as you scan, if you notice that a particular student who often tends to be off task is working, go to that student at the next opportunity and give him or her age-appropriate positive feedback. Or, if a cooperative group is handling a conflict in a responsible way, go over to the group when there is a pause in their interactions and congratulate them on the maturity with which they are handling the situation.

Finally, use visual scanning to identify students who may have questions or otherwise need your assistance. During independent work periods (when you are not engaged with a small group) especially, you want to look for students who have signaled to you that they need assistance. If you ask students to use a flag or open book signal for help (see Module 2, Task 6), you need to show students that the signal actually works. If students find that you don't respond when they signal, they will stop using the signal and will come to you or call out to get your attention instead.

Monitoring is an important component in communicating your expectations and is a critical tool regardless of the type of classroom structure your students may need. You have to know what is going on in your classroom. A classroom that needs high structure, however, will require monitoring at *all* times. In fact, a line you sometimes hear from an experienced teacher with a class needing high structure is, "This class is so tough, you can't take your eyes off them for a second." This is a teacher who understands that continous monitoring is absolutely essential with high-needs students.

Give students feedback on their implementation of expectations (Step 3).

The third step in the process of effectively communicating your behavioral expectations (see Figure 4.3) involves giving students (individually and as a class) clear information about the degree to which they are behaving and/or have behaved as expected for a particular activity or transition (i.e., both during and after each activity or transition). We recommend that you provide positive feedback (in the form of age-appropriate praise) when students are meeting/have met your expectations and corrective feedback (calmly, immediately, and consistently) when they are not meeting/have not met your expectations. Positive feedback serves two vitally important functions—it gives students specific information about what they are doing correctly and it gives them adult attention when they are behaving responsibly. Corrective feedback also serves two vitally important functions—it lets students know that you are monitoring their behavior and it communicates that you are serious (and will be consistent) about your expectations for student behavior.

Providing feedback during an activity/transition:

As you monitor students during an activity or transition, you are likely to notice examples of students meeting your expectations and examples of students not meeting your expectations. Both represent opportunities for you to continue to "teach" students how to meet your behavioral expectations by giving them positive and corrective feedback.

Positive Feedback:

Following are a few quick tips on providing effective positive feedback. (More detailed information is provided in Module 5: Motivation.)

- **Give feedback that is accurate.**
  Do not provide positive feedback unless the individual (or class) has actually exhibited the responsible behavior. If you tell a student that he has been responsible when he has not, you ruin your credibility and lead students to think (justifiably) that your positive feedback means nothing.

- **Give feedback that is specific and descriptive.**
  Tell the student (or the group) exactly what they are doing that is responsible and important. "Alex, Maria, Travis, you are keeping your attention focused on your work. That is a very important part of being successful in this class." Avoid a rote phrase like, "Good job."

- **Give feedback that is contingent.**
  Positive feedback provides useful information on important behaviors. Inform students how the positive behaviors they are demonstrating will contribute to their success and the success of the class. Also, praise students for demonstrating behaviors that are new or difficult.

- **Give positive feedback immediately.**
  Immediacy is important because students need to know *when* they are doing something correctly. In addition, for students who are starved for attention, not getting any attention for meeting expectations will lead to their demanding attention through misbehavior. Positive feedback is most effective when it

occurs very soon after the behavior you are trying to encourage. With primary students in particular, waiting until later to give the feedback will not help to solidify the desired behaviors—by the time you praise them, the students will have forgotten just what it was they did.

- **Give positive feedback in a manner that fits your style.**
  The specific manner in which you give positive feedback does not matter. What is important is that you are specific and sincere. Thus, if you are a bubbly, happy person, your positive feedback should take that form. On the other hand, if you are a more serious and businesslike person, your positive feedback should be given in a more serious, businesslike manner.

Corrective Feedback:

When students (one or more than one) exhibit behavior that does not meet your expectations for that activity, you must correct the inappropriate behavior. To give the most effective correction, consider each instance of not meeting expectations as an instructional opportunity. That is, consider the students' behavioral errors to be similar to errors they might make in math. Most math errors are a function of students not fully understanding a particular concept and/or all the steps in a particular process. Effectively correcting those errors involves reteaching the concept and/or steps. If students fail to meet your behavioral expectations, you should first determine whether it is possible that they did not understand what the expectations were or did not know how to meet the expectations. If the answer to either of those questions is yes, you will need to reteach what your expectations are and/or how students can meet them. If the answer is no, you need to provide corrective feedback. Following are a few quick tips on providing effective corrective feedback. (More detailed information on using corrective feedback is provided in Module 7: Correction Procedures.)

- **Correct the misbehavior immediately.**
  When students are not meeting behavioral expectations, let them know. Do not ignore it and do not wait until the end of an activity/transition/event. While ignoring can be an effective strategy for responding to chronic misbehavior that is designed to elicit attention, when you are trying to establish your expectations at the beginning of the year, students may interpret ignoring as "She was not really serious about how she expects us to behave."

- **Correct the misbehavior calmly.**
  Correcting calmly shows students that you are serious and have high expectations, but that you are also completely in control and will not be rattled by their misbehavior. Emotional corrections, on the other hand, are more likely to give power to the misbehavior and put you in a position of seeming

somewhat out-of-control. Students may think, "When I do this, look how frustrated and angry I can make the teacher."

- **Correct misbehavior consistently.**
  For the first several days of instruction, correct most misbehavior with mild verbal reprimands that focus on the behavior, not the person. Simply restate what the students should be doing at the time. Be direct. Saying something like, "Tina and Adam, you should be working quietly on your lab notebooks at this time," is more appropriate and effective than, "Tina and Adam, you are so immature. I should not have to remind you that this is a work period, not a time to socialize."

If it becomes necessary, because of the severity or frequency of a misbehavior, to use a prearranged corrective consequence, calmly state the misbehavior and the corrective consequence—and then *follow through.*

Providing feedback at the end of an activity/transition/event:

Early in the year, you should plan on ending each activity or transition by giving students feedback about how well they collectively (i.e., as a class) met your *CHAMPs* expectations. That is, when an activity or transition is finished, but before the next activity or transition begins, let the group know whether things went well and they behaved as expected (the way they should for the rest of the year) or whether they need to improve their behavior the next time that particular activity or transition occurs. When an activity goes perfectly, you have a wonderful opportunity to reinforce the class and begin establishing a sense of group pride. "Class, the way this work period went is exactly the way a lab activity of this type should go. Everyone followed safe lab procedures. Conversations at the lab stations were quiet, and all the talking that I heard as I was going around was focused on the lab activity. This is going to be a great class."

If an activity does not go well, describe the specific behaviors that need to be different (without singling out individuals), and set a goal for the next time you have that activity. "Class, during the teacher-directed portion of the math lesson that we have just completed, there were several times that I had to remind people that if they had something to say they need to raise their hand. Please remember that whenever anyone is presenting to the class, whether it is me or a student, there should be no side conversations. Later this afternoon we will be having a science lesson, and during the time that I am demonstrating an experiment, remember, no side conversations and keep your attention focused entirely on whoever is speaking." Avoid statements such as, "Almost everyone remembered the expectation about only talking if you raise your hand and are called on." A statement of this type *is not* positive feedback; it only serves to get students wondering, "Which students were the ones who did not meet the expectations?"

Conclude the day (class period) by orienting students to your end-of-day procedures (see Module 2, Task 4).

Because this is the first day of school, allow plenty of time for this activity. Remember that you may have to take time to help students identify which bus they ride, review materials they need to bring the next day, and make sure they have any and all important papers to take home. You want to put closure on this day in such a way that the students leave your classroom feeling comfortable, eager to return, and with the sense that you are a teacher who will demand that they do their best, but who is also concerned and interested in each of them as individuals.

The strategies presented in this task have been included because we believe that they will help you get your first day of school off to the best start. Remember, the information you present and the atmosphere you establish on "Day One" will yield valuable dividends throughout the school year.

Task 3: Days 2 Through 20 (The First Four Weeks)

During the first month of school, continue to implement the three-step process for communicating expectations, and take the time to verify that students understand what is expected of them.

No matter how clearly and carefully you communicate your *CHAMPs* expectations on the first day of school, few students will fully know exactly how they are supposed to behave after just one day. The way students truly learn your expectations is for you to continue the three-step communication process for a couple of weeks—i.e., beginning each activity and transition with a lesson on the expectations, monitoring student performance during the activity/transition, and giving positive and corrective feedback during and after the activity/transition—to both individuals and the class as a whole. (NOTE: If you are a middle school teacher, remember that your students will be hearing about expectations from four to six other teachers. They are likely to get tired of hearing about expectations; but they are also likely to be confused about such details as which teachers let them talk during independent work and which teachers do not. As you continue to present lessons on your *CHAMPs* expectations, be sure to vary the format of the lessons.)

As the first month of school progresses, the lessons should become increasingly brief and they should focus mainly on any specific expectations that have been problematic (e.g. students talking when the teacher is presenting). You can also use the lesson time to set goals for student behavior. When students seem to fully understand and remember the expectation for an activity or transition, you can start to fade the lessons. For instance, you might introduce the activity or the transition by letting students know that because they have been so responsible you do not need to review the expectation. "Class, the next thing we are going to do is to have a 20-minute work period for you to get going on the math assignment. Since this type of work period has gone so well, I don't even need to review the expectations. Get started working on the assignment that is written on the board."

Another option is to consider using an alternating pattern of lessons—i.e., teach different expectations on different days. For example, during a math lesson on Monday, you might present *CHAMPs* lessons on the teacher-directed and cooperative group portions of the lesson, but not on the independent work period. On Tuesday, you could present a brief *CHAMPs* lesson on independent work and cooperative group activities, but not on teacher-directed instruction. Whenever a particular activity/transition has not gone as smoothly as you would like, plan to use the three-step process to reassert your expectations. If the number of students who have not been meeting the expectations is more than five, plan on reteaching your expectations to the entire class. If only one or two students are having problems, focus the process on those individuals.

By gradually reducing the length and frequency of your *CHAMPs* lessons and by shifting your focus to individuals or small groups who may need more review than others, you gain more time for instruction. Before you cease all *CHAMPs* lessons for any given activity or transition, however, you should verify whether or not students fully understand your expectations for that activity or transition. The final part of this task provides suggestions for administering a quiz or conducting student interviews to determine the degree to which students understand your expectations.

The second step in the communication cycle for expectations—monitoring student performance—should be maintained at a very high level. (NOTE: As stated in Module 3, if a class requires only a low structure management plan, you can get by with less direct monitoring than if the class needs medium or high structure.) Whatever the degree of monitoring your students need, however, you should plan on continuing to circulate and visually scan during all activities and transitions throughout the year.

During the first several days of instruction, you should plan on giving students very frequent feedback on how they are (or are not) meeting your expectations—i.e., the third step in the communication process. In fact, this might almost be an ongoing monologue. With classes needing low structure, you can begin to reduce the amount of positive feedback given to the class and to individual students as soon as any given activity or transition has gone well for several consecutive days. In addition, the corrective feedback can be reduced to simply stating the name of a student who is not meeting your expectation. For example, if two students are talking when they should be listening to a lesson, you may be able to correct the error by saying the names of the two students, making brief eye contact, and getting on with your lesson. On the other hand, if your class needs medium or high structure, you should probably keep the frequency of positive feedback and the descriptive clarity of corrective feedback at a very high level for a long time (minimally for the entire first month of school).

Examples of the Three-Step Communications Cycle

Following are explanations of how you might implement the three-step communication cycle during the first month of school with three different sets of expectations: (1) expectations regarding student behavior in response to your attention signal; (2) expectations regarding student behavior during independent work periods when you are otherwise occupied; and (3) expectations regarding student behavior when they are with specialists. The basic processes described can be used (as is or modified as appropriate) for communicating all your expectations.

Communicating expectations for student behavior in response to your attention signal.

For the first several days of school, frequently review your attention signal and your expectations for student behavior when you give the signal. Whenever you give the signal, check your watch or the clock. If the students respond with silence, stillness, and attention in less than five seconds (and every student raised his/her hand), thank them for their cooperation. "Class, that only took four seconds. Some of you who were moving toward the back of the room stopped, turned around and looked at me immediately. That was exactly the way to respond to this signal. The reason I needed your attention is to let you know that . . . "

If the students do not respond appropriately within five seconds, do not repeat the signal and do not say anything. Simply wait with your hand raised, and make it obvious that you are looking at the time. When the class is finally silent, provide corrective feedback. "Class, some students immediately stopped what they were doing and raised their hand. However, it took 18 seconds from the time I gave the signal until everyone stopped talking and gave me their attention. That is too long. By continuing to talk you were being disrespectful to the students who gave me attention immediately, because you wasted their time. Next time I give this signal, to be respectful of me and of your classmates, stop what you are doing immediately. Now, the reason I needed your attention was to let you know that . . . ."

For several days, provide frequent positive feedback to students for following the signal. If students are taking too long to respond to the signal, provide additional instruction and practice opportunities. If, after a few days of this kind of positive and corrective feedback, students are still not responding quickly enough to your signal, inform the class that you are going to start implementing a consequence for not paying attention to the signal. If it is only two to four students who are not responding to the signal, assign those individuals "time owed" off of recess (for elementary level) or after class (for middle school). If more than four students are not responding to the signal, have the entire class owe time. Make the time owed equal to the number of seconds wasted (i.e., the number of seconds beyond five after you gave the signal). For example, if it takes the class 18 seconds to be fully compliant, they would owe 13 seconds (18 minus 5 seconds). When it is time for recess (or a break between classes), the entire class must wait quietly for 13 seconds. This procedure usually quickly generates enough peer pressure that students start responding to the attention signal within the five-second limit.

For a class that is having a great deal of difficulty responding to the signal, you might optionally add a positive component. For example, you could let the class know that each time all students respond appropriately to the signal within the five-second time, the class earns a point. When they have earned 10 points, the class will get five minutes extra recess.

Communicating expectations for student behavior during independent work times when the teacher is otherwise engaged (e.g., working with a small group).

Teaching students how to behave responsibly during independent work times can be difficult. Working independently tends to be especially hard for young students when their teacher is engaged in another activity (e.g., teaching a small reading group). One solution, if you have a teaching assistant, is to have this person supervise students doing seatwork and working at learning centers while you are with a small group. If this is a possibility, you need to prepare the instructional assistant and the students. During the first few days of school, have your assistant watch as you supervise the whole class for the first ten minutes of an independent work period. Make a point of demonstrating how you answer questions, reinforce on-task behavior, and correct misbehavior. For the remainder of the work period, switch roles—i.e., have the assistant supervise students as you observe and give feedback to him/her. After a few days, you can start the small group work—and have the assistant supervise the other students for the entire period. When you have a system like this, be sure to schedule time (at least once per week) for you and your assistant to discuss how things are going during these independent work periods. Encourage the assistant to ask questions and raise concerns. "I am not quite sure how to respond to Barry. I think he is depending too much on my help. What do you think I should do?"

If you do not have an assistant who can supervise students doing independent work while you are with a small group, you will have to teach your students how to function without direct supervision. We recommend that you plan on spending at least three days "rehearsing" with students what it will be like when you are teaching the small group. "Class, each day at this time, I will be working with a group of students over here. Most of you will be at your seats working on the papers that I will give you. Every one of you has the papers we just went over and you know what you are going to be working on. Today, I will be walking around and helping you if you need it and I will be commenting about how well you are working. Usually, I will not be able to do this, because I'll be busy with the students in the small group, but today . . ." Make a point of praising students frequently for keeping their attention focused on their work.

After three days of rehearsal, spend another two to four days training students how to implement the strategy of "Finish what you know, then come back to anything you are not sure of." During these work periods, modify the rehearsal so that students cannot get help from you (even though you are available). If a student asks for help, give a reminder about the strategy. "Todd, you will need to ask someone at your table for help. Remember that on most days I'll be working over in the reading circle." Frequently praise students for keeping their attention on their work and for getting their questions answered without needing to involve you.

After a few days of this sort of rehearsal, you should be ready to begin conducting your small groups. When you first start working with small groups, you may want to modify your schedule just a bit. That is, if you will typically be working with each group for 30 minutes, consider making it only fifteen minutes initially; then spend the remaining 15 minutes circulating among students working independently to give positive and corrective feedback. NOTE: If you group students homogeneously by ability, you can probably work with your lowest group for the full 30 minutes from the beginning. These are the students who are likely to have the greatest difficulty staying on task. The students working independently while you are working with the lowest group may very well be academically able and mature enough to function independently for the full 30 minutes.

If you don't have an assistant and you don't think your students are likely to be able to work independently, you might consider asking some fifth or sixth grade teachers if a couple of their responsible students could come to your room each day during independent work times to circulate and help answer questions.

Communicating expectations for behavior when students are with specialists.

Specialists in areas such as media, P.E., computer, and music may be in a unique (and difficult) position in terms of teaching their behavioral expectations. In many cases, these specialists see all the students in a school—but only for one or two 20- to 30-minute period(s) per week. This means that the teaching time for expectations lessons that a classroom teacher has for a particular activity in one week (e.g., five math lessons) will take a specialist five weeks. Furthermore, because students only see the specialist once (or twice) a week, they are more likely to forget many of this teacher's expectations from the first meeting to the second. Therefore, we suggest that elementary classroom teachers coordinate with the specialists who see their students. Following are some general suggestions for achieving efficient and effective coordination.

- Each specialist should provide all classroom teachers with a written explanation of how students should enter his/her setting (e.g., the gym or the computer room) and a written list of two or three important rules for his/her class.

- Immediately before students go to a particular specialist, the classroom teacher should tell the class where they are going and the name of that teacher. The classroom teacher should also go over the written expectations, and make it very clear that she/he expects students to behave responsibly. The classroom teacher might say something such as:

"Class, the next thing we are going to do today is go to the gym for Physical Education class. The P.E. teacher this year is Ms. Simonson. When we go to the gym, we will go quietly in lines, just the way we go to the cafeteria. When we get to the gym, you need to stay in your lines and wait outside the gym with me until Ms. Simonson comes to tell you what you should do and where you should go. Ms. Simonson will go over her rules for safe and responsible gym behavior with you, but she asked me to let you know that her two most important rules are: (a) Keep hands, feet, and objects to yourself; and (b) Freeze and listen for directions when you hear her blow the whistle. During P.E., Ms. Simonson is the teacher. I fully expect you to give her the same level of respect and cooperation you demonstrate in the classroom. Now I'll excuse you by tables to line up and wait quietly at the door. Everyone at Table 4 is waiting quietly. You may line up. Table . . ."

- There should be a formal and public transfer of authority from the classroom teacher to the specialist. That is, students should see and hear an interaction between the classroom teacher and the specialist that sounds something like:

Class Teacher: *"Class, this is Ms. Simonson. Every Monday and Thursday at this time you will get to be with her. Ms. Simonson, I have let the class know that I expect them to behave responsibly during their time with you and I have told them your two most important rules. Class, I will be back here to meet you in 30 minutes. I will look forward to hearing a good report from Ms. Simonson.*

P.E. Teacher: *"Thank you Mr. Hasad. I appreciate your having gone over my rules. I am looking forward to getting to know such a responsible group of students. Now class, in just a moment we will enter the gym and each of you should . . . "*

- When the time with the specialist is over, the specialist should publicly hand authority back over to the classroom teacher and inform the teacher of how well the class did. "Mr. Hasad, this class did a wonderful job in P.E. today. The only thing I hope they will work harder on is remembering to freeze, even their mouths and voices, when they hear the whistle. I am looking forward to seeing all of you again next Monday."

- These procedures should be implemented for at least the first four times the students go to a particular specialist. Thus, if students see the specialist twice a week, you would do this for a minimum of two weeks; if they see the specialist once a week, you would do it for a minimum of four weeks.

Verify that students understand the behaviors expected from them.

During the second or third week of school, we recommend that you take some time to systematically determine whether your students really understand what you want from them. The information you get will help you decide whether you need to continue actively teaching your *CHAMPs* expectations or if you can eliminate the lessons because students have mastered the content. If you find that most of your students are able to accurately answer specific and detailed questions about your *CHAMPs* expectations (verbally or on paper), then you can rapidly fade the process of teaching/reviewing the expectations. However, if you learn that a significant percentage of students cannot answer your questions, or cannot answer them correctly, you should continue to conduct *CHAMPs* lessons on a reasonably regular basis.

Making the effort to determine students' understanding of your expectations (i.e., giving a quiz and/or conducting interviews) will do more than provide you with information on whether your students fully understand the expectations. By the very fact that you are willing to take the time to do one or both of these activities, you further communicate to students the importance you place on their knowledge of the *CHAMPs* expectations.

We have identified two main procedures for verifying students' understanding (or lack thereof) of expectations: (1) conducting one-on-one interviews with a few individual students; and/or (2) giving all students a short, written quiz. We strongly suggest you use at least one of these procedures. We recommend that you consider using both. On the following pages, you will find directions and materials for giving a quiz and for conducting interviews on *CHAMPs* expectations.

Giving a Quiz

A written quiz is a relatively simple way to get information from all the students in your class(es) on their knowledge of your expectations. A major advantage of the quiz (as opposed to individual interviews with a few students) is that you can get information from all students in a relatively short period of time. The major disadvantage is that some of the students who do poorly on the quiz may actually know the expectations perfectly well, but have trouble with reading and/or writing. For this reason, a quiz is probably not suitable for grades 2 and lower.

DIRECTIONS:

1. **Decide on the format of the quiz.**
   Your choices are true/false, multiple choice, fill in blank, short essay, or some mix of the preceding formats. Base your decision on both the type of format you

typically use for academic purposes (meaning your students will be familiar with the format) and on the type of format you think will yield the most useful information.

2. **Determine the specific content you want to investigate.**
   Choose one or two activities and one or two transitions to be the focus of your quiz. The most useful information may come from targeting those activities/transitions that have the most complex expectations and/or that seem to be giving students the most difficulty. In terms of the nature of the items, examine your written *CHAMPs* worksheets (see Module 3) for the kinds of details you want to see if students know. That is, your questions should target issues such as whether students can talk during the activity/transition, what kind movement (if any) is allowed, etc. In terms of the number of items, you want to keep the quiz to something that your students can complete in approximately ten minutes.

3. **Prepare your students to take the quiz.**
   Explain to the students that you are giving a quiz that will help you identify if the class understands some of the important expectations within your class. Make sure they know they are not being graded, but the more errors on the quiz the greater the likelihood that you will provide additional practice and explanation of expectations for student behavior.

Figure 4.4 is a sample quiz on expectations that might be used in a fifth grade classroom.

Figure 4.4: Sample Quiz on Expectations

Name ____________________ Date ______________

Circle the letter for the best answer to each of the questions below.

1. When you enter the classroom first thing in the morning, . . .

a. you should be completely silent from the moment you enter the room.

b. you can talk quietly to other students about school work, but must get silent when you get to your seat.

c. you can talk quietly about anything, but when the bell rings you should be in your seat and can talk only about the challenge problem on the overhead projector.

d. you can talk loudly about anything, and when the bell rings you should get to your seat within two minutes and then get quiet.

2. In Room 9, you can use the pencil sharpener . . .

a. only before and after class.

b. before and after class and during independent work periods.

c. anytime you need to.

d. you can not use the pencil sharpener without teacher permission.

3. When the teacher gives the attention signal, "Class, your attention please," you should . . .

a. be silent with eyes on the teacher within five seconds.

b. be silent with eyes on the teacher within ten seconds.

c. be silent with eyes on the teacher within twenty-five seconds.

d. loudly tell other students to be quiet and pay attention to the teacher.

4. During the time the teacher is presenting lessons and is speaking to the class, you should:

a. talk quietly to someone near you and only get out of your seat to sharpen your pencil.

b. talk quietly to someone near you and not get get our of your seat for any reason.

c. talk only if you have been called on by the teacher and can get out of your seat if you want a drink of water or need supplies.

d. talk only if you have been called on by the teacher and should not get out of your seat for any reason (unless you have been given permission).

Figure 4.4: Sample Quiz on Expectations (continued)

Page 2 Sample Quiz on Expectations

5. **Active participation during the time the teacher is presenting lessons should look and sound a certain way. Circle any of the items that describe active participation. You should have six items circled when you are done with this question.**
   a. Sit up straight or lean forward.
   b. Raise your hand if you have something to say.
   c. Answer questions when called on.
   d. Write notes to your friends.
   e. Write notes to keep in your binder that will help you study for tests.
   f. Tell people who are talking that they need to be quiet and listen.
   g. Have toys and things on your desk that will help entertain you during the lesson.
   h. Keep your eyes on the person speaking or on the class notes you are writing (notes you will use for studying for the test).
   i. Let your mind wander wherever it wishes to go.
   j. Talk while the teacher is talking.
   k. Be respectful toward the teacher and other students in what you say and how you act.

Interviewing Students

Interviewing students can provide more detailed and slightly more reliable information than a written quiz. If, during an interview, you are unsure from a student's answer whether she really understands a particular expectation, you can ask additional questions. The interview format also allows students who struggle with written tests to provide more accurate information about what they really know. The major disadvantage of interviews is that they are more time consuming since you can only do one interview at a time. Because of the time issue, we suggest that you only interview a representative sample of about six students.

DIRECTIONS:

1. **Identify two major classroom activities and two major transitions that occur daily (or at least three times per week) in your classroom.**
   Choose activities/transitions that are particularly complex and/or seem to be particularly troublesome for students. Classroom activities might include opening activities, teacher-directed instruction (whole class and/or small group), independent seatwork, class discussions, cooperative groups, work in learning centers or lab stations, and so on. Transitions might include coming in the room at the beginning of the day (period), handing in materials, moving to/from small group

work, going to the library, cleaning up the classroom, getting books out and open to a particular page, getting ready for dismissal, and so on.

2. **Develop interview questions addressing specific aspects of the *CHAMPs* expectations for the two classroom activities and two transitions that you have selected.**
   Feel free to use the reproducible interview template shown in Figure 4.5. (A completed sample template with one teacher's interview questions is shown in Figure 4.6.) As suggested for the quiz items, base your questions on the issues covered in the *CHAMPs* worksheets that you have completed (see Module 3).

3. **Identify a representative sample of students.**
   Choose about six students to interview. Select three students who are academically average or higher. Select three students who are academically lower and/or who have demonstrated some misbehavior.

4. **Decide on a time and format for conducting the interviews.**
   Identify a time when you would be free to conduct the interviews. If you cannot be completely free of supervising your class, plan to conduct the interviews while the class is doing independent work or working in cooperative groups. Because the interviews will probably take about five minutes per student, it may take more than one day to complete them. NOTE: You may wish to work with a colleague and interview each other's students.

5. **Prepare students for the interviews.**
   The whole class: Describe what you will be doing and why. Emphasize that no one is in trouble, rather that you want to see how clear you have been in communicating what students need to do to be successful. Let them know that you would like to be able to meet with all the students to talk about this, but because of time constraints, you can only meet with a few.

   The individual students you are interviewing: Identify the activity or transition and then proceed with your questions. "Each day during math, I begin the lesson by presenting information on the overhead projector. I would like to ask you some questions about what you and the other students should be doing during that time. Think about if we had a new student—and what you would tell him/her about how we do things. For example, what should a student do when he has a question? What should a student do. . ."

Figure 4.5: Reproducible

Student Interview

Student:________________________ Date:____________

CLASSROOM ACTIVITY: ________________________

QUESTIONS:	STUDENT RESPONSES:

CLASSROOM ACTIVITY: ________________________

QUESTIONS:	STUDENT RESPONSES:

TRANSITION: ________________________

QUESTIONS:	STUDENT RESPONSES:

TRANSITION: ________________________

QUESTIONS:	STUDENT RESPONSES:

Figure 4.6: Completed Sample

Student Interview Protocol

Student: ______________________ **Date:** ______________

CLASSROOM ACTIVITY: Teacher-directed math

QUESTIONS:	STUDENT RESPONSES:
• Can you talk to another student while I am teaching? • What should you do if you have a question or don't understand something? • When I say, "Work on this problem", what should you do? • Can you get out of your seat for any reason? • How do you show that you are actively participating in the lesson?	

CLASSROOM ACTIVITY: Independent seatwork in math

QUESTIONS:	STUDENT RESPONSES:
• Can you talk to another student while you are doing your work? - about what? - how loud a voice? • What should you do if you need my help? • Can you get out of your seat for any reason? • How do you show that you are actively participating in this part of the lesson?	

TRANSITION: Beginning class, before & after bell

QUESTIONS:	STUDENT RESPONSES:
• What should you do when you come into the room and are waiting for the bell to ring? • Where should you be when the bell rings? • While we are going through calendar, sharing, etc., - can you get out of your seat? - can you talk to people at your table? • What should you do if you want to say something to the class?	

TRANSITION: Getting book out and open

QUESTIONS:	STUDENT RESPONSES:
• When I say get your math book out and open, how do you know which page? • What should you do if you ever do not have your book? • How long should it take for everyone to have books open and ready? • Is it OK to talk to your neighbor as you are finding the page? - Why not?	

Task 4: Special Circumstances

Be prepared to teach your CHAMPs expectations to any new students who enter your class, and be prepared to develop and teach all students your expectations for any unique events that may occur.

We have emphasized the importance of defining, teaching, monitoring student performance, and giving students feedback on your expectations for their behavior. In addition to the information we have presented thus far, there are two other types of circumstances involving behavioral expectations that have not yet been discussed. Therefore, in this task, we offer suggestions for dealing with students who enter your class after you have taught your expectations (e.g., students who enter your class after the first few weeks of school). We also provide information on how to define and communicate expectations for any "unique" events that students may be participating in (e.g., field trips, assemblies, having a classroom guest speaker, etc.).

Teaching Expectations to New Students

The first two weeks of school are the most important time for teaching behavioral expectations and classroom routines. However, most of you will experience some degree of flux in your student population over the course of the year. That is, you will have at least one student leave and at least one new student enter your class. Many schools have such high student mobility rates that less than half the students in a class at the beginning of the year are still there at the end of the year. When a new student enters your classroom, some form of orientation (similar to what you provide for all students during the first two weeks of school) will be essential to get the student off to a successful start. We recommend that you plan ahead how you will do this. In fact, the higher you expect your student mobility rate to be, the more prepared you need to be to teach your expectations to new students.

To help you, we describe four basic strategies that can be implemented at a classroom level. (NOTE: We have also included the description of a schoolwide strategy—for schools in which there are likely to be several new students each week). If you anticipate getting only one to three new students during the year, implementing the first two strategies is probably sufficient. On the other hand, if you are likely to have quite a few new students entering your class during the year, we would suggest that you consider implementing at least three of the following strategies.

Teach the New Student Individually

The most common and basic method of orienting a new student to your class is for you to simply teach the new student your expectations yourself. To do this, meet with the student for a couple of minutes immediately before each major activity/transition for several days to a week. Tell the student what will be happening and explain your *CHAMPs* behavioral expectations for that activity/transition. At the conclusion of the activity/transition, let the student know how she/he did, and orient him/her to the next activity/transition.

The advantage of this approach is that it generates frequent contact between you and a new student during the student's first week in class. The disadvantage is that it requires a great deal of your time. If you are likely to get only one to three new students during the year, pairing this approach with Reteach the Entire Class is probably both reasonable and effective. However, if you will have many new students during the year, it will be impractical (to say nothing of being a disservice to the rest of the class) for you to take that much time with each new student.

Reteach the Entire Class

You can use the need to orient a new student as an opportunity to go over the *CHAMPs* expectations for all activities and transitions with the entire class. For one day, immediately before each activity and each major transition, ask students to volunteer to share some information about expected behaviors and procedures with the new student. "Please raise your hand if you can tell Sandra one of the important expectations for independent work periods during math class." Call on students until all the important information has been reviewed. If students leave out something critical, add it yourself.

This procedure has several advantages. The new student gets important information, and the information is reviewed and reinforced for the other students. Having students present the information communicates that the expectations are shared by the class, not just the teacher. Finally, taking a couple of minutes to do this before each activity/transition makes a statement that you believe that student knowledge of the right way to do things is important enough to take time for.

The main disadvantage is that if you have to do it more than once every four to six weeks, it will take too much class time. In addition, students may get tired of discussing the same expectations over and over. Therefore, if you do this for one new student, and then get another new student two weeks later, do not repeat the procedure. Another disadvantage is that if you use this procedure by itself, a new student will only get one day of orientation. You will not want to take the entire class' time to orient a new student for more than one day, but there are so many expectations and routines in the typical class that the student is not likely to remember all the details by the second day at a new school. Therefore, even if you use this procedure, use one of the other procedures (e.g., Teach the New Student Individually or The Buddy System) as well.

The Buddy System

With this procedure, you give individual class members the responsibility of orienting new students to the routines and procedures of the class. "Paul, this is Rico. Rico is a student who really understands and follows the procedures that will help you be successful in this class. Throughout the day (class period), you two have permission to quietly talk—even at times that talking is usually not allowed. Paul, if you have a question about how we do things, you can ask me or quietly ask Rico. Rico, anytime during the next week that something is going on that may be new to Paul, please quietly explain what we are doing and why." If you plan on using this procedure, and are likely to have a lot of new students during the year, take time in the second or third week of school to talk to the entire class about how you may call on them individually to help orient a new student. Be sure to not always use the same student as the "Buddy"—i.e., call on different students as the year progresses.

The advantage of this approach is that it takes pressure off you to spend class (instructional) time with a new student. In addition, it communicates your expectation and belief that your students fully understand and implement your expectations. A possible disadvantage is that you will not have enough contact with a new student for that student to feel a real connection with you. If you use the Buddy System, make a point of frequently interacting with and getting to know any new student (e.g., checking on his/her work, asking how she/he is doing, seeing if she/he has any questions, etc.).

A "Welcome to Our Class" Video

If you anticipate a high rate of student mobility, it may be worth taking time to have your students develop an orientation video at the beginning of the year. The amount of time required to plan and direct this activity will vary, depending upon your own style and preferences. Some teachers may assign the task to a small group of students and give them only a broad outline of topics to cover. Other teachers may guide the entire process, and only involve class members as "actors" to demonstrate procedures. If you think this might be a reasonable option for you, plan to "produce" the video about the third week of school. By then, procedures and routines should be well established, and developing the video can help solidify and reinforce the important expectations for the class.

An advantage of this procedure is that it can help create a sense of class pride and unity—along with being great fun and potentially very entertaining. New students can be given the video to view at school (with a school counselor or a peer "Buddy") or to take home to view it with their families.

The major disadvantage to an orientation video is that it can be time consuming to develop and, without monitoring and guidance, some students may get overly silly during the production process. Use your own judgment regarding the trade-off between time spent up front developing such a video and time saved later in welcoming and orienting new students.

A "Newcomers Club" (a schoolwide plan)

If your school has extremely high rates of student mobility, it may be worth proposing some form of orientation to the whole school. For example, at a large elementary school in California that gets between 3 and 20 new students every week, a highly skilled bilingual paraprofessional has been trained to run the "Newcomers Club" every morning. This paraprofessional (who has other responsibilities later in the day) spends the first two hours each morning with any new students and their families. When a new student and his/her family arrive, they are introduced to the principal who greets them and, in turn, introduces them to this paraprofessional. They go to a classroom that has been converted to serve as the "Newcomers Club" and "Parent Room" (very bright and welcoming).

In this relaxed setting, the paraprofessional shows a video (in either English or Spanish) that greets and welcomes the student and his/her family. The paraprofessional then takes the student and his/her family on a walking tour of the school, including a brief visit to the classroom the student will go to later in the morning. After the tour, they go back to the Parent Room to discuss expectations, play a couple of age-appropriate games, and/or resolve any questions the student and family may have. Both the student and the family are invited to come to the Parent Room or to the principal with any questions or concerns that may come up.

The Newcomers Club was very time consuming to develop initially, however, it has created an incredibly invitational and relaxed introduction to the school. In schools with no designated welcoming personnel, a new student arriving at the school can feel as though she/he is being shuffled from person to person and "plopped" into a new classroom!

The teacher is still responsible for orienting the student to the classroom expectations and routines, but the overall responsibility for welcoming and orientation is taken care of at the schoolwide level.

In schools with a moderately high rate of student mobility (say 5-20 new students each month), a Newcomers Club might be run on a regular, but less frequent, basis (e.g., every other Thursday afternoon for an hour or more). The school counselor or a well trained paraprofessional can gather all students who have enrolled in the previous two weeks and spend time with them as a group—going over expectations, answering questions, touring the grounds, introducing them to the nurse, the custodian, the principal, and so on. The key to making this procedure work is that it be highly invitational and welcoming.

Teaching Expectations for Unique Events

In addition to knowing the behavioral expectations for major classroom activities and common transitions, students will need to know how they are expected to behave during any unique events (e.g., field trips) that will occur. If you have not taught your class the expectations for a particular event, misbehavior may be likely—not because students are willfully disobedient, but because they do not have the knowledge/skills to behave in a manner that you consider responsible. For example, imagine taking your unprepared third grade students to an assembly to hear a speaker. If your class is one of the first to arrive, students may have to wait five to ten minutes. Some students may start conversations with friends two or three rows away; others may get bored and start pushing and shoving each other. As the assembly begins, many of the students may continue their inappropriate behaviors. You try to get them to quiet down and listen to the speaker, but soon things feel out-of-control. On the other hand, if one to two weeks before the assembly you had defined, and started teaching, how you expected students to behave during the assembly, they would know that they were only allowed to quietly converse with someone no more than "a 12-inch voice" away, and that they needed to stop talking and pay attention once the principal walked to the microphone.

As soon as you know that your students will be participating in some special event (for which they have not been taught behavioral expectations), you need to start defining and then teaching your expectations. Because this will be, by definition, a special event, the first step should be to identify the specific types of situations students are likely to be engaged in during the event. This may involve doing some advance research to find out about the nature of the event and the types of experiences students will encounter. Figure 4.7 shows the kind of event analyses you might come up with for an assembly and for a field trip to a hydroelectric dam.

Figure 4.7: Sample Special Events Analyses

EVENT: ASSEMBLY	EVENT: FIELD TRIP
Leave the classroom	Leave the classroom
Go down hall as a group	Go down hall as a group
Enter the auditorium and get seated	Wait for the bus
Converse while waiting	Ride the bus

EVENT: ASSEMBLY	EVENT: FIELD TRIP
Get silent when things begin	Get off bus, wait for tour guide
Listen/participate in the program	Listen to guide provide orientation
Show appreciation at end	Move to different locations with the guide
Be excused	Watch the ten-minute film
Go back to class	Tour the NOISY parts of the dam
	Questions/discussion with tour guide
	Eat in the picnic area
	Ride the bus home
	Return to class/dismissal

Once you have identified the major situations for the special event, the next step is to use the *CHAMPs* acronym to define your behavioral expectations for each of those situations. Then, of course, you need to start communicating your expectations to students. For each situation you have identified, teach students the *CHAMPs* expectations so that they know exactly what constitutes responsible behavior. Keep in mind that simply telling students your expectations is not as effective as modeling, role-playing, and discussion.

The greater the complexity of the event or the more problems that have been associated with that type of event, the more days you should "rehearse." For a simple situation (e.g., a guest speaker), a brief orientation the day before and short review immediately prior to the event is probably sufficient. However, if students had a problem the last time they were engaged in a similar event, we recommend that you plan on teaching and reviewing expectations for at least four or five consecutive days.

If the situation and/or your expectations are complex, or if the event involves potential danger, or if there are many different components to the event (e.g., the field trip in Figure 4.7), you definitely should plan to teach your expectations for at least five days. You should plan to break the teaching down, so that each day you introduce a few of the expectations. For example, teaching expectations for something like the preceding field trip example might be organized as follows:

Day 1: Take about ten minutes and discuss and practice the *CHAMPs* expectations for the following:

- Leaving the classroom
- Going down the hall as a group
- Waiting for the bus
- Riding the bus
- Getting off bus, waiting for the tour guide

Day 2: The ten minute lesson would include a review of the content taught the day before and introduce:

- Being silent while the guide is providing orientation
- Moving to different locations with the guide
- Watching the ten-minute film

Day 3: Review the previous two lessons and introduce and mentally prepare students for staying calm and keeping their voices down (i.e., no shouting) while:

- Touring the NOISY parts of the dam

Day 4: Review content covered in the three previous lessons and introduce expectations for:

- Questions/discussion with the tour guide
- Eating in the picnic area
- Riding the bus home
- Returning to class/dismissal

Day 5: Put all of the above information together and introduce the content objectives for the event (i.e., what you want students to learn from the trip).

Module 4: The First Month

Self-Assessment Checklist

Use the worksheet on the following pages to identify which (or which parts) of the tasks described in this module you have completed. For any item that has not been completed, note what needs to be done to complete it. As appropriate, translate your notes onto your planning calendar in the form of specific actions that you can take (e.g., August 17, make sign for classroom.)

COMPLETED	TASK	NOTES & IMPLEMENTATION IDEAS
	FINAL PREPARATIONS I reviewed and completed the essential tasks from Modules 1 - 3. That is, I have ... • Developed and posted Guidelines for Success (M1, T2) • Created positive expectations for all students (M1, T3) • Reviewed the basic principles of behavior management (M1, T6) • Determined the level of structure for my class (M1, T7) • Developed a regular daily schedule (M2, T1) • Arranged the physical space in the classroom (M2, T2) • Identified an attention signal (M2, T3) • Developed beginning and ending routines (M2, T4) • Identified and posted classroom rules (M2, T5) • Developed procedures for managing student work (M2, T6) • Created a Classroom Management Plan (M2, T7) • Defined and prepared lessons on behavioral expectations (M3, T1, T2, and T3)	
	I have developed a modified daily (class) schedule for the first day of school. I have made a sign for my classroom.	

COMPLETED	TASK	NOTES & IMPLEMENTATION IDEAS
	FINAL PREPARATIONS (CONTINUED) I have prepared an initial activity for students to work on when they enter the room. I have prepared a plan for dealing with families who may want to take my time on the first day of school.	
	DAY ONE I have thought about how I will display my Day One Schedule—on the board, an overhead transparency, or flip chart. I have thought about how I will greet students individually as they enter the room. I have thought about how I will get students' attention as soon as the bell rings. I have thought about how I will communicate essential classroom information in the first ten minutes of the day (class). I have thought about how I will teach my attention signal. I have thought about how I will begin teaching students my behavioral expectations for activities and transitions. I have thought about how I will monitor student performance of the behavioral expectations (during activities and transitions) using circulating and visual scanning. I have thought about how I will give individual students and the entire class positive feedback about their behavior during and after activities and transitions. I have thought about how I will give individual students and the entire class corrective feedback about their behavior during and after activities and transitions.	

COMPLETED	TASK	NOTES & IMPLEMENTATION IDEAS
	DAYS 2 - 20 (THE FIRST FOUR WEEKS) I have thought about how I will use the three-step process of teaching, monitoring behavior, and giving feedback to communicate my behavioral expectations during the first month of school. • If I am an elementary teacher, I have thought about how I will help students learn the behavioral expectations of the specialists with whom they will have class. I have thought about how I will verify that my students understand the behavioral expectations I have of them. I have prepared a quiz that can be administered to all the students. I have arranged to conduct interviews with a sample of students.	
	SPECIAL CIRCUMSTANCES I have thought about how I will teach behavioral expectations to students who enter my class. Possibilities include: • teaching the student individually; • reteaching the entire class; • using a buddy system; • making a "Welcome to Our Class" video; and • working to establish a schoolwide "Newcomers Club." I have thought about how I will define and teach behavioral expectations for any unique events in which my students will participate (e.g., field trips).	

Module 4: First Month

Peer Study Worksheet

With one or more of your colleagues, work through the following discussion topics and activities related to the tasks in Module 4. If necessary, refer back to the text to get additional ideas or for clarification. (See the Module 1 Peer Study Worksheet for suggestions on structuring effective discussion sessions.)

Task 1: Final Preparations

A. ONLY IF YOU HAVE TIME, have group members share what they have done in terms of final preparations for the first day of school. Specifically, individual members may want to share ideas for an initial activity that students can work on when they arrive and how they plan to deal with families who want to take their time on the first day.

Task 2: Day One

A. ONLY IF YOU HAVE TIME, have group members share their ideas and plans for displaying their Day One Schedule, greeting students as they arrive, getting students' attention when the bell rings, communicating essential information in the first 10 minutes, and teaching their attention signal.

B Have group members discuss how they will begin to use the 3-step process (of teaching, monitoring behavior, and giving feedback) to communicate behavioral expectations.

Task 3: Days 2 - 20 (The First Four Weeks)

A. Have group members who are elementary teachers share suggestions for helping their students learn the behavioral expectations of specialists (e.g., music, P.E., etc.)

B. Have individual group members share any quizzes and/or interview protocols they have developed to verify student understanding of behavioral expectations. Group members should give each other feedback. If applicable, work in pairs and arrange to interview each other's students.

Task 4: Special Circumstances

A. Have group members share ideas on how they can teach their behavioral expectations to new students who enter their classrooms. In particular, discuss the viability and logistics of creating individual "Welcome to Our Class" videos, and the viability and logistics of establishing a schoolwide "Newcomers Club."

B. Have individual group members share any behavioral expectations they have developed for unique events that have happened and/or will happen.

MODULE 5: MOTIVATION

When you implement effective instruction and positive feedback, you motivate students to demonstrate their best behavior.

Introduction

To motivate is defined as, "to provide an incentive, to move to action, to drive forward." In this module, we describe six tasks that are designed to enhance your efforts to implement effective motivational procedures with your students (i.e., to move them to do their best academically, and to encourage them to exhibit responsible and successful behavior). We believe that the procedures presented can help you maintain the motivation of students who already follow the rules and do their best on assignments, increase the motivation of students who do nothing or only enough to "get by," and generate the motivation to behave responsibly in students who tend to misbehave. In order for you to better understand and implement the tasks in this module, we start by explaining several important concepts about motivation in the Introduction.

The first concepts to understand are that: (1) when a behavior is engaged in repeatedly, it demonstrates a level of motivation to engage in that behavior; and (2) if a behavior does not occur, it demonstrates a lack of motivation to engage in that behavior. This concept is always true, regardless of what an individual may think or say about his or her behavior. For example, a person may repeatedly complain about his job and even say that he is unmotivated to go to work—but if he goes to work regularly, he shows that he is, in fact, motivated to go to work. Likewise, a person may say she is motivated to paint as a hobby, but if she never gets out her paints and brushes, she is not, in fact, motivated to paint. This does not mean that the man will never lose his motivation to go to work or that the woman will never regain her motivation to paint, but that, for the present, their behavior indicates motivation to do otherwise.

The importance of this concept for teachers is its implication that the student who repeatedly misbehaves is, at the moment, more motivated to misbehave than to behave responsibly, and that the student who does nothing is more motivated to do nothing than to work at completing assignments. It means that you, as the teacher, will need to increase these students' motivation to behave responsibly and complete assignments, respectively. The tasks in this module are designed to help you do that.

NOTE

Another implication of the concept is that if your efforts to increase students' motivation to engage in the appropriate/desired behaviors are ineffective, you will also need to work at decreasing their motivation to engage in the inappropriate/undesired behaviors. Specific suggestions for how to do that are included in Module 7: Correction Procedures.

A second important concept about motivation is that most people are motivated to engage in a particular behavior by a complex mix of intrinsic and extrinsic factors. A person can be said to be "intrinsically" motivated when she engages in a behavior and the pleasant consequences that occur during and/or after the behavior are "related to the essential nature of that behavior." Thus, a person who is intrinsically motivated to read, reads because he likes to learn new things, enjoys a good story, and finds curling up with a good book relaxing. The person who is intrinsically motivated to ski, skis because she finds the speed exhilarating, the fresh air pleasant, and the feeling of exhaustion at the end of a challenging day gratifying.

Extrinsic motivation, on the other hand, is when someone engages in a behavior due to pleasant consequences occurring during and/or after the behavior that are not related to the essential nature of the behavior. For example, babies tend to utter "mama" and "dada" more frequently than other sounds because of the reactions (e.g., smiles, tickles, and looks of delight) these sounds elicit in the most significant people in their lives. Or, a college student will continue to attend and write papers for a class that she does not like because she wants a certain grade, and because doing well in the class will move her toward her desired goal of a diploma. Or, a six-year-old child will make his bed to get lavish praise from his mom and dad regarding how responsible, hard-working, and helpful he is.

Some people believe that the only valid kind of motivation is intrinsic motivation, and that teachers should not give students praise and rewards (extrinsic motivators) of any kind. We address this (mistaken) belief in more detail in Task 4, but for right now, we would simply like to say that the line between intrinsic and extrinsic motivation is not as distinct as some people think. In fact, as stated earlier, for most behaviors motivation is usually a mix of intrinsic and extrinsic factors. Although the person who reads a lot may do so for the intrinsic rewards of the task, he may also enjoy the compliments he gets from others on his breadth of knowledge—much of which was learned from reading. The frequent skier may find that, in addition to enjoying the exhilaration etc. of skiing itself, she also enjoys having others comment on her skill or ask her advice on how to handle a particularly challenging slope. The baby learning to talk makes "mama" and "dada" sounds because making those sounds is fun, not just because of the reactions of others. And, the college student who attends class and writes papers does so not only because of the grades and diploma, but because the class is sometimes genuinely interesting and useful.

As a teacher, what this means is that when you have students who are unmotivated to work or to behave responsibly, you need to try to enhance both their intrinsic (e.g., make a science lesson more interesting) and extrinsic (e.g., provide age-appropriate positive feedback) motivation—and in this module, we provide suggestions on how to do both.

A third important concept about motivation has to do with the relationship between one's intrinsic motivation to engage in a task and one's proficiency at that task. Thus, a skilled woodworker is more likely to find spending time in a workshop more intrinsically reinforcing than the person who has never learned to use tools. Similarly, the skilled musician is more likely to find daily practice intrinsically reinforcing than the person who has only played for three weeks. In addition, an individual who has experienced success at learning many different new skills in the past, is more likely to be motivated to try to learn something new in the future than someone who has experienced repeated failure. The student who has had a lot of academic success is more likely to feel excited about the "challenge" of a tough course than the student who has failed at academic pursuits in the past.

The very important implication of this concept for teachers is that in the early stages of learning something new or when learning something difficult, some students (particularly those who have experienced frequent past failure) are not likely to be intrinsically motivated to engage in the behaviors necessary to learn the skill or knowledge.

A further refinement of the concept is the "Expectancy X Value" theory of motivation. First used by Feather, N.T., (1982), this theory explains a person's motivation on any given task as a function of the following formula:

Expectancy multiplied by Value equals Motivation

In the formula, "expectancy" is defined as "the degree to which an individual expects to be successful at the task" and "value" is defined as "the degree to which an individual values the rewards that accompany that success." The power of this theory is its recognition that a person's level of motivation on any given task is a function of both how much the person wants the rewards that accompany success *and* how much he or she expects to be successful.

Many teachers, when trying to ascertain why a student is unmotivated to behave responsibly or complete assignments, for example, tend to ascribe the lack of motivation to issues involving the value component of the formula only. "Nothing seems to motivate him. He doesn't care about getting good grades. He takes no pride in his accomplishments. He doesn't care about free time or stickers or positive notes home. I even tried to put him on a point contract where he could earn time to play a game with a friend, or time on the computer, but he just said he didn't really care about games or computers. I guess there isn't anything else I can do." What these explanations fail to take into account is that if the student thinks he will not succeed at behaving responsibly or completing assignments (expectancy), his motivation will be very low or nonexistent.

Please note that the value factor in the formula can include extrinsic rewards (e.g., money, time stickers, awards, grades) and/or intrinsic rewards (e.g., sense of accomplishment, enjoyment of the task, pride in a job will done, sense of having fulfilled one's duty, and so on). A key implication of the theory is that if the rate for either one of the factors—expectancy or value—is zero, no matter what the rate of the other factor is, the motivation will be zero.

Let's say that both expectancy and value could be calibrated on a scale of 0 to 10, with 0 representing the lowest possible rate and 10 representing the highest possible rate of each. When a value rate and an expectancy rate for any given task are multiplied together they will equal a number between 0 and 100, which can be thought of as the percent of motivation a person has for that task. A key implication of the theory is that if the rate for either one of the factors, expectancy or value, is zero, it won't matter what the rate of the other factor is, motivation will be zero. See the examples below:

Expectancy Rate	10	X	Value Rate 10	=	100% Motivation
Expectancy Rate	10	X	Value Rate 0	=	0% Motivation
Expectancy Rate	0	X	Value Rate 10	=	0% Motivation

Another aspect of the theory for you to understand is that the rates for both expectancy and value will be defined by what a student believes, not what you think they should be. For example, you may know that the student is absolutely capable of being successful if he would simply try. However, if the student believes he cannot be successful (i.e., his expectancy is around 0), motivation will be low to nonexistent.

Whenever a student is unmotivated to do something (complete work, try out for a team, participate in class discussions, enter a science competition, or behave more responsibly), you should try to determine whether the lack of motivation stems from a lack of value (intrinsic and extrinsic), a lack of expectancy, or a lack of both. Specifically, if you need to increase a student's motivation to complete academic tasks, determine whether or not the student is capable of being successful at the tasks. If he or she is not, you may need to modify the tasks so that the student will be able to succeed. *How* you can modify academic tasks is beyond the scope of this program, but there are people in your district who can help with strategies in modifying instruction to make success possible for the student.

We believe that the "Expectancy X Value" theory can be a particularly useful way of thinking about behavior and motivation for teachers. To develop your understanding of it, we suggest that you periodically take the time to analyze activities you personally are motivated and unmotivated to do. When thinking about something you are highly motivated to do, identify the value you place on engaging in and completing the activity and the expectancy of success you have before engaging in it. When you think about an activity that you are not motivated to do, see if you can determine whether it is the expectancy rate, the value rate, or both that is low. Try to identify any activities for which you value the rewards, but avoid doing because your expectancy of success is low. Analyzing your own motivation (or, for some types of activities, your own lack of motivation) will help you develop a deeper understanding of your students' motivation.

In summary, as you review the tasks in this module and consider your students' motivation (or lack of motivation), keep the following concepts in mind. First, the students' behavior will let you know what they are motivated to do and what they are not motivated to do. As necessary, you will have to work on increasing their motivation to engage in appropriate/desired behaviors and/or decrease their motivation to engage in inappropriate/undesired behaviors. Second, when trying to increase student motivation to behave appropriately, use procedures that address both intrinsic and extrinsic motivation. Third, remember that students' motivation to engage in any behavior will be related to the degree to which they value the rewards of engaging in that behavior and their expectation of succeeding at the behavior.

The six tasks presented and explained in this module are:

TASK 1: Enthusiasm
Present the tasks/behaviors that you want students to engage in, in a manner that will generate enthusiasm (and intrinsic motivation) on the part of students.

TASK 2: Effective Instruction
Implement effective instructional practices to keep students interested and academically engaged.

TASK 3: Noncontingent Attention
Use every opportunity possible to provide each student with noncontingent attention.

TASK 4: Positive Feedback
Give students positive feedback in a variety of ways on their progress/success in meeting behavioral and academic goals.

TASK 5: Intermittent Celebrations
Periodically reward both individual students and the whole class with some kind of "celebration" that acknowledges their progress/success in meeting behavioral and academic goals.

TASK 6: Ratio of Interactions
Plan to interact **at least** three times more often with each student when he or she is behaving appropriately than when he or she is misbehaving (i.e., at least a 3:1 ratio).

Immediately following the explanations of the tasks in this module is a Self-Assessment Checklist designed to help you determine which (or which parts) of the tasks you have done/are doing and which you still need to do. The module ends with a Peer Study Worksheet. This worksheet presents a series of discussion questions and activities that can be used by two or more teachers who want to share information and collegial support as they work to improve their classroom management practices.

Task 1: Enthusiasm

Present the tasks/behaviors that you want students to engage in, in a manner that will generate enthusiasm (and intrinsic motivation) on the part of students.

Think about a motivational coach. In addition to simply teaching his/her players the necessary skills, the effective coach brings a great deal of passion to his/her interactions with the players. For example, think about what an effective coach does and says at the last practice before a big game, during the half-time talks, to individual players and the whole team during the game, after the team has won (e.g., "You did great, but don't get over-confident because next week we face the Cougars and they may be even tougher than the team we just beat."), and after the team has lost (e.g., "Yes we lost, but you played a great game and we can learn from the mistakes we made. We just need to work even harder next week."). The actions of the effective coach are designed to inspire the players and motivate them to try their hardest.

In this task, we discuss four specific strategies you can use, alone or in combination, to increase students' intrinsic motivation. By presenting tasks and behaviors in a manner that will generate student enthusiasm, you can "drive students forward" to succeed.

Explain why or how the task/behavior will be useful to students.
Most people are more motivated to work on a task that has a clear and important purpose than on a task that simply seems like meaningless busywork. Therefore, whenever possible, tell your students why you want them to work on the tasks you assign. For example, when presenting a new math skill, you might emphasize how the skill will help them solve certain types of problems. Or, when presenting an important historical event, you might emphasize how the event has relevance to the current events in the country being studied. If you are trying to get your class to work harder toward one of your Guidelines for Success, you can stress how following the guideline will help them individually to be more successful and will help the whole classroom to be a better place for everyone.

Obviously, your explanations need to be age-appropriate. With kindergarten and first grade students, it may be sufficient to say an activity will be fun or interesting. With eighth grade students it is essential to communicate more precisely what the expected outcome will be and how the task will be useful. It is not necessary to provide this kind of explanation for everything you ask students to do, but you should plan on doing it fairly frequently.

Give students a vision of what they will be able to do eventually.
Students should be aware of the long-term benefits of full and active participation in your class. That is, each student who follows your directions and works hard at the tasks you

assign should know what he/she will be able to do at the end of the year that he/she was not able to do at the beginning. The benefits may involve academic skills, study skills, social skills, or a mix of all three. Your long-range classroom goals (see Module 1, Task 1) may provide examples of things you can let students know they will be learning. For example, with younger students, you might show them the kinds of books they will be able to read and understand, and demonstrate the types of math problems they will be able to complete, and explain how they will learn to keep their attention focused on their work for longer and longer periods of time. With seventh grade history students, you might share how they will be able to understand current events in new ways and how they will learn to take useful notes and study for tests.

Relate new tasks to previously learned skills.
Whenever you introduce a new skill or topic, tell students how the new skill relates to previously learned skills. Students should not feel or think that you are presenting hundreds of unconnected skills or concepts. They need to understand that what you ask them to do at any one time relates to what they have been working on and will be working on. In this way, students can see how what they have already mastered is useful in understanding new skills or topics. When you combine this strategy with the two previous suggestions, you will ensure that students have a continual sense of where they have been and where they are going.

Rally the enthusiasm and energy of students, particularly when you will be asking them to do something difficult or challenging.
Remember, many students will not find it easy to be motivated to do something new and/or something hard. This is where you must make a point of emulating a really masterful coach. Don't be afraid to give some variation of a "Win one for the Gipper" speech (for those of you too young to remember, this comes from an old Ronald Reagan movie in which the coach gives an impassioned speech to a football team before an especially challenging game). A classroom example might resemble the following hypothetical speech given two days before a unit test in science:

> *"Class, in two days we have the unit test in science. This is a tough unit, but I know that you can do it; you can get these important concepts. I want you to do three things in the next two days that will really help you get a good score on the next test. First, work to pay attention in class. We are going to be reviewing the essential information you have to understand, so keep your attention focused. Second, anytime you don't understand something we are reviewing, ask about it. There are no stupid questions. If you are unsure how to ask a question, just ask me to give more information or to explain the idea again in a slightly different way. Third, decide right now how much you are going to study tonight and how much you are going to study tomorrow night for this test. How many minutes are you going to study? Decide—right now! Now, add fifteen minutes to that number. If you were thinking that you would study zero minutes, add 15*

minutes—so you will study at least fifteen minutes tonight and fifteen minutes tomorrow night. If you planned to study 30 minutes each night, make it 45 minutes. Remember, the more you study, the more you learn; and the more you learn, the better you will do on the test!"

Task 2: Effective Instruction

Implement effective instructional practices to keep students interested and academically engaged.

Effective instructional practices are an absolutely integral part of effective behavior management practices. A teacher who implements dull instruction, presents unclear tasks, and/or assigns work that is consistently beyond the ability of some of the students, even if he or she does everything else well in terms of behavior management, is likely to have some students who appear unmotivated, disruptive, or hostile. Effective instruction prevents a great deal of misbehavior because students who are highly engaged in meaningful tasks do not have time to misbehave. In addition, when students are successful, their sense of accomplishment can be so satisfying that they are more motivated to behave responsibly.

We believe all teachers need to learn to ask themselves whether a behavior problem (involving a student or a group of students) might be, at least in part, an instructional problem. While it is beyond the scope of this program to provide comprehensive inservice on effective instructional practices (the topic is far too broad and complex), what follows are brief descriptions of some factors related to effective instruction that can significantly influence student behavior. Those factors include:

- Teacher's presentational style
- Actively involving students in lessons
- Having clear objectives and evaluating student progress
- Ensuring high rates of student success
- Providing students with immediate performance feedback

Teacher's Presentational Style

Teacher behavior can be a big factor in the behavior of students. Students are more likely to pay attention to a teacher who is dynamic, clear, humorous, and excited in class than to a teacher who is confusing, boring, or who talks in a monotone. To help you understand how important a factor teacher presentation can be, think back to how you felt about the interesting, and the boring, teachers you had in high school or college.

Although some teachers will naturally be better presenters than others, every teacher can and should strive to make their presentations more interesting to students. A reasonable goal to set for yourself is to be a slightly better presenter every year. Look at the suggestions below, then pick one or two you will practice and work to improve over the course of this year.

- Vary your tone of voice—avoid being monotone.
- Vary the intensity of your presentation—sometimes act excited, sometimes act calm and relaxed.
- Use humor—try to make at least some part of every lesson fun or funny.
- Clarify lesson purpose—make sure students know what they are supposed to be learning and why it is important.
- Clarify information—be very direct about the key concepts students need to understand. The more direct your communication the better.

Actively Involving Students in Lessons

Don't talk too much. When you speak for more than a few minutes without getting students involved in some way, the less motivated students will tend to tune you out. Following are some simple strategies for getting students involved, even during teacher-directed lessons.

- Ask questions.
- Give students tasks to work on in pairs.
- Present mini-tasks for students to work on independently.
- Give mini-quizzes.
- Set up role-plays.
- Present guided practice of tasks students will work on later.

Having Clear Objectives and Evaluating Student Progress

You should always know exactly what you want your students to know or be able to do as a result of the lessons you teach and the tasks you assign. Think about classes you have taken in which you found out that what the teacher did in class had nothing to do with the tests and assignments that were used to evaluate your performance. Most people find this very discouraging.

Start planning your lessons by first thinking about how you will evaluate students. For example, before you begin a two-week science unit, create the test students will take at the end of the unit (or look at it, if you are using a published test that goes with your textbook). After creating/looking at the test, you will know the key vocabulary words, concepts, and operations that you need to directly teach during instruction. You can then make sure that any tasks you assign will help students practice those vocabulary words, concepts, and operations. For those who question this as "teaching to the test," we would reply that a test should cover the material you want students to learn, and so should your instruction. In fact, a clear and consistent match between instruction and evaluation is a hallmark of effective teaching.

Ensuring High Rates of Student Success

All students learn faster when they get predominantly correct answers—on both oral and written tasks. While it is true that students should be challenged with difficult tasks, it's also true that students who constantly face tasks on which they make lots of errors will get discouraged over time. We suggest that you try to provide clear enough instruction and frequent enough practice opportunities to ensure that students will get approximately 90% correct on most tasks.

In situations where you know that students are likely to make high numbers of errors, you should plan to provide more teacher-directed instruction. You can do this whether you are working with students in small groups (while the other students work independently) or with the whole class. Consider the following example involving a whole class math lesson. Your original plans may call for about 15 minutes of teacher-directed instruction and 30 minutes of independent work, during which students would work on the assignment. During the teacher presentation portion you realize that many students are confused and do not seem to understand. If you were to stick with your plan, many students are likely to make lots of errors, and some will become discouraged. Several students may seek your help during the independent work period. Since many students are confused, a better approach would be to change your plan. Instead of giving 30 minutes of independent work, you might say, "Class, since this is such a difficult assignment, I am going to walk you through the first ten problems. Anyone who wants to work ahead may do so, but I invite anyone who is still confused to do them together with me. Watch me do item 1, then copy what I have done."

Providing Students With Immediate Performance Feedback

When students practice a task, they need to receive information on the parts of the task they are doing correctly and the parts they are doing incorrectly—as quickly as possible. If you have students do an assignment on a new math concept, but do not get their corrected papers back to them for a week or more, they will learn little. A student who is making mistakes needs to know it as soon as possible if he is going to learn from those mistakes. During an oral class exercise, you should provide this kind of performance information to students immediately. Likewise, feedback regarding correct and incorrect responses during guided practice in class should be immediate. When you assign written tasks that are to be done independently, be sure to correct the papers within one or two days, and then go over the corrected papers when you return them. "Class, look at the papers I just handed back. Quite a few people had trouble with Question #5. Let's look at why. When you do a problem like this, keep in mind that . . ."

Level of Classroom Structure and Effective Instruction

Effective instruction is important regardless of whether your classroom will be high, medium, or low structure. However, it is essential if your students need a highly structured classroom. High-needs students are more likely to be easily discouraged and are more likely to have a low expectancy of success on tasks. Your instructional practices will need to be especially effective to keep all students feeling successful and highly motivated. If you have a highly structured management plan, pay particular attention to the suggestions in this task regarding:

- Having clear objectives and evaluating student progress
- Ensuring high rates of student success
- Providing students with immediate performance feedback

Task 3: Noncontingent Attention

Use every opportunity possible to provide each student with noncontingent attention.

It is very important for you to make an effort to provide every student with attention that is not contingent on any specific accomplishment. Contingent positive attention (as described in Tasks 4 and 5) involves interacting with and giving feedback to students when they have accomplished or demonstrated improvement on important behavioral or academic goals. Noncontingent attention, on the other hand, involves giving students time and attention not because of anything they've done, but just because you notice and value them as people. Ways of giving noncontingent attention include greeting your students when they enter your room, calling on students during class, showing an interest in the thoughts, feelings, and activities of your students.

The benefits of noncontingent attention should be obvious. Like all of us, students need to be noticed and valued—and when they feel noticed and valued, they are more likely to be motivated to engage in appropriate behaviors. The benefits to you, then, include: a) feeling more connected to your students; b) providing students with a model of pleasant supportive social interactions; c) improved student behavior; and d) making each day much more pleasant (i.e., improved classroom climate for you and the students).

At first glance, you may wonder how simply saying "hello" and making an effort to talk to students can improve their behavior. Dr. Vern Jones (1998), a leading expert on student discipline and motivation, explains it as akin to "putting something in the bank." Each time you interact with a student and show an interest in him or her as a person, you "make a deposit." When you have "invested" enough (i.e., had enough of the right type of interactions so that the student feels valued by you), the student is more likely to want to follow your rules and strive to achieve your Guidelines for Success. In addition, if you make enough deposits, there will be "reserve capital" for those times that you may have to make a "withdrawal" when a student misbehaves. Whether the withdrawal consists of a gentle reprimand, a discussion, or a consequence designed to help improve the student's behavior, the more you have "invested" in the student, the more likely he or she is to understand that you are trying to help him or her. "Mrs. Jacobsen cares so much about me she is taking the time to help me learn to be responsible. I want to do what she is asking me to do." When nothing has been invested, the student may feel that you are simply trying to control his/her behavior. "Mrs. Jacobsen wants me to sit down and be quiet because she doesn't like me. Well, heck with her. I'll do whatever I want, whenever I want. She can't make me sit down." Noncontingent attention helps you build a spirit of cooperation between yourself and your students.

Showing an interest and acting friendly does not mean trying to be a friend or a peer. You are the teacher, and you do not want to be so friendly that you seem to be an equal. You are the one in authority and the one who needs to intervene if there are rule violations. However, as the one in authority you want to communicate that you value and are interested in every one of your students as individual people.

Following are more detailed explanations of some ways to give your students noncontingent attention.

Greet students.
This is the simplest, but perhaps most important, way to provide noncontingent attention. As students enter your room first thing in the morning (or at the beginning of class), you can say such things as, "Hello, Jonathan. Good morning Wachera. Francine, how are you today? You know, I'm tired this morning too. You and I may have to nudge each other to stay awake in class. Maria, Jacob, Tyrone, good to see you today." You may not be able to greet every student each day, but you should try to greet enough students each day that over the course of a week every student will have been greeted.

Elementary teachers should continue to greet their students throughout the day—i.e., greet a few students when they come in from recess, or after music class, or when they return from lunch. Middle school teachers should attempt to greet at least five to eight students per class, as students enter the room. You can also make a point of greeting your students when you see them in the hall. They may barely respond (some students will be self-conscious if they are with friends), but they will notice if you don't take the time to acknowledge them.

Show an interest in students' work.
During independent work periods, when no one needs immediate assistance, go to individual students (or cooperative learning groups) and look at the students' work. Taking a few seconds to look at what a student is doing demonstrates that you are interested in the student and her work. Sometimes you may offer praise in this context; other times you can simply say something like, "I am looking forward to reading this when you are finished, Tamai."

Invite students to ask for assistance.
Occasionally ask individual students how they are doing in class. If anyone indicates that he or she is having trouble, arrange a time for that student to get some additional help from you. For those who say they are doing fine, let them know that if they ever have trouble, they should not hesitate to come see you. If you make an offer of assistance to every student in the first couple of months of school, you communicate that you are aware of them as individuals and that you are available to them.

Whenever time permits, have a conversation with a student or a group of students. Having a conversation demonstrates (even more than just a greeting) that you are interested in your students—their experiences and their ideas. Brief social interactions create an emotional connection between you and your students, and they are not hard to do. For example, if three students enter your middle school classroom at the beginning of the passing period, you can casually chat with them as you stand at the door and greet other entering students. As you are escorting your second grade class to lunch, you might talk quietly with a couple of students as you go down the hall (unless students are not supposed to converse in the halls). Find out about your students' individual interests, and ask about them (e.g., ask a student about her soccer game the previous evening). Periodically share something about yourself. "My son played goalie for his team in college. What position do you like to play?"

Make a special effort to greet or talk to any student with whom you've had a recent interaction regarding a misbehavior.
This kind of gesture on your part communicates that what happened before is now past and that you do not hold a grudge. It also lets the student know that you are prepared for a fresh start. For example, if you had to talk to a student about being disruptive immediately before lunch, that student should definitely be one of the five or six students you greet when the class comes back after lunch. "Aaron, good to see you. How are you doing?" A greeting in these circumstances actually decreases the probability that the student will misbehave in the next instructional activity.

Level of Structure and Noncontingent Attention

This is one of the few tasks in this program in which the level of classroom structure makes absolutely no difference. That is, whether your students need high, medium, or low structure, you owe it to every individual to interact with them as frequently as possible in a manner that is friendly, inviting, and personable.

Task 4: Positive Feedback

Give students positive feedback in a variety of ways on their progress/success in meeting behavioral and academic goals.

Among the most important practices an effective teacher engages in is letting students know about their behavioral and academic progress and/or success. In Module 1 (Task 6), we identified five major actions a teacher can take in an effort to improve student behavior. One of those is to "implement procedures designed to encourage responsible behavior." Giving positive feedback is a powerful way to encourage responsible behavior. When done well, positive feedback confirms for students that they are on the right track and increases the probability that they will strive to demonstrate the same behaviors in the future. In this task we discuss five hallmarks of effective positive feedback. If you incorporate these suggestions into the positive feedback you give your students, you can significantly increase the probability that your feedback will encourage and motivate students to behave more responsibly in the future.

Feedback should be accurate.

Effective positive feedback will be related to a behavior, or set of behaviors, that did, in fact, occur. When an individual receives positive feedback about something he or she did not actually do, the feedback is basically meaningless. If you comment (orally or in a note) to a student that his accuracy in completing math assignments is improving, you need to be sure that the student's accuracy is really improving. If you note that a student demonstrated improved self control by staying in her seat during an entire instructional period, be sure that the student did stay in her seat.

Feedback should be specific and descriptive.

When giving positive feedback, be sure to tell students exactly what they did. That is, feedback should be information laden—confirming for a student what it was she did and what was important or useful. If you want to let a cooperative group know they have done well, describe the specific behaviors that were exhibited. When writing a note regarding a student's paper, identify the specific things he did that contributed to the quality of the paper.

Specific descriptive feedback lets the student know which aspects of his/her behavior you are commenting on. Simply writing, "Excellent paper" at the top of a paper, with no other notes, does not give the student any information about what aspects of the paper lead to your positive reaction—i.e., was it the effective use of figurative language? The organization? The choice of vocabulary? The creative use of the overall ideas? The use of topic sentences? The clarity of the descriptive language?

Following are some common mistakes teachers make when providing positive feedback. All of them can be avoided by providing specific descriptions of student behavior.

The "Good Job" syndrome.

It's easy for teachers to fall into a simple repetitive phrase that they use over and over and over, to give positive feedback. There are two problems with this. First, most simple phrases such as "Good job," "Nice work," "Yes," or "Fantastic" provide no specific information (e.g., what exactly the student did that was useful or important). Second, when a particular phrase is overused, it becomes like background noise—and students will cease to "hear" it.

Making judgments or drawing conclusions about the student.

Be very cautious about stating, or implying, that a student is "good" or "smart" or "brilliant." When a student answers a difficult question, it can be tempting to say something like, "Allison, you are so smart." The problem is that a statement like this not only doesn't provide specific information about what the student did, but it may imply to the student that if she had not come up with that particular answer, you might not think of her as smart. It's far more effective to say, "Allison, you applied the formula, performed a series of computations, and came up with the correct answer."

Calling attention to yourself.

Some teachers praise by saying, "I like the way you . . . " Even when what follows specifically describes the student's behavior, that initial phrase may inadvertently be taken by students to mean that they should behave to "please" you. In fact, what you are working towards is for students to behave in particular ways because it will help them be successful learners. Another problem with an "I like the way you . . " type of phrase, is that some students might get the idea that you "like" them when they are good, which in turn could imply you don't like them when they are not good. Keep the focus of your feedback on the student and what she did, not on your likes and dislikes. The one exception to this is when a student does something particularly helpful to you. In that circumstance, feel free to let the student know that you appreciate his/her help. For example, if you drop some papers and a student helps you pick them up, it is reasonable and logical to say something like, "Thank you for helping me pick those up. I appreciate having such a thoughtful student."

Feedback should be contingent.

The student behavior you provide feedback on should have some level of importance. That is, it should not be an overly simple behavior for the individual who demonstrated it. To understand why, imagine that someone you know and respect (e.g., a favorite college professor, your minister, your boss) sees you drive into a parking lot and, as you step out of your car, comes over to you and says, "Excellent left turn into this parking lot. You used your turn signals, you checked your blind spot and you controlled your speed as you pulled into the parking space to ensure that you did not scratch the car on either side of you." This feedback may be accurate, but it is also likely to be at best meaningless, and at worst insulting to you. It implies that these driving behaviors are something special, when to an experienced driver, making a left turn into a parking lot and a successful turn into a parking space are really no big deal. You would probably wonder why the person was being so gushy and excited about something that you have done successfully many times. It's even possible that receiving this meaningless (or insulting) feedback would reduce your respect for that person.

There are three major circumstances which contribute to positive feedback being contingent. The first is when the feedback occurs while someone is learning a new skill or behavior. If you had a good teacher when you were first learning to drive, that person may have occasionally given you positive feedback similar to the statements in the previous example. The difference is that, because you may have only driven once or twice before, those statements were probably not at all insulting or meaningless—they provided specific and descriptive confirmation of what you did correctly.

Feedback is also contingent when it refers to a behavior that requires effort—whether or not it is a new behavior. For example, imagine that you have been making a concerted effort to increase your helpfulness around the house (because your partner has been carrying more than his/her fair share). If your partner expresses gratitude for the extra help and/or shares his/her appreciation that the household chores are more equally divided, that positive feedback is unlikely to be meaningless or insulting to you. The behavior isn't new or particularly complex (after all, putting socks in the hamper is not exactly rocket science), but it does take effort to change a bad habit. Feedback that acknowledges one's efforts is likely to be valued by the person receiving the feedback, and can lead to maintaining or increasing the frequency of the behavior in the future.

The third circumstance in which positive feedback will be contingent is when it concerns a behavior (or set of behaviors) about which the individual is proud. For example, think about a time when you handed in a paper on which you felt that you had done an especially good job. Chances are that when you got the paper back, you looked at the score, and then went through the paper page by page to see if the instructor had written any comments. For most people, any positive comments received in these circumstances are not viewed as meaningless or insulting. In fact, it is quite likely that you would be pleased by the comments, particularly if the instructor described which parts of the paper were well thought out or well written.

Feedback should be age-appropriate.

Obviously the way you give feedback to a kindergarten student will be somewhat different than the way you give it to an eighth grade student. For example, you can use more sophisticated vocabulary to describe behavior with older students. And, in terms of being contingent, it is more appropriate to focus on advanced behaviors (and combinations of behaviors) with older students. At the same time, it's important with older students to be careful not to embarrass them when providing positive feedback. Middle school students, in particular, may feel a great deal of peer pressure to fit in and be whatever the current word for "cool" happens to be. Think about the thousands of messages students get that suggest that being good is "geeky." If you provide feedback in a way that embarrasses a student, it not only won't be positive (i.e., encouraging), it actually may discourage the student from behaving responsibly in the future. For example, many students will avoid behaving responsibly if they are praised in a way that results in them being accused of being the "teacher's pet." If a student (or students) seems to be embarrassed when you give positive feedback, consider experimenting with one or more of these suggestions:

- **Use a quiet voice** when providing feedback to individuals. If students feel you are making a public display of them, it may increase the possibility that they will feel embarrassed in front of their friends.
- **Be brief.** If you go on too long, accepting the praise graciously may be difficult.
- **Be somewhat businesslike.** Simply state the positive behavior(s) the student engaged in. If you sound too excited or pleased when you praise, it can make a student feel like, "I pleased the teacher—goody goody."
- **Avoid pausing and looking at the student after you praise.** A pause can seem to imply that you expect the student to respond, and this puts a student in a difficult position. "Should I smile, should I say thank you?" Smiling or saying thank you in front of peers can be socially embarrassing, especially to a student who has an image of being "tough." Such a student will often make a smart-aleck comment or engage in misbehavior to reassert to peers how tough and bad she is.

Feedback should be given in a manner that fits your own style.

The previous information may have given the impression that there is one right way to give positive feedback. Nothing could be further from the truth. There is plenty of room for individual style, even when you incorporate our recommendations. A teacher who has a more businesslike personality can and should employ a more businesslike style of providing positive feedback. A teacher who tends to be excited and energetic may be somewhat more "cheerleader-like" when giving feedback. And a soft-spoken teacher's feedback will probably be softer than that of a more boisterous teacher. In most cases, if you are comfortable with your style of giving feedback, your students will probably be comfortable as well. In fact, you probably only have to consider the preceding tips on age-appropriate and nonembarrassing feedback if your students are responding to your current style with embarrassment. If your students are not responding well to your current style of positive feedback, you may need to make some minor adjustments.

Level of Structure and Positive Feedback

The greater the number of risk factors your class has, the greater your need to manage student behavior via positive as opposed to punitive means. With a low structure class, you may be able to get away with relatively low rates of positive feedback and still have students behave responsibly. We do not recommend this, but you can probably do it and students will be fine. If your students come from relatively stable situations and families, in which they receive encouragement to work hard and behave responsibly, they may work hard and behave well without getting much positive feedback from you—although they probably will not feel much joy or experience high levels of motivation.

However, when students need high structure (i.e., the class has many risk factors), frequent positive feedback is essential. Without the feedback, some students will not know exactly what you want from them. Furthermore, if students are trying to meet your academic and behavioral expectations and they do not receive any feedback that you notice what they have done, some of them will cease striving to meet the expectations. "I try to do what she wants and she never even notices. Why should I bother?" The greater the number of high-needs students, the greater the need for you to provide frequent positive feedback that follows the recommendations within this competency.

Students who Respond Negatively to Positive Feedback

Some students may respond negatively to a teacher's efforts to provide positive feedback. For example, shortly after being told that he is behaving in a mature and responsible manner, a student may exhibit his worst behavior. This can lead a teacher to decide that the student should not be given any future positive feedback or acknowledgment. Actually, this is a relatively common phenomenon for which there are several possible explanations. What follows is a brief presentation of a few of those reasons and some suggestions about what you might do with a student like this to reduce the probability that he or she will continue to react badly to positive feedback.

One reason a student may misbehave immediately after receiving positive feedback is that he is embarrassed by the feedback. If you suspect this is the case, try modifying your feedback as suggested earlier in this task. See whether making the feedback more private, stating it in a more businesslike or brief way, and/or eliminating pauses after you provide positive feedback results in the student reacting more positively.

The other reasons a student may behave this way tend be more complex and slightly harder to remedy. They include such things as: a) the student has an image of himself as a "tough guy" that he has to uphold; b) the student feels peer pressure to maintain her "bad" image; c) the student has trouble handling success. When you provide feedback to a student who has one or more of these issues, the feedback won't fit the student's image of herself and can make her feel uncomfortable (i.e., terrified by her own success). Exhibiting misbehavior helps a student like this get back to feeling like a trouble-maker or a loser. It may even be that she does not believe that she really is capable of being successful and feels the need to show you that the success was an aberration of some kind. In addition, the misbehavior takes some pressure off by communicating that you can't expect the student to be successful all the time. Regardless of the reason for a student's misbehavior after receiving positive recognition, you can try experimenting with one or more of the following suggestions:

Treat the misbehavior (i.e., the downturn after receiving positive feedback) as a momentary interruption in the student's success.

For example, if you praise a second grade student for the quality of an assignment he completed, and he then tears up the paper and throws it on the floor while you are handing papers to other students, you might say something like, "Jamie, that litter will need to be picked up and put in the trash before you go out to recess."

The key is not to let yourself communicate anger or disappointment. This can be tough. When a student falls apart after you acknowledge his success, it is natural to feel angry or disappointed. You may want to say something like, "Jamie, you were doing so well and now you go and do this sort of thing. I just don't understand and I am very disappointed."

The problem is that this may feed into the student's need to feel like a "tough guy" or a loser. It definitely takes the pressure off the student to continue to succeed—the teacher has once again seen the worst the student has to offer.

At a neutral and reasonably private time, talk to the student about his tendency to misbehave after getting positive feedback.

See if the student can give you any insights into why this occurs. Ask him if he has any suggestions about ways you can give him positive feedback that will reduce the chance that he will feel a need to misbehave afterwards. Try experimenting with any reasonable suggestions the student makes. If the student cannot come up with any strategies for you to try, ask him what he thinks about some of the suggestions included here.

Be more private with (or otherwise modify the form of) the positive feedback you provide to the student.

The student may prefer to get a note rather than public praise. He may prefer to have you give the feedback at the end of the period, rather than during it. He may prefer that you use a signal that only he knows (e.g., scratch your forehead) to let him know he is behaving responsibly.

Switch from giving specific descriptive feedback to simply interacting with the student when she is behaving responsibly.

Say "hello" to the student as she enters class. If she is on task during independent work, don't specifically praise her, but do go over and ask if she has any questions or needs any help. If she has behaved responsibly throughout the morning, don't praise, but ask her if she would be willing to pass out some papers that need to be distributed to the class. At the end of the day, tell her to have a nice evening. This attention, given when she is behaving responsibly, may reinforce the appropriate behavior even though you are not providing specific descriptive positive feedback.

If eliminating the positive feedback is successful (i.e., the student handles the attention as long as no praise is included), continue to withhold praise for at least four weeks while continuing to provide attention to the student. If the student's behavior is improving, gradually introduce subtle praise. Once a day or so, make a matter-of-fact statement about something the student has done. Don't gush or in any way make a big deal, just make a comment. "Thank you for getting that assignment in on time." "That was a creative contribution you made to the cooperative group you were working with." If you see a downturn, back off and return to attention without praise. However if the student is handling it, gradually increase frequency of specific descriptive feedback you give the student.

Task 5: Intermittent Celebrations

Periodically reward individual students and the whole class with some kind of "celebration" that acknowleges their progress/success in meeting behavioral and academic goals.

It can be useful to occasionally do something that "makes a big deal" of a student's (or an entire class') success. These celebrations of progress and/or success can be especially useful for immature students, students with a long history of behavior problems, or students who need to make major behavioral changes. In general, we are talking about giving some kind of a "reward" on some, but not all, occasions when a student or group demonstrates a particularly important behavior. Those of you familiar with behavioral theory may recognize this concept as an intermittent reinforcement schedule.

Some people equate rewarding behavior with bribery, but nothing could be further from the truth. Bribery is the inducement to do something illegal, unethical or immoral. Providing intermittent rewards after students exhibit desired behavior more accurately reflects an attempt by school personnel to recognize and celebrate the students' progress and success. To understand the "power" of this kind of feedback, imagine a second grade student who writes a story that really impresses the teacher. The teacher shows the story to the principal, who in turn calls the student into the office to congratulate him. The principal also calls the student's mother to let her know what a special skill the student demonstrated. This student will remember these events for the rest of his life. (I know, because it happened to me. RS, author.)

What you want to do is use intermittent celebrations of success more frequently when students are in the early stages of learning a new skill or improving an existing skill or whenever they are working on a difficult (for them) behavior. For example, if you are trying to motivate students to increase their rates of work completion, you might occasionally (e.g., on average one out of three times—but be unpredictable) reward the class by, say, letting them out of class one minute early when 100% of the students complete their daily assignments. As the level of work completion improves, you would reduce how often you gave a reward (e.g., an average of one out of six times—remaining unpredictable). Please note that keeping the rewards unpredictable is what will keep them special.

To decide what kinds of rewards might be most effective, determine what is likely to mean the most to your students. The more academically successful and socially mature the students, the greater the chance that some sort of informational feedback will suffice. For example, most successful students in grades 4 and above will appreciate a specific descriptive note on a paper. On the other hand, the less academically successful and socially mature the students, the more likely it is that they will need a more extrinsically valuable reward to be excited about the "celebration."

The essential idea here is that when a student (or a group of students) makes a significant academic or behavioral improvement, you want to give them more than simple verbal praise. You want to provide some form of positive feedback that lets them know that they have accomplished something special. You want to create a sense of celebration about what they accomplished. The key is to use these celebrations as sparingly as possible, but as frequently as necessary (and always unpredictably!) to keep students proud and excited about their achievements.

Figure 5.1 shows a variety of ideas for "intermittent celebrations of success." This chart is used by permission from Sprick (1995). The suggestions in the left hand column are most appropriate for younger students; those in the middle column are appropriate for older students (most will work with younger students as well); and the suggestions in the right hand column are appropriate for whole groups or classes. These lists are by no means comprehensive or complete. For additional ideas, talk to colleagues, read other books, and ask your students.

Level of Structure and Intermittent Celebrations of Success

With students in a low structure classroom (i.e., a class with few risk factors), you can probably maintain motivation primarily with noncontingent attention and positive feedback. If you want to, you can use intermittent celebrations for variety or a sense of change—but do so sparingly. With a medium structure classroom, occasional celebrations can be used as a way to keep students striving to be successful and to keep things interesting and exciting. Finally, if your students have a lot of risk factors and need a high structure management plan, it will probably be essential for you to use intermittent rewards regularly, along with noncontingent attention and positive feedback.

NOTE

For a class needing high structure, even this combination of procedures may not be sufficient to keep students motivated. You may very well also need to implement one or more of the reinforcement systems suggested in Module 8: Classwide Motivation Systems in order to maintain responsible behavior and high levels of enthusiasm.

Figure 5.1: Intermittent "Celebration" Ideas

Ideas for Younger Students (Pre K-4th Grade)	Ideas for Older Students (3rd-8th Grade)	Ideas for the Group
Let student choose a story	Let student teach a portion of the lesson	Let class listen to recorded music during an independent work period
Let student be first in line	Let student tell a joke to the class	Let class select a theme for one day, such as - Dress-up day - Backward day - Opposite day - Hat day
Let student use piano, computer, etc.	Let student supervise or tutor younger students	Let class invite someone to come to class to see completed projects or assignments
Let student dictate a story that someone types and prints for the student to illustrate	Let student repair a broken desk or replace batteries in calculator	Let class work outside
Let student earn extra minutes of recess for entire class	Let student choose a modified or independent assignment	Let class redecorate classroom
Let student wear a sign or a badge	Let student choose a peer with whom to play a board game or computer game	Have a class party
Let student work near a class pet or have hamster (or other caged pet) on desk for the day	Let student leave class a few minutes early	Give everyone in class food/beverage: - Popcorn - Fruit - Crackers - Juice
Let student sit in your chair	Give student a "Certificate of Achievement"	Go to recess or lunch with class
Let student perform for the class	Publicly congratulate (but be careful not to embarrass) student	Have class applaud for themselves
Have class give student applause	Congratulate student in front of another adult	Tell a joke to class
Identify student as "Special Student of the Day"	Give (or loan from the library) student a book that was special to you at the same age	Give class a new freedom or more responsibility (e.g., increased freedom to move about the room)
Allow student to keep a special trophy or stuffed animal on desk for the day	Give student a job or responsibility	Give everyone in class a special pencil or other school supply item
Give student a gift certificate for free ice cream or french fries	Give student a ticket to school dance or sporting event	Read to class
Congratulate student in front of class	Ask the principal or counselor to call student in and congratulate student on classroom success	Give class additional recess or break time
Take student's picture and post it	Send student or parent(s) a letter via the mail	Invite parents to come and watch class demonstrate a particular skill or competency
Draw stars on back of student's hand	Shake student's hand and congratulate in a very adult-to-adult manner	Set up a challenge or competition with another class
Invite student to eat in room with you	Give student a "Free Homework Pass"	Have a pizza delivered to classroom
Give student a paper crown to wear	Write a positive note to student	Teacher wears funny clothes to class
Post banner or poster with student's name and accomplishment	Call student at home to congratulate for classroom success	Schedule a field trip

Task 6: Ratio of Interactions

*Plan to interact **at least** three times more often with each student when he or she is behaving appropriately than when he or she is misbehaving (i.e., at least a 3:1 ratio).*

One of the most essential behavior management strategies is also perhaps one of the most difficult to implement. This strategy involves making the effort to interact with every student more frequently (at least three times more frequently, to be exact) when the student is behaving appropriately than when he or she is behaving inappropriately. To understand why the strategy is so essential (and so difficult) consider the following:

- Some students are starved for attention. Most teachers have direct experience with how demanding of attention some students can be and most have seen the desperate lengths some students will go to get attention.

- For the student who is truly starved for attention, the form of attention may not matter. A reprimand for misbehaving may be just as satisfying of this student's need for attention as positive feedback for behaving responsibly. In fact, not only might being scolded be just as satisfying as being praised, but it may be even more satisfying because the scolding will probably last longer and involve a greater emotional intensity.

- With students who are starved for attention, the behavior you pay the most attention to is the behavior you will get more of in the future. That is, if you have more interactions with students when they are behaving appropriately (i.e., "positive interactions"), you will see an increase in positive behavior over time. On the other hand, if you have more interactions with students when they are behaving inappropriately (i.e., "negative interactions"), you will see an increase in negative behavior over time.

Please note that your interactions with students are considered positive or negative based on the behavior the student is engaged in at the time you attend to him or her. For example, if a student is off task and you say, "Wanda, you need to get back to work or you will not complete your assignment," it would be considered a negative interaction—even if you made the request very pleasantly and your intention was to help the student. It is a negative interaction because the student was engaged in a negative behavior (i.e., being off task) when you initiated the interaction. Some teachers mistakenly believe that if they are being nice to a student it is a positive interaction and if they are acting hostile or sounding angry it is a negative interaction.

It's also important to realize that just because an interaction is considered negative, it does not mean it is wrong. It may, for example, be the most useful way to get the student back on task at the time. However, what you need to understand is that unless you make an effort to interact with this same student when she is on task, the student may learn that it is actually easier to get your attention (which may be what she wants) for being off task than it is for behaving well. Remember, each time you give attention to a student, you may be reinforcing the behavior you are paying attention to—whether the behavior is positive or negative. This is why we recommend that you have as your goal to pay three times more attention to students when they are exhibiting positive behavior than when they are exhibiting negative behavior.

Unfortunately, this is not always easy. In fact, observational studies regularly show that most teachers pay significantly more attention to students' misbehavior than they do to students' positive behavior. In 1986, Dr. Wes Becker wrote about studies he had run with teachers who had been reprimanding and reminding students about out-of-seat behavior during work periods. He encouraged the teachers to reprimand students more immediately and more consistently—"Don't miss a single student who gets out of seat at the wrong time." The teachers assumed this would decrease the out-of-seat behavior. In fact, the number of students getting out of seat at the wrong times actually increased.

Dr. Becker called this phenomenon the "Criticism Trap" because, although the teachers thought they were doing something effective (e.g., reprimanding or issuing a consequence for an inappropriate behavior), the students (who were starved for attention) were getting out of their seats, at least in part, to get their teachers to look at them and talk to them. The students' need for attention was satisfied when their teachers told them to get back in their seats—which they typically did, at least initially. This, of course, tended to reinforce the teachers for reprimanding. "Ah, now I can teach." But before long the students would realize, consciously or unconsciously, that they were not getting attention when they were doing what the teachers wanted, so they would get out of their seats again. The teachers would reprimand again, giving the desired attention, and the students were again reinforced for getting out of their seats.

This quickly becomes a destructive pattern in which everyone gets what they want in the short run. That is, the student gets attention when he violates the teacher's expectations. The teacher gets momentary compliance each time he reprimands. However, when this cycle is allowed to continue, no one gets what they want in the long run. Over time, students behave less and less responsibly and the teacher gets more frustrated and more negative. The only real way out of the "Criticism Trap" is to have more interactions with students when they are behaving responsibly than when they are misbehaving.

If you think you have fallen into the "Criticism Trap" or if you believe that your ratio of positive interactions to negative interactions with students is less than 3:1, consider implementing one or more of the following suggestions for increasing positive interactions. (NOTE: In addition to these suggestions on ways to increase the number of positive interactions with students, you might also want to review Module 7: Correction Procedures for information on how to reduce negative interactions.)

1. Each time you have a negative interaction with a student, tell yourself that you owe that student three positive interactions.

2. Identify specific times during each day that you will give students positive feedback on some aspect of their individual behavior or class performance. For example, you might decide that at the beginning of each math period, you will compliment five or six students.

3. Schedule individual conference times with students to compliment them on their behavioral or academic performances.

4. Make a point of periodically scanning your classroom, specifically "searching" for important reinforceable behaviors that you can acknowledge to students.

5. Identify particular events that occur during the day (e.g. a student getting a drink of water) that will prompt you to observe the class and identify a reinforceable behavior.

6. Make a point to reduce the amount of attention (time and intensity) a student receives for misbehavior and to increase the amount of attention (time and intensity) the student receives when not engaged in misbehavior.

7. Engage in frequent noncontingent positive interactions with the student(s).

In Module 6: Monitor and Revise, we provide suggestions on how you can periodically monitor your ratios of interactions to determine if you have fallen into the "Criticism Trap." For now, just be aware that the behaviors you pay the most attention to are the behaviors that are likely to occur with the most frequency as the year progresses. Consequently, we urge you to make a concerted effort to interact with every one of your students more frequently when the student is engaged in positive behavior than when he or she is engaged in negative behavior.

Level of Structure and Ratio of Positive to Negative Interactions

The higher the level of structure you have determined to be necessary for your students, the greater the probability that at least some of the students will be starved for attention. This, in turn, means that you are likely to have some students who will try to get their attention needs met via misbehavior, which can lead to a pattern of frequent nagging and reprimanding—and the classic spiral into the "Criticism Trap." Therefore, the greater your class' need for structure, the more you need to make an effort to maintain positive interactions at a very high level. That is, this task is *absolutely essential* for classes needing high structure. Maintaining a 3:1 ratio of positive to negative interactions is also important with low structure classes, but it is generally easier to do so because there isn't as much misbehavior to which you need to respond.

Module 5: Motivation

Self-Assessment Checklist

Use the worksheet on the following pages to identify which (or which parts) of the tasks described in this module you have completed. For any item that has not been completed, note what needs to be done to complete it. Then translate your notes onto your planning calendar in the form of specific actions that you can take (e.g., December 2, take time to reflect on how effective my instructional practices are).

COMPLETED	TASK	NOTES & IMPLEMENTATION IDEAS
	ENTHUSIASM I have determined specific ways that I will present tasks and/or behaviors to students, which will generate enthusiasm and intrinsic motivation on their part. These include, but are not limited to: • explaining how the task/behavior will be useful to students; • giving the students a vision of what they will be able to do; • relating the new task/behavior to previously learned skills; • rallying student enthusiasm and energy for the task/behavior; • other	
	EFFECTIVE INSTRUCTION I have identified one or two aspects of my presentation style that I will work to improve over the course of this year. I have made a plan for working on ways to actively involve students in lessons this year. I have determined specific ways in which I ensure that my lessons involve clear objectives and the content of the lessons is reflected in student evaluation instruments.	

COMPLETED	TASK	NOTES & IMPLEMENTATION IDEAS
	I have determined specific ways in which I ensure high rates of student success on tasks. I am prepared to give students immediate performance feedback.	
	NONCONTINGENT ATTENTION I have considered how I will provide each of my students with noncontingent attention—including, but not limited to: • greeting students; • showing an interest in student work; • inviting students to ask for assistance; • having conversations with students, when possible; • making a special effort to talk with any student with whom I interacted regarding misbehavior In my planning calendar, I have noted two to three times during the school year when I will review how well I am doing at providing all students with noncontingent attention.	
	POSITIVE FEEDBACK I have made a plan to ensure that I am incorporating the following characteristics into the positive feedback I give students regarding their academic and/or behavioral performance. • the feedback will be accurate • the feedback will be specific and descriptive • the feedback will be contingent • the feedback will be age-appropriate • the feedback will given in a manner that fits my personal style If any student seems to be responding to my positive feedback with an increase in inappropriate behavior, I am prepared to make modifications to the feedback I am giving.	

COMPLETED	TASK	NOTES & IMPLEMENTATION IDEAS
	INTERMITTENT CELEBRATIONS Based on the level of structure I have determined my students need, I will plan on using intermittent celebrations • rarely • occasionally • frequently I have identified (or have a plan for how I can identify) the kinds of "rewards" that are likely to be most useful with my students.	
	RATIO OF INTERACTIONS I understand how important it is for me to interact with each of my students at least three times more when they are behaving responsibly than when they are misbehaving. I will watch for any tendency on my part to fall into the "Criticism Trap."	

Module 5: Motivation

Peer Study Worksheet

With one or more of your colleagues, work through the following discussion topics and activities related to the tasks in Module 5. If necessary, refer back to the text to get additional ideas or for clarification. (See Module 1 Peer Study Worksheet for suggestions on structuring effective discussion sessions.)

Introduction:

A. As a group, discuss the classroom implications and/or examples of the following four concepts related to motivation:
   - When a particular behavior occurs repeatedly, it demonstrates a level of motivation on the part of the individual(s) to engage in that behavior; and when a particular behavior does not occur, it demonstrates a lack of motivation on the part of the individual(s) to engage in that behavior.
   - In most cases, when an individual engages in a particular behavior, it is prompted by a mix of intrinsic and extrinsic motivational factors.
   - A person's motivation to engage in a particular behavior is affected by the person's proficiency at that behavior.
   - Motivation can be thought of as the result of "Expectancy x Value."

Task 1: Enthusiasm

Have each group member give a specific example of how they will use each of the following strategies to generate student enthusiasm and increase students' intrinsic motivation to engage in desired tasks/behaviors.

- Explaining how the task/behavior will be useful to students.
- Giving the students a vision of what they will be able to do.
- Relating the new task/behavior to previously learned skills.
- Rallying student enthusiasm and energy for the task/behavior.
- Other

Task 2: Effective Instruction

A. Have each group member identify one or two aspects of their presentational style that they intend to work to improve over the course of the year.

B. As a group, create a list of ideas beyond those suggested in this program for actively involving students in lessons.

C. As a group, discuss the relationship among course content, course objectives, and course evaluation.

D. Have each group member describe what he or she will do to ensure high rates of student success.

E. Have each group member share the ways they give students timely performance feedback.

Task 3: Noncontingent Attention

A. Have each group member identify situations (e.g., times of day or types of activities) in which she or he provides noncontingent attention to several or many students.

B. Consider having group members pair up and observe each other for part of a day (e.g., the first ten minutes of the day as students arrive) in order to give each other feedback on the quantity and quality of the noncontingent attention they provide their students.

C. Discuss the feasibility and logistics of encouraging all staff members to make an effort to give individual students as much noncontingent attention as possible.

Task 4: Positive Feedback

A. Have each group member give specific positive and negative examples of positive feedback that reflects each of the following qualities:

- accurate;
- specific and descriptive;
- contingent;
- age-appropriate

B. Have one group member describe a student who reacts badly to positive feedback. As a group, discuss possible strategies.

Task 5: Intermittent Celebrations

A. Have each group member identify whether his or her class is likely to require a rare, moderate, or frequent use of intermittent celebrations to keep students motivated and enthusiastic. Have each person identify two or three reward ideas that would be appropriate for individual students in their class and two to three reward ideas that would be appropriate for the class as a whole.

Task 6: Ratio of Interactions

A. As a group, discuss the concept of the "Criticism Trap," and have individuals come up with specific examples from their experience where this may have been happening.

B. Have each group member identify the specific strategies he or she will employ to ensure that he or she will interact at least three times more often with each student when the student is behaving responsibly than when the student is misbehaving.

MODULE 6: MONITOR AND REVISE

When you monitor what is actually going on in your classroom, you are able to make adjustments to your Classroom Management Plan that will increase student success.

Introduction

This module presents no brand new concepts. Instead, we start by asking you to review your implementation of the following essential concepts that were presented in Modules 1, 2, 3, 4, and 5:

Module 1: Vision
Identifying long-range classroom goals and "Guidelines for Success" will ensure that you and your students know where you are headed.

Module 2: Organization
Establishing well-designed, efficient routines and procedures will prompt responsible and organized behavior from students.

Module 3: Expectations
Identifying and being prepared to teach exactly what you expect from your students during every activity and transition will ensure that students do not have to guess at what constitutes appropriate behavior.

Module 4: The First Month
Implementing the three-step process for communicating expectations allows you to help students learn what your expectations are and how to meet them, and whether they are/are not successfully exhibiting expected behaviors.

Module 5: Motivation
Interacting with every student at least three times more when she/he is behaving responsibly (through noncontingent attention and contingent praise) than when engaged in misbehavior, is one of the most powerful strategies you can employ to ensure a positive and productive classroom environment.

In addition to reflecting on how well you have implemented these important behavior management concepts, at this time you also need to consider:

- Which aspects of your classroom management plan are going well and should be maintained as is.
- Whether there are one or more problem areas indicating that you need to make adjustments in your management plan.
- Whether the level of classroom structure you are currently using should be maintained or revised.

To help you with your decisions about the preceding issues, this module includes a variety of tools for collecting and evaluating objective information (i.e., data) about what is actually occurring in your classroom. Without accurate information, your decisions are likely to be based on hunches, guesses, and/or whatever feels right at the moment. We believe that one of the requirements of professionalism is making informed decisions based on objective information. We'll use another example from the medical profession to explain what we mean.

When you go in for a routine physical examination, your doctor gathers a variety of information—pulse, respiration, blood pressure, urinalysis, cholesterol levels, and so on. Then your doctor evalutes the objective information she has gathered, along with your subjective reports about how you feel, and makes a judgment about your overall health. She may decide that you are just fine, or she may recommend that additional information be collected, or she may suggest that a treatment plan be implemented. Without the objective data, your doctor would be less able to accurately assess your overall health or make useful recommendations regarding your health care options.

The information-gathering tools in this module are designed to give you objective information about the overall "health" of your current Classroom Management Plan. They include the following:

Tool 1: *CHAMPs* versus Daily Reality Rating Scale
This tool allows you to look at each major activity and transition during your day, and evaluate (on a five-point scale) how well students meet your *CHAMPs* expectations for that activity or transition. With the information you get, you will be able to decide whether you need to reteach your *CHAMPs* expectations and/or modify the level of structure you have selected as most appropriate for your students. We suggest that you monitor this

particular aspect of your classroom management plan (i.e., the actual implementation of your *CHAMPs* expectations) several times per year.

Tool 2: Ratio of Interactions Monitoring Form(s)
There are actually three different versions of this tool for determining whether you have fallen into the "Criticism Trap" (i.e., you are inadvertently paying so much attention to student misbehavior that you could actually be perpetuating some misbehavior). The primary form involves documenting your interactions with students during a particular period of time. You can use the supplementary forms to document interactions with a specific student or relative to a specific behavior.

Tool 3: Misbehavior Recording Sheet
Keeping a systematic record of your students' misbehavior for one day (elementary teachers) or for one week (middle school teachers) can help you determine whether the level of structure for your management plan needs adjusting and/or whether one or more of your students (or the whole class) would benefit from a targeted behavior management plan or classwide motivation system. We have included four different versions of this tool so that you can choose the one that will allow you to most easily record misbehavior that occurs in your classroom.

Tool 4: Gradebook Analysis Worksheet
An up-to-date gradebook is a wealth of data. We show you how to compile and analyze the existing data in your gradebook to determine whether individual students are exhibiting chronic problems with absenteeism, tardiness, work completion, or assignment failure. You can use the information from your analysis to make judgments about whether any individual student, or the class as a whole, would benefit from the implementation of a behavior management plan that targets one or more of these problems.

Tool 5: On-Task Behavior Observation Sheet
This simple tool can be used to determine your class' average rate of on-task behavior during independent work times. If students are on task less than 80% of the time, you need to reteach your *CHAMPs* expectations for work periods and/or implement some form of classwide incentive system that will encourage students to use class work times more productively.

Tool 6: Family/Student Satisfaction Survey
Just as many businesses find it worthwhile to look at "customer satisfaction," we believe that you can benefit from knowing how "satisfied" your students and their families are with your classroom. This is a short survey that can be given to families (to discuss with their students) at the end of the year and/or during the year. The information will help you identify whether there are aspects of your classroom management plan that you need to communicate more clearly or do differently.

You are much more likely to use these tools if you build their implementation into your schedule. Therefore, right now STOP AND WRITE THE FOLLOWING PROMPTS IN YOUR PLANNING CALENDAR! Write each prompt on or near the suggested date (although you want to avoid specific dates that are already scheduled for other major activities such as field trips or schoolwide testing).

As the year progresses and you come to a particular prompt on your calendar, go to the specified page(s) in this book and follow the directions for collecting and analyzing the data. For right now, just skim through the rest of this module to familiarize yourself with the included tools. At this point you only need a minimal familiarity with each tool. However, when it is time to actually use a particular tool, plan on carefully reviewing the specific instructions for that tool.

Week 3	Student Interviews or Quiz (Module 4, Task 3)
Week 4 or 5	*CHAMPs* versus Daily Reality Rating (Module 6, Tool 1)
2nd Month	Ratio of Interactions Monitoring (Module 6, Tool 2)
3rd Month (early)	Misbehavior(s) Recording (Module 6, Tool 3)
3rd Month (late)	Gradebook Analysis (Module 6, Tool 4)
4th month	On-Task Behavior Recording (Module 6, Tool 5)
January (early)	*CHAMPs* versus Daily Reality Rating (Module 6, Tool 1)
January (late)	Misbehavior(s) Recording (Module 6, Tool 3)
February (early)	Ratio of Interactions Monitoring (Module 6, Tool 2)
February (late)	On-Task Behavior Recording (Module 6, Tool 5)
March (early)	Gradebook Analysis (Module 6, Tool 4)
April (after spring break)	CHAMPs versus Daily Reality Rating (Module 6, Tool 1)
Last two weeks	Family/Student Satisfaction Survey (Module 6, Tool 6)

Even if you have started the *CHAMPs* program *during* the school year, you can still use the preceding timeline. From today's date, identify the next recommended evaluation activity. Write it, and all the activities suggested for the remainder of the year, on your planning calendar. Implement those activities at the appropriate times.

NOTE

Module 6 does not have a Self-Assessment Checklist because the whole module itself involves self-assessment. Although there is no Peer Discussion Worksheet for this module, we recommend that you share ideas and suggestions regarding the information and tools presented in the module with colleagues.

Tool 1: *CHAMPs* versus Daily Reality Rating Scale

Directions for Use

Determine the degree to which student behavior during daily activities and transitions matches your CHAMPs expectations.

WHY:

- To help you decide whether you need to reteach your *CHAMPs* expectations.
- To help you decide whether your current level of structure fits the needs of your class.
- To help you decide whether you might need some kind of classwide system to increase students' motivation to behave responsibly.

WHEN:

- During the fourth or fifth week of school.
- Shortly after major vacations (e.g., winter and spring breaks).

HOW:

1. Make a copy (or copies) of the appropriate reproducible forms shown in Figures 6.2 and 6.3.
2. Identify (from your plan book or daily schedule) the major activities and transitions that occur during a typical school day, and write each activity and transition on the "Activity" line in one of the form's rating boxes. (See Figure 6.1).

Figure 6.1: Sample from CHAMPs Rating Scale

CONVERSATION	1	2	3	4	5
HELP (TEACHER ATTENTION)	1	2	3	4	5
ACTIVITY *Before the bell*					
MOVEMENT	1	2	3	4	5
PARTICIPATION	1	2	3	4	5

CONVERSATION	1	2	3	4	5
HELP (TEACHER ATTENTION)	1	2	3	4	5
ACTIVITY *Opening/Attend.*					
MOVEMENT	1	2	3	4	5
PARTICIPATION	1	2	3	4	5

CONVERSATION	1	2	3	4	5
HELP (TEACHER ATTENTION)	1	2	3	4	5
ACTIVITY *Teacher Directed*					
MOVEMENT	1	2	3	4	5
PARTICIPATION	1	2	3	4	5

CONVERSATION	1	2	3	4	5
HELP (TEACHER ATTENTION)	1	2	3	4	5
ACTIVITY *Independent Work Period - Math*					
MOVEMENT	1	2	3	4	5
PARTICIPATION	1	2	3	4	5

NOTES

- *Elementary teachers may need several pages, and may wish to spread this evaluation activity across several days. For example, one day the morning activities and transitions could be evaluated, and the next day the afternoon activities could be evaluated.*
- *Middle school teachers should complete a rating scale for each of their classes. You may want to spread this across several days. For example, one day you might conduct the evaluation for first and second periods; the next day, for third and fourth periods; and the third day, for fifth and sixth periods.*

3. Before each activity or transition, briefly review your *CHAMPs* expectations with students (if necessary). Then, immediately after completing the activity/transition, rate the degree to which students met your expectations, using the following rating scale:

   5 = All students met expectations

   4 = All but one or two students met expectations

   3 = Most students met expectations

   2 = About half the class met expectations

   1 = Most students did not meet expectations

NOTE

Some teachers may want to involve students in the rating process. If you choose to do this, explain the purpose and procedures to students ahead of time. Be sure to tell students that their input should have NO references to individual students who did not meet expectations. A reproducible master of an enlarged rating form is provided (see Figure 6.3). It can be used as an overhead transparency if you plan to involve your class in the rating process.

Review the data you have collected and determine which activities or transitions may require re-teaching of expectations. In addition, consider the following information as you interpret your data.

- If all the activities and transitions rated a "4" or a "5," keep doing what you are doing. NOTE: If you wish to give an extra boost to students, you might consider implementing one or more of the classroom motivational systems appropriate for a Low Structure classroom (see Module 8). If you have one or two students whose behavior concerns you, you may need to consider individual behavior management plans (see *Teacher's Encyclopedia of Behavior Management* for suggestions).
- If at least 70% of activities and transitions rated a "4" or a "5," it may be a good idea to implement one or more of the classwide motivation systems appropriate for a Medium Structure classroom (see Module 8). If you have one or two students whose behavior concerns you, you may need to consider individual behavior management plans (see *Teacher's Encyclopedia of Behavior Management* for suggestions).
- If fewer than 70% of activities and transitions rated a "4" or a "5," you should probably implement one or more of the classwide motivation systems appropriate for a High Structure classroom (see Module 8).
- If fewer than 50% of activities and transitions with a "4" or a "5," we recommend implementing one of the classwide systems for a High Structure class and at least two systems appropriate for a Medium Structure class (see Module 8).

Following the two reproducible forms, Figure 6.4 shows a completed sample *CHAMPs* v. Daily Reality Rating Scale—with a brief analysis of its results.

Figure 6.2: Reproducible

CHAMPs versus Daily Reality Rating Scale

Teacher Name: ______________________________ Date: ______________________

Ratings
5 = All students met expectations
4 = All but one or two students met expectations
3 = Most students met expectations
2 = About half the class met expectations
1 = Most students did not meet expectations

CONVERSATION	1	2	3	4	5
HELP (TEACHER ATTENTION)	1	2	3	4	5
ACTIVITY:					
MOVEMENT	1	2	3	4	5
PARTICIPATION	1	2	3	4	5

CONVERSATION	1	2	3	4	5
HELP (TEACHER ATTENTION)	1	2	3	4	5
ACTIVITY:					
MOVEMENT	1	2	3	4	5
PARTICIPATION	1	2	3	4	5

CONVERSATION	1	2	3	4	5
HELP (TEACHER ATTENTION)	1	2	3	4	5
ACTIVITY:					
MOVEMENT	1	2	3	4	5
PARTICIPATION	1	2	3	4	5

CONVERSATION	1	2	3	4	5
HELP (TEACHER ATTENTION)	1	2	3	4	5
ACTIVITY:					
MOVEMENT	1	2	3	4	5
PARTICIPATION	1	2	3	4	5

CONVERSATION	1	2	3	4	5
HELP (TEACHER ATTENTION)	1	2	3	4	5
ACTIVITY:					
MOVEMENT	1	2	3	4	5
PARTICIPATION	1	2	3	4	5

CONVERSATION	1	2	3	4	5
HELP (TEACHER ATTENTION)	1	2	3	4	5
ACTIVITY:					
MOVEMENT	1	2	3	4	5
PARTICIPATION	1	2	3	4	5

CONVERSATION	1	2	3	4	5
HELP (TEACHER ATTENTION)	1	2	3	4	5
ACTIVITY:					
MOVEMENT	1	2	3	4	5
PARTICIPATION	1	2	3	4	5

CONVERSATION	1	2	3	4	5
HELP (TEACHER ATTENTION)	1	2	3	4	5
ACTIVITY:					
MOVEMENT	1	2	3	4	5
PARTICIPATION	1	2	3	4	5

CONVERSATION	1	2	3	4	5
HELP (TEACHER ATTENTION)	1	2	3	4	5
ACTIVITY:					
MOVEMENT	1	2	3	4	5
PARTICIPATION	1	2	3	4	5

CONVERSATION	1	2	3	4	5
HELP (TEACHER ATTENTION)	1	2	3	4	5
ACTIVITY:					
MOVEMENT	1	2	3	4	5
PARTICIPATION	1	2	3	4	5

Figure 6.3: Reproducible

CHAMPs versus Daily Reality Rating Scale

5 = All students met expectations
4 = All but one or two students met expectations
3 = Most students met expectations
2 = About half the class met expectations
1 = Most students did not meet expectations

C ONVERSATION	1 2 3 4 5
H ELP (**T** EACHER **A** TTENTION)	1 2 3 4 5
A CTIVITY:	
M OVEMENT	1 2 3 4 5
P ARTICIPATION	1 2 3 4 5

C ONVERSATION	1 2 3 4 5
H ELP (**T** EACHER **A** TTENTION)	1 2 3 4 5
A CTIVITY:	
M OVEMENT	1 2 3 4 5
P ARTICIPATION	1 2 3 4 5

C ONVERSATION	1 2 3 4 5
H ELP (**T** EACHER **A** TTENTION)	1 2 3 4 5
A CTIVITY:	
M OVEMENT	1 2 3 4 5
P ARTICIPATION	1 2 3 4 5

C ONVERSATION	1 2 3 4 5
H ELP (**T** EACHER **A** TTENTION)	1 2 3 4 5
A CTIVITY:	
M OVEMENT	1 2 3 4 5
P ARTICIPATION	1 2 3 4 5

Figure 6.4: Completed Sample

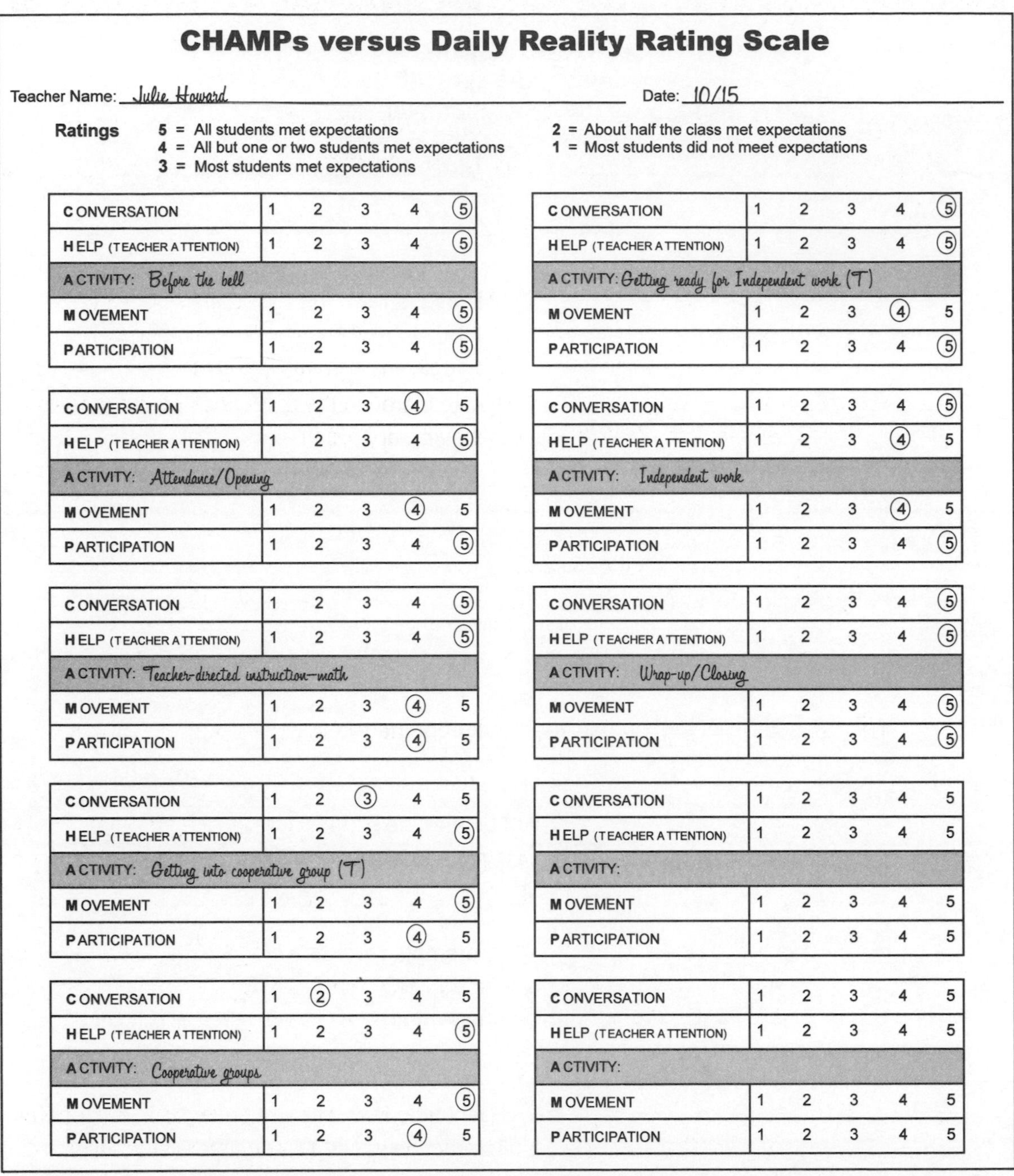

CHAMPs versus Daily Reality Rating Scale

Teacher Name: Julie Howard Date: 10/15

Ratings
5 = All students met expectations
4 = All but one or two students met expectations
3 = Most students met expectations
2 = About half the class met expectations
1 = Most students did not meet expectations

(Circled ratings shown in parentheses.)

ACTIVITY: Before the bell					
CONVERSATION	1	2	3	4	(5)
HELP (TEACHER ATTENTION)	1	2	3	4	(5)
MOVEMENT	1	2	3	4	(5)
PARTICIPATION	1	2	3	4	(5)

ACTIVITY: Getting ready for Independent work (T)					
CONVERSATION	1	2	3	4	(5)
HELP (TEACHER ATTENTION)	1	2	3	4	(5)
MOVEMENT	1	2	3	(4)	5
PARTICIPATION	1	2	3	4	(5)

ACTIVITY: Attendance/Opening					
CONVERSATION	1	2	3	(4)	5
HELP (TEACHER ATTENTION)	1	2	3	4	(5)
MOVEMENT	1	2	3	(4)	5
PARTICIPATION	1	2	3	4	(5)

ACTIVITY: Independent work					
CONVERSATION	1	2	3	4	(5)
HELP (TEACHER ATTENTION)	1	2	3	(4)	5
MOVEMENT	1	2	3	(4)	5
PARTICIPATION	1	2	3	4	(5)

ACTIVITY: Teacher-directed instruction—math					
CONVERSATION	1	2	3	4	(5)
HELP (TEACHER ATTENTION)	1	2	3	4	(5)
MOVEMENT	1	2	3	(4)	5
PARTICIPATION	1	2	3	(4)	5

ACTIVITY: Wrap-up/Closing					
CONVERSATION	1	2	3	4	(5)
HELP (TEACHER ATTENTION)	1	2	3	4	(5)
MOVEMENT	1	2	3	4	(5)
PARTICIPATION	1	2	3	4	(5)

ACTIVITY: Getting into cooperative group (T)					
CONVERSATION	1	2	(3)	4	5
HELP (TEACHER ATTENTION)	1	2	3	4	(5)
MOVEMENT	1	2	3	4	(5)
PARTICIPATION	1	2	3	(4)	5

ACTIVITY:					
CONVERSATION	1	2	3	4	5
HELP (TEACHER ATTENTION)	1	2	3	4	5
MOVEMENT	1	2	3	4	5
PARTICIPATION	1	2	3	4	5

ACTIVITY: Cooperative groups					
CONVERSATION	1	(2)	3	4	5
HELP (TEACHER ATTENTION)	1	2	3	4	(5)
MOVEMENT	1	2	3	4	(5)
PARTICIPATION	1	2	3	(4)	5

ACTIVITY:					
CONVERSATION	1	2	3	4	5
HELP (TEACHER ATTENTION)	1	2	3	4	5
MOVEMENT	1	2	3	4	5
PARTICIPATION	1	2	3	4	5

Analysis:
In this sample, only one activity (Cooperative Groups) and one transition (Getting into Cooperative Groups) have ratings that are less than 4s and 5s. The teacher realizes that the main problem is students talking too loudly so the noise level in the room is excessive. Therefore, she decides to leave her classroom level of structure as it is—Low Structure. However, she also plans to reteach her behavioral expectations, particularly emphasizing how students in each cooperative group can monitor and manage the voice levels within their own groups.

Tool 2: Ratio of Interactions Monitoring Form(s)

Information

Determine whether you are interacting with students at least three times more when they are behaving responsibly than when they are misbehaving.

WHY:

- To help you evaluate whether you have fallen into the "Criticism Trap"—i.e., whether you are responding so frequently to misbehavior that, although the behavior stops in the short run, it is actually increasing over time.
- To help you decide whether you need to increase the number of interactions you have with students when they are behaving appropriately.

WHEN:

- During the second month of school.
- In early to mid-February.

HOW:

1. Make a copy (or copies) of the appropriate reproducible forms in Figures 6.5, 6.6, and 6.7

2. Make sure you thoroughly understand the difference between "positive interactions" with students and "negative interactions" with students. Review the following:

   a) It is the student behavior that prompts the interaction (or that is occurring at the time the interaction is initiated), NOT THE TONE OF THE INTERACTION, that determines whether an interaction is positive or negative.

   b) When you interact with a student who is or has just engaged in appropriate (or desirable) behavior, the interaction would be counted as **Attention to Positive**. Examples include:

Praise	"Owen, you have been using this work time very efficiently and have accomplished a great deal."
Noncontingent attention	"Charlene, how are you today?"
Implementing a positive system	"Theresa and Josh both earned a marble in the jar for the class. They worked out a disagreement without needing my help."

NOTE

This would be counted as two positive interactions because the teacher gave attention to two different students.

c. When you interact with a student who is exhibiting or has just exhibited an inappropriate (or undesirable) behavior, the interaction should be recorded as **Attention to Negative**. Examples include:

Reminders	"Cody, you need to get back to work."
Reprimands	"Hanna, you know that you should be keeping your hands to yourself."
Corrections	"Ty, I don't think you need to tell me about that because I think you can handle that on your own."
Warnings	"Jennifer, if I have to speak to you again about talking in class, I will have to call your mother."
Consequences	"Adam, that is disruptive. You owe one minute off recess."

3. Determine a time of day (approximately 30 minutes) during which you seem to have the most trouble being positive with students, and arrange to record (either audio tape or videotape) that time period for one day.

4. Listen to (or watch) the recording and mark your interactions on the Ratio of Interactions Monitoring Form. To do this, make a tally mark under "Attention to Positive" for each interaction you had with a student (or the class) when the behavior was responsible. Make a tally mark under "Attention to Negative" for each interaction you had with a student (or the class) when the behavior was irresponsible. Do not mark instructions to the group (e.g., "Class, open your books to page 133.") at all. However, do count an instruction to an individual student (e.g., "Beth, please turn out the lights.") as positive if the student was behaving responsibly at the time and negative if the student was misbehaving.

If you wish to get more detailed information, consider using codes instead of simple tally marks for each interaction. For example:

M or F	=	brief attention to an individual male or female student
C	=	brief attention to the class or a group
F/15	=	attention to an individual female lasting approximately 15 seconds
NC	=	Noncontingent attention to an individual (e.g. "Good Morning")
NV	=	Nonverbal attention (e.g. a reassuring smile or a threatening look)

5. Calculate your ratio of positive interactions with students to negative interactions with students. (If you coded your interactions—e.g., by gender, type of instructional activity, specific type of attention, etc.—calculate separate ratios for each category.)

6. Analyze your performance.

- Evaluate whether you achieved an overall 3:1 ratio of positives to negatives.
- Evaluate whether your ratio of positives to negatives varies by category (e.g., it's lower with females than males).
- Evaluate the overall style of your interactions (e.g., corrections too harsh, praise too friendly or insincere-sounding), and whether or not you are comfortable with it.
- Evaluate the contingency of the positive feedback you give to individual students.
- Evaluate whether one or two individuals received most of the negative interactions. If so, plan to use the Ratio of Interactions Monitoring Form (With a Particular Student).
- Evaluate if you had to correct a particular category of behavior (for example, off-task talking) more frequently than other problems. If so, use the Ratio of Interactions Monitoring Form (Regarding a Particular Behavior).

7. Plan a course of action.

- If your overall interactions, or any subset of interactions, do not reflect a 3:1 (positive to negative) ratio, use the strategies following the reproducible forms and make an effort to both decrease attention to negative behavior and increase attention to positive behavior. After approximately two weeks, monitor your interactions again to see if you have achieved the desired 3:1 ratio.

- Once you have successfully modified your ratios, check for an improvement in student behavior. If students are behaving better, congratulate yourself and keep up the good work. If they are not, re-read Module 5: Motivation Procedures, to see if there are any variables regarding student motivation that you have not implemented. In addition, read Module 8: Classwide Motivation Systems, to determine whether a motivation system might be appropriate.

NOTE

Following the blank reproducible Monitoring Interactions forms, Figure 6.8 shows a completed sample form—with a brief analysis of its results.

Figure 6.5: Reproducible

Ratio of Interactions Monitoring Form

(During a Particular Time of Day)

Teacher: ______________________________ Date: ______________

Time of Day: ______________________________

Coding System Used (if any)

Attention to Positive	Attention to Negative

Analysis and Plan of Action:

Figure 6.6: Reproducible

Ratio of Interactions Monitoring Form

(With a Particular Student)

Teacher: ______________________________ Date: ______________

Student's Name: ______________________________

Coding System Used (e.g., to indicate specific activities or transitions)

Note *every* interaction you have with the student

Attention to Positive (Praise and/or non-contingent attention)	Attention to Negative

Analysis and Plan of Action:

Figure 6.7: Reproducible

Ratio of Interactions Monitoring Form

(Regarding a Particular Behavior)

Teacher: ______________________________ Date: ______________

Behavior: ____

Coding System Used (e.g., to indicate gender, activity)

Label the positive and negative behavior that will be monitored (e.g., Attention to Respect and Attention to Disrespect.)

ATTENTION TO POSITIVE	ATTENTION TO NEGATIVE
______________________ (BEHAVIOR LABEL)	______________________ (BEHAVIOR LABEL)

NOTE: Decide if you will use a "Public Posting" (see Module 5) monitoring system, or if you wish to keep a less obtrusive record (e.g., marks made on a clipboard).

Analysis and Plan of Action:

Figure 6.8: Completed Sample

Ratio of Interactions Monitoring Form

(During a Particular Time of Day)

Teacher: Mrs. Hammond Date: October 12

Time of Day: 9:30 to 10:45

Coding System Used (if any)
M = Male
F = Female
N = Nick
C = Class (as a whole)

Attention to Positive	Attention to Negative
M, M, M, F, M, F F, C, F, N, F, M C, M, M, N, F, M	N, N, M, N, F, F, N N, C, M, M, N

Analysis and Plan of Action:

My overall ratio is 1.5:1 so I need to decrease negatives and increase positives to get to 3:1 ratios. (If Nick's data is pulled out, I am almost at 3:1!!)

My interactions with Nick are 1:3 (negative) so I should work on this and monitor my interactions with Nick in a week.

I think my feedback was fine in terms of clarity and style.

INCREASING POSITIVE INTERACTIONS

As necessary, implement one or more of the following strategies:

a. Each time you have a negative interaction, remind yourself that you "owe" three positives.

b. Identify specific times during each day that you will give individual students (or the whole class) positive feedback on some aspect of their behavior or class performance. For example, at the beginning of the math lesson, you might compliment five or six students.

c. Use individual conference times (discussed in the previous session) to compliment individual students on their performance.

d. Frequently scan the room and "search" for important reinforceable behaviors.

e. Identify particular events that occur during the day (e.g. a student getting a drink of water) that will serve as a prompt to observe the class and identify a reinforceable behavior.

f. Reduce the amount of attention (time and intensity) the student receives for misbehavior. Increase the amount of attention (time and intensity) the student receives when not engaged in misbehavior.

g. Interact with the student(s) frequently with noncontingent positives.

DECREASING NEGATIVE INTERACTIONS

As necessary, implement one or more of the following strategies.

a. Identify whether there are aspects of the physical setting, schedule, organization, and so on that you might modify to reduce the probability that students will misbehave. For example, if some students push others in the rush to get out the door, excuse the students by rows or table groups.

b. Try "precorrecting" a misbehavior before it occurs. For example, if you anticipate that students will push each other while leaving the classroom, give a prompt like, "Remember to keep your hands and feet to yourself as you are leaving the room when I excuse the class."

c. Try praising someone doing it the "right way" and intervene only if the misbehaving student does not change the behavior.

NOTE

Your goal is not to eliminate all negative interactions. Some are essential. For example, if a student does not know that a particular behavior is not acceptable, a gentle correction is the most direct and efficient way to provide the information the student needs to be successful. Or, if you have a pre-established corrective consequence for a particular behavior, you must intervene anytime a student exhibits that behavior in order to maintain consistency.

Tool 3: Misbehavior Recording Sheet

Information

Determine whether you need to implement an intervention plan or plans to deal with specific types of student misbehavior.

WHY:

- To help you identify how often, and for what, you are intervening with students regarding their inappropriate behaviors.
- To help you detect any patterns to students' misbehavior (e.g., times of day, day of week, individual students who never misbehave, etc.).
- To give you specific and objective information about individual students' behavior that you can share with the students and their families, if necessary.
- To help you decide whether you might need some kind of classwide system to increase students' motivation to behave responsibly.

WHEN:

- During the early part of the third month of school.
- In mid- to late-January.

HOW:

1. Choose one of the four reproducible forms shown in Figures 6.10, 6.11, 6.12, and 6.13, and make a copy (or copies) of it. (NOTE: You may wish to design your own form.)

   - The first form (Figure 6.10) is a daily record of misbehavior, by hour, organized by student name. This form is appropriate for an elementary teacher. NOTE: If you wish, you can change the headings (i.e., 1st hour, 2nd hour) to reflect particular activities (e.g., math, reading). The idea is for the columns to reflect meaningful divisions in the school day so you can analyze whether certain times/subjects have a greater preponderance of misbehavior.

   - The second form (Figure 6.11) is a weekly record of misbehavior, by day, organized by student name. This form is probably most appropriate for a middle school teacher, who would need one form for each class that will be monitored.

- The third and fourth forms (Figures 6.12 and 6.13) are daily and weekly records of misbehavior (respectively), organized by student seating when desks are arranged in rows, with each square representing a desk. Elementary teachers would use the daily form and use the horizontal lines within a square for individual class activities. Middle school teachers would use the weekly form (one form per class period) and use the horizontal lines within a square for days of the week. Figure 6.9 shows a sample of both elementary and middle school uses for the forms provided in Figures 6.12 and 6.13. (NOTE: If desks are arranged in clusters or a U-shape, you will have to create your form.)

Figure 6.9: Completed Sample of Misbehavior Recording Sheet

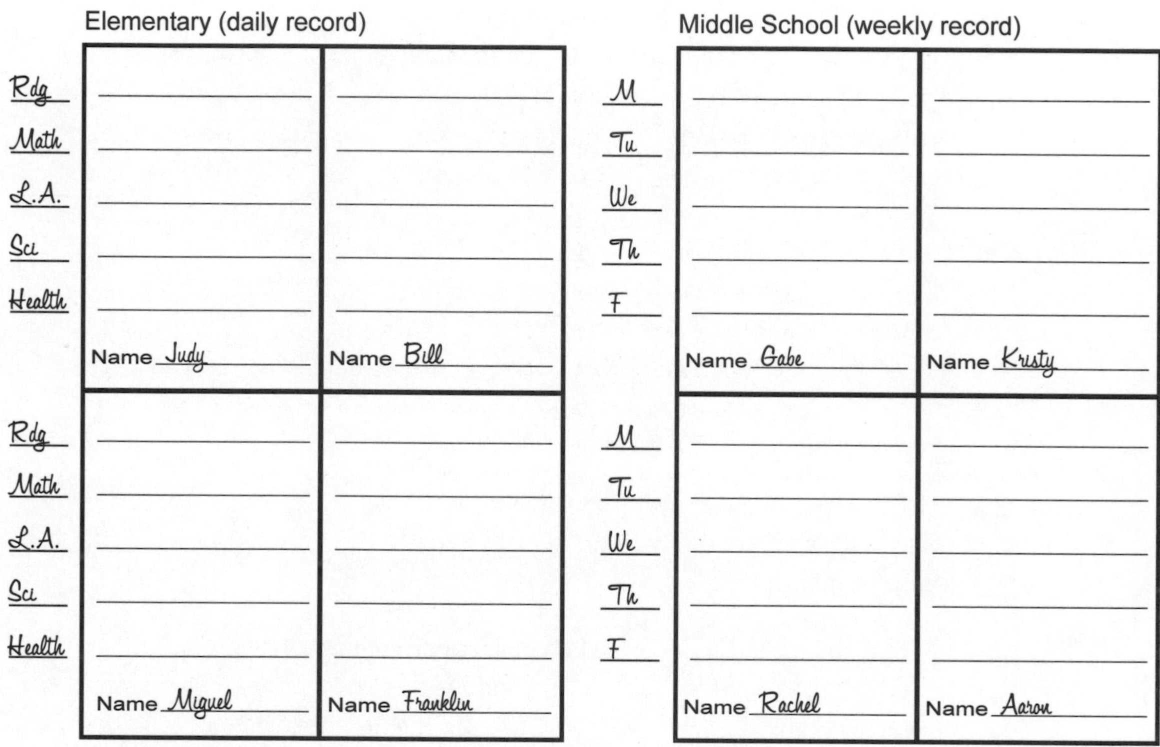

MIDDLE SCHOOL TEACHERS AND ELEMENTARY SCHOOL SPECIALISTS:

You need to decide whether to use a Misbehavior Recording Sheet in one, two, or all of your classes. We recommend doing it with all classes for at least one full week; however, you might try it initially with just one class for a week (probably the class with the most misbehavior). If you find the information useful, you can plan how/when to use the tool with the rest of your classes.

2. Put the appropriate Misbehavior Recording Sheet on a clipboard and plan to keep the clipboard close by for the entire day (if you are an elementary

teacher), or for five days of a particular class period (if you are a middle school teacher).

3. Explain to students that for the entire day (or the next five class periods), you will be recording anytime you have to speak to someone or the whole class about inappropriate behavior.

4. Whenever you speak to a student about a misbehavior, note the specific misbehavior on the form using a coding system such as the following:

O =	Off task	H =	Hands/feet/objects bothering others
T =	Talking	D =	Disruption
S =	Out of seat at wrong time	A =	Arguing

(Build your code so that you have a different letter for each type of major misbehavior you think is likely to happen.)

NOTE

It may appear that you will spend all your time recording. However, remember that you are only going to mark one letter each time you have to speak to a student about misbehavior (it takes about two seconds). The hardest part of this task is not the time involved, but remembering to keep the form near you when you are teaching and while you are circulating throughout the room.

Analyze the data and determine a plan of action.

- You may find that the behavior of some students improves simply because you are keeping records. If so, consider using the Misbehavior Recording Sheet on an ongoing basis. This data will be very useful for discussing behavior with students and their families, determining citizenship grades, and making decisions about your Classroom Behavior Plan.

- Make a subjective decision regarding your level of concern about the amount of misbehavior that is occurring. If you are unconcerned (i.e., the amount of misbehavior is so low that it is not interfering with student learning), do not bother making any changes.

- If you are concerned about the amount of misbehavior in your class, analyze the data from the Misbehavior Record Sheet further. First, determine how much of the misbehavior is exhibited by just a few students. Identify the three students who had the most frequent incidents of misbehavior and calculate the percentage of the total class misbehavior that could be attributed to those students (i.e., divide the total number of misbehaviors exhibited by the three students by the total number of misbehaviors exhibited by the entire class). For example, if the three students' total for two days was 45 and the total for the rest of the students was 16, you would divide 45 by 61 to get a percentage of 74%.

- Once you have identified the percentage of misbehavior exhibited by the top three misbehaving students, use the following criteria to determine the most appropriate action.
  - If more than 90% of the total classroom misbehavior can be attributed to the three individual students, keep your level of structure and procedures as they are. For the one, two, or three individuals with the most misbehavior, consider implementing individual behavior management plans.
  - If 60% to 89% of the total classroom misbehavior can be attributed to the three individuals, review your level of classroom structure and implement one or more classroom motivation systems (appropriate for medium structure). See Module 8. In addition, consider individual behavior management plans for the students whose behavior is the most problematic.
  - If less than 60% of the misbehavior can be attributed to the three individuals (i.e., the problem is classwide), review and implement all the suggestions for high structure classrooms in Modules 1, 2, 3, 4, 5, and 7. In addition, carefully read the information in Module 8 and arrange to implement one or more of the classwide systems appropriate for high structure classrooms.

Following the four reproducible forms, Figure 6.14 shows a completed sample Misbehavior Recording Sheet—with a brief analysis of its results.

Figure 6.10: Reproducible

Misbehavior Recording Sheet

(Daily by Student Name)

Date: ____________________ Reminders: ____

Name	1st Hour	2nd Hour	3rd Hour	5th Hour	6th Hour	Total

Codes:

Figure 6.11: Reproducible

Misbehavior Recording Sheet

(Weekly by Student Name)

Date: ______________________ Reminders: ____

____

NAME	MON.	TUES.	WED.	THURS.	FRI.	TOTAL

Codes:

Figure 6.12: Reproducible

Misbehavior Recording Sheet (Daily by Seating Chart)

Name	Name	Name	Name	Name
Name	Name	Name	Name	Name
Name	Name	Name	Name	Name
Name	Name	Name	Name	Name
Name	Name	Name	Name	Name
Name	Name	Name	Name	Name

Figure 6.13: Reproducible

Misbehavior Recording Sheet
(Weekly by Seating Chart)

Mon					
Tues					
Wed					
Thurs					
Fri					
	Name	Name	Name	Name	Name
Mon					
Tues					
Wed					
Thurs					
Fri					
	Name	Name	Name	Name	Name
Mon					
Tues					
Wed					
Thurs					
Fri					
	Name	Name	Name	Name	Name
Mon					
Tues					
Wed					
Thurs					
Fri					
	Name	Name	Name	Name	Name
Mon					
Tues					
Wed					
Thurs					
Fri					
	Name	Name	Name	Name	Name
Mon					
Tues					
Wed					
Thurs					
Fri					
	Name	Name	Name	Name	Name

Figure 6.14: Completed Sample

Misbehavior Recording Sheet

(Weekly by Student Name)

Date: 11-3 Reminders: On Wed. remind about Fri. test

Class Period: 2

Name	Mon.	Tues.	Wed.	Thurs	Fri.	Total
Anderson, Chantel				T		1
Bakena, Ruben						0
Bell, Justin						0
Carranza, Melinda		T		T	T	3
Cummings, Teresa						0
Demalski, Lee			T			1
Diaz, Margo						0
Etienne, Jerry						0
Fujiyama, Kim						0
Grover, Matthew						0
Henry, Scott	D D T	D O		D T	T	8
Isaacson, Chris						0
Kaufman, Jamie				D		1
King, Mark						0
LaRouche, Janel				T		1
Morales, Maria Louisa				T		1
Narlin, Jenny						0
Neely, Jacob			O	O		2
Nguyen, Trang						0
Ogren, Todd	T T D	D	O O	T	T T	9
Pallant, Jared						0
Piercey, Dawn			T	O	T	3
Reavis, Myra						0
Thomason, Rahsaan	T T		T	T	T T	6
Vandever, Aaron						0
Wong, Charlene						0
Yamamoto, Junko		T		O T		3

Codes: D - Disruption
O - Off task
T - Talking

Analysis and Plan of Action

Scott Henry, Todd Ogren, and Rahsaan Thomason are the students with the most misbehaviors. Together they had a total of 23 misbehaviors for the week. The whole class total (including the three) was 39. That means the misbehaviors of these three students accounted for approximately 59% of the total class misbehavior. This suggests that a medium level of structure is appropriate for the class, which is what the teacher currently had in place. The teacher decided that she needed a classwide motivation system, so she reviewed the information and menu of systems in Module 8. She decided to implement the 100 Squares system. With this system, the teacher will be on the lookout for times when the entire class is behaving responsibly. At such times, she'll have a student draw a number from a jar (like Bingo) and will cross out (or color in) the corresponding number on the 100 square chart. When a whole row of the chart is filled in—across, up or down, or diagonally—the entire class gets a reward. The teacher will also teach the class strategies for gently correcting classmates who are engaging in misbehavior.

Tool 4: Gradebook Analysis Worksheet

Information

Determine whether student tardiness rates, attendance rates, work completion rates, and work quality are satisfactory.

WHY:

- To help you decide whether you need to implement a plan to improve:
- Student punctuality rates; and/or
- Student attendance rates; and/or
- Student work completion rates; and/or
- The quality of student work.

WHEN:

- During the third month of school.
- In early- to mid-March.

HOW:

1. Make a copy (or copies) of the reproducible form shown in Figure 6.15.

2. Calculate rates of punctuality, attendance, work completion, and work quality for each student in your class and record them on a Gradebook Analysis Worksheet.

    - To calculate the punctuality rate for each student, divide the actual number of days the student arrived on time to your class by the total number of days school has been in session through that date.

    - To calculate the attendance rate for each student, divide the actual number of days the student has been at school by the total number of days school has been in session through that date.

    - To calculate the rate of work completion for each student, divide the actual number of in-class and homework assignments the student has turned in by the total number of in-class assignments that have been due through that date.*

    - To calculate the percentage of Quality Work, first determine what you consider to be quality work. You could define quality as any assignment with a passing grade or above (i.e., grades of "D" and above, or you may prefer to define quality as a grade of "C" or above.) For each student, divide the number of assignments that meet your definition of "quality" by the total number of assignments given to date.*

* Elementary teachers should make these calculations for students across all academic content areas.

3. Calculate the Overall Grade Status of each student in your class and record on a Gradebook Analysis Worksheet.

- To calculate the Overall Grade Status simply use your gradebook to determine the current grade of each student. Elementary teachers may choose to eliminate this step, or they can average students' grades across academic content areas.

NOTE

You may want to consider having a responsible intermediate grade student or parent volunteer assist you with tasks 2 and 3. If you do have someone other than yourself do these calculations, replace student names with numbers (for which you have the key) to protect students' confidentiality. This can be done easily by making a photocopy of your gradebook pages with the students' names covered.

---

4. For each area you are evaluating (e.g., attendance, work quality), determine a cut-off percentage that indicates a cause for concern. For example, with punctuality, attendance, & work completion, it may be 90%; for percent of work not meeting your quality standards, it may be 80%).

   Analyze your results and decide upon a plan of action for each area.

   - If only one or two individuals fall below the cut-off percentage in any area, examine any interrelationships among the data. For example, a student may be failing because she is not attending regularly and, therefore, not completing work. Consider implementing some kind of individual intervention. For example, you might:
     - Arrange to discuss the problem with the student.
     - Arrange to discuss the problem with the student and the student's family.
     - Make sure the student is capable of doing assigned tasks independently.
     - Establish an individualized motivational plan for the student.
     - Discuss the problem with your school counselor, your school psychologist, or a district behavior specialist.

- If more than two or three individuals fall below the cut-off percentage in a particular area, consider implementing some kind of whole class intervention(s). For example, you might:
  - Revise and/or reteach your *CHAMPs* expectations for independent work periods. See Module 3.
  - Review and, if necessary, revise your procedures for managing work completion. See Module 2.
  - Publicly post and discuss daily class percentages. See Module 2.
  - Establish a classwide motivation system. NOTE: If in scanning the data for a particular area (e.g., tardiness), you see so many students having problems that you consider it to be a classwide problem, examine the menu of classwide systems in Module 8 for a plan to directly motivate students to improve the particular behavior.

Figure 6.15: Reproducible

Gradebook Analysis

Teacher: ______________________________ Date: ____________________

Student Name or #	% Attendance	% Punctuality	% Work Completion	% Quality Work	Overall Grade Status

Tool 5: On-Task Behavior Observation Sheet

Information

Determine the degree to which the independent work time in your classroom is being used effectively.

WHY:

- To help you decide whether you need to reteach your *CHAMPs* expectations for independent work periods to students.
- To help you identify the possible cause of poor work completion rates and/or misbehavior during independent work periods.

WHEN:

- During the fourth month of school.
- In mid- to late-February.

HOW:

1. Make a copy (or copies) of the reproducible form shown in Figure 6.16.

2. Identify the independent work period(s) that you wish to monitor. Middle school teachers should target any class or classes that are having trouble completing work and/or those with frequent misbehavior.

3. Determine whether you will be conducting your own observation or have a colleague do it (which you would reciprocate at another time).

   Having a colleague collect the data has several advantages. For one thing, you will be available to do whatever you usually do during this work period (e.g., teach a small group or circulate and help students who have questions). In addition, a colleague is likely to be slightly more objective. You may have an unconscious tendency to make students look better or worse than they really are. Finally, exchanging classroom observations with a colleague gives the two of you a great opportunity to share ideas about how to help students improve their overall rate of on-task behavior.

During the observation period, whoever is collecting data should use the "instantaneous time sampling" method of observation. This is a fancy name for the following easy method of data collection:

- The observer is positioned away from high traffic areas and in a place where she/he can easily see students working at their seats. She/he has a blank On-Task Behavior Observation Sheet and a pen or pencil.

- The observer chooses an observation pattern that allows him/her to observe each student in the class a minimum of three times. For example, if students are in rows, the observer might start with the student in the front row to the left. She/he would then look at the next front-row student to the right, and then the next student in the front row—until she/he has observed each student in the front row. Then the observer would go to the students in the second row, moving from left to right; then the third row; and so on. After observing the last student in the back row, she/he would repeat this pattern at least two more times. NOTE: It is important not to skip around, or the data will be less accurate.

- When observing an individual student, the observer only looks at that student for an instant—almost like taking a mental snapshot. Then she/he looks down at the paper and asks her/himself whether the student was on or off task at the instant of observation. If the student was on task, the observer marks a "+" and if the student was off task, she/he marks a "-". Repeat this for every student, following the pattern established in the step above. The idea is for the observer to set up a rhythm with a quick pace, spending no more than three to five seconds on each student —"Look, Think, Mark." Next student, "Look, Think, Mark." NOTE: The mark should reflect what the student is doing *at the moment of being observed*—NOT what she/he was doing a moment before or does a moment after (even if she/he is off task).

- The observer should work through the whole pattern (all students) at least three times, so that every student is observed a minimum of three times. When finished, the Observation Sheet should look something like the example below (from a class with 30 students).

- Notice that no effort is made to record which students were on or off task. The point of this tool is to look at a class average.

5. Determine the percentage of on-task behavior by dividing the total number of on-task marks (pluses) by the total number of marks (pluses and minuses). (In the sample above, this would be 70 divided by 90, meaning that during the observation period, the class was on task approximately 78% of the time.)

6. Analyze the data and, if necessary, determine a plan of action.

- If the class had an on-task rate of 90% or more, provide positive feedback (including telling them how they did) and encourage them to keep up the good work. If you feel that the percentage does not accurately reflect their typical behavior (i.e., they were more on task because they knew they were being observed), let them know that you are pleased with what they demonstrated they could do and that you want them to strive to behave everyday, the way they did when observed. If you know that all of the off-task behavior was exhibited by one or two students, arrange a private discussion with those individuals. Use the time to set improvement goals for the students and, if necessary, to develop individualized management plans to help them learn to manage work times more responsibly.

- If the class had an on-task rate of between 80 and 89%, tell them what the percentage was and let them know that although they did pretty well, there is room for improvement. Together with the students, identify strategies that individual students might use to monitor and improve their own on-task behavior. If you feel that the percentage does not accurately reflect their typical behavior (i.e., they were more on task because they knew they were being observed), let them know that you are pleased with what they demonstrated they could do and that you want them to strive to behave every day the way they did when observed. If you know that all of the off-task behavior was exhibited by one or two students, arrange a private discussion with those individuals. Use the time to set improvement goals for the students and, if necessary, to develop individualized management plans to help them learn to manage work times more responsibly.

- If the class had an on-task rate of less than 80%, tell them what the percentage was and explain that improvement needs to occur. Review your *CHAMPs* expectations for independent work periods, placing special emphasis on what constitutes appropriate "Participation." At a later time, examine your grade book. If, despite their high rates of off-task behavior, the class has high rates of work completion (e.g., above 95%), consider the possibility that you are giving students too much class time to do their assignments. If both on-task behavior and work completion are low, you may want to establish a classwide system to motivate students to improve both their work completion and on-task behavior (see Module 8). Remember, if students are on task (on average) less than 80%, too much valuable instructional time is being lost, and you need to intervene.

NOTE

If, as is possible, the process of monitoring seems to improve student behavior (i.e., the act of being observed motivates students to be more on task than usual) and if you are working with students in grades 4 and above, consider teaching the students how to take this kind of data. Then, periodically ask an individual student (not always the same person) to observe and record. Give the class feedback at the end of the work period. Use this procedure a couple of times per week until the class is consistently 90% on task or higher.

Figure 6.16: Reproducible

On-Task Behavior Observation Sheet

Teacher: ______________________________ Date: ______________

Observer: ______________________________

Activity

Analysis and Plan of Action

Tool 6: Family/Student Satisfaction Survey

Information

Determine how your students and their families perceive various logistic and organizational features of your classroom.

WHY:

- To help you identify those aspects of your classroom program that are working well and those that may need modification.
- To help you identify whether there are aspects of your classroom program that you need to more clearly communicate to students and their families.

WHEN:

- Last two weeks of school.
- (Optional) mid-year.

HOW:

 Make copies of the two-page reproducible form shown in Figure 6.17.

NOTE

The survey can and should be modified to reflect your classroom program and any areas of concern that you may have.

---

2 Determine how you will let families know that the survey is coming and the logistics of how families will receive and return the survey. For example, you could send the surveys home with students and have them returned by students. Or, if your school can budget for postage, you could send the surveys by mail with pre-addressed, postage-paid return envelopes enclosed.

3 When all surveys have been returned, analyze the results. Keep in mind that although the information is subjective opinion, it can help you identify aspects of your classroom that may require further review. For example, if 50% of the families respond that students did not have enough homework, you should carefully consider whether the amount of homework you assign is sufficient. On the other hand, if 60% say the amount of homework is about right, 20% say it's too much and 20% say it's not enough, you can probably assume that

the amount of homework matches the average family's perception of what is appropriate.

NOTE

Giving a survey of this type can be very threatening. As you examine the results, remind yourself that you cannot take critical information personally. Rather, you are looking for patterns of information that will help you fine tune your classroom program.

NOTE TO MIDDLE SCHOOL TEACHERS

Discuss with colleagues whether or not to have a schoolwide survey that goes to all families (as opposed to having individual teachers give their own surveys). If too many individual teachers give their own surveys, a family with two students in the school could end up having to fill out up to twelve surveys!

Figure 6.17: Reproducible

Family/Student Satisfaction Survey

Dear Families:

As we approach this point in the school year, I want to thank you all for your help and support. As a professional trying to meet the needs of all students, I am always looking for ways to improve. You can help by giving me feedback about the strengths and weaknesses you see in my program. Please take a few minutes to fill out the following survey. If possible, please discuss these questions with your child and come up with answers together.

Note there is no place to put your name. I will not know who wrote what unless you wish to sign your name. Once completed, fold the survey in half and have your student return it to the box by my desk. As always, if you wish to talk to me personally, give me a call.

Sincerely,

HOMEWORK:

The amount of homework assigned has been:

☐ Way too much ☐ A bit too much ☐ About right ☐ Not enough

The difficulty of homework has seemed to be:

☐ Way too hard ☐ A bit too hard ☐ About right ☐ Too easy

ASSIGNMENTS AND CLASSWORK:

The amount of in-class work assigned has been:

☐ Way too much ☐ A bit too much ☐ About right ☐ Not enough

The difficulty of in-class work has seemed to be:

☐ Way too hard ☐ A bit too hard ☐ About right ☐ Too easy

Most of the time my child has felt that the work is:

☐ Stupid ☐ Boring ☐ OK ☐ Interesting ☐ Fun

The academic subject my child has liked the most is:

☐ Reading ☐ Spelling ☐ Writing ☐ Math ☐ Science ☐ Social Studies

Please explain why:

The academic subject my child has liked the least is:

☐ Reading ☐ Spelling ☐ Writing ☐ Math ☐ Science ☐ Social Studies

Please explain why:

Family Satisfaction Survey (Page 2 of 2)

CLASSROOM ATMOSPHERE

Most of the time, my student has:

☐ Hated coming to school ☐ Felt that school is OK ☐ Looked forward to coming to school

Please explain why:

My student feels that s/he has been treated with respect by the teacher:

☐ Not often ☐ Most of the time ☐ All of the time

Please explain why:

What might have been (might be) done to make this year a more pleasant and productive experience for your child?

MODULE 7: CORRECTION PROCEDURES

When you treat student misbehavior as an instructional opportunity, you give students the chance to learn from their mistakes.

NOTE

The information in Module 7 is most useful for classroom situations in which student behavior is basically under control, but misbehavior occurs frequently enough to annoy or concern you. If your class is bordering on being out of control, consider holding off on this module for now. Instead, we recommend that you refocus your efforts on defining/communicating your behavioral expectations (see Modules 3 and 4) and implementing a classwide motivation system designed for a class needing high structure (see Module 8).

Introduction

No matter how well you have organized your classroom and no matter how effectively you have communicated your behavioral expectations to students, a certain amount of misbehavior is still bound to occur (although much less so than if you hadn't organized and communicated expectations). Unfortunately, many teachers have the tendency to "react" to student misbehavior in ways that actually lead to more, rather than less, of the inappropriate behavior. This module is based on the idea that if you are able to regard misbehavior as an opportunity to help students learn, you will be more likely to "respond" to the misbehavior effectively. The tasks in the module are designed to help you: (1) differentiate among "classroom rule violations," "early-stage misbehavior," and "chronic misbehavior"; (2) correct early-stage misbehaviors with simple information-giving responses; (3) identify the underlying causes of ongoing or chronic misbehavior; and (4) develop and implement comprehensive intervention plans to reduce the probability that chronic misbehavior will continue. Before describing the Module 7 tasks, we want to present some basic concepts about correcting misbehavior that you should understand.

The first concept has to do with the importance of being prepared ahead of time to deal with student misbehavior. We have found that when teachers know in advance how they will respond to misbehavior, they are much less likely to get annoyed and frustrated and are much more likely to be effective. There are many ways that you can prepare yourself to handle student misbehavior. One is to identify classroom rules that anticipate the misbehaviors most likely to occur, along with appropriate corrective consequences for their violation. Another involves learning about when and how to develop and implement comprehensive intervention plans designed to correct misbehaviors that occur on a regular basis (i.e., chronic misbehaviors). The final way we suggest that you prepare to deal with misbehavior is to familiarize yourself with several simple, yet effective, procedures for responding to those misbehaviors that are neither ongoing nor covered by your classroom rules. If you have a repertoire of procedures at your fingertips, these "early-stage misbehaviors" will not shock you or leave you feeling helpless.

The second concept about correcting misbehavior is that correction procedures can only be considered effective if they reduce the future occurrence of the misbehavior they are intended to address. This is an important concept to understand because it is not uncommon for a teacher to deal with an inappropriate behavior in a way that seems to solve the problem at the moment, but which in the long run actually makes the situation worse. We introduced this phenomenon in Module 5: Motivation when we discussed the "Criticism Trap." In that context, we explained that students who are starved for attention may actually be "encouraged" to misbehave as a result of the repeated attention they get when the teacher corrects them (even though the student may cease the misbehavior for a short time immediately following the correction).

The idea that you need to evaluate the effectiveness of correction procedures based on their impact on students' long-term behavior applies to more than just situations involving attention-seeking misbehaviors. For example, a teacher who sends an extremely disruptive student out of class may feel that he has solved the problem. However, if the student continues to misbehave in the future (e.g. the average number of disruptive incidents per week stays the same or increases), the more accurate conclusion is that being sent out of class is, at best, a neutral event for this student and, at worst, something the student likes to have happen. (NOTE: A result of this is that it is critical for you to collect information about the occurrence of any chronic problem behavior before you attempt to intervene. In addition, you must continue to monitor its occurrence after you have implemented an intervention plan in order to evaluate the effectiveness of your efforts.)

A third major concept about correcting misbehavior is that, because most chronic misbehavior serves a purpose for the individual who engages in it and because there are many different reasons why students misbehave, correction efforts for specific misbehaviors will be more effective if they address the underlying causes of those behaviors. What follows is a list of common reasons why students misbehave. (NOTE: Task 1 of this module provides information on how to determine the category of a misbehavior, and the five remaining tasks include specific suggestions for how to deal effectively with misbehaviors in the various categories.)

- Students may misbehave because they do not know precisely what the teacher expects. (The teacher views a student as disruptive because she gets up to sharpen her pencil while the teacher is speaking, but the student's previous teachers did not mind if students did this.) See Task 2.
- Students may misbehave because they are unaware of when (or how much) they exhibit an inappropriate behavior. (A student doesn't realize that she complains every time the teacher asks her to do something.) See Task 3.
- Students may misbehave because they do not know how to exhibit the appropriate behavior. (A first grade student has never learned to stay seated and bring a task to completion.) See Task 4.
- Students may misbehave because they are starved for attention and have found it is easier to get attention through reprimands than through praise. (A student frequently gets out of his seat and wanders around, so the teacher is continually saying things like, "Allen, how many times do I have to tell you to get back to your seat?") See Task 5.
- Students may misbehave because they generally feel powerless, and have discovered they can get a sense of power by making adults frustrated and angry. (A student talks back and argues with adults, and finds that some peers look up to him as being "bad" or "tough.") See Task 6.
- Students may misbehave in order to get sent out of class because they are afraid of looking stupid at a task. (A student who is disrespectful to the teacher gets sent from class and perhaps even suspended for a week, and so escapes having to do school work.) See Task 6.

The last concept regarding correction procedures has to do with the use of "corrective consequences" when responding to misbehavior. Corrective consequences are "costs" or "penalties" that are imposed on students for each instance of a particular misbehavior. Time out, restitution, and loss of privileges are all examples of corrective consequences. What's important to understand is that while using corrective consequences may be necessary and helpful in managing some student misbehaviors (i.e., keeping them in check), they are highly unlikely to be sufficient to eliminate those behaviors entirely. Think about the effect of speeding tickets on driving behavior. The fact that police issue speeding tickets undoubtedly helps keep car speeds reasonable. However, there are still individuals who drive above the limit. In addition, the only reason that speeding tickets have any effect is because the police maintain continual patrols. If you decide that corrective consequences are indicated for misbehavior in your classroom, keep in mind that some students will continue to push the limits, and that you will have to maintain your other efforts as well. That is, effective corrective consequences can help reduce misbehavior to tolerable levels, but they are NOT miracle cures. (NOTE: Task 6 of this module ends with a "Menu of Corrective Consequences." The menu contains how-to descriptions of effective corrective consequences that can be reasonably used in a classroom setting.)

The six tasks presented and explained in this module are:

TASK 1: Analyze Misbehavior
Be prepared to categorize misbehaviors as early-stage, awareness type, ability type, attention-seeking, purposeful/habitual—and be prepared to use a basic correction strategy (approach) for each category. (Task 1 ends with a Clarifying Responses to Misbehavior form that will assist you in your analysis and planning.)

TASK 2: Early-Stage Misbehaviors
For early-stage misbehaviors, be prepared to respond with one of a repertoire of correction strategies that are designed to provide information.

TASK 3: Awareness Type Misbehaviors
For ongoing misbehaviors that stem from students' lack of awareness of when/how much they are misbehaving, be prepared to develop and implement an intervention plan that includes increasing their awareness of their behavior.

TASK 4: Ability Type Misbehaviors
For ongoing misbehaviors that stem from students' lack of ability or skill, be prepared to develop and implement an intervention plan that includes modifying your expectations or the environment (for physiological inability) or providing instruction on the goal behavior (for lack of skill).

TASK 5: Attention-Seeking Misbehaviors
For ongoing (but mild) attention-seeking misbehaviors, be prepared to develop and implement an intervention plan that includes planned ignoring.

TASK 6: Purposeful/Habitual Misbehaviors
For ongoing misbehaviors that are habitual and/or serve a purpose other than getting attention, be prepared to develop and implement an intervention plan that includes the use of corrective consequences.

The Clarifying Responses to Misbehavior Worksheet at the end of Task 1 and the Self Assessment Checklist at the end of the module will help you preplan your responses to misbehavior. After working through them, you should have a detailed plan for responding calmly, consistently, and productively to any student misbehaviors that may occur. Review the Peer Study Worksheet at the end of this module with a colleague (and, if possible, arrange to observe in each other's classrooms) to help one another fine tune and implement your planned correction procedures.

Task 1: Analyze Misbehavior

Be prepared to categorize misbehaviors as early-stage, awareness type, ability type, attention-seeking, or purposeful/habitual—and be prepared to use a basic correction strategy (approach) for each category.

As noted in the Introduction to this module, the more prepared you are to deal with student misbehavior, the more likely it is that your efforts to eliminate it will be effective. The information in this task is designed to help you begin preparations. We explain how to "categorize" misbehavior, and why and how to use different basic correction approaches for each of the main categories of misbehavior. Suggestions for the specific procedures to use with the various categories of misbehavior are presented in Tasks 2 through 6 of this module.

The first thing you need to do is to differentiate among the general categories of classroom rule violations, early-stage misbehaviors, and chronic misbehaviors. These distinctions are important because the quality and quantity of pre-planning (as well as the nature of your responses) for the different situations are very different.

Classroom rule violations are misbehaviors that are specifically addressed by your classroom rules. Because your classroom rules should address those misbehaviors that you anticipate are most likely to occur, you should also predetermine (and teach students) what corrective consequences will be implemented in case of infractions. For example, if you have a rule that says, "Arrive on time with all your materials," you should also have a plan regarding the "penalty" for students who do not bring their materials. During the year, if a student arrives without materials, you don't have to spend a lot of time trying to figure out what to do—you just calmly and consistently implement the corrective consequence that has been previously identified.

Early-stage misbehaviors are behaviors that are not covered by your classroom rules and that have just started, occur infrequently, or are not particularly troublesome for you. Generally, correcting an early-stage misbehavior will involve telling/reminding the student that the behavior is not appropriate and giving the student information about what she/he should be doing instead. An example of an early-stage misbehavior situation would be if, on the third day of school, one student makes a very sarcastic comment about some aspect of the lesson you are teaching. If you do not have a rule about sarcastic comments and if this is the first time the student has behaved this way, you can probably correct the problem by simply letting the student know that such remarks are not appropriate. By their very nature, early-stage misbehaviors will vary tremendously, and it is neither reasonable nor possible for you to preplan for every eventuality. We suggest that you prepare for this general category of misbehaviors by becoming familiar with a variety of effective information-giving strategies that you can use in various situations. In Task 2: Early-Stage Misbehaviors, we provide "how-to" information on such basic correction strategies as proximity, verbal reprimand, use of humor, and so on.

Chronic misbehaviors are behaviors that occur repeatedly across days or weeks and/or early-stage behaviors for which simple correction strategies were not effective. For example, think about a student who gets angry and refuses to participate in the current classroom activity. If this happens once in September, once in December, and once in February, you could treat each instance as an early-stage misbehavior. However, if the student behaved that way five times during the first week of school, it should be identified as a chronic misbehavior.

Correcting chronic misbehaviors requires more of your time and effort. In fact, with chronic misbehaviors you should be prepared to analyze the "nature" (i.e., the cause and/or purpose) of the behavior and to develop and implement a comprehensive "intervention plan." The following steps represent the overall approach that we recommend for any misbehavior that you identify as chronic. Following the list of steps are detailed explanations of each step.

1. Analyze the "nature" of the target (problem) behavior. Collect data (if you have not already done so).

2. Develop a preliminary behavior change plan (i.e., intervention) based on your analysis.

3. Discuss your preliminary intervention plan with the student and, if appropriate, with the student's family.

4. Implement the intervention plan for at least two weeks. Monitor student behavior so that you can evaluate the plan's effectiveness.

NOTE

If you are worried about more than one chronic misbehavior, start by listing and prioritizing them. For example, say that your biggest behavioral concerns are: a) many students who do not complete their work; b) one student who is overtly disrespectful to you and his peers; c) a few students who make disruptive noises; and d) quite a few students who blurt out without raising their hands. You should identify which of the problems is your first concern, which is your second concern, and so on. Then, you can work through the planning steps for the most problematic behavior. That is, you would analyze the cause/purpose of the behavior and develop and implement an intervention plan for it. Implement a plan to use for just the first behavior for a few days to a week—or until you are comfortable with it. Next, analyze, develop, and implement your plan for the second problem behavior. Implement each plan long enough that you will not feel overwhelmed by trying to develop and implement too many different plans too quickly.

Intervention Planning Steps

STEP 1: Analyze the "nature" of the target (problem) behavior. Collect data if you have not already done so.

When you are concerned about a particular behavior, but do not have any data to support your concern, you need to collect information about the behavior before you develop an intervention plan. Module 6: Monitor and Revise has monitoring tools for recording the frequency of a behavior. If the target behavior is one that lasts a long time (e.g., a student is out of seat for extended periods of time), you should use a stop watch to get duration data. The objective data you collect on the target misbehavior will help you define the problem more precisely, and will give you a baseline from which you will be able to make judgments about the effectiveness of any intervention plan you implement.

If the target problem is unclear—i.e., you are not sure exactly what about the behavior bothers you, keep anecdotal records for a few days. Anecdotal notes are brief descriptions of specific situations that trouble you. Once you have notes from several incidents over a few days, you will usually be able to clarify the nature of the problem behavior well enough that you can then collect more objective data on its frequency or duration.

The next part of your analysis is to determine the cause and/or purpose of the misbehavior. As noted in the introduction to this module, knowing the cause/purpose of a misbehavior is important because correction procedures that are effective with some behaviors may not be effective with other behaviors. For example, if a student is misbehaving because she wants attention, giving that student corrective consequences each time she misbehaves is not likely to work because she is getting what she wants—attention. Using planned ignoring will be far more effective in this case. On the other hand, if a student continually gets out of her seat because she does not realize that it is inappropriate and/or she does not know how to stay in her seat, then ignoring her out-of-seat behavior is not likely to change that behavior. This student needs information—she needs to be taught what the appropriate behavior is and how she can exhibit that appropriate behavior.

We have identified four subcategories of chronic misbehavior. These subcategories are: (a) awareness type misbehaviors; (b) ability type misbehaviors; (c) attention-seeking misbehaviors; and (d) purposeful/habitual misbehaviors. What follows are descriptions of the four categories and brief introductions into the general correction approach that tends to be most effective with each. (Specific suggestions for how to effectively intervene with misbehavior in each of these subcategories are presented in Tasks 3-6.)

Awareness Type Misbehaviors:

Sometimes a student seems to be willfully misbehaving, when in fact the student is unaware of the behavior she exhibits. An example of an awareness type misbehavior might be a seventh grade student who always responds argumentatively to corrective feedback—at school for behavioral and academic performance, and (according to her parent) at home as well. The teacher tries the early-stage correction strategy of discussing the problem with the student, but sees no improvement in her behavior. Since this student responds negatively *every time* she is given corrective feedback and since initial efforts to correct the behavior with information have been ineffective, it is reasonable to assume that the student may not be aware of how negatively she reacts when she is given corrective feedback.

When a student engages in ongoing misbehavior because of a lack of awareness, the intervention plan needs to include making expectations clear, helping the student become aware of his/her behavior, and, if necessary, providing incentives to encourage the student to change his/her behavior. Information on how to develop this kind of intervention plan is covered in Task 3.

Ability Type Misbehaviors:

Sometimes a student who exhibits a behavior does so because he or she is unable or does not know how to exhibit the desired behaviors. The following scenario describes a student whose misbehavior may be related to an inability to exhibit the desired behavior:

> *A very active first grade student is rarely able to stay in one place for more than two or three minutes at a time, regardless of the activity. He has been evaluated by a physician who suggested that effective behavioral interventions be implemented as the best way to determine whether medication may be necessary/helpful. Because the student's misbehavior is pervasive across a range of activities it is reasonable to assume that the student may lack the knowledge and skill to be able to stay in one place for a longer period of time.*

When students misbehave due to issues of ability, you must first ascertain whether the student is physiologically capable of exhibiting the desired behavior. If she/he is capable, then the intervention plan needs to include giving the student the necessary skills/knowledge. If the student is not physiologically capable of exhibiting the behavior, there need to be modifications made to the student's environment and/or adjustments made in the expectations. Information on how to effectively intervene with ability type misbehaviors is provided in Task 4.

Attention-Seeking Misbehavior:

Attention-seeking misbehaviors are behaviors that a student engages in to satisfy his/her (often unconscious) need for attention. Chronic blurting out, excessive helplessness, tattling, minor disruptions, and so on are examples of behaviors that may be attention-seeking in nature. When a student is seeking attention via misbehavior, any intervention effort that involves giving the student attention when he is misbehaving is likely to actually reinforce the inappropriate behavior. Planned ignoring, which is designed to reduce or eliminate the attention the student receives for engaging in misbehavior while giving the student frequent attention when he is not engaged in misbehavior, should be part of any intervention plan for this category of misbehavior. More information on using planned ignoring to deal with attention-seeking misbehavior is presented in Task 5.

Purposeful/Habitual Misbehavior:

When chronic misbehavior does not stem from a student's lack of awareness or ability, and is not being exhibited because the student wants attention, then you need to assume that it is serving some other purpose for the student. For example, some students misbehave to escape from something aversive (e.g., a student wants to avoid doing academic tasks that he believes he will fail). Other students use misbehavior to demonstrate and achieve a sense of power and control (e.g., a student talks back and argues with adults to look tough in front of friends). Still other students may engage in misbehaviors that provide competing reinforcers (e.g., a student reads during instructional lessons because he enjoys reading silently more than participating in the lesson). There are also some students for whom misbehavior becomes so habitual that the original purpose of the misbehavior is unclear or no longer relevant. For example, a student who has successfully engaged in attention-seeking behaviors for years, may continue to misbehave even when planned ignoring is implemented because the inappropriate behaviors are firmly established in her behavioral repertoire.

With truly purposeful and/or habitual misbehavior, you will probably need to include the use of corrective consequences for the misbehavior as part of your intervention plan. Task 6 provides information on developing an effective intervention plan for this category of misbehaviors. Included in the information are guidelines for using corrective consequences and a "menu" of specific consequences that you might use.

STEP 2: Develop a preliminary behavior change (i.e., intervention) plan based on your analysis.

Once you have developed a hypothesis about why the target behavior may be occurring, review the decision-making chart shown in Figure 7.1. Think about the target misbehavior as you examine the chart. Then go to the information in this module that pertains to that misbehavior. (NOTE: Figure 7.1 is designed to guide you to the appropriate procedures that will fit the nature of the target problem.)

Figure 7.1: Analysis of Chronic Misbehavior

When a misbehavior is enough of a problem to be considered chronic, ask:
Is the behavior a problem of awareness?
Yes
Task 3
1. Develop a signal to cue the student about the misbehavior.
2. Develop a monitoring and/or evaluation record.
3. Provide feedback.
No
Is the behavior a problem of ability?
Yes
Task 4
1. Decide if the desired behavior is physiologically possible.
2. If yes, conduct lessons to teach the desired behaviors.
3. If no, make accommodations.
4. Provide feedback.
No
Is the purpose of the behavior to get attention?
Yes
Task 5
1. Give no attention to misbehavior.
2. Provide attention when the student is not misbehaving.
No
The behavior serves some other purpose for the student. So...
Task 6
Implement planned consequences!
1. Further analyze purpose of the misbehavior.
2. Meet the student's needs in positive ways.
3. Calmly and consistently implement pre-planned corrective consequences.

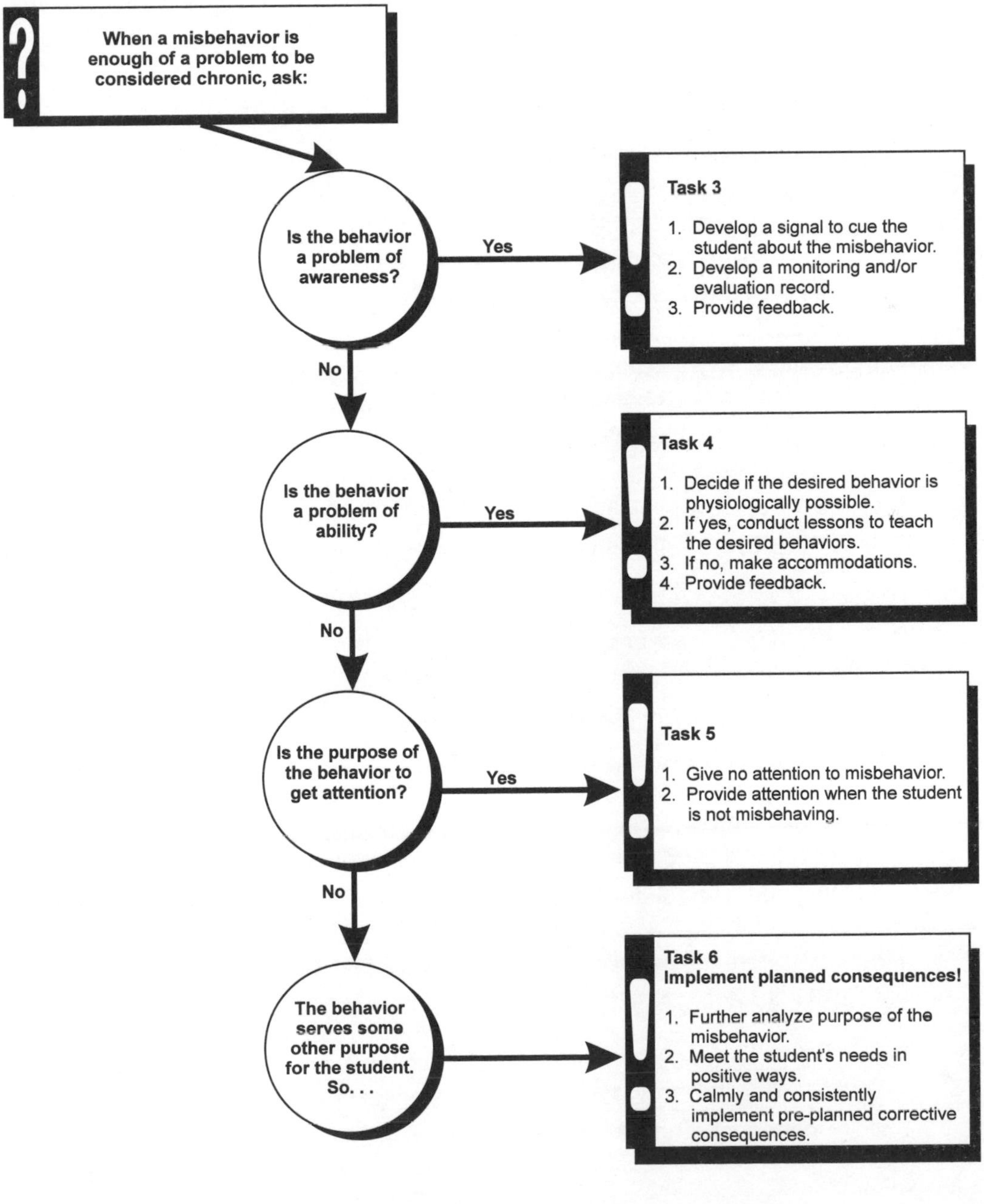

Use the suggestions in Tasks 3, 4, 5, or 6 (or modify them as necessary) to develop a preliminary plan for improving the target behavior. Although the specific procedures for each subcategory of chronic misbehavior (awareness, ability, attention-seeking, and purposeful) are different from each other, there are two fundamental types of procedures that should be included in all intervention plans. First, you need to include procedures for encouraging the positive opposite of the misbehavior. For example, if the target misbehavior is disrespect, the intervention plan should identify how you will encourage (and increase) demonstrations of respectful behavior by the student. Second, your plan needs to specify exactly how you will respond to instances of the misbehavior in ways that allow you to be calm, consistent, and brief. Once you have a preliminary plan (using the information in Tasks 3 through 6), then you can continue with the remaining planning steps.

STEP 3: Discuss your preliminary intervention plan with the student (and, if appropriate, the student's family).

Prior to implementing an intervention plan for any chronic misbehavior, you should schedule a time to discuss your concerns about the target behavior and your proposed plan with the student (or the entire class, if the behavior is being exhibited by many students). You need to decide whether or not to include the student's family in the discussion. If the behavior involved is quite serious (e.g., the student is hitting other students or is verbally abusive), the family should definitely be asked to participate. On the other hand, if the behavior is a relatively minor one (e.g., the student is restless and over-uses the pencil sharpener and the drinking fountain), it may not be necessary to include the family. If you are not sure about involving the family, we suggest that you include them.

During the discussion, define the target behavior for the student as clearly as you can. Whenever possible describe the behavior in observable terms and share any objective data about the behavior that you have collected (e.g., "Troy, you have hit, poked, or kicked someone eight times in two days."). Avoid making statements that imply judgments (e.g., "Tommy, you are so bad most of the time, something has to be done."). After you have explained the nature of the problem, present your proposed plan. Make sure the student (and the family, if present) understands all aspects of the proposed plan. We strongly recommend that you invite ideas for improving the plan from the student (and family). Incorporating reasonable suggestions will give the student (and family) a sense of ownership in the plan and will demonstrate that you want the student (and family) to be active partners in these efforts to improve the student's behavior.

Figure 7.2 is a reproducible template for structuring a phone conversation with a student's family about joining you and the student for a discussion of this kind. Following the reproducible template, Figure 7.3 shows a completed template.

Figure 7.2: Reproducible

Chronic Problems—Request for Conference

1. Introduce who you are and provide an appropriate greeting:

2. Inform that you are calling about a problem:

3. Describe the problem (avoid labeling or passing judgment):

4. Describe why it is a problem (keep the focus on the student, not yourself or the other students):

5. Present why you think a conference would be useful and specify if the student should attend the conference:

6. Inform the family if other school personnel (or other agency personnel) will be in attendance:

Date of this contact: ______________________________

Time and place for the conference: ______________________________

Figure 7.3: Completed Sample

Chronic Problems—Request for Conference

1. **Introduce who you are and provide an appropriate greeting:**

   Hello, Mr. Houser? This is Ms. Grier, Toby's teacher. May I take just a moment of your time?

2. **Inform that you are calling about a problem:**

   I am calling because I want to speak with you about something that happened at school today.

3. **Describe the problem (avoid labeling or passing judgment):**

   Today during science class, Toby was working with a group of three other students. They got into a disagreement that led to Toby getting quite angry at one of the female students in the group, a student named Melissa. Now, there is nothing wrong with disagreements and even anger, but Toby called Melissa some very inappropriate names that can not be tolerated in school. He threatened to hurt her. Although this incident was the worst, Toby has gotten angry on a couple of other occasions as well.

4. **Describe why it is a problem (keep the focus on the student, not yourself or the other students).**

   Even though he is only in second grade, he needs to learn that when he is angry, calling names and threatening others is not acceptable school behavior.

5. **Present why you think a conference would be useful and specify if the student should attend the conference:**

   I think it would help Toby to realize how serious this behavior is if you and/or Mrs. Houser would come to school to meet with Toby and me. Together we can decide on a plan for helping Toby behave more responsibly.

6. **Inform the family if other school personnel (or other agency personnel) will be in attendance:**

   Because making threats is so serious, I feel we need to ask Ms. Nestor, the principal, to join us.

Date of this contact: *January 14, 11:50 a.m.*

Time and place for the conference: *Ms. Nestor's office at 2:00 p.m.*

STEP 4: Implement the intervention plan for at least two weeks. Monitor student behavior so that you can evaluate the plan's effectiveness.

Once you have analyzed the behavior, developed a preliminary plan, and had a discussion with the student (and family), you are ready to implement the plan. We recommend that you keep your plan in effect for at least two weeks. During that time, continue to collect objective (frequency or duration) data on the behavior so that you can determine whether or not the problem is improving. Do not be alarmed if the behavior gets worse during the first week. This sometimes happens, even with a plan that eventually will be successful. For example, when you first begin ignoring an attention-getting behavior, the student is likely to try even harder to get attention by misbehaving more frequently. If you persist, eventually, the student will learn that responsible behavior leads to more attention than the former misbehavior.

After two weeks, evaluate the situation. If the behavior is getting better, continue to implement your plan. It is very important to remember that most successful behavior changes occur gradually, getting a little better each week. However, if you have seen no behavioral improvement after two weeks, try modifying one or more aspects of your plan. You might even ask the student for ideas on what would make the plan more effective. Whenever you make a change in your intervention plan, implement the new plan for a minimum of two weeks, and continue to evaluate effectiveness.

Students are more likely to learn to behave responsibly when misbehavior is corrected in a planned (as opposed to spur-of-the-moment) manner. Taking the time to analyze your students' misbehaviors will increase the likelihood that your responses will be calm, consistent, and brief—all of which will increase your chances of helping students learn to improve their behavior. To help you plan for misbehaviors, we have prepared a Clarifying Responses to Misbehavior worksheet (see Figure 7.4). With this worksheet, you list the misbehaviors that are currently occurring in your classroom, in order from greatest to least concern. You then proceed through a series of systematic steps in which you identify the cause/purpose of the behavior and identify a proposed response to it. For those behaviors that seems to require the use of corrective consequences, you also identify what the proposed consequences will be. When you have used this worksheet to address all the problem behaviors in your classroom (which may take some time), you will have a comprehensive and well thought-out plan for dealing with misbehavior.

Figure 7.4: Reproducible

Clarifying Responses to Misbehavior

1. In the first column, list all misbehaviors currently occurring in your classroom. Begin with behaviors that are of greatest concern (e.g., they interfere with instruction; they are detrimental to the students; they really bother you, etc.) and continue the list through to those of least concern. List the behaviors in as specific and observable terms as possible. For example, ADHD would be listed as "fidgety, poking others, off task, etc."

2. Label each behavior listed. That is, for each behavior identify whether:
The student(s) is trying to get adult or peer attention (label in column 2 as "Attn.")
The student(s) is not able to or does not know how to exhibit the appropriate or desirable behavior (label in column 2 as "Aware").
Some other factor may be involved (label in column 2 as "Purp" for Purposeful/Habitual

3. For each behavior, identify a proposed response to the misbehavior. For attention-seeking behavior, consider ignoring. For problems of ability/awareness, consider gentle verbal reminder or redirection. Purposeful/Habitual problems will probably require a consequence.

4. For each behavior that requires a consequence, specify a proposed consequence.

1. List Problems (greatest to least concern). If the behavior is exhibited by one or two individuals, write their names. If the behavior is exhibited by three or more students, indicate "class."	Label each as Awareness, Ability, Attention, or Purposeful.	Identify a proposed response (e.g. Reprimand, Redirect, Ignore, Consequence).	When a consequence is indicated, identify a proposed consequence (e.g., loss of point, demerit, time owed, time out, etc.)

Task 2: Early-Stage Misbehaviors

For "early-stage" misbehaviors, be prepared to respond with one of a repertoire of correction strategies that are designed to provide information.

One of the basic concepts underpinning this module is that preplanning how you will respond to misbehavior will make your corrections more effective. This is true even for early-stage misbehavior—i.e., behaviors for which you do not have a predetermined consequence or an intervention plan. Because it is not possible to preplan for every potential early-stage misbehavior, the information in this task is designed to help you develop a repertoire of simple correction strategies to use with a misbehavior that is in the very early stages. The basic rule for early-stage misbehavior is try the easy thing first. In general, the easiest correction strategies involve simply giving the student information about what he/she should be doing at that moment. If you try a simple correction strategy and it solves the problem (i.e., the problem does not occur or only rarely occurs in the future), then there no longer is a problem—end of discussion. If the misbehavior continues across a period of days or weeks, then you are no longer looking at an early-stage problem and you need to look at the situation more systematically and analytically.

What follows is a "menu" of correction strategies that are appropriate for early-stage misbehaviors. If you take the time to familiarize yourself with these strategies, you will be prepared to respond effectively when faced with an early-stage misbehavior.

Proximity

The proximity correction strategy is based on the same rationale as having highway patrol officers on the roadways. That is, most people, even those who tend to exceed the speed limit, are more likely to follow the speed limit when a police officer is near. In the classroom, proximity involves simply going over to where students are engaged in misbehavior. The misbehavior is likely to cease as you get near, because your proximity at that moment will prompt the students to stop exhibiting the misbehavior and start exhibiting the desired behavior. The more you move throughout your room in unpredictable ways, the better able you will be to correct misbehavior through proximity.

For example, if you are presenting a lesson and a couple of students begin talking to each other rather than listening to you, you might start walking over to that part of the room—while continuing to present the lesson. If the students quit talking while you are on the way, continue the lesson from where you are, and then move to different place in the room or back to the front. After a few minutes, make eye contact with the students who had been talking.

You may even want to compliment them for listening and participating (although in middle school this may be inadvisable if you think it would embarrass them in front of peers).

Gentle Verbal Reprimand

To use a gentle verbal reprimand, simply go over to the student or students engaged in a misbehavior and quietly remind/tell them what they should be doing at that moment. For example, if the two students in the previously described scenario did not stop talking as you moved in their direction, you might quietly say to them, "Johanna, Alexander, if you have something to say, you need to raise your hand and wait to be called on." Effective verbal reprimands have the following features:

- They are short. They cause only a very brief interruption in the lesson.
- They are given when you are physically near misbehaving students—not from across the room.
- Their tone and content are respectful.
- They are clear and unequivocal.
- They state the expected behavior, rather than accusing the student(s) of the misbehavior.
- They are given in a way that creates the illusion of privacy. (You don't want to try to make it truly secret or the other students will try to hear what you are saying to the misbehaving student, but you also do not want to make it seem that you are putting the student on public display.)

Discussion

Sometimes you may need to talk with a student about a misbehavior in a way that is more detailed and lengthy than a reprimand. For example, if a student makes a disrespectful comment as you are presenting a lesson, you may want to have a talk with the student about the importance of treating each other respectfully.

The major rule about discussions is that they are usually best if they occur at a neutral time. In fact, there are several reasons why having a discussion immediately after a misbehavior tends to be ineffective: a) you leave the rest of the class waiting; b) you give the misbehaving student too much immediate attention; c) the student is likely to be defensive; and, d) you are likely to be somewhat frustrated or angry. It is far more effective to wait until later, when the class is engaged in independent work or even after class, and then privately discuss the situation with the student. During your meeting, be sure to discuss with the student better ways that she/he could handle similar situations in the future.

Family Contact

A very important and potentially effective early-stage correction procedure is a family contact. When making contact with the family regarding misbehavior, keep the following suggestions in mind:

- Provide an objective description of the behavior, not a judgment about the student.
- Suggest that it would be useful if the family discussed the behavior with the student and communicated the expectation that the student will behave more responsibly in the future.
- Avoid implying that the student should be punished at home or that the family should "make" the student behave.
- Create a sense that you and the family can work as partners in helping the student reduce misbehavior and succeed in your class.

Figure 7.5 (at the end of this task) is a reproducible template that outlines the content to cover in an early-stage family contact. Following the blank template, Figure 7.6 shows a sample template that has been completed by a fifth grade teacher.

Humor

Humor can be a powerful and effective way to respond to misbehavior—especially with older students. For example, consider a situation in which a student makes a "smart-aleck" comment on the second day of school as the teacher is presenting a lesson. If the teacher is quick-witted enough, she might be able to respond to the student's comment in a way that will make the student himself laugh, and a tense moment will have been diffused. Please note that we are not talking about sarcasm or ridicule here. The sensitive use of humor will bring people closer together. Sarcasm or ridicule will make a student feel angry and hostile that you have made a joke at his expense.

If you do use humor in response to a misbehavior, you should plan on talking to the student later—to make sure that he understands that his behavior was not acceptable and that you expect him to behave more responsibly in the future. In addition, you can check to see that you did not embarrass the student with your humorous comment. For example, with a situation similar to the one in the last paragraph, you might say something like, "Thomas, today in class you made a comment and then I made a joke out of what you said. First, I want to make sure that I did not embarrass you with what I said. Well good, I'm glad. I owe it to every student to treat them as respectfully as I expect them to treat me. If I ever do anything that feels disrespectful to you, please come and talk to me about it. Now, I need to ask that in the future you raise your hand when you have something to say in class and that you make an effort to see that your comments treat me respectfully. I appreciate humor in the classroom, and I suspect that you will be someone who will not only contribute to our lessons, but also get us to see the humor in different situations as well. Thanks for taking the time to talk to me. I'm looking forward to seeing you in class tomorrow."

Praise Someone Behaving Responsibly

If one student is misbehaving, it can sometimes be effective to use descriptive praise addressed to one or more students behaving responsibly at that moment. "Gayle, Rashonda and Paul are doing a great job of following my direction to come to the rug for story time." This technique is most likely to be successful in the primary grades. In fact, it can actually backfire at middle school level if the praised students are embarrassed.

Restitution

The goal of restitution is for a misbehaving student to learn that if her behavior causes damage, then she needs to repair that damage. If a student writes on a desk, she should have to wash that desk. If a student is rude to a guest speaker, she should be required to apologize, in writing, on the phone, or in person, to the guest speaker. If you use the restitution strategy, try to make it clear to the student that what you are asking her to do (e.g., apologizing to the guest speaker) is not a punishment but a reparation (i.e., an attempt to repair any damage her rudeness may have caused—in terms of the guest speaker's opinion of students in the school).

An Emotional Reaction

Exhibiting an emotional reaction (e.g., anger) is a strategy that should be used very sparingly (not more than twice a year with any group of students), and not at all in the first five or six weeks with a new class. It is appropriate to use with a group, but not with individuals. For example, say that most of the students in a class that is usually a pleasure to work with start acting silly while a guest speaker is in the room. It might not be bad to let the class know that you are angry and disappointed in them. If the class has never seen you angry before, it may have a bit of a shock effect and help improve the class' behavior in the future.

The reason we recommend that you not use this particular strategy with an individual student is the risk that you will be dealing with an individual who is seeking power via misbehavior. Getting an adult angry can be a powerful motivating force for this kind of student. The reason not to use the procedure at the beginning of the school year is that showing students anger or frustration too early in the year may encourage the class to "act up" more in the future because they think it is fun or funny to watch you get angry. Finally, if you overuse the procedure (e.g., more than twice a year), it will lose any power it may have had. An emotional reaction will "shock" students only if they rarely see it. On the other hand, if students are used to seeing you get angry repeatedly, they are more likely to think, "There he goes again, blowing his stack over nothing."

Whichever correction strategy you use to respond to an early-stage misbehavior, be sure that when the students who engaged in the misbehavior begin to behave responsibly, you give them positive feedback. Students need to see that you notice positive behavior more than misbehavior. Also, remember that if one or more of these strategies does not solve the problem quickly, you will need to develop and implement an intervention plan that is based on a more thoughtful analysis of the misbehavior (see Task 1).

Early-Stage Problems—Family Contact

1. **Introduce who you are and provide an appropriate greeting:**

2. **Inform that you are calling about a problem:**

3. **Describe the problem (avoid labeling or passing judgment):**

4. **Describe why it is a problem (keep the focus on the student, not yourself or the other students). Emphasize that you know the student can be successful.**

5. **If appropriate, ask if the family has any insight into why the problem may be occurring. If so, adjust the remainder of this call based on what you learn.**

6. **Make suggestions about what the family might do with this information:**

Date of the contact: ______________________________

Notes on the contact: ______________________________

Figure 7.6: Completed Sample

Early-Stage Problems—Family Contact

1. Introduce who you are and provide an appropriate greeting:

Hello, Mrs. Thompson? This is Mr. McLemore, Rob's teacher. How are you today? I'll bet that new baby is keeping you very busy. How is she doing? May I take just a moment of your time?

2. Inform that you are calling about a problem:

I am calling because I wanted to speak with you about a problem that has been going on at school.

3. Describe the problem (avoid labeling or passing judgment):

For the last two days, Rob has not been doing his work in class. He sits at his desk and stares out the window, talks with his neighbor, and plays with his pencil. When I remind him to get to work, he will work if I am standing right there, but as soon as I go to do something else, he quits working again. Today he didn't finish any of his assignments.

4. Describe why it is a problem (keep the focus on the student, not yourself or the other students). Emphasize that you know the student can be successful.

I am concerned because Rob is a very able student. I don't want him to develop the bad habit of wasting class time. To succeed in school, he will need to learn to keep his attention on his work.

5. If appropriate, ask if the family has any insight into why the problem may be occuring. If so, adjust the remainder of this call based on what you learn.

One of the reasons I am calling is to find out if you know of anything that might be bothering Rob or that could be distracting him from his classwork.

6. Make suggestions about what the family might do with this information:

I am not calling so that you will "punish" him. I am just concerned about him and hope you will talk to him about the problem. Let him know that he is capable of being successful in my class, but he has to keep his attention focused and do his work. Please tell him I called and that I am looking forward to seeing him tomorrow. I will call you in a few days to let you know how Rob is doing. If you want to talk to me, feel free to call me. The best time to reach me is between 3:30 and 4:00 any afternoon but Tuesday.

Date of the contact: September 27,

Notes on the contact: Mrs. Thompson couldn't tell me any particular reason that Rob has been so inattentive the last two days. She said she would talk to him, find out if anything was wrong, and encourage him to pay attention to his work.

Task 3: Awareness Type Misbehaviors

For ongoing misbehaviors that stem from students' lack of awareness of when/how much they are misbehaving, be prepared to develop and implement an intervention plan that includes increasing their awareness of their behavior.

When a student misbehaves because he isn't aware of when or how often he is engaging in an irresponsible behavior, your intervention plan should focus on increasing the student's awareness of his behavior. It is not appropriate to use traditional corrective consequences (i.e., "punishers") in this situation. In fact, using corrective consequences for this category of misbehaviors is analogous to punishing students who make mistakes on math assignments without letting them know that they were making errors. When a student lacks awareness of his misbehavior, you need to make sure the student understands how he is supposed to behave, and then help the student learn to recognize when he is misbehaving.

If you determine that a student's misbehavior stems from a lack of awareness, we suggest that you develop and implement a four phase intervention plan. The four phases are summarized below, and then explained in detail.

- Make sure the student knows what behavior you expect him to exhibit (the target or goal behavior).
- Respond to instances of the misbehavior in a manner that lets the student know that he is not meeting the goal.
- Monitor the student's behavior so that you, the student (and the student's family) will have an objective basis for discussing progress.
- Provide positive feedback when the student is successful (or makes improvements). If positive feedback doesn't seem sufficient to motivate the student to stop exhibiting the behavior, consider using some type of incentive (reward).

❶ Make sure the student knows what behavior you expect him to exhibit (the target or goal behavior).

When you meet to discuss the situation with the student (and the family), be sure to explain the behavior you want the student to demonstrate. Emphasize, in age-appropriate ways, the benefits to the student of demonstrating this new behavior. Be prepared to identify actions you will take to help the student learn the new behavior. You might also consider writing the behavioral goal into an informal contract, using something like the reproducible Goal Contract form shown in Figure 7.7. NOTE: Information on goal setting procedures you can use with all your students is provided in Module 8: Classwide Motivation Systems.

Figure 7.7: Reproducible

Goal Contract

Student's Name ______________________________ **Date** ______________

A goal for you to work on is to ______________________________

____

You can show you are working on this goal by:

A. ______________________________

____

B. ______________________________

____

C. ______________________________

____

____

Student's Signature

____

Teacher's Signature

Goal Contract

Student's Name ______________________________ **Date** ______________

A goal for you to work on is to ______________________________

____

You can show you are working on this goal by:

A. ______________________________

____

B. ______________________________

____

C. ______________________________

____

____

Student's Signature

____

Teacher's Signature

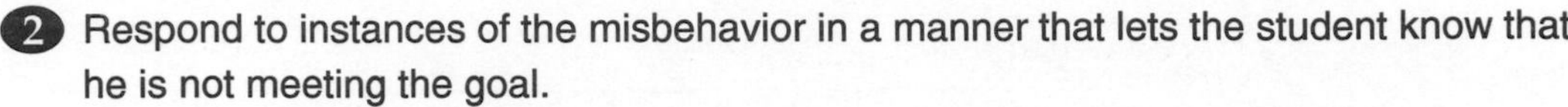

2 Respond to instances of the misbehavior in a manner that lets the student know that he is not meeting the goal.

As has been stated earlier, students should not be "punished" for behavioral mistakes that are related to a lack of awareness or ability. Instead, each time an "error" occurs, you want to give the student information about the inappropriate behavior and what he should do instead. Following are descriptions of several information-based correction strategies. Choose one (or more) that you can use to provide the student with information that will help him be more successful in the future. Remember, just like a student learning to correct errors in math, a student learning a new behavior may make frequent errors and need to be corrected each time.

- **Gentle verbal reprimands**

  Reprimands were discussed in detail in Task 2. Remember that effective reprimands are brief, proximate (close), respectful, clear, and reasonably private. Provide a verbal description of what the student should be doing. When students make errors in math, one of the most effective correction procedures is to tell them what they should have done, e.g., "You need to remember to carry the ten from the ones column over to the tens column."

- **Redirection**

  Redirection involves guiding the student back to what she should be doing instead of misbehaving. Instead of verbally reminding the student, you literally direct the student to the desired activity. For example, if a young student is not where she should be, you might go over and guide her back to her seat, while complimenting other students for showing self-control by staying in their work areas. Or, if you have a low functioning special education student who tends to wave his hands in front of his face (or engage in some other sort of self-stimulatory behavior), you might simply take one of his hands, put a pencil in it, and then redirect him to the work on his desk. All of this can (and should) be done without giving the student very much attention.

- **Signal**

  If a student seems truly unaware of when he is engaging in a misbehavior, it can be very helpful to use a verbal or nonverbal signal to cue the student. For example, if you have a student who hums while doing seatwork, the signal might be to say his name and subtly shake your head "no." Tell the student that whenever he notices you using that signal, it means that he is humming and needs to stop. (Note: You might want to have the student help you identify an appropriate signal when you first meet to discuss the situation.)

- **Precorrection**

  When there seems to be a good chance that a student will exhibit the misbehavior in a particular situation (based on prior history), you might consider using a precorrection to help the student be successful. Before the student has had a chance to exhibit the misbehavior in a typically problematic situation, give her information that will increase the probability that she will exhibit a responsible behavior. For example, if a student has trouble accepting corrective feedback, you could use something like the following precorrection just before you return papers. "Sheila, I am about to hand back some papers I have graded. You solved most of the problems correctly, but you do have a couple of errors that need to be fixed. Give some thought to the neutral or positive ways of reacting to corrections we discussed. I am sure you will be able to manage your reaction in a responsible way."

3. Monitor the student's particular behavior so that you, the student (and the student's family) will have an objective basis for discussing progress.

When a student tends to be unaware of engaging in a misbehavior, being able to discuss his progress (or lack of progress) will be an important part of increasing the student's awareness. Thus, if a student is not aware of how frequently he engages in a behavior, you should probably keep a continuous record of the number of incidents that occur each day. You can chart each day's total and arrange to periodically review the chart with the student. In some cases, it can be beneficial to give the student a recording sheet and have him mark each incident. However, if the student is unlikely to keep an accurate record or would be embarrassed to record his behavior in front of peers, you should do the recording. Arrange to meet with the student at the end of each day to chart the incidents and discuss progress. For more ideas on this type of recording and for a sample of a recording sheet, see Module 6: Monitor and Revise, Tool 3. (NOTE: In addition to the monitoring forms provided previously, sometimes it can be useful to track a positive and a negative behavior concurrently. Figure 7.8 shows a reproducible monitoring sheet that can be used to record both appropriate and inappropriate reactions (e.g., to corrective feedback).

Figure 7.8: Reproducible

Monitoring Reactions to Correction

Appropriate/Inappropriate Reactions Tally

Name ______________________

Week of ______________________

Behavior to be counted ______________________

____

Monday

Appropriate Reactions

1 2 3 4 5 6 7 8 9 10
11 12 13 14 15 16 17 18 19 20

Inappropriate Reactions

1 2 3 4 5 6 7 8 9 10
11 12 13 14 15 16 17 18 19 20

Tuesday

Appropriate Reactions

1 2 3 4 5 6 7 8 9 10
11 12 13 14 15 16 17 18 19 20

Inappropriate Reactions

1 2 3 4 5 6 7 8 9 10
11 12 13 14 15 16 17 18 19 20

Wednesday

Appropriate Reactions

1 2 3 4 5 6 7 8 9 10
11 12 13 14 15 16 17 18 19 20

Inappropriate Reactions

1 2 3 4 5 6 7 8 9 10
11 12 13 14 15 16 17 18 19 20

Thursday

Appropriate Reactions

1 2 3 4 5 6 7 8 9 10
11 12 13 14 15 16 17 18 19 20

Inappropriate Reactions

1 2 3 4 5 6 7 8 9 10
11 12 13 14 15 16 17 18 19 20

Friday

Appropriate Reactions

1 2 3 4 5 6 7 8 9 10
11 12 13 14 15 16 17 18 19 20

Inappropriate Reactions

1 2 3 4 5 6 7 8 9 10
11 12 13 14 15 16 17 18 19 20

Appropriate/Inappropriate Reactions Tally

Name ______________________

Week of ______________________

Behavior to be counted ______________________

____

Monday

Appropriate Reactions

1 2 3 4 5 6 7 8 9 10
11 12 13 14 15 16 17 18 19 20

Inappropriate Reactions

1 2 3 4 5 6 7 8 9 10
11 12 13 14 15 16 17 18 19 20

Tuesday

Appropriate Reactions

1 2 3 4 5 6 7 8 9 10
11 12 13 14 15 16 17 18 19 20

Inappropriate Reactions

1 2 3 4 5 6 7 8 9 10
11 12 13 14 15 16 17 18 19 20

Wednesday

Appropriate Reactions

1 2 3 4 5 6 7 8 9 10
11 12 13 14 15 16 17 18 19 20

Inappropriate Reactions

1 2 3 4 5 6 7 8 9 10
11 12 13 14 15 16 17 18 19 20

Thursday

Appropriate Reactions

1 2 3 4 5 6 7 8 9 10
11 12 13 14 15 16 17 18 19 20

Inappropriate Reactions

1 2 3 4 5 6 7 8 9 10
11 12 13 14 15 16 17 18 19 20

Friday

Appropriate Reactions

1 2 3 4 5 6 7 8 9 10
11 12 13 14 15 16 17 18 19 20

Inappropriate Reactions

1 2 3 4 5 6 7 8 9 10
11 12 13 14 15 16 17 18 19 20

When a student's behavior problem involves more qualitative than quantitative issues (i.e., how well rather than how much), it can be useful to have the student use some kind of a self-evaluation monitoring form—on which she can rate the "quality" of a given behavior at particular times during the day (or even just at the end of the day). Figure 7.9 is a reproducible self-evaluation sheet that would be appropriate for a student who is learning to keep his desk and work area neat and organized. The reproducible form shown in Figure 7.10 could be used by a student who is learning to participate more actively in class.

NOTE

If you decide to incorporate student self-evaluation into your intervention plan, set the system up so that the student will have a good chance of earning a high rating most of the time. For example, if a student who is rating himself on how well he used in-class work times only gets to evaluate himself once for the whole day, he may have to give himself an overall poor rating. However, if it is set up so that he evaluates his behavior for each thirty-minute work period throughout the day, he is likely to feel more successful overall. That is, although there may be some time periods that he has to rate himself low, there should also be several work times during the day for which he can give himself a high rating.

Figure 7.9: Reproducible

Desk Neatness Self-Evaluation

Name ________________________________ **Date** ____________

Directions: Check off how your desk rates against our definitions of "Neat" and "Messy."

A Neat Desk	A Messy Desk
□ The top is clean.	□ The top has pencil marks or smudges and dried glue.
□ All papers are in a notebook or in the folder to take home.	□ There are loose papers (some done, some unfinished, some blank paper).
□ There are books in a neat stack and there are not too many.	□ There are books thrown in (many library books or books from home).
□ Pencils, scissors, erasers, and any other little things are in the pencil box.	□ Pencils and other little stuff are loose in the desk.
□ No toys or other little junk are in the desk.	□ Toys and other little junk are cluttering the desk.

If your desk was neat without having to do any "last minute" cleaning, have the teacher sign here:

Teacher Signature ________________________________

Desk Neatness Self-Evaluation

Name ________________________________ **Date** ____________

Directions: Check off how your desk rates against our definitions of "Neat" and "Messy."

A Neat Desk	A Messy Desk
□ The top is clean.	□ The top has pencil marks or smudges and dried glue.
□ All papers are in a notebook or in the folder to take home.	□ There are loose papers (some done, some unfinished, some blank paper).
□ There are books in a neat stack and there are not too many.	□ There are books thrown in (many library books or books from home).
□ Pencils, scissors, erasers, and any other little things are in the pencil box.	□ Pencils and other little stuff are loose in the desk.
□ No toys or other little junk are in the desk.	□ Toys and other little junk are cluttering the desk.

If your desk was neat without having to do any "last minute" cleaning, have the teacher sign here:

Teacher Signature ________________________________

Figure 7.10: Reproducible

Self-Evaluation on Class Participation

PARTICIPATION EVALUATION RECORD

Name____________________

Date ____________________

Rating Scale

0 Did not participate verbally and did not take notes

3 Participated verbally at least once, but did not take notes

6 Took notes, but did not participate verbally

9 Participated verbally at least once and took notes

Directions: For each subject, circle the number that best describes your level of participation.

Subject: ____________________
0 3 6 9

Subject: ____________________
0 3 6 9

Subject: ____________________
0 3 6 9

Subject: ____________________
0 3 6 9

Subject: ____________________
0 3 6 9

Subject: ____________________
0 3 6 9

Subject: ____________________
0 3 6 9

PARTICIPATION EVALUATION RECORD

Name____________________

Date ____________________

Rating Scale

0 Did not participate verbally and did not take notes

3 Participated verbally at least once, but did not take notes

6 Took notes, but did not participate verbally

9 Participated verbally at least once and took notes

Directions: For each subject, circle the number that best describes your level of participation.

Subject: ____________________
0 3 6 9

Subject: ____________________
0 3 6 9

Subject: ____________________
0 3 6 9

Subject: ____________________
0 3 6 9

Subject: ____________________
0 3 6 9

Subject: ____________________
0 3 6 9

Subject: ____________________
0 3 6 9

4 Provide positive feedback when the student is successful (or makes improvements). If positive feedback doesn't seem sufficient to motivate the student to stop exhibiting the behavior, consider using some type of incentive (reward).

Throughout the day, as the student demonstrates success or takes steps toward success, provide positive verbal feedback. Increased awareness requires that the student know when she is doing well. Furthermore, without positive feedback, the student may get discouraged by the corrective feedback you provide when she makes an error.

If you do not see progress (the misbehavior decreasing as the goal behavior increases) within a couple of weeks, consider establishing a simple system of reward-type incentives. For example, a student who is learning to keep a work area organized and materials neat could be given a point for each day that her area is neat. When she accumulates a certain number of points she gets a predetermined reward.

Task 4: Ability Type Misbehaviors

For ongoing misbehaviors that stem from students' lack of ability or skill, be prepared to develop and implement an intervention plan that includes modifying the expectations or environment (for physiological inability) or providing instruction in the goal behavior (for lack of skill).

Sometimes a student misbehaves because he/she is either physiologically unable to exhibit the appropriate (goal) behaviors or does not know how to do so. The most effective intervention plans in these situations will include a reasonable response to the underlying cause of the situation. That is, if a student is physically or neurologically not able to exhibit the desired behavior, then your intervention must involve making modifications to the student's environment and/or adjusting your expectations. If the student is capable of the behavior, but does not know how to exhibit it, your intervention must involve teaching the student. In either case, implementing corrective consequences for this category of misbehavior is inappropriate at best and inhumane at worst.

When you believe that a student's misbehavior stems from a lack of ability, the first thing you need to ascertain is whether or not the student is capable of learning to exhibit the goal behavior. This is essential because if a student is not physiologically capable of exhibiting the goal behavior, establishing a plan (even a positive plan) to change the student's behavior would be cruel. Instead, you need to adjust your rules and expectations.

Consider the following two examples. First, imagine that you have a student in your class who is permanently confined to a wheelchair due to a spinal cord injury. You probably also have some kind of school rule to the effect of, "Students will walk in the halls." It is obviously completely inappropriate for you to expect this student to "walk" in the halls. It makes no sense to think that you could use either corrective consequences or positive incentives to get the student to walk rather than wheel himself in the halls. In fact, the idea of trying to "change" this student's behavior is actually inhumane. What you do is adjust the rule to fit this student's capabilities. That is, you learn to live with this situation with this student.

A more difficult example would be a case in which you have a student who is diagnosed with Tourette's Syndrome in your class. When reviewing this student's records, you see the notation that teachers are supposed to "ignore outbursts such as barking, snorting, or swearing" done by this student in class. Your first thought might be that such a recommendation is ridiculous. However, the only way a student with Tourette's Syndrome can control these kinds of behaviors is through the use of medication—and in some cases, medication does not completely eliminate them. Therefore, what you have to do is learn to live with this student and his disability.

If you are unsure whether a desired behavior is within a student's physiological capability, you need to check with your special education staff, school psychologist, and/or the student's physician(s).

NOTE

Unlike individuals with Tourette's Syndrome, children who have been identified as having Attention Deficit Disorder (ADD)—with or without Hyperactivity (ADHD)—are capable of learning to control their behavior. Although a student with this diagnosis may have some ability type problems, those problems can be treated using some of the strategies outlined below.

In this task, we present a four-phase process for helping students who exhibit misbehavior that is related to a lack of ability—but for whom the desired behaviors are physiologically possible. The four phases are summarized below and then explained in detail.

- At a neutral time, have a discussion and/or provide lessons on the goal behavior(s).
- Correct errors in a manner that provides instruction.
- Make accommodations to increase the student's chance of success.
- Provide positive feedback when the student is successful (or makes improvements). Set up reward-type incentives if simple positive feedback seems insufficient to motivate the student.

1 At a neutral time, have a discussion and/or provide lessons on the goal behavior(s).

At least three days per week, conduct lessons with the student. Use the lessons to model and have the student practice the goal behavior. Keep in mind that when a student lacks the ability to demonstrate a particular behavior, just talking about it will not be enough for the student to really learn it. Coaches know this. The coach who wants a beginning basketball team to learn about free throws not only provides step-by-step demonstrations of the process, but actually has the players use a ball and practice the skill. And, the coach does not do this just one time. He or she provides repetition and practice daily across a period of weeks.

If it does not seem possible for you to provide the instruction yourself, talk to your administrator. Maybe an instructional aide could cover your class for ten minutes a day, or maybe the school counselor could conduct the lessons with the student. In fact, if several students in the building have the same ability-type problem, the counselor might even run a small group session. For example, if there are one or two students in each of three first grade classes who have trouble staying on task and in their seats, the counselor (or another skilled person) could arrange to provide a daily twenty-minute lesson specifically on "staying on task" for all five or six students.

2 Correct errors in a manner that provides instruction.

Punishing students for exhibiting misbehaviors when they have not yet learned to exhibit a positive alternative is silly and potentially cruel. It is far more sensible and far more likely to improve the behavior if you respond to instances of misbehavior (i.e., correct) with a correction strategy such as proximity, gentle reprimands, a cueing signal, or redirection (all of which have been described in previous tasks in this module). For example, if you have a student who has been labeled ADD and who tends to "drum" on his desk, you might pre-arrange to give him a signal each time he starts to drum. Teach him that when he sees you give the signal, he needs to stop drumming.

3 Make accommodations to increase the student's chance of success.

Determine whether there are modifications you might make in terms of the daily schedule, class structure, behavioral expectations, classroom physical arrangements, your interactions with the student, and so on that would make it easier for the student to be successful. For example, with the first grader who has trouble staying in one place for more than a few minutes at a time, you might make a masking tape box on the floor around the student's desk. You could then tell student that this is his office and that if he feels the need to move around and/or get out of his seat, he can do so as long as he stays in his "office." In effect, what you are doing is expanding the range of what is acceptable behavior for the student, yet keeping parameters that reduce the possibility the student will disturb others.

4 Provide positive feedback when the student is successful (or makes improvements). Set up reward-type incentives if simple positive feedback seems insufficient to motivate the student.

Throughout the day as the student demonstrates success, or takes steps toward success, give him/her positive verbal feedback. Students who exhibit this category of misbehavior need information that lets them know when and what they are doing well. Without this positive feedback component, these students may feel overwhelmed and/or discouraged by the corrective feedback they receive when they make errors. If the student fails to make progress within a couple of weeks (i.e., the misbehavior is not decreasing and the goal behavior is not increasing), you might also want to consider establishing a simple reward-type incentive system. For example, you might do something like have the first-grade student with the masking tape office earn one point for each hour that he stays in his office (unless given permission to go outside the boundary). He could accumulate points, and then "spend" them on activities he particularly enjoys.

Task 5: Attention-Seeking Misbehaviors

For ongoing (but mild) attention-seeking misbehaviors, be prepared to develop and implement an intervention plan that includes planned ignoring.

An attention-seeking misbehavior is a mild, recurring behavior that a student knows is unacceptable, but engages in as a way to get teacher or peer attention. Chronic blurting out, excessive helplessness, tattling, minor disruptions, and so on are examples of behaviors that may be attention-seeking in nature. When a student is seeking attention via misbehavior, responding with a correction strategy or corrective consequence will necessarily give the student attention, and may actually end up reinforcing the student for misbehaving. The strategy that is most likely to "correct" attention-seeking misbehavior is planned ignoring. (NOTE: Planned ignoring is NOT appropriate for early-stage attention-seeking behavior. Instead, you want to give the student information—in hope of stopping the behavior before it becomes chronic.)

With planned ignoring, you reduce or eliminate the attention a student receives for engaging in misbehavior, while concurrently giving the student frequent attention when he or she is not engaged in misbehavior. The goal is for the student to learn that using misbehavior to get attention is ineffective, but that behaving responsibly results in frequent and very satisfying attention. Planned ignoring is not the same as tolerating a student's misbehavior. Tolerating misbehavior implies that one has given up expecting a change and has decided to "live with" the misbehavior. Planned ignoring is a conscious strategy applied by the teacher in an effort to change the misbehavior. What follows are suggested steps for implementing planned ignoring as part of an intervention plan designed to help a student learn to get his/her attention needs met without engaging in misbehavior.

1. Ascertain whether ignoring is an appropriate response.

   To determine if ignoring is the best strategy for the problem behavior, ask yourself the following questions:

   - **Is the misbehavior really attention-seeking in nature?**

     If the student's misbehavior is due to a lack of ability or awareness, ignoring will not work and can even be somewhat cruel. Not paying attention to a misbehavior caused by lack of awareness or ability is as inappropriate as ignoring math mistakes made by students. Without correction, students assume they are doing things correctly. If a student tattles on other students because he is trying to help, then he needs lessons and feedback about the difference between tattling and social responsibility. On the other hand, if the student fully understands that a behavior is not acceptable, but uses the misbehavior as a way to seek or demand attention from teacher or peers, then planned ignoring is likely to be effective.

- **Is the behavior itself acceptable, and the problem is with the amount (frequency or duration) of the behavior?**

Sometimes the issue with attention-seeking behavior is not that the behavior itself is inappropriate, but rather that the frequency or duration that student engages in the behavior is problematic. For example, say you have a student who asks a lot of questions and is always seeking teacher assistance. While you do not want to discourage the student from asking questions or seeking assistance, if he asks for help more than is necessary, that is learned helplessness.

You cannot ignore a student's questions or requests for assistance. You could not justify such action to the student, his family, or to your building principal. What you can do with a problem of excess, though, is to specify what a reasonable amount of the behavior would be. Using the previous example, you could first determine how much this student asks for help compared to other students of similar intellectual ability. For a couple of days, keep a record of how many times the target student asks for help and how many times one or two similar students ask for help. At the end of the second day, you might have a record that looks something like the following:

Mark		**Olivia**		**Rose**	
Mon.	Tues.	Mon.	Tues.	Mon.	Tues.
19	17	3	4	4	2

This objective information shows you that your concern is warranted. It also lets you know that your goal should be to get Mark to the point where he asks for help no more than five times during a day. You might set up a system in which each day, you give Mark fifteen tickets. Every time he asks for help, he has to give you one of the tickets. When all his tickets are gone, you will not be able to help him—that is, you will ignore requests for assistance that are in excess of the current limit. Conversely, each ticket he has left over at the end of the day will be worth one minute of time to help you after school or during recess. Once he is consistently staying below 10 requests in a day, you can modify the system so that he will only get ten tickets per day. You would continue the system until the student is only getting five tickets each day.

- **Is the misbehavior so severe (e.g., hitting) that ignoring is not an appropriate strategy?**

  Sometimes a behavior that is attention-seeking in nature is so severe that you cannot responsibly ignore it. For example, if a student is hitting other students, you must intervene. Or, if a student's disruptive behavior is so severe that lessons cannot continue, you must intervene. When an attention-getting misbehavior is that severe, you need to treat it as "purposeful/habitual" and include the use of corrective consequences (see Task 6). Remember, though, that the student wants attention, so when you assign a consequence make every effort to do so in a manner that gives the student as little attention as possible. In addition, be sure to make a concerted effort to give the student frequent attention when he is not engaged in misbehavior. The goal is for the student to learn that, although he will get attention for misbehavior, it is less attention and less satisfying attention than what he can easily get for behaving responsibly.

- **Will you ignore the behavior from all students or just from the target student?**

  If the behavior is exhibited chronically by one or two students, and intermittently by several others, you should ignore any student who exhibits it. For example, if blurting out without raising a hand is a problem for quite a few students, make a classwide announcement that you are going to ignore blurting out and only call on students who remember to raise their hands. However, if the behavior is exhibited primarily by one student, plan to ignore that student when she engages in the misbehavior, and give verbal reprimands to any other student who exhibits the misbehavior.

  Once you determine that a behavior is attention-seeking and that ignoring would be an appropriate correction strategy, the next step is to develop an intervention that includes using planned ignoring. To develop an effective plan, you need to give careful thought to and specify for yourself exactly which behaviors you will ignore, which you will assign corrective consequences, and which you will encourage. For example, you might end up with a list something like the following:

BEHAVIOR TO IGNORE	BEHAVIOR REQUIRING CONSEQUENCE	BEHAVIOR TO ENCOURAGE
Blurting out	Bothering other students	Raising hand
Silly noises	Hitting	Hands/feet to self
Tapping pencil	Kicking	Working quietly
		On task
		Getting immediately to work
		Following directions

2 Discuss the proposed plan with the student.

When the problem involves only one student, arrange to meet with that student (and if appropriate, with the student's family). During the meeting, describe the problem behavior and your proposed plan to ignore it. Be sure to make it clear that your intent is not to ignore the student as a person, but the behavior the student should be managing without attention from you. Explain that because you have such high expectations for the student's ability to manage this behavior, you are not going to give reminders and/or assign consequences. Do inform the student that if he engages in more severe misbehaviors that cannot be ignored (e.g., bothering others, hitting, and kicking), you will assign corrective consequences. Finally, let the student know that you will be looking for opportunities to give him your time and attention when he is behaving responsibly.

Decide whether or not you need to discuss the fact that you will be ignoring the target student's behavior (e.g., noises and blurting out) with the entire class. If you believe this to be necessary, inform the student during your initial meeting. Make sure the student knows that you will present the plan in a way that communicates that everyone in the class has behaviors to work on and that his is getting attention in positive ways. If you discussed ignoring as a strategy during your first two weeks of school, review the key concepts you taught the students—most notably that ignoring is a strategy used to help a student learn to manage his/her own behavior.

If the situation involves a behavior that is exhibited by many students, inform the entire class that you will use ignoring as a strategy. Emphasize that ignoring does not mean the behavior is acceptable. Rather, explain that you are using ignoring because this particular behavior is so clearly unacceptable that you should not have to take your valuable time to tell students not to do something they know they should not do. Keep the tone of this discussion complimentary rather than accusatory (i.e., communicate high expectations).

3 When the misbehavior occurs, continue what you are doing and provide positive feedback to other students.

Once you have informed the student of your plan to ignore, give no attention to the misbehavior. Some teachers feel a need to tell the student each time, "I am ignoring you now." DO NOT DO THIS! Telling a student that you are ignoring him is giving him attention. Give no attention at the time of the misbehavior. Do not shrug, sigh, or act exasperated. Teach. Present lessons. Give your attention to students who are doing the responsible thing at that moment. With primary age students, you can even overtly praise students who are doing what you want. "Brett, you are keeping your attention focused on your work and you are working quietly without making any unnecessary noise."

If other students pay attention to the student engaged in misbehavior, give a gentle verbal reprimand. "James, Adam can take care of himself, and the most helpful thing you can do right now is mind your own business or do your own work." If another student laughs at the target student, you might say something like, "Belinda, please don't laugh. Your laughter might encourage Carla to continue clowning around and that would not be helpful to Carla. Mind your own business and do your own work."

IMPORTANT!!

During the first several days of using planned ignoring, you should expect the behavior to get worse before it begins to get better. Believe it or not, when a behavior gets worse it is a good sign that the strategy will eventually work. Remember, the student has received attention for exhibiting this behavior in the past, and that attention has been very satisfying. What's happening now is that when the student exhibits the behavior, she is not getting attention. The logical response from the student is to try harder to get your attention using the behavior that has been so successful in the past. If you continue to ignore, eventually the student will learn that if she really wants attention, she needs to behave responsibly.

Be consistent. Ignoring intermittently is worse than not ignoring at all. For example, if you have decided to ignore blurting out, ignore all blurting out. If you ignore it the first five times it happens, and then get frustrated and assign a consequence on the sixth time, you simply teach the student to be more persistent—"The teacher will eventually give me attention if I misbehave long enough."

A common question regarding ignoring is "What if I am ignoring a student's noises and blurting out, and then he hits someone?" The answer is that, under those circumstances, you should implement your consequence for hitting. This is not inconsistent. In fact, it is the reason we encourage you to develop lists of behaviors to ignore, behaviors requiring consequences, and behaviors to encourage. You need to be prepared to consistently ignore the behaviors that will benefit from ignoring. However, if the student exhibits a behavior that you pre-decided to have consequences for, then you need to stop ignoring and implement the consequence.

4 When the attention-seeking misbehavior ceases, give the student attention.

You need to demonstrate to the student that responsible behavior results in attention. Therefore, shortly after the student begins behaving responsibly (for primary students, within a minute or two; for intermediate and middle school students, within five minutes), give the student attention. Either praise the responsible behavior or just go over and talk to the student for a few moments. "Carla, you are working so quietly, I thought I would come over and see if you had any questions or needed any help. No? Well, OK, but if you need anything, raise your hand and I'll be right over."

5 Maintain frequent interactions with the student when he is not misbehaving.

In Module 5: Motivation, we explained the importance of providing at least three times more attention to positive behavior than negative behavior. This is *essential* whenever you are using planned ignoring. If the student does not experience lots of attention when behaving responsibly, he will simply step up the severity of misbehavior until you cannot possibly ignore him (e.g., he will start hitting other students). You must praise this student frequently and give him lots of noncontingent attention.

6 Monitor the student's behavior to determine whether progress is being made.

At least once per week, count the frequency or record the duration of this behavior. After two weeks of using planned ignoring, evaluate whether the situation is improving. If it is not, continue the ignoring and increase the amount and intensity of attention you provide when the student is not misbehaving. If there is still no improvement after another two weeks, abandon planned ignoring as a strategy and treat this misbehavior as purposeful and/or habitual (see Task 6).

Task 6: Purposeful/Habitual Misbehaviors

For ongoing misbehaviors that are habitual and/or serve a purpose other than getting attention, be prepared to develop and implement an intervention plan that includes the use of corrective consequences.

Chronic misbehavior may occur for reasons other than a lack of awareness or ability, or a need for attention. For example, chronic misbehavior may help a student avoid something aversive or demonstrate and achieve a sense of power and control. There are also cases when the original purpose of a student's misbehavior is no longer relevant and the student misbehaves just because the inappropriate behaviors have become firmly established in his/her behavioral repertoire.

When ongoing misbehavior is truly purposeful and/or habitual, it will probably be necessary to use corrective consequences (i.e., punishers) to help the student learn that the misbehavior has negative costs. The use of corrective consequences alone, however, is not likely to be sufficient to change a student's behavior. Therefore, in addition to using corrective consequences, an intervention plan for purposeful/habitual misbehaviors needs to include efforts to remove any positive or satisfying aspects of engaging in the misbehavior for the student as well as efforts to continually demonstrate that positive behavior leads to positive results.

The remainder of this task describes intervention planning guidelines for purposeful/habitual misbehavior. The information addresses the three important components of an intervention plan for this type of misbehavior: a) removing any positive/satisfying aspects of demonstrating the misbehavior; b) demonstrating to the student that positive behavior leads to positive results; and c) responding to the misbehavior by assigning appropriate corrective consequences. The final section of the task is a "Menu of Classroom-Based Corrective Consequences" in which you will find descriptions of several consequences that can reasonably be used in a classroom setting.

NOTE

If chronic misbehavior is exhibited by a number of students in your class, you should plan to use one or more of the corrective consequences described in the menu at the end of the module, and to implement one or more of the classwide motivation systems described in Module 8.

---

1 Remove any positive/satisfying aspects of demonstrating the misbehavior.

Remember that the misbehavior you want to change has served a purpose for the student. For example, a student may misbehave in order to be removed from class and escape doing the academic work, or a student may not participate in class because he enjoys reading his book more than listening to the lesson. As you develop your intervention plan, you need to ensure that the student will no longer get whatever it is that he or she has been getting from the misbehavior. If a student has gotten power by engaging in arguments with you, your plan will need to address how you will avoid engaging in arguments with this student. If a student has been using misbehavior to escape from doing his work, you will need to ensure that the corrective consequence included in your intervention plan does not result in the student getting out of work. If a student does not complete work because he plays with toys at his desk, part of your plan must be that there are no toys at his desk. If a student enjoys hurting other people's feelings with mean comments, you will need to train yourself and the other students to not take his critical comments personally ("Sticks and stones may. . .").

2 Continually demonstrate to the student that positive behavior leads to positive results.

In addition to making sure that the student will not benefit from the misbehavior, your intervention plan should also specifically address how you can continually demonstrate to the student that responsible behavior is worthwhile. This can include efforts to meet the student's needs in positive ways and efforts to increase the student's motivation to behave responsibly.

- **Meet the student's needs in a positive way.**

  Once you identify what purpose a student's misbehavior is serving, you need to try to find some positive way of satisfying that purpose. For example, if a fourth grade student talks back to adults as a means of seeking power, you might ask the student if he would be willing to be a positive help around the school and use his power to help the school be a better and safer place. You could give the student a choice among several different jobs (e.g., being a tutor for a younger student, teaching and refereeing soccer games during the primary recess, or serving as a fire drill assistant to the principal). Job options such as refereeing soccer games during recess have other potential benefits because a counselor could use the time as an opportunity to "train" the student in how to be a positive leader for the younger students. Along with the use of appropriate corrective consequences if the student does talk back, having a positive position of power can solve this kind of problem behavior in a couple of months.

  If a student is seeking to escape academic work, you need to ask yourself whether the student is capable of doing the work successfully. If not, you should modify his assignments or get some kind of help for the student so he will begin to experience success.

When a misbehavior involves competing reinforcers, you can arrange for the student to have access to the desired reinforcers when he has met your expectations. For example, if the student likes to read novels rather than do his work, you might allow him to read when his other work is completed, or occasionally give the student an alternative assignment that involves reading a novel and giving a report to the class.

- **Increase the student's motivation to behave responsibly.**

For some students, a change in the type and/or frequency of positive feedback from you may be sufficient to increase the student's motivation to behave responsibly (see Module 5: Motivation). In other cases, it may be necessary to establish some form of positive feedback system—in which the student earns rewards for exhibiting positive behavior. For ideas on classwide systems, see Module 8: Classwide Motivation Systems. For ideas on individual contracts and systems, see Sprick and Howard (1995). An example of an individual system (for increasing homework completion) from this resource is shown in Figure 7.11.

Figure 7.11: Individual Motivation System (Less Disruptive)

Individual System to Increase Homework Completion

When a student is not concerned about the designated consequences of failing to turn in completed homework and/or does not value the sense of satisfaction that comes with completing and turning in required work, you may need to implement a system of external incentives (i.e., rewards and consequences) to motivate him to turn in completed homework on time.

1. **Establish a structured system for reinforcing the appropriate behavior and providing a consequence for the inappropriate behavior.**

   a. With the student, create a list of rewards he would like to earn. The rewards may need to be relatively high in perceived value in order to create a powerful incentive to motivate the student to get his homework completed on a regular basis. To get some ideas for the list, watch what the student does during less structured times in class—what does he do when he has choices? Or you can ask the student for his preferences.

   You might also have the student read through the list of your ideas and then together discuss the possibilities. If the student's parent(s) will be working with you and the student on the plan, maybe some of the reinforcers could be things the parent(s) provide at home (e.g., having a friend spend the night, a later curfew, additional money for clothing, etc.).

   b. Assign "prices" (in points) for each of the rewards on the list and have the student select the reward he would like to earn first.

   The prices should be based on the instructional, personnel, and/or monetary cost of the items. Monetary cost is clear—the more expensive the item, the more points required to earn it. Instructional cost refers to the amount of instructional time lost or interfered with by a particular reward. Thus, an activity which causes the student to miss part of academic instruction should require more points than one the student can do on his own free time. Personnel cost involves the time required by you and/or other staff to fulfill the reinforcer. Having lunch with the principal, therefore, would cost more points than spending five minutes of free time with a friend.

   The prices must be low enough that the student will think, for example, "You mean all I have to do is _____, and I can earn _____!" If the desired reinforcers are priced too high and would take the student too long to earn (from his perspective), he may not be any more motivated to complete his homework than he was without the system.

   c. Develop a homework completion self-monitoring form and establish a system to translate each successfully filled in space into points. For example, the student might earn one point each for accurately recording the assignment, the due date, and the necessary materials (three points total). When the assignment is completed and turned in, the student might earn another five points, making each homework assignment worth a total of eight points.

   Larger assignments or projects, such as writing a report, could be broken down into steps, each with its own line and due date on the monitoring form. For example, the outline, the note cards, the rough draft, and the final draft could be treated as separate assignments, each worth eight points—making the whole report worth a possible 32 reinforcement points.

   d. When the student has accumulated enough points to earn the reward he has chosen, he "spends" the points necessary and the system begins again. That is, he selects another reward to earn and begins with zero points.

2. **Respond consistently to the inappropriate behavior.**

   a. Gently correct the student when he fails to turn in his homework.

   b. Establish consequences (in addition to any predetermined class-wide consequences) for not being responsible for his homework. The most obvious consequence would be that if the student does not turn in the work, he fails that assignment. However, that consequence alone may be too abstract and delayed to affect the student's behavior in the short run. Another, and more immediate, consequence will probably be necessary (e.g., the student must stay in from recess/breaks and/or stay after school until the work is caught up).

   If the parent(s) are working with you on the reinforcement portion of the plan, you can consider asking them to implement a consequence at home as well, such as grounding the student until he is caught up with his work. However, this is only appropriate if the parent(s) are also reinforcing the student—the parent(s)' role should never be only punitive.

   c. When neither home-based nor school-based consequences are possible, for whatever reason, it puts more pressure on the positive aspects of the intervention to ensure that the plan is powerful enough to motivate the student to complete his homework—despite the lack of consequences for not turning it in.

3. **Use reinforcement to encourage appropriate behavior.**

   a. Give the student increased praise and attention for turning in completed homework on time.

   b. In addition, show interest and enthusiasm about how the student is doing on the system. "Salvador, every day this week you have earned all eight points for every assignment. Congratulations! You should be very proud of your organizational skill."

3 Implement corrective consequences that are appropriate to the problem behavior.

When misbehavior is purposeful/habitual, you need to carefully plan how you will respond to specific instances of the behavior. If you do not preplan what your response will be, there is a high probability that you may inadvertently reinforce the misbehavior. The following suggestions can help you choose and implement an effective corrective consequence—one that will help the student learn that engaging in misbehavior has a logical cost associated with it. (NOTE: At the end of this task is a descriptive menu of possible corrective consequences you can implement in your classroom.)

- **Plan to implement the corrective consequence consistently.**

  If corrective consequences are going to reduce or eliminate purposeful/habitual misbehavior, they must be implemented *consistently*. When you implement a corrective consequence only some of the times the student exhibits the misbehavior, the consequence (no matter how severe) is not likely to change the behavior. In fact, it may even make things worse than if there was no consequence at all. Anytime a student is able to engage in a misbehavior and not receive the designated consequence, he is likely to feel a sense of satisfaction. "Getting away with it" can be great fun and the student may find he likes "playing games" to see how frequently he can engage in the behavior and not get caught.

  Teachers tend to implement corrective consequences based on an accumulation of misbehavior. Thus, what ends up controlling the use of consequences is teacher emotion. The student "gets away" with it the first five times he is disruptive; then on the sixth time, the teacher gets mad and implements a consequence. What happens is, the first several times the behavior does not "bother" the teacher, but by the sixth time the teacher is "fed up"! While understandable, this leads to grossly inconsistent responses. To change purposeful and/or habitual misbehavior you need to define specific behaviors that are not acceptable and then implement corrective consequences for those behaviors each time, regardless of how you feel about the behavior at the time.

  Your goal is to develop clear expectations of what behaviors are unacceptable so that you can be consistent. If you are concerned about disruptions, specify the precise behaviors you consider disruptive. Also be sure to identify examples of noise and class participation that are not disruptive. If your concern is a student who is disrespectful, describe specific ways the student has been disrespectful and ways the student could have behaved in the same situations that would have been respectful. Creating a T-chart that specifies responsible and irresponsible behavior can help. Use the chart when discussing your expectations and consequences with the student. Figure 7.12 is a sample T-chart for a student who makes disruptive noises. (NOTE: Many of the behaviors on this chart would need to be demonstrated by you so that the student could see and hear the difference.)

Figure 7.12: Sample T-Chart for Disruptive Behavior

RESPONSIBLE NOISE	DISRUPTIVE NOISE
. **Putting paper in the trash.**	. **Wadding up paper.**
. **Getting paper out.**	. **Tearing up paper.**
. **Quietly opening/closing notebook rings.**	. **Snapping open/closed notebook rings or slamming notebook on desk.**
. **Writing, sharpening pencil at breaks.**	. **Tapping pencil.**
. **Raising hand, waiting to be called on, using an appropriate volume level.**	. **Blurting out, without raising hand or waiting to be called on.**
. **Working quietly.**	. **Humming, making "clicking" noises with tongue.**
. **Once or twice a work period, asking a neighbor a work-related question.**	. **Talking about anything other than work during work periods.**

Once you have developed a T-chart and discussed what constitutes responsible and irresponsible behavior with the student, be sure to implement the designated corrective consequence *every* time the student exhibits one of the irresponsible behaviors on the list. Be aware that your greatest tendency to be inconsistent will not occur on a "bad day" when you are tired, but rather on a "good day" when you are feeling relaxed and refreshed. On good days, the behavior is not going to be as likely to bother you and so you may be inclined to let it go—i.e., to ignore it. DO NOT DO THIS. The student needs to know that each time he engages in the misbehavior the consequence will be implemented, whether or not the behavior bothers you at a particular moment.

- **Make sure the corrective consequence fits the severity and frequency of the misbehavior.**

When deciding on the corrective consequence that you will implement, you need to choose one that matches the severity of the problem. You can start by examining the irresponsible behaviors listed on your T-chart. Choose a consequence that fits even the mildest example of the unacceptable behavior. All too often, teachers pick a consequence that is so harsh they are unwilling to implement it when the occasion arises. "Now Joanie, stop that because I do not want to have to give you a detention." This leads to inconsistency. You want a consequence that is mild enough that you will be comfortable implementing it every time the student exhibits one of the irresponsible behaviors. As you think about your choice of a consequence, look at each example of the misbehavior listed on your T-chart. If the consequence seems too harsh for any of those examples of irresponsible behavior, you may need to select a milder consequence. When determining the severity of consequences, err on the side of making consequences too mild—because you may not follow through on consequences that are overly harsh.

Whatever corrective consequence you choose, plan to implement the consequence in the same way for all of the behaviors within that category. In other words, if you have decided to use "demerits," all disruptive acts should result in one demerit. Do not create a situation in which some disruptive acts get one demerit and some get three—which would mean that every time the student is disruptive you will have to explain why you have assigned one or three demerits. If you decide to use "time owed" as a consequence for a student who tends to be disrespectful, have each infraction equal the same amount of time owed (e.g., one minute). Do not set it up so that some instances of disrespect cost one minute, while others cost five minutes. You do not want to put yourself in the position of having to explain why one misbehavior equals one minute owed and the next equals five minutes owed. Again, if you err on the side of consequences that are too mild, you are more likely to follow through than if the consequences are too harsh.

In addition to matching the corrective consequence to severity of the infraction, you also need to consider the frequency of the infraction. For example, at first glance it might seem reasonable to say that every time a student is disruptive the student loses five minutes from recess. However, if the student is likely to be disruptive seven times in a day and you only have one fifteen minute recess, that student will end up not having to "pay" for each infraction. In fact, by the middle of the morning, the student might very well have already lost her entire recess, and justifiably decide that there is no reason to even bother to behave. Furthermore, when consequence severity does not match misbehavior frequency, you might be more inclined to be inconsistent in implementation. For example, by the second infraction you might start thinking that you'll let some of the behaviors go by because you don't want the student to lose her entire recess too soon. Overly harsh consequences make consistency difficult for most teachers. You are better off setting it up so that the student loses one minute of recess for each infraction. This way, even if the student has a bad day, you will be likely to consistently implement the consequence. "Joanie, that is disruptive. You owe another minute."

- **Plan to implement the consequence unemotionally.**

  With purposeful and/or habitual misbehavior there is a high probability that the student has learned that she can make adults frustrated, hurt or angry. If you get angry when correcting the student, your anger may actually reinforce the student's misbehavior. When a student feels hostility toward adults, seeing the adult frustrated or exasperated can be highly satisfying. For a student who feels powerless, getting an adult angry on a regular basis provides a huge sense of power and control. You need to strive to implement corrective consequences unemotionally so your reactions do not give the student the idea that misbehavior is a way to achieve power over you.

- **Plan to interact with the student briefly at the time of a misbehavior. Never argue.**

  When a student misbehaves, your interaction with that student should last less than five seconds. Simply state the misbehavior and state the consequence. A common mistake is to explain and justify. All explanations should be done in your initial discussion with the student, or in a regularly scheduled follow-up meeting.

  If you think the student will have a tendency to argue or deny that he exhibited the misbehavior, tell the student during your initial discussion that at the time of an incident you will not argue or negotiate and that you will ignore any attempts on his part to do so. At the same time, let the student know that if he ever wants to speak to you about something he thinks is unfair, he can make an appointment to see you before or after school. Once you have made this clear, if the student tries to argue, simply remind him that he can make an appointment to see you. Then resume teaching.

  Although keeping interactions brief may be a difficult habit to get into, you will find that it allows you to keep your focus where it belongs—on teaching and on providing positive feedback to all students when they are meeting your expectations. Think about the consequence you are planning to use for a misbehavior. If you cannot imagine implementing that consequence without lengthy explanations or negotiations at the time of the misbehavior, you may need to select a different consequence.

Implement the three component plan.

Once you have the behaviors (positive and negative) and consequences well defined, ask yourself some "what if" type questions. What if the student objects? What if the parents object? Will my administrator support me if there are objections? What if the behavior increases for a few days; can I still follow through with this consequence? Do I need to explain this consequence to the entire class? Will I apply the consequence to anyone who exhibits this behavior or just to the target student? The more issues you can identify and address, the greater the likelihood that your intervention plan will be effective (i.e., help reduce, and eventually eliminate, the misbehavior). Discuss any "what if" questions you cannot answer with your school administrator or building counselor. Do not implement any intervention plan until you know you can follow through on all aspects of the plan. Remember that your plan needs to address how you will eliminate (or reduce) the probability that the student will get positive benefits from engaging in the misbehavior and how you will see that the student experiences positive benefits from exhibiting responsible behavior.

Once all aspects of your plan have been developed and all potential difficulties have been resolved, meet with the student (or class if the consequence will be implemented classwide) to explain what will happen each time she engages in the misbehavior. Make sure the student knows the cost of choosing to exhibit the misbehavior in the future, but keep the tone of this discussion positive. Remember, we recommend that you implement an intervention plan consistently for at least two weeks. Collect data on the behavior during this two week period to determine if the behavior is getting better or worse. Even if things seem to get worse for a few days, do not switch to a different consequence right away. After two weeks, if the behavior is about the same or getting worse, go through the planning steps again and make necessary modifications. Monitor the behavior for two more weeks. If the behavior improves, continue what you are doing. If the behavior still has not improved, consider implementing a motivation system to encourage the student to improve his/her behavior in addition to trying a new corrective consequence.

A Menu of Classroom-Based Corrective Consequences

The following pages contain descriptions of effective corrective consequences that can be implemented in a classroom setting. Each description includes a brief explanation of what the consequence is and how to use it. Remember, when using corrective consequences be sure to assign them consistently and calmly (i.e., unemotionally), and while interacting with the student as briefly as possible.

NOTE

Never use a corrective consequence that involves humiliation or ridicule of the student, and avoid using academic tasks as corrective consequences (e.g., extra math homework or writing an essay).

Time Owed

When a student misbehaves and you have to intervene, some of your time is wasted. Therefore, a reasonable corrective consequence is to have the student lose time from an activity she/he values, (e.g., off of recess or after school). "Time owed" is an appropriate and effective corrective consequence for misbehaviors that occur frequently (e.g., disruptions, talking during lessons, name calling, or disrespectful behavior) and for behaviors that tend to involve duration (e.g., a student is out of his seat for a period of time, or a student takes an excessive amount of time to comply with a direction). In these types of situations, the time a student owes will be equal to the time spent misbehaving.

To use this corrective consequence, you will have to decide when the time owed will be paid back. It needs to be a time that the student values. For example, with an elementary student who likes recess, time owed from recess is an easy and logical choice. If your schedule does not include recesses or if the misbehaving student prefers not to go to recess, possible alternatives are after school, during passing periods between classes, or from free time activities. It is important that the time NOT be paid in such a way that it may interfere with the student's time with another teacher. Thus, if keeping middle students after class for more than one minute would mean that a student would not be able to get to his/her next class on time, you should plan not to keep any student for more than one minute. Similarly, an elementary student should not be assigned to repay time owed during P.E. class if this would reduce the time the student spends with the P.E. teacher.

Another decision you will need to make is how much time will be owed for each infraction. As a general rule, you want to keep the amount of time short enough that you will not hesitate to implement the consequence each time the student misbehaves. When making this decision, also keep in mind the amount of time you have access to that can be used as a penalty. Thus, elementary teachers might have students owe one minute per infraction, while middle school teachers (who can't keep students after class for more than one minute) may use 15 seconds owed for each infraction. Although 15 seconds might sound almost silly, it is actually a pretty long time for an adolescent who wants to be in the hall talking with friends; and it allows you to assign the consequence for up to four infractions. Middle school teachers may need to establish a policy such as "Each infraction will cost 15 seconds of time owed, and if there are more than four infractions, the student will be assigned to After-School Detention." When dealing with behaviors that last for a period of time, establish a minute by minute correspondence, with the number of minutes owed corresponding directly to the number of minutes the student engages in the misbehavior.

A final decision with this corrective consequence is what to have the student do when repaying the time owed. As a general rule, we recommend that you have the student do nothing. During a "first time," you may wish to use the time to discuss the misbehavior and ways the student could behave more responsibly in the future. Do not do this regularly, however, as the one-on-one interaction time with you may become reinforcing to the student and actually serve to perpetuate the misbehavior.

Time-out

Many people think that the purpose of "time-out" is to send the student to an aversive setting. That is not the case. The actual purpose of time-out is to remove a misbehaving student from the opportunity to earn positive reinforcement. That is, the goal is to communicate to the student that if he engages in the misbehavior, he will not get to participate in the interesting, productive, and enjoyable activities from which he is removed. The obvious implication here is that instruction and classroom activities need to be interesting, productive and enjoyable. Following are descriptions of four different types of time-out that are appropriate for different logistical situations and different ages of students.

Time-out from a favorite object (primary level):

When developing your intervention plan, you might ask the student if he would like to bring a favorite object, such as a stuffed animal, to class to watch her work and follow the rules. Initially the object is placed on the student's desk. If the student misbehaves, the object is removed and placed on the teacher's desk facing away from the student. When the student begins behaving appropriately, the object is returned to the student's desk. Rhode, et al. (1992) describe this as a Bumpy Bunny Time-Out. If you are concerned that the student might play with the object, explain to the student that playing with the object will mean that the object goes to time-out on your desk. Another option is to initially place the object near the student (e.g., on a bookshelf near where the student sits). If the student misbehaves, the object would be taken to a different part of the room and placed facing away from the student. When the student begins to behave responsibly again, you would return the object to the shelf near the student so that it can "watch" the student behaving responsibly.

Time-out from small group instruction (elementary level):

If a student misbehaves during small group instruction, you can have the student push back her chair so that she is not physically part of the group. You should conduct the next minute or two of instruction in as fun and reinforcing a manner as you possibly can. You want the student to feel that she is missing out on the privilege of participating in something that is enjoyable and beneficial.

Time-out at desk (elementary level):

If a student misbehaves, ask the student to put his head down on his desk and close his eyes for a short period of time (e.g., two minutes). This form of time out is very mild, but can be effective for relatively minor problems such as a student who tends to cause disruptions during instructional periods or during independent seatwork.

Time-out in class—isolation area (elementary and middle school levels):

In this option, you establish a "time-out area" in a low traffic part of your classroom. It can be as simple as having a chair off to the side of the room, or it can involve something like having an area behind a screen—arranged so that you can see the student, but he cannot see the majority of his classmates.

With all the options, you should keep the length of any time-out brief, and you should not allow the student to take work to the time out area. For primary students, a two- or three-minute time-out is best; for intermediate and middle school students, the optimal time is five minutes. When using this consequence, each time a student misbehaves, she/he should be instructed to go to time-out. The time-out period does not begin until the student is in the area, seated and quiet.

If you think the student is unlikely to go to time-out, and the student is old enough to understand time owed, establish that when instructed to go to time-out, he has one minute to get there and get settled. Any time longer than one minute will result in the student owing the extra amount of time off of recess or after school. If the student is unlikely to understand time owed (as in the case of a kindergarten student or a student with cognitive deficits), plan to conduct a few "practice sessions" in which you model, and have the student role-play going to time-out. If you conduct sessions like this, be sure the student knows he has not done anything wrong, and that you are just pretending so that he can learn how to go to time-out when you need to ask him.

Time-out in another class (elementary or middle school levels):

For students who are likely to misbehave during an in-class time-out (e.g., the student will clown around to get other students to laugh at her), it may be necessary to assign the student to time-out in another class. To do this, you need to find a teacher with a room near yours who has a class with fairly mature students. It could be a younger grade or an older grade, but should probably not be your exact grade level.

If the student misbehaves in your rooms, she should be sent to the "time-out teacher's room." This teacher should have a prearranged spot for the student—e.g., a chair in a low traffic area of the class—and should preteach his/her class to ignore the student when she enters. The time-out teacher should not be required to stop teaching his/her class or do problem solving with the misbehaving student. The idea behind this procedure is simply that the student is less likely to "show off" for students in a different class (especially a different grade level class).

Restitution

Restitution, which was presented as a correction strategy for early-stage problems in Task 2, can also be effective with chronic purposeful misbehaviors if they involve damage to property or to social relationships. That is, if a student engages in behavior that causes damage, a logical consequence is that the student has to repair the damage. For example, if a student makes a mess in the restroom (e.g., using paper towels to plug a sink so water runs all over the floor), requiring the student to use a mop to dry the floor is more logical than having the custodian clean up the mess.

NOTE

You probably cannot have the student use chemicals such as disinfectants, but he can certainly use a mop and bucket. When used with ongoing misbehavior, the "amount" of the restitution should increase with successive instances of misbehavior. Thus, if a student wrote on a desk, you might have him wash the desk. If he did it a second time, you would have him wash all the desks in the class.

Positive Practice

Positive practice (or overcorrection) is an appropriate corrective consequence to use with infractions for which having the student practice the responsible behavior would be effective. An obvious example is if a student runs in the halls, ask her to go back and walk. A student who runs in the halls repeatedly might be required to spend time during recess or after school practicing walking in the halls.

Response Cost—Loss of Points

If you use any kind of a point system in your class, you might want to set it up so that certain infractions result in point "fines." More detailed information on how to use point systems as a management tool is provided in Module 8: Classwide Motivation Systems. In addition to their usefulness in promoting motivation, point systems also provide you with another corrective consequence option.

An example of a simple way to use a point system as a corrective consequence is to set it up so that the student starts each day with twenty points. Every time you have to speak to him about the problem behavior, he loses a point. At the end of the day, you write the number of points he has left on a special note that goes home with him. Each remaining point equals ten minutes of television/video game time (or some other privilege the student enjoys) at home. The less the student misbehaves, the more points he has at the end of the day, and the more television time he gets. Obviously, this system depends on family cooperation. Also, because your main interaction with the system is to give the student attention when he has misbehaved, you will need to make a concerted effort to pay attention to the student when he is not misbehaving.

Response Cost Lottery

This is a variation on a response cost consequence that can be used in situations where there are three or four students in class who have challenging behaviors. You give those students, or even every student in the class, a certain number of tickets (e.g., ten) at the beginning of each day (or each week for middle school level). Each time a student misbehaves, that student loses a ticket. At the end of the day (or week), the students write their names on all their remaining tickets and place them in a container (hat, bowl, box) for a drawing. The name of the student on the ticket drawn gets a treat or a small reward. The more tickets a student has, the greater his/her chances of winning.

Detention

Detention is usually a schoolwide system that involves assigning a student to spend a set amount of time (e.g., 40 minutes) in a non-stimulating setting. Most schools that use detention have their detention periods after school and/or before school and/or during lunch. When used as a schoolwide procedure, any teacher can assign any student to detention. Often, detention is structured so that the students in detention are required to do academic tasks during the period. One problem with detention is that students may find it reinforcing if they happen to have friends assigned to the same detention. As with any corrective consequence you try, keep records. If you are repeatedly assigning the same student to detention across a period of weeks, then this particular corrective consequence is not working for this student, and you should modify your correction plan to include a more effective consequence.

Demerits

Demerits essentially represent negative points, which when accumulated, result in the loss of a privilege or the imposition of a negative consequence. Demerits can be used to soften a pre-determined consequence that might otherwise be overly harsh for a single example of a misbehavior. For example, if the consequence for talking in class is after-school detention (which seems rather harsh for a single instance), the teacher is likely to respond to that behavior inconsistently—sometimes ignoring the behavior, sometimes threatening ("If you keep talking I am going to have to give you a detention"), and maybe finally giving the detention. The use of demerits might allow the teacher to set up a more consistent policy. For example, a middle school teacher might tell students that each time he has to speak to a student about talking in class (or other minor disruptions), that student will get a demerit. If a student gets four demerits within one week, it equals an after-school detention. The teacher is more likely to intervene every time there is a disruptive behavior (because the response for each single incident is reasonable), meaning more consistency.

Another way to use demerits (which may be especially useful for elementary teachers) is to set it up so that all students who have no more than five demerits get to participate in a free time activity at the end of the day (but those with six or more do not get to participate). You could even up the ante by arranging to give a special treat to each student who had no more than one demerit.

Office Referral

Referring a student to the administrator should be used only in cases involving the most severe misbehaviors—i.e., physically dangerous behavior and/or illegal behavior. If you think there may be other behaviors for which you might want to send a student to the office, you should discuss these circumstances with the administrator ahead of time, so that she/he can coordinate a plan for when the student is sent to the office.

Module 7: Correction Procedures

Self-Assessment Checklist

Use the worksheet on the following pages to identify which (or which parts) of the tasks (including the introductory concepts) described in this module you have completed. For any item that has not been completed, note what needs to be done to complete it. Then translate your notes onto your planning calendar in the form of specific actions that you can take.

COMPLETED	TASK	NOTES & IMPLEMENTATION IDEAS
	INTRODUCTORY CONCEPTS If my class is bordering on being out-of-control, before considering the information in Module 7, I will: • review, and modify as necessary, the organizational variables of my classroom (Module 2); • review, and redefine as necessary, my behavioral expectations (Module 3); • review my use of the 3-step process for communicating expectations (Modules 3 and 4); • consider implementing a classwide motivation system to encourage students to behave responsibly (Module 8). I understand the importance of the following concepts related to correcting misbehavior: • My efforts to eliminate/reduce misbehavior will be more effective if I have considered how I will correct inappropriate behaviors ahead of time. • The only way I can judge the effectiveness of my correction efforts is by whether a targeted behavior decreases over time. • There are many causes of/purposes for misbehavior and my correction efforts will be more effective if they address the cause or purpose of the targeted behavior. • Although corrective consequences may be necessary and useful in managing some misbehavior, used alone they are not likely to eliminate the targeted misbehaviors.	

COMPLETED	TASK	NOTES & IMPLEMENTATION IDEAS
	ANALYZE MISBEHAVIOR I understand the difference and can distinguish among classroom rule violations, early-stage misbehaviors, and chronic misbehaviors. I understand that, in general, I should be prepared to assign corrective consequences for classroom rule violations, use informaton-giving corrections in response to early-stage misbehaviors, and develop and implement an intervention plan that addresses the underlying causes of/purposes for chronic misbehavior. I understand that the steps in dealing with chronic misbehaviors are to: • analyze the "nature" of the problem, which will include collecting data; • develop a preliminary plan based on that analysis; • discuss my preliminary plan with the student (and family); • implement the intervention plan for at least two weeks, while monitoring student behavior to determine progress. I understand and can explain the following subcategories of chronic misbehavior: awareness type, ability type; attention-seeking; and purposeful/habitual. I have listed (or will list) all the misbehaviors that are currently occurring in my classroom, in order from greatest concern to least concern, and for each misbehavior I have identified its cause or purpose and how I will respond when it occurs. For behaviors that require the use of a corrective consequence, I have also identified what the proposed consequence will be.	

COMPLETED	TASK	NOTES & IMPLEMENTATION IDEAS
	EARLY-STAGE MISBEHAVIORS I have a repertoire of information-giving correction strategies to use with early-stage misbehaviors that include: • Proximity • Gentle verbal reprimands • Discussion • Humor • Restitution • Emotional reaction When implementing any early-stage correction strategy, I am careful to always treat students with dignity and respect.	
	AWARENESS TYPE MISBEHAVIORS I understand that with misbehaviors that stem from a student's lack of awareness of when (or how much) he or she is engaging in a misbehavior, I should use the following steps: • Make sure the student knows the behavior I expect (the goal behavior). • Respond to instances of the misbehavior in a way that lets the student know that he or she is not meeting the goal. • Monitor the student's misbehavior so that I will have an objective basis for discussing progress with the student (and family). • Give the student positive feedback when he or she is successful, and consider some type of incentive system if necessary.	

COMPLETED	TASK	NOTES & IMPLEMENTATION IDEAS
	ABILITY TYPE MISBEHAVIORS I understand that with ability type misbehaviors the first thing I need to do is ascertain whether or not the student is physiologically capable of exhibiting the goal behavior. If the student is not capable, then I must modify the environment and/or adjust my expectations. I understand that if a student misbehaves due to a lack of knowledge, I should use the following steps: • At a neutral time, have a discussion and/or provide lessons about the goal behavior. • Respond to instances of the misbehavior in a way that provides instruction to the student. • Make accommodations to increase the student's chance of success. • Provide positive feedback when the student is successful, and set up an incentive type system if necessary.	
	ATTENTION-SEEKING MISBEHAVIORS If a student exhibits a mild ongoing misbehavior that seems to stem from a need for attention, I will first ask myself the following questions: • Is the misbehavior really attention-seeking in nature? • Is the behavior itself acceptable and the problem is with the amount of the behavior? • Is the misbehavior too severe to ignore? • Will I ignore the behavior from all students or just the target student?	

COMPLETED	TASK	NOTES & IMPLEMENTATION IDEAS
	After determining whether or not ignoring is an appropriate response to an attention-seeking behavior, I will implement the following steps: • I will develop a plan to ignore and then present that plan to the student (and family). • I will respond to *all* instances of the misbehavior by ignoring the target student, continuing what I was doing, and providing positive feedback to other students. • I will give the target student attention when the attention-seeking misbehavior ceases. • I will maintain frequent interactions with the target student when he or she is not misbehaving. • I will monitor the target student's behavior to determine whether progress is being made.	
	PURPOSEFUL/HABITUAL MISBEHAVIORS For chronic misbehavior that does not stem from a lack of awareness or ability or a need for attention, I will develop and implement a comprehensive intervention that: • includes an effort to remove any positive/satisfying aspects of demonstrating the misbehavior for the student. • includes an effort to continually show the student that positive behavior leads to positive results. • includes the use of appropriate corrective consequences to help the student learn that engaging in misbehavior has a logical cost to it.	

Module 7: Correction Procedures

Peer Study Worksheet

With one or more of your colleagues, work through the following discussion topics and activities related to the tasks in Module 7. If necessary, refer back to the text to get additional ideas or for clarification. (See Module 1 Peer Study Worksheet for suggestions on structuring effective discussion sessions.)

Tasks 1-6: Preplan for Misbehavior

A. Have each member of the group bring a completed Clarifying Responses to Misbehavior worksheet (Figure 7.4). Taking turns, have each individual "walk through" one of the behaviors on his/her worksheet. That is, have the person describe the behavior, explain what he/she labeled the behavior (i.e., Awareness, Ability, Attention, Purposeful) and why, a proposed response to the behavior, and, if the response calls for corrective consequences, what the proposed consequence will be. Have the rest of the group give feedback.

MODULE 8: CLASSWIDE MOTIVATION SYSTEMS

When you implement classwide systems appropriate to the collective needs of your students, you can enhance student motivation to behave responsibly and strive for success.

Introduction

In Module 5: Motivation, we suggested basic strategies for promoting student motivation—i.e., using effective instructional practices and giving students meaningful and relevant positive feedback on their behavioral and academic progress. This module extends those suggestions by explaining when and how to implement an effective classwide "system" (or systems) to increase student motivation to behave responsibly and/or strive to achieve goals such as your Guidelines for Success (see Module 1, Task 2). A "classwide system" is an organized and systematic set of procedures designed to have an impact on all the students in your class. We believe there are many circumstances for which using a classwide system to enhance motivation is not only appropriate, but may even be necessary. For example:

- The behavior of many students in your class is challenging in many different ways—not following directions, wasting class time, disrespect, and so on.
- Students are, for the most part, responsible, but quite a few students have a problem with one specific behavior (e.g., work completion or talking during work periods).
- Your class behaves responsibly enough, but students have
- grown somewhat apathetic.

In this module, we provide information on how to decide which basic kind of system (i.e., nonreward-based or reward-based) you should use, and on how to implement, maintain, and fade a reward-based system. In addition, we offer

Elementary Sample:

Mr. Harn's third grade class was bordering on out-of-control. Before the year began, he thought a medium level of structure would be appropriate for his students. By the third week of school, it was clear that the initial procedures he had set up were not sufficient. He began keeping the Daily Record of Misbehavior (see Module 6) and determined that he needed to revise his level of classroom structure to high and that he needed to implement a classwide motivation system appropriate for a high structure class to further encourage students to behave responsibly. After reading the descriptions of the various systems in the menu, he decided that the "Whole Class Points" system would work well for his students and fit his own personal style. With this system, Mr. Harn awarded one point to the class for each 15 minute period during which all the students behaved appropriately. For each point the class earned, Mr. Harn moved the "rocket" on the rocket chart up one space. When the class earned ten points, (i.e., the rocket had moved ten spaces), the students got five minutes of extra recess and the rocket was moved back down to the launch pad, ready for another "take-off." Once the system was implemented, Mr. Harn noticed significant improvement in the students' behavior. Periodically he would change the theme of the chart—going from a rocket scenario to a race car scenario to a speedboat scenario. Over time, he also gradually added more spaces on the chart before students got their reward, and began increasing the time students were required to behave appropriately. After the students had earned a number of rewards and were demonstrating consistent improvements in their behavior, Mr. Harn held a class meeting and together he and the class decided to switch to an intermittent type system involving Classroom Lottery Tickets.

a "menu" of easy-to-implement classwide systems from which you can choose the one (or ones most appropriate for your particular situation.

Unlike the previous modules, this module contains only one task. It is:

Be prepared to effectively employ a classwide system (or systems) to increase motivated and responsible student behavior.

To help you accomplish this task, Module 8 presents information and suggestions on the following topics:

1. Deciding whether to use a nonreward-based or a reward-based system.
2. Effectively choosing, designing, and implementing a reward-based system, and,
3. Effectively maintaining and fading a reward-based system.

This basic information is followed by a menu of different systems that can be easily used in a classroom. For each item on the menu, we describe what the system is designed to accomplish, the level of classroom structure (high, medium, or low) for which it is most appropriate, and the specifics of how to use it. While the menu itself is arranged alphabetically, Figure 8.1 lists the included systems according to their most appropriate level of classroom structure (low, medium, and high). The module ends with a Self-Assessment Checklist and a Peer Study Worksheet that will assist you in implementing the strategies within this module.

Figure 8.1: Motivation Systems by Level of Classroom Structure

APPROPRIATE SYSTEMS FOR CLASSES NEEDING LOW STRUCTURE	APPROPRIATE SYSTEMS FOR CLASSES NEEDING MEDIUM STRUCTURE	APPROPRIATE SYSTEMS FOR CLASSES NEEDING HIGH STRUCTURE
Goal Setting Procedures: . Teacher sets goals for individual students . Teacher guides students in the process of setting their own goals . Teacher guides students in setting classwide goals	. 100 Squares . Group Response Cost . Lottery Tickets . Mystery Behavior of the Day . Public Posting (Classwide) . Public Posting (Individual) . Self-Evaluation of On/Off Task Behavior . Target and Reward a Specific Behavior . Team Competition with Response Cost Lottery	. Behavioral Grading . Economic Simulation . Reinforcement Based on Reducing Misbehavior . Whole Class Points

Decide whether you need a nonreward-based or a reward-based system

Classwide motivation systems generally fall into one of two categories:

1. Nonreward-based systems, which potentially improve students' desire to behave responsibly and achieve goals by enhancing their intrinsic motivation.

2. Reward-based systems, which use extrinsic reinforcers to increase student motivation to behave responsibly and strive for goals.

If your students are, for the most part, behaving responsibly, completing most of their work, and exhibiting cooperation, they do not need extrinsic rewards to be motivated. In a class that is functioning this well, students are demonstrating daily that they are intrinsically motivated to meet classroom expectations. With such a class, a nonreward-based system such as goal setting is perfectly reasonable. In fact, goal setting can be a very effective strategy for not only maintaining, but also enhancing already acceptable levels of motivation. Goal setting procedures are designed to give students something to strive for, so they do not fall into patterns of "going through the motions" in the classroom. If you do not need a reward-based system for your students (because the class is already behaving so responsibly), go directly to the descriptions of various goal setting systems in the menu and decide which one seems most appropriate for you and your class.

On the other hand, if you are frustrated by the amount of student misbehavior or the lack of student productivity in your class, your students are demonstrating that they are not intrinsically motivated to behave responsibly. Implementing a system in which students can earn extrinsic rewards for responsible behavior may be just what is needed to encourage them. A reward-based system may provide the incentive needed to "light a fire" under students and get them moving in a more positive and productive direction.

NOTE

If you have any doubts, the data from one or more of the monitoring procedures in Module 6 (e.g., the CHAMPs v. Daily Reality Rating Scale or the Record of Misbehavior Sheet) can help you confirm the need for a motivation system based on extrinsic rewards.

Even if you determine that your class needs or would benefit from a reward-based motivation system, you may find yourself reluctant to implement a system that depends upon extrinsic rewards. Some people have concerns about the use of rewards (or reward-based systems) to improve student behavior. What follows is an attempt to answer some of the most commonly raised questions related to using rewards. We hope that the information provided will help you understand how a reward-based system (or systems) can, usefully and effectively, be incorporated into your Classroom Management Plan. After looking over the following questions and answers, read the sections on effectively choosing and implementing a reward-based system, and maintaining and fading a reward-based system. Then review the menu and choose the system or systems that you want to use (or modify for use).

Answers to Common Concerns About Using Structured Rewards

Q: Shouldn't students work without needing rewards?

A: Yes, they should, but some don't. When you can motivate students by making your expectations clear and your instruction effective, that's what you should do. If all your students seem to be working up to their fullest potential, you do not need and probably should not implement a reward-based system. However, if you have some (or many) students who are not working as hard or as well as you think they should and you have done what you can to make expectations clear and instruction compelling, your choices are limited. You can let the students fail, or you can continue to try to increase their intrinsic motivation to behave, or you can experiment with using rewards.

Q: Isn't rewarding behavior the same as bribery?

A: Emphatically not! A bribe is an offer of payment, usually monetary, to do something illegal, unethical, or immoral. For example, if a building contractor offers to pay a building inspector "under the table" to ignore inadequate or unsafe aspects of a construction project, that is a bribe. Establishing a system in which students are rewarded for improving their rates of school work completion is not bribery. It is more analogous to someone getting a diploma for completing college or a getting a paycheck for doing a job.

Q: Won't students get hooked on the rewards?

A: Possibly—which is why we say that if you can sufficiently motivate your students without using rewards, you should do so. It is also why we recommend that if you do find that you need some form of reward system, you always keep your focus and enthusiasm for the system on what students are *doing*, not on what they are earning. Initially, the students may work mainly for the reward, but if you make a point of emphasizing their accomplishments, eventually most of them will begin to work for the sense of satisfaction in a job well done—whether they earn rewards or not.

Q: Isn't intrinsic motivation better?

A: Maybe. Nobody really knows. However, as was stated in Module 5: Motivation, most behaviors are the result of a complex mix of both intrinsic and extrinsic motivation. The basic rule we suggest for teachers is: If you can't motivate students intrinsically, then use extrinsic rewards to get the desired behavior established.

Q: Won't giving students rewards reduce their intrinsic motivation?

A: Possibly. When students are already exhibiting desired behaviors, using high-powered rewards *may* slightly reduce their willingness to work without rewards. Therefore, as stated earlier, if students are intrinsically motivated to meet your expectations, do not use structured rewards; use goal-setting procedures. However, if less structured methods have failed or seem likely to fail to motivate students to behave responsibly, you should consider the use of structured rewards.

Using a Reward-Based System

Once you decide that a reward-based system would be appropriate and/or helpful in improving your students' motivation, it's important to carefully choose, implement, maintain, and eventually fade the system(s) you use. In fact, reward-based systems, like all other aspects of your classroom behavior plan, will be effective or ineffective depending on how well you do those things. We suggest that you read through the following information on using a reward-based system before you read the menu of suggested systems. Then you will be prepared to choose, or design, a system that best fits the needs of your class and implement, maintain, and fade the system effectively.

As you choose your system, you need to keep in mind that some systems are regular and highly systematic in terms of how students earn the rewards (e.g., "If you do ___, then you earn ___."), while other systems involve giving students rewards intermittently (and unpredictably). With intermittent systems, it's more like "Some of the times you do ___, you might earn ____." Regular systems tend to be more appropriate and/or necessary when you are trying to motivate a class needing high structure, but they can also be harder to fade than intermittent or unpredictable systems. Intermittent reward systems are often sufficient for medium structure classes. What you want to do is select the "least complex" system that seems likely to "grab" the interest of your students and get them exerting gentle peer pressure to succeed (e.g., getting students saying things to each other like, "Allan, quit talking or you will make us lose a point.").

All reward-based systems (regular and intermittent) require maintenance, even after they are up and running. It's like having a car. No matter how well engineered your vehicle is, you still have to put fuel in it and make sure it gets the occasional oil change, brake job, and tune-up. In fact, you wouldn't expect your car to run without gas and periodic mechanical work. Unfortunately, some teachers think that once a motivation system is in place, it should pretty much run by itself. It won't. Furthermore, in most cases using a reward-based system should be a temporary measure that you employ to get the class into a pattern of successful behavior. Your eventual goal should be to gradually fade it so that it is your students' intrinsic motivation that is maintaining their responsible and/or enthusiastic behavior.

What follows are tips on how you can effectively choose and implement a reward-based system, keep it running well, and eventually fade it altogether.

Tips for effectively choosing (designing) and implementing a reward-based system

Make sure the system is appropriate for and interesting to students.

In addition to deciding whether students need a system in which the rewards are awarded regularly or intermittently, you want the system to be one that the students find compelling. For example, the Whole Class Points system described in the menu can be made visually stimulating (like the rocket chart example) and exciting to primary students, but is probably too "babyish" for most middle school classes. Conversely, if you were to try to use the Behavioral Grading system with a first or second grade class, many of the students probably wouldn't understand how the system works because grading is a somewhat abstract concept. The goal is to design a system that students find exciting and/or to which they find themselves drawn.

Make sure the rewards students will be working for are highly motivating.

If the reward a class is working toward is not something students care about (or something most students want to earn), your system is not likely to be effective. You want to use "high power" rewards—i.e., rewards that students will want badly enough that they will be "motivated" to try to meet your expectations to earn the reward. Therefore, you need to identify rewards that the whole class will want to earn. Examples include: free time; extra recess; getting out of class two minutes early; a reduction in a number of problems and/or questions assigned for homework; and so on.

Sometimes it can be useful to have students help you come up with the rewards for the class. For example, you might conduct a brainstorming session and ask students to identify things that they (as a class) could get or do when all students demonstrate responsible behavior. During a brainstorming session, write down any suggestion that any student makes (unless it is obscene or disrespectful). Continue the activity for at least five to ten minutes so that a variety of ideas can be generated. When the brainstorming session is complete, go back and eliminate any items that are too expensive or otherwise unrealistic. Some of the items on your final list will probably have more "value" than others. For example, some may cost money while others do not; some may cut into more class time than others, and some may involve more time from school personnel than others. When you first implement your system, do not hesitate to start with rewards that have a pretty high value. You want the system to be exciting enough that most of the students feel it is in their best interest to improve their behavior.

Set the system up in ways that make student success likely.

Students must believe that they have a high probability of achieving success. If students think their chances of earning a reward are low, they are not likely to change their behavior—even if the reward is one they really want. (Think about the concept of "Motivation = Expectancy X Value" that was discussed in Module 5: Motivation.)

One way to increase the probability of student success is to ensure that any time limits involved are short enough that students can meet your criteria. For example, say a fifth grade teacher implements a system in which the class can earn one point for each day that the entire class behaves responsibly. Students may (reasonably) believe that they will never earn any points because the chances that they will make it a full day without someone "messing up" are slim. This system is likely to fail because the students will never feel motivated enough to make it work. The system would be stronger (and probably more effective) if it were set up so that the class would earn a point for each hour, or even for each half hour, that all students behave responsibly.

Another way to have students believing that success is possible is to make the "cost" of earning the rewards relatively "inexpensive"—for the students. In other words, students need to see that they will get a reward relatively quickly if they meet your expectations. For example, say you establish a system where your second graders can earn extra recess time by getting 25 points, but the most number of points they can earn in a day is 5. That means that, at best, the students will have to work for a whole week before they will get extra recess time. For second grade students, this may be too long for any payoff. When you choose your system, remember that if the students believe that it is going to take too long to earn the reward, they may have an attitude of, "Why bother." In the second grade example, the extra recess would be more likely to motivate students if it cost 8 points rather than 25 points. The less mature your students, the more immediately obtainable the rewards will need to be if the system is going to be effective.

NOTE

Once the students are consistently behaving the way you expect, you can and should make the time intervals longer and/or the rewards more "expensive," as part of the process of gradually fading the system (see the tips on effectively maintaining and fading a reward-based system in this module).

Avoid systems with arbitrary time limits.

A weakness of many reward-based systems is that they include an unnecessary and arbitrary time limit—i.e., a time by which the points need to be earned in order to receive the reward. For example, consider a system in which a class can earn 5 points per day if everything goes extremely well, and if the class earns 15 points by Friday, the students get the last 15 minutes of class as "earned time" with snacks. The (arbitrary) time limit in this system creates several potential problems. First of all, if students have trouble behaving well early in the week, they may know by Wednesday morning that they cannot possibly earn the reward that week. That means they have no incentive to behave well on Wednesday afternoon, Thursday, and Friday. Or, students might do so well that they have 15 points by the end of the day Wednesday—and at least some of them are going to realize that they can misbehave all they want on Thursday and Friday because the reward has already been earned. Still another potential problem with a time limit is the difficult decision you will face if the class has earned 14 points by Friday afternoon. If you give them the reward (because they came so close), they learn that you do not follow through on what you say (i.e., they cannot really trust you). However, if you do not give them the reward, meaning that they will be starting back at zero points on Monday, they may feel so discouraged that they won't even want to try at all.

All of these potential problems can be eliminated by simply eliminating the time limit. For example, the same system would be much stronger if it were set up that as soon as the class earns 15 points, students will get the last 15 minutes of class as earned time with snacks. They might earn the points within three days or it could take them a couple of weeks, depending on how well everyone manages their own behavior.

Carefully organize the entire system before you begin implementation.

When things are not going well behaviorally, many teachers will rush to implement a motivation system to improve the situation. To implement an effective system, you need to give careful thought to what you are going to do and/or want to do, and then develop a preliminary mental implementation plan. Once you have created your mental plan, put it into writing. The act of writing out the procedures can help you to identify possible weaknesses with the system and/or issues that are unaddressed. As you identify those problems or issues, resolve them—make decisions. For example:

> *What will I do if one student repeatedly behaves in a way that prevents me from giving the point or reward to the entire group? Well, I will give that student a warning and tell him that his continued misbehavior will not prevent the group from earning points. At the same time, when the class earns the reward, he will not get to participate in the reward activities. If necessary, I will set up an individualized behavior management contract.*

After you have a written a plan that addresses all the questions or issues you can think of, discuss the plan with a colleague. Speak to someone who is teaching (or has taught) the grade level you teach. Ask him or her to listen to your proposed plan with a critical ear. Encourage this person to identify any weaknesses or unanswered questions in your plan.

Make sure your expectations for student behavior are clear and that you have adequate procedures for monitoring student behavior.

Even a well-designed reward system can fail if the expectations for student behavior within the system are unclear. The biggest reason for this is that, without clearly defined behavioral expectations, you may be inconsistent in determining whether students have met the criteria for earning their reward. That is, you may award "points" on one day, when you are in a good mood, but the next day when you are feeling more frustrated, you don't award any points (even though the students behaved the same way). This sort of inconsistency is very destructive to motivation. Students are likely to stop trying to meet expectations that are unclear and inconsistent.

In addition to having clear expectations, you must have adequate procedures for monitoring student behavior. In fact, the only way you can reasonably implement a reward-based motivation system is if you can adequately monitor student behavior. For example, if you have a system intended to address student behavior on recess (e.g., your class can earn one point for each recess during which everyone in the class follows the rules)—then you either need to be out with students during recess or have some way to get information from the playground supervisors at the conclusion of each recess. If there is some aspect of your students' behavior that you cannot adequately monitor, that behavior should not be part of your system.

Teach the students how the entire system works.

Before you implement any system, prepare one or more lessons to teach the students how the system works. When students don't understand all aspects of a system, there is very little chance it will motivate them—particularly the cognitively low and/or least mature students. In preparing the lessons, if you find that the system seems too complicated for students to grasp, you probably need to revise it. If you can't make it more clear, concise, and easy to understand, then you probably need a different system.

After you teach students how the system will work, verify that they understand. Ask questions to determine their level of understanding. If there are specific aspects of the system that are confusing, reteach those aspects. In addition, you might want to give students an opportunity to suggest refinements or modifications. If students make suggestions that would strengthen the system, incorporate those suggestions. For example, if students suggest reward ideas that would increase their interest in the system, you should seriously consider their ideas.

Make sure that you believe that the system will help improve student behavior.

Your students are very likely to meet your expectations regarding the system. If you believe the system will work, the students will pick up on your optimism. Likewise, if you believe the system will probably fail, the students will sense that you do not expect them to be successful. It's in your best interest to be optimistic. Even if the system does not work initially, an optimistic attitude will lead you to try to identify refinements and modifications to the system that will make it work. On the other hand, with a pessimistic attitude you are likely to give up if the system does not result in immediate and drastic improvement in student behavior. Remember: "Optimists are wrong just as often as pessimists, the big difference is they have a lot more fun."

Tips for effectively maintaining and fading a reward-based system

Keep your energy and enthusiasm about the system high.

You are the fuel that keeps the system supplied with energy to run. If you don't "fill 'er up" with your excitement, interest, and support, students are very likely to lose interest (even if the rewards they are working toward are compelling).

Keep your focus on the students' behavior rather than the rewards they earn.

The energy and excitement that you invest in the system, and in acknowledging student successes, should be concentrated on "Look at what you did" rather than "Look at what you get." By keeping your focus on the students' improved growth, maturity, progress, and so on, you increase the chances that the students will begin working less for the "reward" and more for their sense of satisfaction in meeting expectations successfully.

Continue using other motivational strategies at a high level.

In Module 5: Motivation, we presented a number of basic strategies for establishing and maintaining student motivation. All the classwide systems for boosting motivation discussed in this module require that you maintain your use of the following basic strategies:

- Present activities/tasks in a manner that induces student motivation.
- Use effective instructional practices and present tasks in interesting ways.
- Provide frequent noncontingent attention.
- Provide frequent positive feedback that is contingent, specific, descriptive, and age-appropriate.
- Pay more attention to every student when he or she is engaged in responsible behavior than when he or she is engaged in misbehavior (minimally, a ratio of 3:1).

When a system has been successful for a period of time, start making it more challenging.

Once student behavior improves to the point that your class is successfully meeting your expectations most of the time, you need to modify the system so that it is more challenging—or students may get bored with it. For example, say a third grade class is implementing the Whole Class Points rocket chart system. Initially it is set up so that every 15 minutes the teacher's timer will go off, and if students have met the teacher's expectations for responsible behavior during the 15-minute interval, the class earns a point. When the class has earned ten points, they get one of the rewards. If the class is regularly earning a point during most intervals (say above 80% of the time), you need to make things slightly more challenging. The next time the students earn a reward and the rocket is moved down to zero, inform the class that after the rocket gets to the moon the next time, the system will change. Instead of a rocket chart, it will be a race car chart, and instead of ten spaces "to reach the moon," there will be 13 spaces before the race car reaches the "finish line." By increasing the difficulty, you make earning the next reward slightly more challenging.

It's important to give students plenty of advance notice before making this kind of modification. As you explain the increased number of spaces, emphasize to students that you are making the change because they have been successful. Be careful not to sound apologetic about this change. If any students complain, let them know that the system, like many things in life, will be challenging and may increase in difficulty, but emphasize that they have the skills to still earn the reward quickly. Increasing the difficulty (e.g., more points required) is the first of many steps you will take in fading the system.

Another way to make the system more challenging is to make the criteria for earning points harder. For example, with the rocket chart system, you might go from monitoring in 15-minute intervals to monitoring in 20-minute intervals. Or, you could increase the number of behaviors being monitored. For example, you could add the behavior "Treating everyone with respect" as an additional criteria for determining whether the class will earn a point for a given interval. The following chart shows how you might make gradual changes in something like the rocket chart system. (NOTE: These changes would be phased in over a period of several months.)

15 minute intervals	10 points required for reward
15 minute intervals	13 points required for reward
20 minute intervals	13 points required for reward
20 minute intervals	18 points required for reward
"Treating everyone with respect" added to expectation	
30 minute intervals	18 points required for reward
30 minute intervals	25 points required for reward
45 minute intervals	25 points required for reward
45 minute intervals	35 points required for reward
60 minute intervals	35 points required for reward

Remember, you do not want to increase a system's difficulty until students have been consistently successful. If you make things too difficult before students feel somewhat in control of their own success, they may be inclined to give up and stop trying to meet the expectations.

By making changes like these gradually, you make the system increasingly "lean" (i.e., students demonstrate highly responsible behavior for relatively small extrinsic rewards). Notice that in the preceding example, students start out working in 15-minute intervals and needed ten points for a reward. This means that 150 minutes of responsible behavior earned students a reward. A few months later, the same class is working in 45-minute intervals and needs 25 points for a reward. That means 1125 minutes of responsible behavior for a reward.

Once a system is fairly "lean," modify it to be based on intermittent rewards.

Some of the systems in the menu that are identified as appropriate for medium structure classrooms involve the use intermittent rewards—or rewards that are given only on some occasions (rather than every time) that performance criteria are met. Moving to intermittent rewards is another step in making your motivation system "more difficult." For example, you could propose that the Whole Class system be replaced by the 100 Squares system. With this change, you do not increase the time interval. Instead, when you feel the class is working well, you have a student draw a number and you fill in the space for that number on the 100 Squares chart. When the class completes a line (across, up/down, or diagonally) they earn a reward. The intermittent nature of the system—no timer, you draw a number intermittently—moves the class even closer to the way rewards work in less structured settings.

Once a class is working successfully for intermittent rewards, consider adding (or switching to) one of the goal setting systems described in the menu.

Goal setting is one of the last "steps" in fading students from the support of extrinsic rewards to a reliance on their intrinsic motivation. While you are still using a system of intermittent rewards, begin setting individual goals for each student (or have the students set their own goals) and help the class to set a classwide goal. Then, make a point of providing frequent positive feedback to students for meeting the goals. Once you have motivated students to be striving toward their individualized goals, and you are maintaining high rates of positive feedback to individuals and the whole class, you will be very close to being able to abandon any kind of reward-based system altogether.

When appropriate, have a class discussion about abandoning the use of the reward-based system.

When the class seems ready (i.e., most students seem to take pride in behaving responsibly), arrange to conduct a whole class discussion on whether students feel they can continue to behave responsibly without getting rewards. If the tone of the discussion suggests that most students think they can maintain their responsible behavior without a system, set a classwide goal such as:

> *We, the students in Room 14, can behave responsibly and we will strive to meet our Guidelines for Success without needing a reward system.*

When students can agree to this kind of classwide goal, you can stop using a reward-based system. However, you do need to continue providing *frequent* positive feedback, and an occasional special treat when the class is exhibiting ongoing responsible behavior. (See Intermittent Celebrations of Success in Module 5).

Menu of Classwide Systems

What follows in this module are descriptions of a variety of classwide systems for increasing student motivation. Think of this as a menu of procedures. As you read through the "menu," you can note those systems that fit the level of structure that your class needs and that look interesting to you. Then, you can choose the system or systems (or design your own) that you can implement in your classroom to improve the motivation of your students.

The systems are presented in alphabetical order in the menu itself. However, for your convenience, they are presented in table form in Figure 8.2, according to the classroom level of structure for which they are most appropriate.

Figure 8.2: Motivation Systems by Level of Classroom Structure

Appropriate Systems for Classes Needing Low Structure	Appropriate Systems for Classes Needing Medium Structure	Appropriate Systems for Classes Needing High Structure
Goal Setting Procedures: . Teacher sets goals for individual students . Teacher guides students in the process of setting their own goals . Teacher guides students in setting classwide goals	. 100 Squares . Group Response Cost . Lottery Tickets . Mystery Behavior of the Day . Public Posting (Classwide) . Public Posting (Individual) . Self-Evaluation of On/Off Task Behavior . Target and Reward a Specific Behavior . Team Competition with Response Cost Lottery	. Behavioral Grading . Economic Simulation . Reinforcement Based on Reducing Misbehavior . Whole Class Points

NOTE

Several of the systems described in the following menu have been taken or adapted from The Tough Kid Book, *by Rhode, Reavis, & Jenson (1992). This excellent book and its corresponding* Tough Kid Tool Box *are filled with many useful ideas on managing the behavior of difficult students.*

100 Squares (Medium Structure)

This "intermittent reward" system, which is a combination of tic-tac-toe and bingo, is designed to acknowledge the behavior of the entire class. It is especially useful when trying to improve student behavior regarding a specific rule (e.g., "Work during all work times").

To set it up you need a white board or a flip chart, on which you will draw a large 10 square by 10 square grid (i.e., a chart with 100 spaces—see Figure 8.3). Place the grid in a prominent place in the room. Get two containers (e.g., bowl, hat, sack) and 100 small tokens such as poker chips, Formica samples, small tag board squares, popsicle sticks, etc. On each of the tokens, write a number from 1 to 100, and place all of them into one of the two containers.

Figure 8.3: Sample of 100 Squares

Sample of 100 Squares

1	2	3	4	5	6	7	8	9	10
11	12	13	14	15	16	17	18	19	20
21	22	23	24	25	26	27	28	29	30
31	32	33	34	35	36	37	38	39	40
41	42	43	44	45	46	47	48	49	50
51	52	53	54	55	56	57	58	59	60
61	62	63	64	65	66	67	68	69	70
71	72	73	74	75	76	77	78	79	80
81	82	83	84	85	86	87	88	89	90
91	92	93	94	95	96	97	98	99	100

On *some* occasions when the entire class is working well, stop what is going on and have a student draw one of the tokens from the full container. Identify the number written on the token, and then fill in—e.g., initial or color—the space on the chart that has the same number. Put the token into the empty (second) container. When ten squares in a row—horizontally, vertically, or diagonally—have been filled in, the entire class gets one of the group rewards that have been identified (e.g., by you or during a class brainstorming session). Once a full line has been completed and a reward given, erase the initials in the squares (or put up a new grid on the flip chart), put all the drawn tokens back into the original container, identify (you choose or have the class vote) the next reward students will work toward, and begin the system again.

Have a different student draw the number each time—so that eventually every student will have gotten to do so. In the early stages of using the system, try to have at least ten drawings per day, but *never* have a drawing unless everyone in the class is doing well at that particular moment. "Class, right now everyone is seated, with eyes on the overhead and anyone who wants to talk is remembering to wait to be called on. Mica, would you please draw a number from the bowl and tell me the numbered space that should be initialed."

After the class has earned at least six or more rewards, modify the system to make the chart an 11 X 11 grid with 121 spaces (and add the additional tokens). This will allow you to continue to hold frequent drawings, but it will also mean that it will take longer for students to earn a reward. As time goes on, if the system continues to have a positive effect on student behavior, you can make the chart a 12 X 12 grid with 144 spaces, and eventually even a 15 X 15 grid with 225 spaces. At some point, plan to have a class discussion to see if students want to continue the system. If they think they can continue to behave responsibly without needing the system, let them know that you will periodically give them free time (or other favorite rewards). If students want to continue the system, double the number of tokens in the container—so that there will be two tokens for each number. If a number is drawn and that space is already filled in, the token just goes into the second container. This doubling of tokens makes the actual reward harder to earn and moves students one step closer to working without the system.

This system is more interesting than one in which you simply fill in successive boxes because part of the anticipation is that students will be hoping that the number drawn will be one that brings a row closer to completion.

NOTE

Be sure to clarify that the students who draw the numbers are doing so for a class, not an individual, reward.

Behavioral Grading (High Structure)

This system involves keeping records on each individual student's behavior and translating those records into "grades." It is a classwide system in that every student is "graded" on the same behaviors, but it is individualized in that each student receives his/her own grades. This is an especially useful system with middle school students. It may also be effective with fourth and fifth grade students, but is likely to be less effective with primary grade students than some of the other systems in this menu, such as Whole Class Points. The behavioral "grades" may be incorporated as part of students' academic grades, or they may stand alone as something like "citizenship grades." We recommend that with middle school students the behavior grade be included as a percentage of the student's overall grade (e.g., 20% of the science grade, 50% of the P.E. grade).

This system depends on accurate and systematic record keeping. A Record of Misbehavior Sheet (see Figure 6.11 in Module 6, Tool 3) is a very effective tool to use with this system. First, identify the three or four particular misbehaviors that you wish to address (i.e., reduce/eliminate) at a classwide level. Then identify three or four positive traits or behaviors you wish encourage to at a classwide level. (Note: The positive traits may correspond directly to your Guidelines for Success.) For each positive and each negative behavior, assign a code that you will use to record occurrences of that behavior on your record sheet without having to write the entire word. Figure 8.4 shows a sample of such a code:

Figure 8.4: Sample of Codes for Behavioral Grading

MISBEHAVIOR	CODE	POSITIVE TRAIT	CODE
Off task	o	Do Your Best (Effort)	E
Talking (at wrong time)	t	Be responsible	B
Swearing	s	Respect/Cooperation	R

Elementary teachers can use a Daily Misbehavior Record Sheet, Figure 6.10, and middle school teachers can use a Weekly Misbehavior Record Sheet, Figure 6.11. Then, each time you speak to a student about a misbehavior, mark the appropriate code next to that student's name in the appropriate column. Whenever you provide positive feedback to a student, identify the positive trait his/her behavior demonstrated (e.g., on-task behavior might be an example of "doing one's best"), then mark the appropriate code.

Elementary teachers who use this system might (optionally) put a weekly record form, which corresponds to your Daily Record Sheet, on each student's desk. Whenever you mark a positive or negative behavior on your record sheet, have the student(s) put a tally mark in the appropriate column on his/her form. This sheet can be sent home at the end of the week so the student's family can see how much positive and corrective feedback has been given to the student during the week. Figure 8.5 shows a sample of what the form for students' desks might look like—keeping in mind, of course, that the columns would be labeled with the specific positive and negative behaviors you are monitoring. (NOTE: We suggest running your week from Friday of one week through Thursday of the following week. That way, you can send the sheets home every Friday.)

Figure 8.5: Sample

Name ______________________________ **Week of** ______________

COOPERATION	RESPONSIBILITY	EFFORT	TALKING	OFF TASK	SWEARING

For middle school students, you would enter a score of between 0 and 20 points each week, based on their behavior. To determine each student's weekly points, assume that each student starts each new week with 15 points (or 75% of the total possible for the week, roughly a grade of C). During the week, students lose one point for each misbehavior and gain one point for each positive behavior that you notice and comment on. There may be some days when nothing is coded for a student, and other days when several things are coded. Only record the times you talk directly to a student about one of the targeted (positive or negative) behaviors. At the end of the week, figure each student's total by adding points to and/or subtracting points from the student's baseline of 15, based on your records of the student's behavior for the week. In the sample presented in Figure 8.6, notice that the week begins on a Friday. If you compute students' point totals on Thursday evening, they get the results on Friday—which reduces the delay in giving them feedback.

Figure 8.6 shows a sample Weekly Record Sheet in which the coding is based on the sample described earlier. That is, an "E" stands for Effort, a "T" for talking, and so on. Note that the first student, Gina, has three positive comments and four negative. Therefore her total for the week is 14 (15-4+3=14). The next student, Frank, has six positive codes and no negative, however his weekly total is only twenty points rather 21 (15+6=21). This makes sense when you think about how most teachers grade an essay that is worth 100 points. No matter how good an individual student's essay is, if there are only 100 points possible, the student will not get more than 100 points. With this behavioral grading system, a student can never get more than 20 points or less than 0 points for any particular week.

Figure 8.6: Completed Sample

Portion of Completed Weekly Record Sheet

Name ______________________ Week of ____________

NAME	FRIDAY	MONDAY	TUESDAY	WEDNESDAY	THURSDAY	TOTAL
Andersen, Gina	ss	EE	s	sB		14
Bendix, Frank	R	R	EE	EE	B	20
Bigornia, Brad	o		B		R	16
Collias, Zona	t	B tt	ttt		BR	12

If you were using this system as part of students' academic grades, these points would be added into your gradebook just like homework and test scores. If the points are to be used only to determine citizenship grades, the weekly scores would be kept separate from your academic grades. Then, you would total them at the end of the grading period and determine percentages. That is, students who got 90% of the total possible points would receive an A, those who got 80% would receive a B, and so on. Regardless of how you use the system, students should get weekly information on their current point total and their current grade status.

There are several advantages to this type of motivation system. First, simply by scanning your completed daily or weekly record sheet, you can monitor the nature of your interactions with students. Are you paying more attention to positive behavior or negative behavior? Are there some students with whom you rarely ever interact? Are there some students you only interact with in a corrective capacity? Every week, you can quickly consider these issues as you review the data, and then make plans for any necessary adjustments in your behavior for the following week. Another advantage to this type of system is that it provides you with a lot of specific and objective data that you can share with families (e.g., during parent conferences or when speaking to a family about a behavioral problem that has been occurring). Finally, we think you will find that students may tend to take your praise and your corrections more seriously when they know that you are keeping a record of their behaviors—appropriate and inappropriate—and that the record will be reflected in their grades.

Economic Simulation (High Structure)

In this type of system, you use pretend money and create a mini-economy in your classroom. Students are "paid" for their behavior, and can use the money to "purchase" a variety of possible items. This can be a useful system in grades 2-8 for reducing frequent, but minor misbehavior, such as off-task behavior, talking in class, put downs, and so on.

You can make this type of system simple or complex. In its simplest form, it functions as a "response cost" type of system. That is, every student starts the week with a certain amount of "money in the bank." During the week you use a Misbehavior Record Sheet to monitor the inappropriate behavior of individual students. Each misbehavior "costs" the student who exhibited it one dollar. At the end of the week, you determine students' "payout." Any student who has had no recorded misbehaviors receives ten dollars. (NOTE: Figures 8.7 and 8.8 are reproducible masters of "*CHAMPs* Bucks," in one and five dollar amounts respectively. You can use these reproducible masters to "mint" your class money or you may prefer to design your own money.) A student who misbehaved six times would receive four dollars and a student who misbehaved once would receive nine dollars. The money can be spent on items in a student store (pencils, stickers, erasers, certificates for computer time, and so on.) Plan to give "bonuses" (e.g., one or two extra dollars) to individual students who have been following rules and striving toward the Guidelines for Success. Be careful not to be inadvertently discriminatory, though. Every student should get some "bonuses" every now and then.

In a slightly more sophisticated version of this system, students can also be "paid" for completing academic work and/or demonstrating responsible behavior. For example, you might pay students two dollars for each assignment completed (more for any major projects). If you want to include something like this, you will need to record the positive feedback you give students in addition to recording their misbehavior. (See the information on "Behavioral Grading System" for suggestions on how to manage this kind of recording.) Then have each student start each day with a certain number of dollars (say five), to which they will add one dollar for each positive behavior or subtract one dollar for each negative behavior. To start students might be paid daily, but as they get familiar with the system, this can be modified to a weekly "pay day."

If you wish, once the basic system is running smoothly and showing positive effects, you might also use it as a way to teach students about how the real economy works—by gradually adding in other features. For example, every two weeks you could add in one or more of the features below:

- Establish "savings accounts" for students.
- Establish "checking accounts" for students.
- Charge students "rent" for their desks.
- Require students to "buy" certain supplies (e.g., pencils, art paper, etc.).
- Have students "purchase" certain privileges.
- Arrange to pay extra for special projects (extra credit assignments).
- Establish charitable foundations to which students can contribute.
- Assess taxes on the money students are paid.
- Give every student a class job for which she/he is paid, for example:
    - Managers of student store
    - Accountants (helping you compute payments)
    - Bankers (managing savings accounts)
    - City Council (paid from taxes collected)
    - Supply managers
    - Tutors or helpers who go to assist in kindergarten
    - Real estate agents (determining and collecting rents for desks)
    - Zoologist (caring for class animals)
    - Computer maintenance
    - Graphic artists (preparing bulletin boards and displays)

Figure 8.7: CHAMPs Bucks (reproducible master)

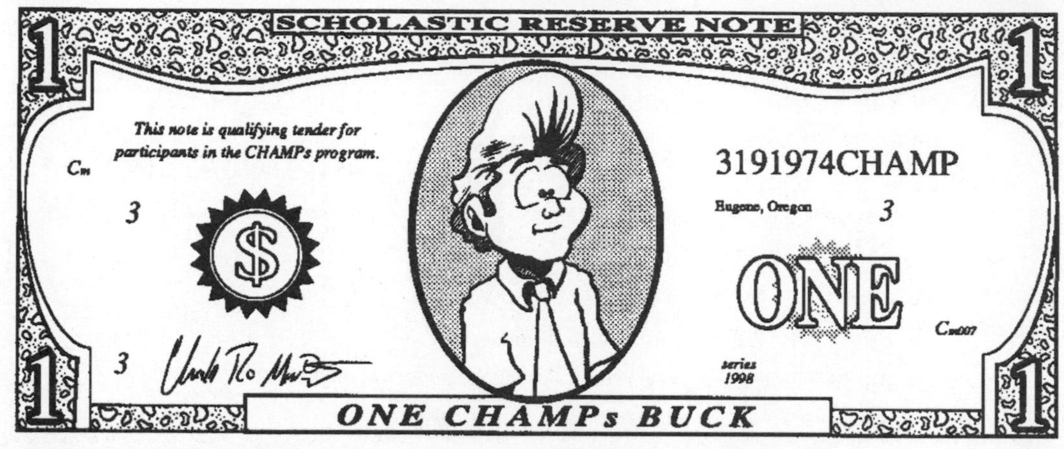

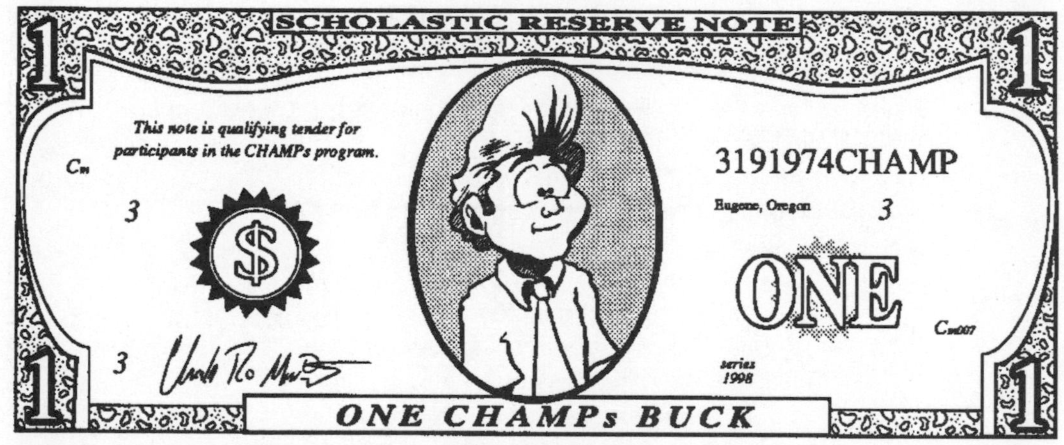

Figure 8.8: CHAMPs Bucks (reproducible master)

Goal Setting Procedures (Low Structure)

Goal setting involves helping students learn to strive for positive goals they can achieve. Goals can be academic, behavioral, or a mix of both. Because the focus tends to be on increasing desired behaviors (as opposed to reducing negative behaviors), goal setting systems are generally most appropriate for classes in which students need only a low structure management plan. If a class is exhibiting frequent misbehavior, there is probably not sufficient intrinsic motivation among students in the class for goal setting procedures to have much of an impact. On the other hand, if a class is for the most part behaving responsibly, there is by definition a significant amount of intrinsic motivation being demonstrated. When this is the case, use of goal setting procedures can often extend and channel that intrinsic motivation in productive directions.

Using a goal setting system in which you set goals for each student (and share them with the individual students) represents a "first level" of implementation. More sophisticated versions would involve having the students themselves set goals for the class as a whole and eventually teaching students to set their own goals.

We recommend that you work with a class for at least one full month before implementing any goal setting system.

Teacher Sets Goals for Students

To use this procedure (i.e., in which you set the goals), go through your class list student by student, and give thought to what you want for each student. That is, think about what attitude, behavior, or trait would help each individual student be more successful. What follows is a list of the kinds of goals you might identify for different students:

- To complete more work.
- To write more neatly.
- To follow directions (without arguing).
- To get along better with other students (be less bossy).
- To be willing to take more risks—accept more challenges.
- To have a more positive attitude—complain less.
- To accept and learn from mistakes.
- To stay focused on work during class.
- To talk only at appropriate times.
- To demonstrate more self control (anger management).
- To master basic multiplication/division facts.
- To be more independent and self-reliant.

- To interact more with other students (be less shy).
- To be more creative.
- To be willing to try new things.

You can use the reproducible form shown in Figure 8.10 to record goals for each of the students in your class. Write the name of each student on the form. Then take 15 to 30 seconds per student and think about what that student most needs to learn. Think about the lasting legacy you want to leave with this student. "If I could only help her learn one thing, it would be to teach her to . . ." Leave the "Priority" column on the form blank for the time being. If you can't think of a goal for a particular student, skip that student and come back to him/her later. When you go back, try to identify why you could not come up with something. For example, if you could not come up with something because the student is already such a hard-working and responsible individual, you might set a goal about the student continuing to be highly motivated (e.g., "to continue to do her best, and to continue to be such a hard working, creative, and cooperative student"). If you do not know a student well enough to identify a goal, do not set a goal for the student, but set one for yourself to get to know that student better. This task of identifying a goal for each student (and going back to the students requiring more thought) should take between 15 and 30 minutes.

Once you have identified a goal for each student, the next step is setting priorities. That is, you need to determine which of the students' goals have an element of urgency to them and which represent goals that are merely desirable. You should plan on committing greater time and attention to helping the students who may not be successful in school and work if they do not achieve their goal and/or learn the skill or trait. On the other hand, when a goal is less urgent (i.e., the student will probably do fine whether or not she/he improves in this particular skill or trait), it will not require as much time or attention from you. This step of prioritizing students' goals is essential because you cannot do all things at once.

You will notice that the "Priority" column on the Goal Setting Form calls for rating each student's goal with a 1+, 1, 2, or 3. Figure 8.9 is a guide for determining which rating would be most appropriate, and for identifying the corresponding action you should take to help the student achieve the goal.

Figure 8.9: Determining Priorities for Goals

	Urgency for the Student	Action by the Teacher
1+	This student must immediately learn to meet this goal in order to succeed in my classroom and in the future.	I will meet with the student and family, fill out a Goal Contract, provide frequent positive feedback, and may set up an individualized contract.
1	This student would benefit greatly from learning to meet this goal.	I will meet with the student, fill out a Goal Contract and provide frequent positive feedback when the student strives to meet the goal.
2	This student might benefit from learning to meet this goal.	I will provide frequent positive feedback when the student strives to meet the goal.
3	This student is going to be fine whether she/he learns to meet this goal or not.	I will provide occasional positive feedback when the student strives to meet the goal.

NOTE

Be careful about identifying too many 1+s. We suggest that for goals with this priority level you arrange to have a student/family conference concerning the goal. If you identify eight or more students with 1+ priority level goals, the class probably needs a more involved (i.e., a reward-based) motivation system than goal setting.

Following the reproducible master in Figure 8.10 is a sample of a completed Goal Setting form (Figure 8.11).

Figure 8.10: Reproducible

Goal Setting Form

Student Name	Goal	Priority 1+, 1, 2, 3

Figure 8.11: Completed Sample

Goal Setting Form

Student Name	Goal	Priority 1+, 1, 2, 3
Alex Andrews	Be less hostile and verbally aggressive	1+
Anna Daniels	Be more relaxed about grades	2
Tricia Engelmann	Learn to use humor appropriately & supportively	2
Larry Fine	Be more tolerant of those with less ability	2
Ben Frank	Complete and hand in work	1+
Angela Gomez	Hand in neater work	2
Nancy Wong	Use more creativity	2
Benjamin Brown	Learn to manage classtime better	3
Steve Canfield	Be more confident	3
Lana Moler	Be more independent	1
Jennifer Nakir	Do more than the minimum	2
Robert Pedersen	Build others up rather than put them down	2
Matthew Stein	Stay at task in seat	2
Peggy Stone	Get to school on time	1
Paul Templeton	Interact with other students	2
Emily Vowell	Get homework in on time	1
Brian Wood	Speed up rate of work completion	2
Jan Brown	Less disruptive	1
John Jackson	Work independently for longer periods	3
Lonnie Hall	Ask for help when needed	2
Timothy Smith	Avoid fighting, work on getting along	1

Once you have identified a goal for each student and have specified priority levels for all the students' goals, you need to determine how you will make students aware of the goals you hope they will achieve. One way is to have a conference with each student, during which you can discuss the goal and provide the student with a written, or as appropriate (e.g., kindergarten students, a pictorial), description of the goal. Now, there are probably many of you thinking (shouting!), "I don't have time to meet with every student! I have 30 students!" That's where the prioritizing comes into play. You should definitely plan to meet with the students who have the highest priority goals, the 1+s. In fact, we recommend that for students with 1+ goals, you try to meet not only with the individual student, but with the student's family. For students who have level 1 priorities, you should also meet with the student, but you do not need to involve the family. You can hold off on scheduling meetings for the students who have level 2 and 3 priority goals. In fact, we recommend that you only meet with these students if you can free up the time.

When you meet with a student (or the student and his/her family), complete a Goal Contract. A reproducible master of a Goal Contract is provided in Figure 8.12. To fill out a goal contract, first identify the overall goal—which will probably be what you wrote for the student on the Goal Setting Form. However, if your goal for the student was framed in terms of something the student should not do, transform the goal into a positive statement of what the student should do (e.g., "Stop being disruptive" would become "Participate responsibly in lessons and study times."). Then, *and this is very important*, list three specific ways the student can demonstrate that she/he is striving to achieve the goal. You will also want to have a rationale in mind that you can present to the student, about how striving to achieve this goal will help him/her. Communicate all of this information to the student during your conference.

Figure 8.12: Reproducible

Goal Contract

STUDENT'S NAME ______________________________ DATE ______________

A GOAL FOR YOU TO WORK ON IS TO ______________________________

____

YOU CAN SHOW YOU ARE WORKING ON THIS GOAL BY:

A. ____

____

B. ____

____

C. ____

____

____
STUDENT'S SIGNATURE

____
TEACHER'S SIGNATURE

Goal Contract

STUDENT'S NAME ______________________________ DATE ______________

A GOAL FOR YOU TO WORK ON IS TO ______________________________

____

YOU CAN SHOW YOU ARE WORKING ON THIS GOAL BY:

A. ____

____

B. ____

____

C. ____

____

____
STUDENT'S SIGNATURE

____
TEACHER'S SIGNATURE

Another way that you can share your goals with students is by having mini-conferences—that is, taking time during independent work periods to briefly inform individual students of the goals you hope to see them strive to achieve. You might use mini-conferences with students who have level 2 and 3 priority goals.

Finally, you can communicate your goals for students (somewhat indirectly) by looking for and capitalizing on opportunities to give each student positive feedback related to the behavior/trait that you hope to help him/her achieve. This method of communication works, even if you have not yet had a goal conference (or a mini-conference) with the student. When a student exhibits behavior that reflects the identified goal, comment on it. For example, if your goal for a student was for him "to talk only at appropriate times," and the student's participation while a guest speaker was in the room was appropriate, you might say, "Jamal, while our guest artist was here this morning I noticed that you gave him your full attention. You only talked during the times that he wanted you to discuss things at your table, and when you raised your hand to be recognized. That demonstrated a great deal of respect for the speaker." Whether or not you've had a goal discussion or completed a goal contract with a student, feedback of this nature will help the student realize that this is a behavior that you are monitoring and that you feel is important for him to learn. Providing this type of contingent, descriptive, and immediate positive feedback is also extremely valuable after you have conducted a goal conference with a student.

We recommend that elementary teachers go through this entire goal setting process once a month. Middle school teachers might also plan to use the process once a month, but for a different class each month—so that you end up thinking about goals for each of your classes once or twice a year. (Remember, whether you are a middle school or elementary teacher, wait to use goal setting as a classwide motivation system until you have worked with your students for at least a month.) As you repeat the goal setting process, your goal(s) for a particular student may vary from time to time. If a student has not made progress on the goal, or has made some progress but still has further to go, maintain the same goal. If the student has met your goal, consider setting a new goal. Each time you go through the process, you should restate the priorities, and conduct conferences with students who have level 1+ and 1 priority goals, and mini-conferences with students who have level 2 and 3 priority goals. For all students, give positive feedback when you see the student taking steps toward the goal.

HELPFUL HINT

Keep your filled-out Goal Setting Form handy and review it a couple of times each week. This will remind you of what specific behaviors you are looking for with each of the students in the class.

Teacher Guides Students in Setting Goals

Once students understand the concept of striving to achieve a goal, you can conduct one or more lessons to teach students how to set their own goals. Begin by discussing the importance of goal setting. Remind students that they have been working hard to achieve the goals that you have set for them. Then explain that learning to set goals and striving to meet them is a skill that can be very beneficial and can help them succeed in school, in work situations, and in life.

Have students identify and discuss some short term goals they might want to achieve for themselves. Encourage students to focus on school-based goals—however, let them know that setting goals for themselves in areas outside of school (e.g., sports, hobbies, etc.) can also be very useful. You may want to put some sample goals on the board to provide ideas for students who might have trouble coming up with goals of their own. Pass out copies of the Goal Contract. Have each student write an overall goal and three ways to demonstrate that she/he is trying to achieve the goal. If you do the activity yourself along with your students (i.e., complete a Goal Contract for yourself), you validate the students for their efforts. Once students have completed a goal contract, tell them to keep a copy of their goal on their desk or on the front cover of a notebook so they will be reminded frequently of the goals they are striving to achieve.

For a couple of days after this session, try to meet with each student to discuss his/her goal contract. If a student has set an unreachable goal, help him/her to make the goal more realistic. Record each student's goal on a blank version of the Goal Setting Form, so that you have a summary of all the students' goals on one or two pages. Once you have signed all the contracts and have summarized all the students' goals, watch for any opportunity to give students positive feedback on their efforts to achieve their goals (as you did when you set the goals for students).

If this process proves useful (i.e., behavior is improving, motivation is increasing), repeat once each month.

Teacher Guides Students in Setting a Classwide Goal

Consider guiding your students in a process of setting a classwide goal. The goal might involve reducing a classwide problem (eliminate teasing), increasing a positive behavior (e.g., improve classroom climate through increased positive interactions), or participating in a service project (e.g., make regular visits to a retirement home). Put a reasonable time limit on achieving the goal so that you and the class will have a specific date to evaluate their success.

Establishing and actively working toward a common goal as a group is a powerful way to increase students' sense of purpose and belonging. It can build classroom pride and create a powerful sense of community.

Group Response Cost (Medium Structure)

This is a simple system that can be used very effectively to reduce one specific misbehavior that tends to be exhibited by several different students in the class and/or to improve a group's behavior in terms of following directions and/or being efficient during transitions.

To use the system to reduce a common group misbehavior (e.g., use of profanity), first set up a special time in the afternoon for a fun group activity—e.g., an extra ten minutes of recess. Then take index cards and on each card write times, in 30 second intervals from zero to ten minutes. Thus, on one card you would write 0 seconds, on the next 30 seconds; on the next you would write one minute; and then one and one-half minutes, two minutes, and so on until you reach ten minutes. Tell students that each day the class will start out with ten minutes of extra recess, but that any time you hear profanity, they will lose 30 seconds of that recess. Take your stack of cards (with the "ten minutes" card on top) and demonstrate how when you hear profanity, you will take the top card and move it to the back of the stack, leaving the "nine and one-half minutes" card on top. The time shown on the top card at recess time will be how much extra recess the class gets that afternoon.

When using this system to improve a behavior such as "following directions" or "being efficient during transitions," make up cards for ten extra minutes of recess (as described above). Let students know that when you give a directive for a transition (e.g., "Everyone get out your math books and a blank piece of paper."), they will have a reasonable amount of time (say one minute) in which to comply, but that any time it takes them beyond the one minute will come off of the ten minute extra recess time. Then, after you give your first directive in a day, wait for one minute. If the class is ready, thank students for their efficiency. If students are not ready, hold up the stack of cards with the "ten minute" card showing. Every 30 seconds, move the top card to the back of the stack. Continue this process, without saying a word, until all students are ready. After you give the next directive for a transition, wait the allotted time, and then pick up the stack of cards. After 30 seconds, move the top card (which, for example, may be nine minutes) to the back of the stack. The idea is that over the course of a day, each block of 30 seconds that students waste will cost them 30 seconds off the extra recess period.

Because this system is predominately punitive (taking time away from the extra recess), you really need to make a concerted effort to provide students with frequent positive attention, positive feedback, and even intermittent rewards (see Module 5) when they behave appropriately. Too much focus on a negative behavior without frequent positive interactions can backfire on you—i.e., students may try to lose the ten minutes quickly just to frustrate you and see what you will do next.

This system is most likely to work when there are more than three or four students who exhibit one specific misbehavior. If there are only one, two, or three students who are causing the problem, you would be better off setting up individualized plans (both positive and corrective) with those students. The system is also unlikely to be powerful enough to be effective if your class frequently exhibits many different misbehaviors.

Lottery Tickets (Medium Structure)

A relatively simple, but highly effective way to specifically encourage appropriate behavior (or a specific positive behavior) is with an "intermittent" weekly lottery reward system.

Each week on an unpredictable basis, present individual students who are following the rules/demonstrating responsible behavior with lottery tickets for a weekly drawing (Figure 8.13 shows a sample and Figure 8.14 is a reproducible master of multiple lottery tickets).

Figure 8.13: Sample Lottery Ticket

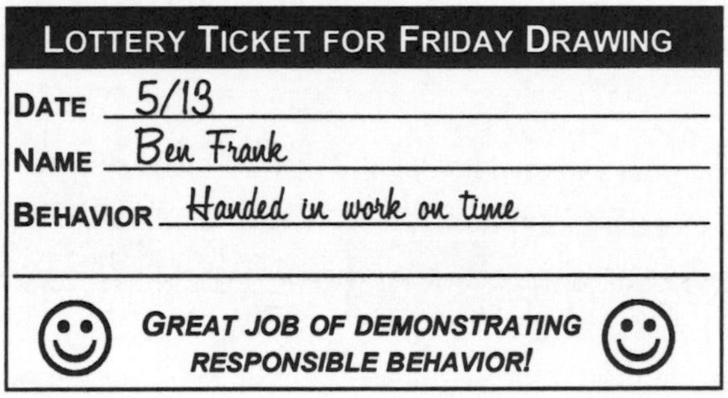

LOTTERY TICKET FOR FRIDAY DRAWING

DATE 5/13

NAME Ben Frank

BEHAVIOR Handed in work on time

☺ GREAT JOB OF DEMONSTRATING RESPONSIBLE BEHAVIOR! ☺

Figure 8.14: Sample Lottery Ticket

LOTTERY TICKET FOR FRIDAY DRAWING	LOTTERY TICKET FOR FRIDAY DRAWING
DATE ____	DATE ____
NAME ____	NAME ____
BEHAVIOR ____	BEHAVIOR ____
GREAT JOB OF DEMONSTRATING RESPONSIBLE BEHAVIOR!	GREAT JOB OF DEMONSTRATING RESPONSIBLE BEHAVIOR!

LOTTERY TICKET FOR FRIDAY DRAWING	LOTTERY TICKET FOR FRIDAY DRAWING
DATE ____	DATE ____
NAME ____	NAME ____
BEHAVIOR ____	BEHAVIOR ____
GREAT JOB OF DEMONSTRATING RESPONSIBLE BEHAVIOR!	GREAT JOB OF DEMONSTRATING RESPONSIBLE BEHAVIOR!

LOTTERY TICKET FOR FRIDAY DRAWING	LOTTERY TICKET FOR FRIDAY DRAWING
DATE ____	DATE ____
NAME ____	NAME ____
BEHAVIOR ____	BEHAVIOR ____
GREAT JOB OF DEMONSTRATING RESPONSIBLE BEHAVIOR!	GREAT JOB OF DEMONSTRATING RESPONSIBLE BEHAVIOR!

LOTTERY TICKET FOR FRIDAY DRAWING	LOTTERY TICKET FOR FRIDAY DRAWING
DATE ____	DATE ____
NAME ____	NAME ____
BEHAVIOR ____	BEHAVIOR ____
GREAT JOB OF DEMONSTRATING RESPONSIBLE BEHAVIOR!	GREAT JOB OF DEMONSTRATING RESPONSIBLE BEHAVIOR!

LOTTERY TICKET FOR FRIDAY DRAWING	LOTTERY TICKET FOR FRIDAY DRAWING
DATE ____	DATE ____
NAME ____	NAME ____
BEHAVIOR ____	BEHAVIOR ____
GREAT JOB OF DEMONSTRATING RESPONSIBLE BEHAVIOR!	GREAT JOB OF DEMONSTRATING RESPONSIBLE BEHAVIOR!

When you give a ticket, have the student write his/her name and the date on it. Be sure to tell the student exactly why he or she is getting the ticket so that he or she can write a brief description (e.g., "Consistent homework completion"). Have the student put the completed ticket into a container for a drawing that will occur at the end of week. Each Friday, before the drawing, identify two rewards you think students would like (e.g., a coupon for free ice cream and 15 minutes of computer time). At the time of the drawing, announce the first reward and draw a lottery ticket from the container. The student whose name is on that ticket receives the reward. Repeat the process for the second reward. Throw away (or better yet recycle) the tickets that still remain in the container. The next Monday, start giving out tickets for that week's drawing.

With this type of system, it is important to watch that you are not being discriminatory. For example, it would be easy to inadvertently harbor a grudge towards individual students who have been especially troublesome (during the current week or in the past), and "not notice" their positive behavior. It can also be easy to fall into the trap of noticing the small improvements of your more difficult students and the great leaps of your high achievers, but failing to recognize (or acknowledge) the ongoing, sustained effort of your average students.

Mystery Behavior of the Day (Medium Structure)

This simple and creative intermittent reward-based system was developed by Ms. Pat Gagnon, a 4th grade teacher in Springfield, Oregon. Each morning Pat decides on a particular positive behavior or trait that she will look for that day (e.g., "Helping Others"). The students know that she will be watching for some behavior, but she does not tell them what the day's behavior/trait is. During the day, she watches for, and notes to herself, examples of students exhibiting the "mystery behavior." Toward the end of the day, she puts a small treat on the desks of the students she "caught" exhibiting the behavior. After the rewards are given, she has the class spend a few minutes trying to guess what the Mystery Behavior was for that day. Whether or not students guess correctly, Pat tells them what the behavior was and lets them know that she will be looking for a different Mystery Behavior the next day.

You can add to the level of interest in this system by having a large envelope with the words "Mystery Behavior of the Day" prominently displayed in the room. Before the students arrive each morning, write the behavior or trait you will look for that day on a piece of paper and place it in the envelope. At the end of the day, after students have discussed what they think the Mystery Behavior was, have one of the students who earned a treat that day draw the piece of paper from the envelope and announce the behavior. You might even want to encourage the student to add a bit of fanfare—like an Academy Awards ceremony—"And, the Mystery Behavior for today is. . ."

When using this system, be sure to vary the Mystery Behavior so that every student will get recognized periodically. That is, be very careful that no student goes too long without being "caught" exhibiting one of the Mystery Behaviors.

Classwide Public Posting (Middle Structure)

When there is one specific behavior you want to increase (e.g., homework completion) or decrease (e.g., use of student-to-student put downs during class), you can overtly chart that behavior in a place and in way that all students can see it. This is especially useful when a specific problem is exhibited by quite a few students in the class (as opposed to a problem that only a couple of students exhibit). Public posting makes everyone aware of how pervasive a problem is, and gives the entire group positive feedback when the situation improves.

For example, if you have a middle school class that is having trouble with frequent name calling, laughing at peers' mistakes, and other forms of student-to-student disrespect, you could start by keeping a simple tally of the total number of disrespectful actions that occur each day for three days. After the three days, you would post a chart with the data from the first three days. Posting the chart serves as the impetus for holding a class discussion about the problem, the benefits of reducing the negative behavior, and strategies that individual students might employ to help reduce the problem. In this example, one strategy that you could share would be that individuals should avoid laughing when someone calls someone else a name or otherwise puts somebody down. Each day, you would keep a simple count of the number of disrespectful incidents, and at the end of the day you would record that data on the chart. At least twice a week when you post the data, you could initiate a short discussion about whether the problem is getting better, getting worse, or staying about the same. If the situation is staying the same or getting worse, you could have students discuss other actions they can take to help reduce the problem.

As noted before, public posting can also be effective for helping you increase a positive behavior (e.g., daily work completion). To use it for this purpose, start by determining the class' daily percentage of completed work turned in on time for one week. You can do this by simply counting the number of assignments turned in on each day in a given week and dividing that number by the total number of assignments that should have been turned in that day. This figure is the class' percentage of work completion for that day. Record that first week's worth of data on a chart you have placed prominently in the room. Use the initial record to prompt a discussion of the importance of work completion, the benefits to each individual for completing his/her work, and strategies individuals can use to help increase (if necessary) their own work completion. Then compute the class' daily percentage of work completion and plan to record it on the chart the next day. At least twice a week, preferably daily, discuss the data on the chart and whether the percentage of work completion is increasing, decreasing, or staying about the same.

Individual Public Posting (Middle Structure)

Publicly posting student performance data has been demonstrated to be an effective means of improving performance in academic areas such as math, reading, and language arts. To use this system, create a large chart with each student's name on it, and with places to record scores. For example, you might have a chart on which you record each individual student's best score every week on a timed math exercise. At the end of the week, have each student enter his/her best score for that week in the correct space on the chart. Have individual students compare their best score for the current week to their best scores from previous weeks. When using public posting of individual data, it is important to emphasize (and to keep emphasizing) that the purpose of the system is not for students to compete with each other, but for each student to compete against his/her own personal best. Some of you may be concerned that this type of system will humiliate those students who are struggling academically. The fact is, it is the lowest 50% of your students who are likely to make the most significant gains in achievement. Nonetheless, if you are considering this system, discuss it with your administrator first to determine if it is an acceptable practice in your school district.

Reinforcement Based on Reducing Misbehavior (High Structure)

This system is designed to reward an entire class for significant reductions in the total number of misbehaviors that occur on any given day. It is particularly effective when many different students in the class exhibit a wide variety of misbehavior.

To implement the system, use either a Daily or Weekly Misbehavior Recording Sheet (see Module 6, Tool 4) and keep data on class misbehavior for at least five days. Design a chart on which you have spaces to record the data from those five days, plus at least another 20 or 30 days. Then determine the average number of misbehaviors per day that occurred during your five-day baseline period (i.e., add the total number of misbehaviors you recorded and divide by five).

From the average number of incidents that have been occurring daily, build a sliding scale for awarding points. Create the scale so that if the average number of incidents (or more) occurs, students earn no points, but as progressively fewer incidents occur, students earn an increasing number of points that can be applied to a reward. For example, if you found that the average number of incidents for the five days was 33 (obviously this hypothetical class has a lot of misbehavior), your point scale might look like the following:

More than 32 incidents	= 0 points
22-32 incidents	= 1 point
15-21 incidents	= 2 points
7-14 incidents	= 3 points
3-6 incidents	= 4 points
1-2 incidents	= 5 points
0 incidents	= 6 points

Post the chart, and point out to students the number of incidents that occurred over the preceding five days. Explain your concern, and inform students that you are willing to provide the class with some rewards if they will work on reducing the amount of misbehavior that occurs each day. Then show students your scale of number of incidents and corresponding points.

Next, have students brainstorm a list of class reward ideas. Once you have a reasonable list, set prices for each of the possible rewards (in terms of how many points will be required to get each reward). The price-setting needs to be done by you, and you should base the "prices" on the instructional, personnel, and/or monetary costs of the items. Monetary cost is clear—the more expensive the item, the more points should be required to earn it. Instructional cost refers to the amount of instructional time lost or interrupted as the result of a particular reward (e.g., an extra ten minutes of recess means ten minutes less instructional time). Any reward that results in the class having to miss academic instruction should "cost" more points than one that does not (e.g., one the class can do during recess time). Personnel cost refers to the time required of you and/or other staff to give the reward. An extra recess that required arranging for extra supervision would cost more than letting students have music playing during an independent work period.

Have the class vote on the rewards. The one that receives the most votes is the reward students will work for first. The items that received the second and third most votes will be the second and third rewards that students will have a chance to win.

Each day, keep a careful count of the number of incidents of misbehavior. At the end of the day, record the total number of misbehavior incidents, and tell the class how many points they earned that day. Each day let students know the total number of points they have accumulated to date. When the class has enough points, they get the designated reward. Then the system starts again, and they have zero points. Remind the class of the next reward they are working toward (e.g., the item that got the second most votes).

Self-Evaluation of On/Off-Task Behavior (Middle Structure)

With this system, you monitor students' on-task and off-task behavior during instructional activities. It is particularly appropriate when your students do not exhibit a great deal of overt misbehavior, but also do not use their work time well. That is, quite a few students in the class tend to sit and do nothing or converse instead of doing their work or participating actively in instructional activities.

Before you use this system, it's important to have provided lessons on your *CHAMPs* expectations for teacher-directed instruction, independent work periods, and cooperative groups (see Modules 3 & 4). Once you have thoroughly taught students what "on-task" behavior looks like and sounds like, which may take several weeks, use the reproducible master of the "Self-Evaluation of On- & Off-Task Behavior" form (see Figure 8.15) and make copies of the form for each student.

To use the system, set a timer at the beginning of each work period—for anywhere from 1 to 30 minutes. When the timer goes off, each student evaluates whether she/he was on task or off task at that moment, and then circles the "next" number in the appropriate column of the recording sheet. After you have given students an opportunity to do their recording, instruct them to get back to work, and reset the timer. Vary the amount of time you set the timer for—so students never know exactly when they will be evaluating their behavior.

Before you implement the system, be sure to explain to students how it works. Teach them how to evaluate whether they were on task or off task and how to accurately fill out the form. Then, each time the timer goes off, monitor a few students (not always the same ones!) to see if they are recording accurately. When you are monitoring, if you disagree with a student's rating, discuss your assessment of the situation with the student. Never argue, but do encourage students to be honest with themselves in their ratings. You can teach students in grades 5 and above how to calculate their own daily percentage (divide the total on-task numbers circled by the total of both on-task and off-task numbers circled). With younger students, you will probably have to calculate the percentage for them. Have each student keep a graph of his/her daily on-task percentage and encourage students to try to improve their performance from one day to the next. Use the procedure for a couple of weeks.

NOTE

This procedure can be used with kindergarten and first grade students, by making the focus on "Being in the Right Place" versus "Being in the Wrong Place"—and evaluating whether students were in their seats during seatwork time, on the rug during story time, in line when it is time to line up, and so on. With young students, however, it may be better to set the system up as a group count (how many students were in the right place when the timer went off?), in which the group earns a point if everyone is "in the right place" when the beeper goes off. Have a place on a chalkboard or flip chart to record the students' accumulated total of points. Then, when the class gets a predetermined number of points, the class gets a treat or a special activity.

An alternative to using a timer (and having to reset it each time) is to use "beeper tapes." These are audio tapes, usually 30 minutes in length, which are blank except for 2-15 randomly recorded beeps. You can make your own "beeper tapes" using an audio cassette recorder, a clock with a second hand, and some means of making a noise (e.g., a doorbell, hitting a chime, hitting an empty glass with a spoon). You may want to have a variety of tapes on hand. For example, you might have two tapes on which the beeps occur at regular intervals (one with beeps every 5 minutes and one with beeps every 12 minutes) and two or three tapes on which the beeps occur at irregular intervals (one with 2 beeps, one with 8 beeps, and one with 12 beeps).

Figure 8.15: Reproducible

SELF EVALUATION OF ON- & OFF-TASK BEHAVIOR																			
NAME ____________________ DATE ____________________																			
ON TASK										OFF TASK									
1	2	3	4	5	6	7	8	9	10	1	2	3	4	5	6	7	8	9	10
11	12	13	14	15	16	17	18	19	20	11	12	13	14	15	16	17	18	19	20
MY PERCENTAGE OF ON-TASK BEHAVIOR FOR TODAY WAS: ______%																			

SELF EVALUATION OF ON- & OFF-TASK BEHAVIOR																			
NAME ____________________ DATE ____________________																			
ON TASK										OFF TASK									
1	2	3	4	5	6	7	8	9	10	1	2	3	4	5	6	7	8	9	10
11	12	13	14	15	16	17	18	19	20	11	12	13	14	15	16	17	18	19	20
MY PERCENTAGE OF ON-TASK BEHAVIOR FOR TODAY WAS: ______%																			

Target and Reward a Specific Behavior (Middle Structure)

This simple classwide behavior management system is useful when there is one specific behavioral problem that is exhibited by quite a few different students (e.g., name calling/put downs). For a couple of days, count the number of times the targeted behavior occurs. Don't bother to count how many incidents any individual student has, just the total number of incidents for the day (or class period in middle school).

After two days, share the information you have collected with students and tell them that you need them to reduce the frequency of this misbehavior. Guide the class in the process of setting a realistic improvement goal for themselves (e.g., reducing the number of daily incidents from 40 to 32). Students may be tempted to set an unrealistic goal, such as reducing the number of incidents from 40 per day to 0. Explain that if they don't set a reasonable goal—say, no more than 32 incidents—they will make it very difficult to achieve their goal. Explain that a realistic goal increases their chances of success. Also tell them that once they achieve their initial (reasonable) goal, they can start setting more challenging goals for themselves.

Using a list of classwide rewards that has been generated by the class, create a "Grab Bag." Write each of the rewards on a small card, and put all the cards in a container. On any day that the class meets their goal, one of the students gets to draw a card from the container. The class receives the reward on the card. When you are ready to start moving students toward fading the system, let them know that you have put some cards into the container that say, "Congratulations! Today you have the satisfaction of having attained your goal." Explain that if one of these cards is drawn, students will not get an actual reward that day. Instead, it will give them the opportunity to learn that there are many things people do in life, not for any reward, but simply for the satisfaction of doing something well. The more of these cards you add, the closer you move students toward eliminating the system completely.

A Variation: Mystery Motivators (Medium Structure)

A variation of the system "Targeting a Specific Misbehavior" is called "Mystery Motivators." This variation makes the system even more of a "gamble," which may mean that it is more interesting and compelling for some classes. Using an invisible ink pen, make an "X" on approximately 60% of the school days on a calendar for the next month. (NOTE: Invisible pens are available at novelty stores. They also come with the *Tough Kid Tool Box*, Jenson, W.R. (1994) available from Sopris West.) Then choose one of the rewards from the list generated by the class and write it on a card, which you place in an envelope labeled "Mystery Motivator." Do not tell students what reward is written on the card. On those days when the class meets its behavior goal, one student gets to "color" in that day on the calendar to see if there is an X (previously invisible) in the square. If there is an X, have another student open the Mystery Motivator envelope and announce which Mystery Motivator the class earned. If there is no X when the calendar square is colored in, you will enthusiastically congratulate students on meeting their goal, but the Mystery Motivator is not awarded (or revealed). If there are days in which the class does not meet the goal (i.e., there were too many incidents of the misbehavior), students do not even get to check whether there was an X. If the system is effective, you can begin fading it during the second month by putting fewer Xs on the calendar (i.e., creating fewer chances to get an extrinsic reward).

Team Competition with Response Cost Lottery (Middle Structure)

A system involving team competition (i.e., groups of students compete against each other) can be useful for reducing a minor, but annoying behavior (e.g., students blurting out or other minor disruptions). Of course, whenever you do anything with teams—especially when the competition involves academic and/or behavioral performance—it's important to ensure that the teams themselves are as comparable as possible. Thus, you should assign students to teams rather than letting them self-select their teams, and you should make sure that no team is overloaded with "problem" or "extremely responsible" students.

To use this system, divide students into four to six teams. Have each team give itself a team name (but do not allow any gang affiliation names). At the beginning of each day, every team receives a certain number of tickets (e.g., ten). Have the students write their team's name on their tickets. Then, whenever a student misbehaves, take a ticket from his/her team. At the end of the day, collect the remaining tickets from each team and put them in a container for a lottery drawing. The team whose name is on the winning ticket earns the reward for the day. (A list of desired rewards can be generated by the class.) Start the system over the following day.

Whole Class Points (High Structure)

In this system you provide feedback, both positive and corrective, to the entire class at regular intervals. For each interval during which the behavior of the class met your expectations, the group earns a point. Once the group has earned a predetermined number of points, the entire class gets a reward. This is an excellent system to use when you have quite a few immature students in the class. However, it is not a good choice if most of your class behaves well, but two or three students are responsible for most misbehavior.

The first thing you need to determine when using this system is the duration of the interval you will use (e.g., each hour, each half hour, each quarter hour, etc.). The less mature your class (regardless of grade level), the shorter the intervals should be. For example, with a relatively immature group of students, you may need intervals as short as 15 minutes. You also need to determine how you will keep track of the duration—i.e., what will prompt you that it's time to evaluate behavior. Possibilities include: an alarm on your watch; a kitchen timer; or a preprogrammed classroom computer.

Next, have a class brainstorming session to identify possible rewards. Eliminate unreasonable suggestions and then set "prices" for how many points it will take to earn various reward items/activities. Your prices should be based in part on the length of the interval you are using (e.g., if you use 15-minute intervals, the rewards should "cost" more than if you use 60-minute intervals). Prices should also be based on the monetary, instructional, and personnel costs the various rewards entail. Thus, a two-hour movie with popcorn will be more "expensive" than five minutes of extra recess.

The last consideration is how you will keep track of the points. With most elementary classes, some kind of graphic representation (chart) on a bulletin board or flip chart can be very effective. You might want to relate the theme of the chart to the content of something the class is currently studying. For example, you could track points using a rocket on its way to the moon, a covered wagon on the way to Oregon, or a whale migrating to Baja. Figure 8.16 shows this system with a space motif.

Figure 8.16: Rocket Point Chart

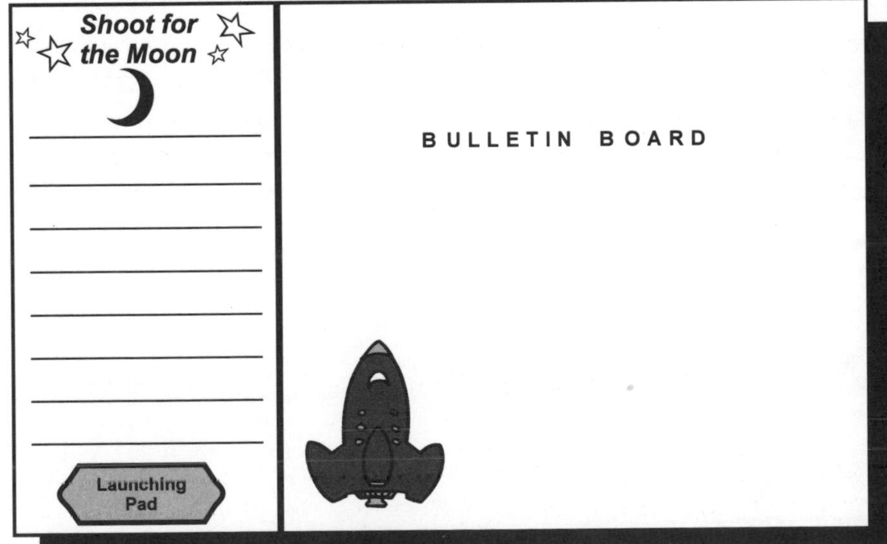

Reprinted with permission from Sprick, R.S. (1991). *The Solution Book: A Guide to Classroom Discipline*.

Another graphic representation idea that might be appropriate for an intermediate class studying biology in science could be to have a visual that shows parts of a cell—each of which will be "labeled" as soon as the class earns so many points. In fact, the various labels could cost different amounts (e.g., the cell wall costs five points, the chromosomes ten points, the cytoplasts three points, and so on). When the entire cell has been labeled, the group earns the reward. See Figure 8.17.

Figure 8.17: Parts of a Cell Point Chart

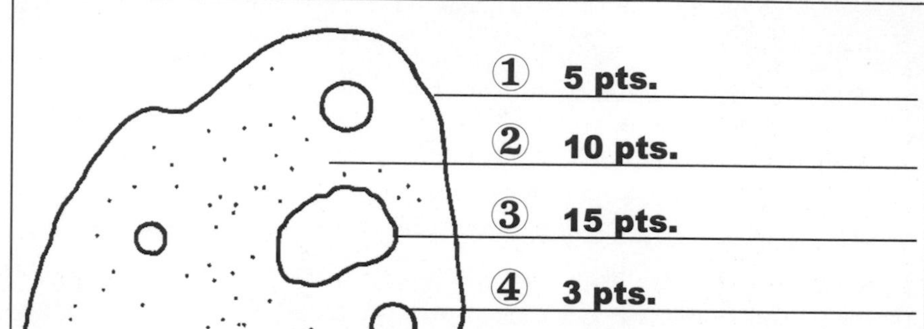

If you are a middle school teacher, use your own judgment about whether your students would be "motivated" by this kind of graphical point tracking. If you don't think they would, simply devote a small corner of the chalkboard to recording the points ("4th period: 6 points.")

Once these various decisions have been made, implementation is fairly simple. At the conclusion of each interval (e.g., when the timer goes off after 30 minutes), review the behavior of the entire class for the preceding 30 minute period. If students met your expectations (think about your *CHAMPs* expectations), the group earns two points. If all but one or two students met your expectations, the group earns one point. If more than one or two students failed to meet expectations, the group earns zero points. If the group earns anything less than two points, describe the inappropriate behaviors that led to your assessment—but do not name names of students who misbehaved. "Because I had to give several of you reminders about talking during quiet study time, the group does not get any points for this time period. However, I am resetting the timer, and I am sure that in the next 30 minutes you will be able to earn two points."

If student behavior does not improve, increase the amount of positive feedback you give to individual students and to the class during each interval. If there is still insufficient improvement, consider using shorter intervals (15 minutes rather than 30). When the class has earned a reward, begin the system again by having the class vote on the next reward. You can keep the system interesting for students by changing the theme periodically—that is, you do not want to use a cell motif or rocket motif for more than a couple of weeks at a time.

Module 8: Classwide Motivation Systems

Self-Assessment Checklist

Use the worksheet on the following pages to identify which (or which parts) of the tasks described in this module you have completed. For any item that has not been completed, note what needs to be done to complete it. Then translate your notes onto your planning calendar in the form of specific actions that you can take (e.g., November 1, decide if my class needs a reward-based motivation system).

COMPLETED	TASK	NOTES & IMPLEMENTATION IDEAS
	EFFECTIVELY EMPLOY A CLASSWIDE MOTIVATION SYSTEM I have evaluated, subjectively and/or with systematic monitoring tools, the behavior and motivation level of my students.	
	I have carefully considered whether my students would benefit from a nonreward-based or a reward-based motivation system.	
	If a nonreward-based system is appropriate, I am prepared to use some form of goal-setting with my students.	

COMPLETED	TASK	NOTES & IMPLEMENTATION IDEAS
	If a reward-based system is needed, I have reviewed the information on how to use a reward-based system so that I am prepared to: • choose (design) a system that is appropriate to the needs of my students; • implement the system in a way that will enhance its effectiveness with my students; • maintain the system so that it continues to have a positive effect on my students' motivation; and • eventually fade the system, so that students' improved behavior and/or increased motivation stems primarily from their own intrinsic motivation.	

Module 8: Classwide Motivation Systems Peer Study Worksheet

With one or more of your colleagues, work through the following discussion topics and activities related to the tasks in Module 8. If necessary, refer back to the text to get additional ideas or for clarification. (See the Module 1 Peer Study Worksheet for suggestions on structuring effective discussion sessions.)

Introduction:

A. Have each group member share whether his/her class needs (or could benefit from) a nonreward-based motivation system or a reward-based system—and explain how he/she reached that decision. Other group members should provide feedback.

B. Each group member who has decided that goal-setting is appropriate for his/her students should explain how he/she plans to implement the system—including how he/she will conduct conferences with students.

C. Each group member who has decided that a reward-based system is needed for his/her students should share the specifics of any system(s) that he/she plans to use. Other group members should provide feedback.

Menu

A. As a group, review the various systems presented in the menu. Discuss how they might be implemented in your individual classrooms, and how you might address any issues/problems that seem likely.

B. Have individual group members share other "system" ideas that they have found to be effective.

WHAT THE RESEARCH SAYS

Teachers Establish Smooth, Efficient Classroom Routines

Teachers:

A. Plan rules and procedures before the school year begins and present them to students during the first few days of school.

B. Begin class quickly and purposefully, with assignments, activities, materials and supplies ready for students when they arrive.

C. Require students to bring the materials they need to class each day and assign storage space as needed.

D. Establish routines for handling administrative matters quickly and efficiently, with minimum disruption of instructional time.

E. Make smooth, rapid transitions between activities throughout the class period or school day.

F. Circulate around the room during seatwork activities, keeping students on task and providing help as needed.

G. Conduct periodic review of classroom routines and revise them as needed.

Allen (1986); Anderson (1980); Armor et al. (1976); Bain, Lintz, and Word (1989); Bielefeldt (1990); Brophy (1979, 1983, 1986); Brophy and Good (1986); Brown, McIntyre, and McAlpine (1988); Doyle (1986a); Edmonds (1979a); Emmer and Evertson (1980, 1982); Evertson (1982, 1985); Evertson and Harris (1992); Evertson et al. (1985); Gersten and Carnine (1986); Good and Brophy (1986); Hawkins, Doueck, and Lishner (1988); Hawley et al. (1984); Kounin (1977); Leinhardt, Weidman, and Hammond (1987); Medley (1978); Rosenshine (1983); Rosenshine and Stevens (1986); Sanford, Emmer and Clements (1983); Sanford and Evertson (1981); Wang, Haertel, and Walberg (1993-1994)

Teachers Interact with Students in Positive, Caring Ways

Teachers:

A. Pay attention to student interests, problems, and accomplishments in social interactions both in and out of the classroom.

B. Encourage student effort, focusing on the positive aspects of students' answers, products, and behavior.

C. Communicate interest and caring to students both verbally and through such nonverbal means as giving undivided attention, maintaining eye contact, smiling, and nodding.

D. Encourage students to develop a sense of responsibility and self-reliance. They give older students, in particular, opportunities to take responsibility for school-related activities and to participate in making decisions about important school issues.

E. Share anecdotes and incidents from their experience and appropriate to build rapport and understanding with students.

Agne, Greenwood, and Miller (1994); Allen (1986); Anderson (1985); Bain, Linz, and Word (1989); Bain and Jacobs (1990); Cooper and Good (1983); Cooper and Tom (1984); Cotton (1992); Doyle (1986a); Edmonds (1979a,b); Emmer and Evertson (1980, 1981a); Glatthorn (1989); Good (1987); Good and Brophy (1984); Gottfried and Gottfried (1991); Hawkins, Doueck, and Lishner (1988); Kearns (1988); Marshal and Weinstein (1985); McDevitt, Lennon, and Kopriva (1991); Midgley, Feldaufer, and Eccles (1989); Mills et al. (1989); Mortimore and Sammons (1987); Mortimore et al (1988); Pecukonis (1990); Rutter et al. (1979); Taylor, S.E. (1986-87); Teddlie et al. (1989); Wang, Haertel, and Walberg (1993-1994); Weinstein and Marshall (1984); Woolfolk and Brooks (1985).

Teachers Provide Incentives, Recognition, and Rewards to Promote Excellence

Teachers:

A. Define excellence by objective standards, not by peer comparison. They establish systems for consistent recognition of students for academic achievement and excellent behavior.

B. Relate recognition and rewards to specific student achievements and use them judiciously. As with praise, teachers are careful not to use unmerited or random rewards in an attempt to control students' behavior.

C. Provide incentives and rewards appropriate to the developmental level of students, including symbolic, token, tangible, or activity rewards.

D. Make certain that all students know what they need to do to earn recognition and rewards. Rewards should be appealing to students, while remaining commensurate with their achievements, i.e., not too lavish.

E. Present some rewards publicly and others privately; Some immediately and some delayed to teach persistence.

F. Make some rewards available to students on an individual basis, while allowing others to earned by groups of students—as in some cooperative learning structures.

Bain, Lintz and Word (1989); Brophy (1980, 1986a, b, 1987, 1988b); Brophy and Good (1986); Cameron and Pierce (1994); Canella (1986); Emmer and Everston (1980, 1981a); Evertson (1981); Evertson, Anderson, and Anderson (1980); Gettinger (1983); Good (1984b); Rosenshine and Stevens (1986); Rosswork (1977); Rutter et al. (1979); Slavin (1980, 1984,1988, 1989, 1991, 1994).

Teachers Set Clear Standards for Classroom Behavior and Apply Them Fairly and Consistently

Teachers:

A. Set standards which are consistent with or identical to the building code of conduct.

B. Let students know that there are high standards for behavior in the classroom, and explain rules, discipline procedures, and consequences clearly.

C. Provide written behavior standard and teach and review them from the beginning of the year or the start of new courses.

D. Establish rules that are clear and specific; they avoid vague or unenforceable rules such as "be in the right place at the right time."

E. Provide considerable reteaching and practice of classroom rules and procedures for children in grades K-3.

F. Involve older students in helping to establish standards and sanctions.

G. Apply consistent, equitable discipline for all students, making certain that sanctions are clearly linked to students' inappropriate behavior.

H. Teach and reinforce positive, prosocial behaviors and skills, including self-control skills, especially with students who have a history of behavior problems.

I. Stop disruptions quickly, taking care to avoid disrupting the whole class.

J. Focus on students' inappropriate behavior when taking disciplinary action—not on their personalities or histories.

K. Handle most disciplinary matters in the classroom, keeping referrals to administrators to a minimum.

L. Participate in training activities to improve classroom management skills.

Allen (1986); Anderson (1980); Bain, Lintz, and Word (1989); Bielefeldt (1990); Brophy (1979, 1983, 1986a); Brophy and Good (1986); Cotton (1990b); Doyle (1986b); Emmer and Evertson (1981a,b); Emmer and Aussiker (1989); Emmer (1982); Evertson (1985,1989); Evertson and Harris (1992); Gettinger (1988); Good and Brophy (1986) Gottfredson, Gottfredson, and Hybl (1993); Hawkins, Doeck, and Lishner (1988); Kounin (1977); Lemming (1993); Mayer (1993); Medley (1978); Render, Padilla, and Krank (1989); Rutter et al. (1979); Sanford and Evertson (1981); Solomon et al. (1988); Teddlie, Kirby, and Stringfield (1989); Vincezi and Ayrer (1985).

The above material is reprinted with permission from Effective Schooling Practices: A Research Synthesis, 1995 Update. This excellent summary of school and teacher effectiveness literature was compiled by Kathleen Cotton. To order copies of this resource, call or write:

Document Reproduction Service
Northwest Regional Educational Laboratory
101 S.W. Main Street, Suite 500
Portland, Oregon 97204
503-275-9519

Reproducible

CHAMPs Icons

PRESENTATION
BOOK

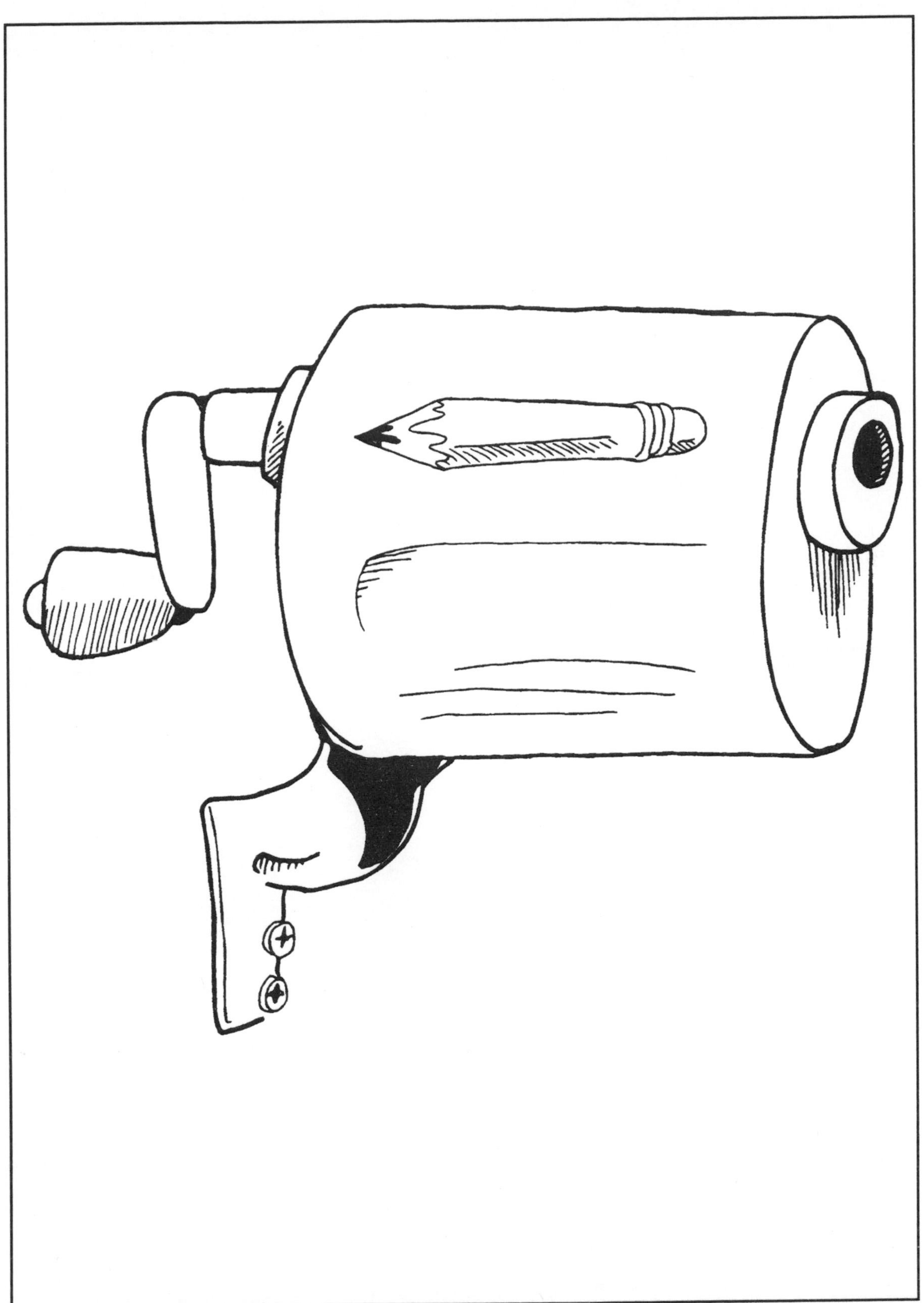

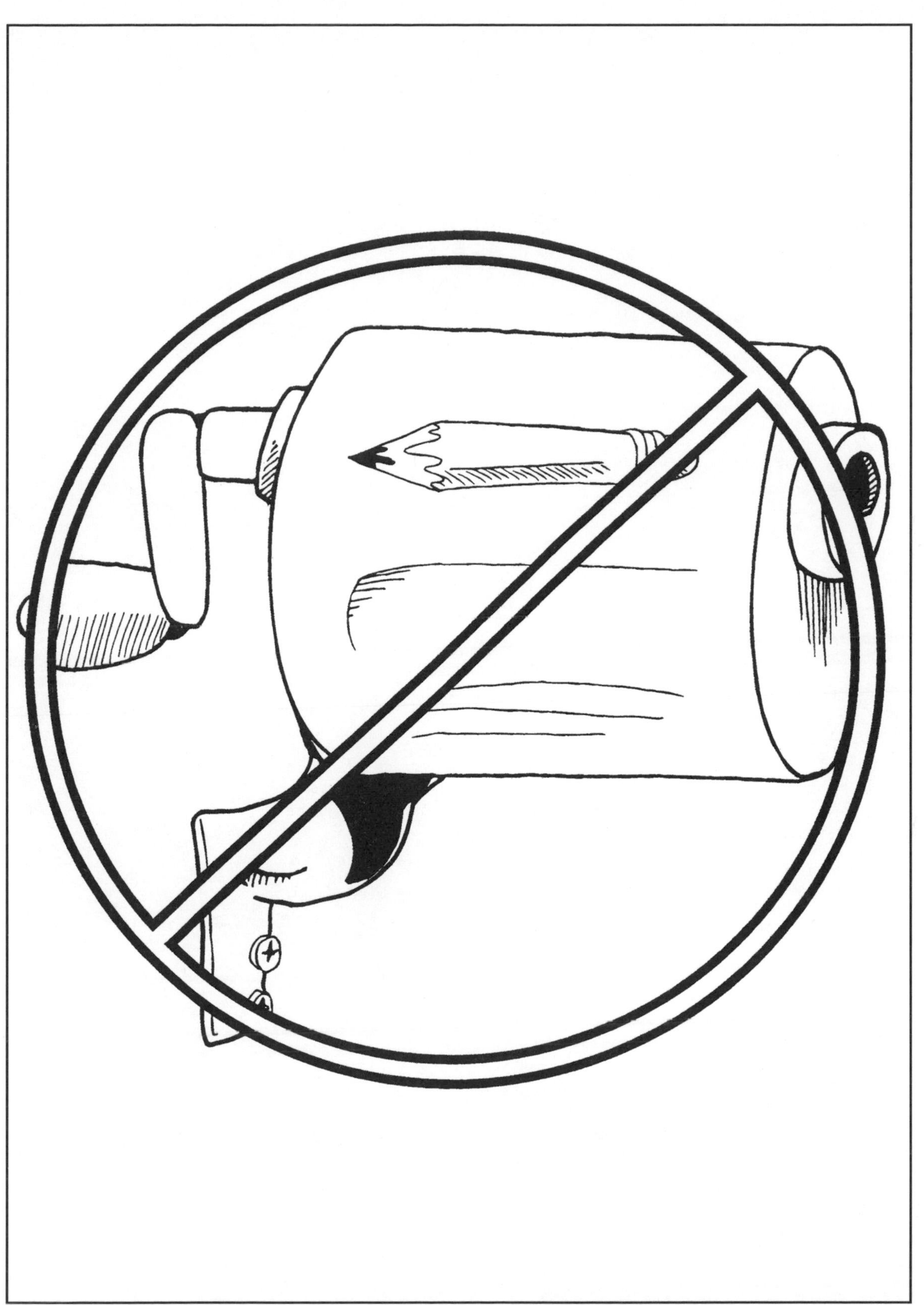

IN

PLEASE
HELP

Board Work
ABC
123

Clean Up
SHINE
GAMES
GAMES
GAMES
SUPER FUN!

Gym

Library
THE PLANETS
GIVE A HOOT
READ
PIRATES
PIRATES
MAPS
MYSTERIES
DOGS!
ART

Line Up

Group
SEPTEMBER

Free Play

Snack

Music

Seat Work

REFERENCES

Agne, K.J., Greenwood, G.E., and Miller, L.D. "Relationships Between Teacher Belief Systems and Teacher Effectiveness." *The Journal of Research and Development in Education* 27/3 (1994): 141-152

Allen, J.D. "Classroom Management: Students' Perspectives, Goals, and Strategies". *American Educational Research Journal* 23:3 (Fall 1986): 437-459.

Anderson, C.S. The Investigation of School Climate. In *Research on Exemplary Schools*, edited by G.R. Austin and H. Garber. Orlando, FL: Academic Press, 1985, 97-126.

Anderson, L.W. "Learning Time and Educational Effectiveness." *NASSP Curriculum Report 10:2* (December 1980) (ED 210 780).

Archer, A. and Gleason, M. (1990). *Skills for School Success.* North Billerica, MA: Curriculum Associates.

Armor, D., Conry-Oseguera, P., Cox, M., King, N., McDonnell, L., Pascal, A., Pauly, E. and Zellman, G. *Analysis of the School Preferred Reading Program in Selected Los Angeles Minority Schools.* Santa Monica, CA: Rand Corporation, 1976 (ED 130 243).

Bain, H.P. and Jacobs, R. *The Case for Smaller Classes and Better Teachers.* Alexandria, VA: National Association of Elementary School Principals, 1990 (ED 322 632).

Bain, H., Lintz, N., and Word, E. *A Study of First Grade Effective Teaching Practices from the Project Star Class Size Research. A Study of Fifty Effective Teachers Whose Class Average Gain Scores Ranked in the Top 15% of Each of Four School Types in Project STAR.* 1989 (ED 321 887).

Becker, W.C. (1986). *Applied psychology for teachers.* Chicago: Science Research Associates.

Bielefeldt, T. "Classroom Discipline." *Research Roundup* 5:2 (February 1990) (ED 318 133).

Brophy, J.E. "Classroom Management Techniques." *Education and Urban Society* 18:2 (February 1986a): 182-194.

Brophy, J.E. "Classroom Organization and Management." *The Elementary School Journal* 83:4 (March 1983): 265-285.

Brophy, J.E. "Educating Teachers About Managing Classrooms and Students." *Teaching and Teacher Education* 4:1 (1988a): 1-18.

Brophy, J.E. "Research Linking Teacher Behavior to Student Achievement: Potential Implications for Instruction of Chapter 1 Students." *Educational Psychologist* 23:3 (Summer 1988b): 235-286 (ED 293 914).

Brophy, J.E. "Synthesis of Research on Strategies for Motivating Students to Learn." *Educational Leadership* 45:2 (October 1987): 40-48.

Brophy, J.E. "Teacher Behavior And Its Effects." *Journal of Educational Psychology* 71:6 (December 1979): 733-750 (ED 181 014).

Brophy, J.E. "Teacher Influences on Student Achievement." *American Psychologist* 4:10 (October 1986b): 1069-1077.

Brophy, J.E. *Teacher Praise: A Functional Analysis.* East Lansing, MI: The Institute for Research on Teaching, 1980 (ED 181 013).

Brophy, J.E. and Good, T.L. Teacher Behavior and Student Achievement. In *Handbook of Research on Teaching*, Third Edition, edited by M.C.Wittrock. New York: Macmillan, 1986, 328-377.

Brown, S., McIntyre, D., and McAlpine, A. "The Knowledge Which Underpins the Craft of Teaching." Paper presented at the Annual Meeting of the American Educational Research Association, New Orleans, LA, April 1988 (ED 294 872).

Cameron, J. and Pierce, W.D. "Reinforcement, Reward, and Intrinsic Motivation: A Meta-Analysis." *Review of Educational Research* 64:3 (Fall 1994): 363-423.

Cannella, G.S. "Praise and Concrete Rewards: Concerns for Childhood Education." *Childhood Education* 62:4 (March/April 1986): 297-301.

Cooper, H.M. and Good, T.L. *Pygmalion Grows Up: Studies in the Expectation Communication Process.* New York: Longman Press, 1983.

Cooper, H.M. and Tom, D.Y.H. "Teacher Expectation Research: A Review with Implications for Classroom Instruction." *The Elementary School Journal* 85:1 (September 1984): 77-89.

Cotton, K. *Developing Empathy in Children and Youth.* Close-Up #13. Portland, OR: Northwest Regional Educational Laboratory, 1992 (ED 361 876).

Cotton, K. *Effective Schooling Practices: A Research Synthesis: 1995 Update.* Portland,OR: Northwest Regional Educational Laboratory. 1995.

Cotton, K. *Preventing and Treating Alcohol, Drug, and Smoking Addiction: Research on Effective Practices.* Portland, OR: Northwest Regional Educational Laboratory, 1990a.

Cotton, K. *Schoolwide and Classroom Discipline*. Close-Up #9. Portland, OR: Northwest Regional Educational Laboratory, 1990b.

Doyle, W. "Classroom Organization and Management." In *Handbook of Research on Teaching*, Third Edition, edited by M.C.Wittrock. New York: Macmillan, 1986a, 392-431.

Doyle, W. Effective Secondary Classroom Practices. In *Reaching for Excellence: An Effective Schools Sourcebook*. Washington, DC: National Institute of Education, May 1986b.

Edmonds, R.R. "Effective Schools for the Urban Poor." *Educational Leadership* 37:1 (October 1979a): 16-24.

Edmonds, R.R. "Some Schools Work and More Can." *Social Policy* 9 (1979b): 28-32.

Edmonds, R.R. and Frederiksen, J.R. *Search for Effective Schools: The Identification and Analysis of City Schools That Are Instructionally Effective for Poor Children*, 1979 (ED 170 396).

Emmer, E.T. *Management Strategies in Elementary School Classrooms*. Austin, TX: Research and Development Center for Teacher Education, 1982 (ED 251 432).

Emmer, E.T. and Aussiker, A. School and Classroom Discipline Programs: How Well Do They Work? In *Strategies to Reduce Student Misbehavior*, edited by O.C. Moles. Washington, DC: Office of Educational Research and Improvement, U. S. Department of Education, 1989, 105-142 (ED 311 608).

Emmer, E.T. and Evertson, C.M. *Effective Management at the Beginning of the School Year in Junior High Classes*. Report No. 6107. Austin, TX: Research and Development Center for Teacher Education, University of Texas, 1980 (ED 241 499).

Emmer, E.T. and Evertson, C.M. "Synthesis of Research on Classroom Management." *Educational Leadership* 38:4 (January 1981a): 342-347.

Emmer, E.T. and Evertson, C.M. *Teacher's Manual for the Junior High Classroom Management Improvement Study*. Austin, TX: Research and Development Center for Teacher Education, University of Texas, 1981b.

Emmer, E.T., Sanford, J.P., Clements, B.S., and Martin, J. *Improving Classroom Management In Junior High Classrooms: An Experimental Investigation*. Austin, TX: Research and Development Center for Teacher Education, University of Texas, 1982 (ED 261 053).

Evertson, C.M. "Differences in Instructional Activities in Higher and Lower Achieving Junior High English and Math Classes." *Elementary School Journal* 82/4 (March 1992): 329-351.

Evertson, C.M. "Improving Elementary Classroom Management: A School-Based Training Program for Beginning the Year." *Journal of Educational Research* 83/2 (November/December 1989): 82-90.

Evertson, C.M . *Organizing and Managing the Elementary School Classroom.* Austin, TX: Research and Development Center for Teacher Education, University of Texas, 1981 (ED 223 570).

Evertson, C.M. "Training Teachers in Classroom Management: An Experimental Study in Secondary School Classrooms." *Journal of Educational Research* 79:1 (September/October 1985): 51-58.

Evertson, C.M. "Differences in Instructional Activities in Higher and Lower Achieving Junior High English and Math Classes." *Elementary School Journal* 82/4 (March 1982): 329-351.

Evertson, C.M., Anderson, C., and Anderson, L. "Relationship Between Classroom Behavior and Student Outcomes in Junior High Mathematics and English Classes." *American Elementary Research Journal* 17:1 (Spring 1980): 43-60.

Evertson, C.M. and Harris, A.L. "What We Know About Managing Classrooms." *Educational Leadership* 49/7 (April 1992): 74-78.

Evertson, C.M., Weade, R., Green, J.L., and Crawford, J. *Effective Classroom Management and Instruction: An Exploration of Models.* Washington, DC: National Institute of Education, 1985 (ED 271-423).

Feather, N.T. (Ed.) (1982). *Expectations and actions.* Hillsdale, NJ: Erlbaum.

Fister, S.L. and Kemp, K.A. (1995). *The One-Minute Skill Builder: Improving Student Social Skills.* Longmont, CO: Sopris West.

Gersten, R. and Carnine, D. "Direct Instruction in Reading Comprehension." *Educational Leadership* 43/7 (April 1986): 70-78.

Gettinger, M. "Methods of Proactive Classroom Management." *School Psychology Review* 17:2 (1988): 227-242.

Gettinger, M. "Student Behaviors, Teacher Reinforcement, Student Ability, and Learning." *Contemporary Educational Psychology* 8:4 (October 1983): 391-402.

Glatthorn, A.A. *Secondary English Classroom Environments.* Greenville, NC: North Carolina State University and East Carolina University, 1989.

Good, T.L. Teacher Effects. In *Making Our Schools More Effective: Proceedings of Three State Conferences.* Columbia, MO: University of Missouri, 1984a.

Good, T.L. "Two Decades of Research on Teacher Expectations: Findings and Future Directions." *Journal of Teacher Education* 38:4 (July/August 1987): 32-47.

Good, T.L. and Brophy, J.E. *Looking in Classrooms*, Third Edition. New York: Harper & Row, 1984b.

Good, T.L. and Brophy, J.E. School Effects. In *Handbook of Research on Teaching*, Third Edition, edited by M.C. Wittrock. New York: Macmillan, 1986, 570-602.

Gottfredson, D.C., Gottfredson, G.D., and Hybl, L.G. "Managing Adolescent Behavior: A Multiyear, Multischool Study." *American Educational Research Journal* 30:1 (Spring 1993): 179-215 (ED 333 549).

Gottfried, A.E. and Gottfried, A.W. "Parents Reward Strategies and Children's Academic Intrinsic Motivation and School Performance." Paper presented at the Biennial Meeting of the Society for Research in Child Development, Seattle, WA, April 1991 (ED 335 144).

Hartwig, L. and Meredith, G. (1994). *Got It!: Seven Steps for Teaching Students To Get on Top of Their Problems*. Longmont, CO: Sopris West.

Hawkins, J.D., Doueck, H.J., and Lishner, D.M. "Changing Teaching Practices in Mainstream Classrooms to Improve Bonding and Behavior of Low Achievers." *American Educational Research Journal* 25:1 (Spring 1988): 31-50.

Hawley, W.D., Rosenholtz, S.J., Goodstein, H., and Hasselbring, T. "Good Schools: What Research Says about Improving Student Achievement." *Peabody Journal of Education* 61:4 (Summer 1984): entire issue.

Huggins, P. (1990). *The ASSIST Program: Affective/Social Skills: Instructional Strategies and Techniques*. Longmont, CO: Sopris West.

Jenson, W.R., Rhode, G., and Reavis, H.K. (1994) *The Tough Kid Tool Box*. Longmont, CO: Sopris West.

Jones, V.Y. and Jones, L.S. (1998). *Comprehensive Classroom Management: Creating Communities of Support and Solving Problems* (5th ed.). Needham Heights, MA: Allyn & Bacon.

Kearns, J. "The Impact of Systematic Feedback on Student Self-Esteem." Paper presented at the Annual Meeting of the American Educational Research Association, New Orleans, LA, April 1988 (ED 293 897).

Kounin, J. S. *Discipline and Group Management in Classrooms*. Huntington, NY: Krieger Publishing, 1977.

Leinhardt, G., Weidman, C., and Hammond, K.M. "Introduction and Integration of Classroom Routines by Expert Teachers." *Curriculum Inquiry* 17/2 (Summer 1987): 135-176

Leming, T.J. "In Search of Effective Character Education." *Educational Leadership* 51:3 (November 1993): 63-71.

Marshall, H.H. and Weinstein, R.S. *It's Not How Much Brains You've Got, It's How You Use it: A Comparison of Classrooms Expected to Enhance or Undermine Students' Self- Evaluations.* Washington, DC: National Institute of Mental Health/Chicago, IL: Spencer Foundation, 1985 (ED 259 027).

Mayer, G.R. "A Dropout Prevention Program for At-Risk High School Students: Emphasizing Consulting to Promote Positive Classroom Climates." *Education and Treatment of Children* 16:22 (May 1993): 135-146.

McDevitt, T.M., Lennon, R., and Kopriva, R.J. "Adolescents' Perceptions of Mothers' and Fathers' Prosocial Actions and Empathic Responses." *Youth and Society* 22:3 (March 1991): 387-409.

Medley, D.M. *Teacher Competence and Teacher Effectiveness: A Review of Process Product Research.* Washington, DC: American Association of Colleges for Teacher Education, 1978.

Midgley, C., Feldlaufer, H., and Eccles, J.S. "Student/Teacher Relations and Attitudes Toward Mathematics Before and After the Transition to Junior High School." *Child Development* 60:4 (August 1989): 981-992.

Mills, R.S. and Grusec, J.E. "Cognitive, Affective, and Behavioral Consequences of Praising Altruism." *Merrill-Palmer Quarterly* 35:3 (July 1989): 299-326.

Mortimore, P. and Sammons, P. "New Evidence on Effective Elementary Schools." *Educational Leadership* 45:1 (September 1987): 4-8.

Mortimore, P., Sammons, P., Stoll, L., Lewis, D., and Ecob, R. *School Matters.* Berkeley, CA: University of California Press, 1988.

Paine, S.C. (1983). *Structuring your classroom for academic success.* Champaign, IL: Research Press.

Pecukonis, E.V. "A Cognitive/Affective Empathy Training Program as a Function of Ego Development in Aggressive Adolescent Females." *Adolescence* 25:97 (Spring 1990): 59-76.

Render, G.F., Padilla, J.N.M., and Krank, H.M. "Assertive Discipline: A Critical Review and Analysis." *Teachers College Record* 90:4 (Summer 1989): 607-630.

Rhode, G., Jenson, W.R., and Reavis, H.K. (1992). *The Tough Kid Book: Practical Classroom Management Strategies.* Longmont, CO: Sopris West.

Rosenshine, B. "Teaching Functions in Instructional Programs." *Elementary School Journal* 83/4 (March 1983): 335-351

Rosenshine, B. and Stevens, R. Teaching Functions. In *Handbook of Research on Teaching,* Third Edition, edited by M.C.Wittrock. New York: Macmillan, 1986, 376-391.

Rosswork, S. "Goal-Setting: The Effects on an Academic Task With Varying Magnitudes of Incentive." *Journal of Educational Psychology* 69:6 (December 1977): 710-715.

Rutter, M., Maughan, B., Mortimore, P., and Ouston, J. *Fifteen Thousand Hours: Secondary Schools and Their Effects on Children.* Cambridge, MA: Harvard University Press, 1979.

Sanford, J.P., Emmer, E.T., and Clements, B.S. "Improving Classroom Management." *Educational Leadership* 40/7 (April 1983): 56-60.

Sanford, J.P. and Evertson, C.M. "Classroom Management in a Low SES Junior High: Three Case Studies." *Journal of Teacher Education* 32:1 (January/February 1981): 34-38.

Sheridan, S.M. (1995). *The Tough Kid Social Skills Book.* Longmont, CO: Sopris West.

Slavin, R.E. "Cooperative Learning." *Review of Educational Research* 50:2 (Summer 1980): 315-342.

Slavin, R.E. "Cooperative Learning and Student Achievement." *Educational Leadership* 46:2 (October 1988): 31-33.

Slavin, R.E. Cooperative Learning and Student Achievement. In *School and Classroom Organization*, edited by R.E. Slavin. Hillsdale, NJ: Erlbaum, 1989.

Slavin, R.E. "Group Rewards Make Groupwork Work." *Educational Leadership* 48:5 (February 1991): 89-91.

Slavin, R.E. "Quality, Appropriateness, Incentive, and Time: A Model of Instructional Effectiveness." *International Journal of Educational Research* 21 (1994): 141-157.

Slavin, R.E. "Students Motivating Students to Excel: Cooperative Incentives, Cooperative Tasks, and Student Achievement." *The Elementary School Journal* 85:1 (September 1984): 53-63.

Solomon, D., Watson, M.S., Delucchi, K.L., Schaps, E., and Battistich, V. "Enhancing Children's Prosocial Behavior in the Classroom." *American Educational Research Journal* 25:4 (Winter 1988): 527-554.

Sprick, R.S. *Cafeteria Discipline: Positive Techniques for Lunchroom Supervision.* (Video Program). Eugene, OR: Teaching Strategies, 1995.

Sprick, R.S. *Playground Discipline: Positive Techniques for Recess Supervision.* (Video Program). Eugene, OR: Teaching Strategies, 1990.

Sprick, R.S. *STP: Stop, Think, Plan, A School-wide Strategy for Teaching Conflict Resolution Skills* (Video Program). Eugene, OR: Teaching Strategies, 1995.

Sprick, R.S. *The Solution Book: A Guide to Classroom Discipline.* Chicago: Science Research Associates, 1981.

Sprick, R.S. and Colvin, G. *Bus Discipline: A Positive Approach* (Video Program). Eugene, OR: Teaching Strategies, 1992.

Sprick, R.S. and Howard, L.M. *Substitutes: Planning for Productivity and Consistency.* (Video Program). Longmont, CO: Sopris West, 1996.

Sprick, R.S. and Howard, L.M. *The Teacher's Encyclopedia of Behavior Management: 100 Problems/500 Plans.* Longmont, CO: Sopris West, 1995.

Sprick, R.S., Howard, L., Wise, B.J., Marcum, K., and Haykin, M. (1998). *The Administrator's Desk Reference Of Behavior Management* (Vols. 1-3). Longmont, CO: Sopris West.

Sprick, R.S., Sprick, M.S., and Garrison, M. *Foundations: Establishing Positive Discipline Policies, Vol. I: The Process, Vol. II: Sample Policies, and Vol. III: The Workbook* (Video program). Longmont, CO: Sopris West, 1993.

Sprick, R.S., Sprick, M.S., and Garrison, M. *Interventions: Collaborative Planning for Students At-Risk.* Longmont, CO: Sopris West, 1993.

Taylor, S.E. "The Impact of An Alternative High School Program on Students Labeled 'Deviant'." *Educational Research Quarterly* 11:1 (1986-87): 8-12.

Teddlie, C., Kirby, P.C., and Stringfield, S. "Effective Versus Ineffective Schools: Observable Differences in the Classroom." *American Journal of Education* 97:3 (May 1989): 221-236.

Vincenzi, H. and Ayrer, J.G. "Determining Effective Schools." *Urban Education* 20:2 (July 1985): 123-132.

Walker, H.M., Colvin, G., and Ramsey, E. (1995). *Antisocial Behavior In School: Strategies And Best Practices.* Pacific Grove, CA: Brooks/Cole.

Walker, H.M., McConnell, S., Holmes, D., Todis, B., Walker, J., and Golden, N. (1983). *The Walker Social Skills Curriculum: The ACCEPTS Program.* Austin, TX: Pro-Ed.

Walker, H.M., Todis, B., Holmes, D., and Horton, D. (1998). *The Walker Social Skills Curriculum: The ACCESS Program.* Austin, TX: Pro-Ed.

Wang, M.C., Haertel, G.D., and Walberg, H.J. "What Helps Students Learn?" *Educational Leadership* 51:4 (December 1993-January 1994): 74-79.

Weinstein, R.S. and Marshall, H.H. *Ecology of Students' Achievement Expectations. Executive Summary.* Berkeley, CA: California University/Washington, DC: National Institute of Education, 1984 (ED 257 806).

Woolfolk, A.E. and Brooks, D.M. "The Influence of Teachers' Nonverbal Behaviors on Students' Perceptions and Performance." *The Elementary School Journal* 85:4 (March 1985): 513-528.

INDEX

N

O

P

R

U

V

W